W9-AWX-905

Published by Our Sunday Visitor Publishing Division, Our Sunday Visitor, Inc.
Published 2015.

21 20 19 18 17 16 3 4 5 6 7 8 9 10

Our Sunday Visitor Publishing Division, Our Sunday Visitor, Inc., 200 Noll Plaza, Huntington, IN 46750; 1-800-348-2440

ISBN: 978-1-61278-967-5 (Inventory No. T1731)
LCCN: 2015946963

Cover design: Lindsey Riesen
Cover art: Shutterstock
Interior design: Amanda Falk

PRINTED IN THE UNITED STATES OF AMERICA

TO THE READER

This Catholic edition of the New Revised Standard Version of the Bible has been authorized by the National Conference of Catholic Bishops in the U.S.A. and by the National Council of the Churches of Christ in the U.S.A. It has received the ecclesiastical approval of the Catholic Bishops of both the United States and Canada. The undersigned, who prepared this edition, is a member of the Revised Standard Version Bible Translation Committee as well as an active member and past president of the Catholic Biblical Association of America.

Roman Catholics are already familiar with the accuracy and elegance of the New Revised Standard Version, first published in 1990. It has previously appeared in two major types of edition: an edition of the Old and New Testaments alone, the Bible of most Protestants; and an edition of the Old and New Testaments with the Apocryphal/Deuterocanonical Books placed between the two Testaments. The text of the latter edition received the Imprimatur (official approbation) of the United States and Canadian Catholic Bishops. The New Revised Standard Version is truly an ecumenical translation, for it was produced by Roman Catholic, Eastern Orthodox, Protestant, and Jewish scholars. Because of this Catholic presence no change in the translation was requested for this edition....

Roman Catholics will welcome this edition of the New Revised Standard Version of the Bible for personal reading and study as well as liturgical usage. Based on the latest manuscript discoveries and critical editions, it offers the fruits of the best biblical scholarship in the idiom of today while being sensitive to the contemporary concern for inclusive language when referring to human beings.

ALEXANDER A. DI LELLA, O.F.M.
Andrews-Kelly-Ryan Distinguished Professor of Biblical Studies
The Catholic University of America

September 30, 1992
Feast of St. Jerome

The Gospel According to
MATTHEW

The Genealogy of Jesus the Messiah

1 An account of the genealogy[a] of Jesus the Messiah,[b] the son of David, the son of Abraham.

2 Abraham was the father of Isaac, and Isaac the father of Jacob, and Jacob the father of Judah and his brothers, 3 and Judah the father of Perez and Zerah by Tamar, and Perez the father of Hezron, and Hezron the father of Aram, 4 and Aram the father of Aminadab, and Aminadab the father of Nahshon, and Nahshon the father of Salmon, 5 and Salmon the father of Boaz by Rahab, and Boaz the father of Obed by Ruth, and Obed the father of Jesse, 6 and Jesse the father of King David.

And David was the father of Solomon by the wife of Uriah, 7 and Solomon the father of Rehoboam, and Rehoboam the father of Abijah, and Abijah the father of Asaph,[c] 8 and Asaph[d] the father of Jehoshaphat, and Jehoshaphat the father of Joram, and Joram the father of Uzziah, 9 and Uzziah the father of Jotham, and Jotham the father of Ahaz, and Ahaz the father of Hezekiah, 10 and Hezekiah the father of Manasseh, and Manasseh the father of Amos,[e] and Amos[f] the father of Josiah, 11 and Josiah the father of Jechoniah and his brothers, at the time of the deportation to Babylon.

12 And after the deportation to Babylon: Jechoniah was the father of Salathiel, and Salathiel the father of Zerubbabel, 13 and Zerubbabel the father of Abiud, and Abiud the father of Eliakim, and Eliakim the father of Azor, 14 and Azor the father of Zadok, and Zadok the father of Achim, and Achim the father of Eliud, 15 and Eliud the father of Eleazar, and Eleazar the father of Matthan, and Matthan the father of Jacob, 16 and Jacob the father of Joseph the husband of Mary, of whom Jesus was born, who is called the Messiah.[g]

17 So all the generations from Abraham to David are fourteen generations; and from David to the deportation to Babylon, fourteen generations; and from the deportation to Babylon to the Messiah,[h] fourteen generations.

The Birth of Jesus the Messiah

18 Now the birth of Jesus the Messiah[i] took place in this way. When his mother Mary had been engaged to Joseph, but before they lived together, she was found to be with child from the Holy Spirit. 19 Her husband Joseph, being a righteous man and unwilling to expose her to public disgrace, planned to

---

a Or *birth* *b* Or *Jesus Christ* *c* Other ancient authorities read *Asa* *d* Other ancient authorities read *Asa* *e* Other ancient authorities read *Amon* *f* Other ancient authorities read *Amon* *g* Or *the Christ* *h* Or *the Christ* *i* Or *Jesus Christ*

dismiss her quietly. 20 But just when
he had resolved to do this, an angel of the Lord appeared to him
in a dream and said, "Joseph, son
of David, do not be afraid to take
Mary as your wife, for the child
conceived in her is from the Holy
Spirit. 21 She will bear a son, and
you are to name him Jesus, for
he will save his people from their
sins." 22 All this took place to fulfill
what had been spoken by the Lord
through the prophet:

23 "Look, the virgin shall conceive
and bear a son,
and they shall name him
Emmanuel,"

which means, "God is with us."
24 When Joseph awoke from sleep,
he did as the angel of the Lord
commanded him; he took her as his
wife, 25 but had no marital relations
with her until she had borne a son;[j]
and he named him Jesus.

The Visit of the Wise Men

2 In the time of King Herod, after Jesus was born in Bethlehem of Judea, wise men[a] from the
East came to Jerusalem, 2 asking,
"Where is the child who has been
born king of the Jews? For we observed his star at its rising,[b] and
have come to pay him homage."
3 When King Herod heard this, he
was frightened, and all Jerusalem
with him; 4 and calling together all
the chief priests and scribes of the
people, he inquired of them where
the Messiah[c] was to be born. 5 They
told him, "In Bethlehem of Judea;
for so it has been written by the
prophet:

6 'And you, Bethlehem, in the
land of Judah,
are by no means least among
the rulers of Judah;
for from you shall come a ruler
who is to shepherd[d] my
people Israel.' "

7 Then Herod secretly called for
the wise men[e] and learned from
them the exact time when the star
had appeared. 8 Then he sent them
to Bethlehem, saying, "Go and
search diligently for the child; and
when you have found him, bring
me word so that I may also go and
pay him homage." 9 When they had
heard the king, they set out; and
there, ahead of them, went the star
that they had seen at its rising,[f] until
it stopped over the place where the
child was. 10 When they saw that the
star had stopped,[g] they were overwhelmed with joy. 11 On entering
the house, they saw the child with
Mary his mother; and they knelt
down and paid him homage. Then,
opening their treasure chests, they
offered him gifts of gold, frankin-
cense, and myrrh. 12 And having
been warned in a dream not to
return to Herod, they left for their
own country by another road.

The Escape to Egypt

13 Now after they had left, an
angel of the Lord appeared to Joseph in a dream and said, "Get up,
take the child and his mother, and
flee to Egypt, and remain there
until I tell you; for Herod is about

j Other ancient authorities read *her firstborn son*
a Or *astrologers*; Gk *magi* *b* Or *in the East*
c Or *the Christ* *d* Or *rule* *e* Or *astrologers*; Gk *magi* *f* Or *in the East* *g* Gk *saw the star*

to search for the child, to destroy
him." 14 Then Joseph[h] got up, took
the child and his mother by night,
and went to Egypt, 15 and remained
there until the death of Herod. This
was to fulfill what had been spoken
by the Lord through the prophet,
"Out of Egypt I have called my
son."

The Massacre of the Infants

16 When Herod saw that he had
been tricked by the wise men,[i] he
was infuriated, and he sent and
killed all the children in and around
Bethlehem who were two years old
or under, according to the time that
he had learned from the wise men.[j]
17 Then was fulfilled what had been
spoken through the prophet Jeremiah:
18 "A voice was heard in Ramah,
wailing and loud lamentation,
Rachel weeping for her children;
she refused to be consoled,
because they are no more."

The Return from Egypt

19 When Herod died, an angel
of the Lord suddenly appeared in
a dream to Joseph in Egypt and
said, 20 "Get up, take the child and
his mother, and go to the land of
Israel, for those who were seeking
the child's life are dead." 21 Then
Joseph[k] got up, took the child and
his mother, and went to the land
of Israel. 22 But when he heard that
Archelaus was ruling over Judea in
place of his father Herod, he was
afraid to go there. And after being
warned in a dream, he went away
to the district of Galilee. 23 There
he made his home in a town called
Nazareth, so that what had been
spoken through the prophets might
be fulfilled, "He will be called a
Nazorean."

The Proclamation of John the Baptist

3 In those days John the Baptist
appeared in the wilderness of
Judea, proclaiming, 2 "Repent, for
the kingdom of heaven has come
near."[a] 3 This is the one of whom
the prophet Isaiah spoke when he
said,
"The voice of one crying out in
the wilderness:
'Prepare the way of the Lord,
make his paths straight.' "
4 Now John wore clothing of camel's hair with a leather belt around
his waist, and his food was locusts
and wild honey. 5 Then the people
of Jerusalem and all Judea were going out to him, and all the region
along the Jordan, 6 and they were
baptized by him in the river Jordan,
confessing their sins.
7 But when he saw many Pharisees and Sadducees coming for
baptism, he said to them, "You
brood of vipers! Who warned you
to flee from the wrath to come?
8 Bear fruit worthy of repentance.
9 Do not presume to say to yourselves, 'We have Abraham as our
ancestor'; for I tell you, God is able
from these stones to raise up children to Abraham. 10 Even now the
ax is lying at the root of the trees;
every tree therefore that does not
bear good fruit is cut down and

h Gk *he* *i* Or *astrologers*; Gk *magi*
j Or *astrologers*; Gk *magi* *k* Gk *he* *a* Or *is at hand*

thrown into the fire.
11 "I baptize you with[b] water for
repentance, but one who is more
powerful than I is coming after me;
I am not worthy to carry his sandals. He will baptize you with[c] the
Holy Spirit and fire. 12 His winnowing fork is in his hand, and he will
clear his threshing floor and will
gather his wheat into the granary;
but the chaff he will burn with unquenchable fire."

The Baptism of Jesus

13 Then Jesus came from Galilee
to John at the Jordan, to be baptized
by him. 14 John would have pre-
vented him, saying, "I need to be
baptized by you, and do you come
to me?" 15 But Jesus answered him,
"Let it be so now; for it is proper
for us in this way to fulfill all righteousness." Then he consented.
16 And when Jesus had been baptized, just as he came up from the
water, suddenly the heavens were
opened to him and he saw the Spirit
of God descending like a dove and
alighting on him. 17 And a voice
from heaven said, "This is my Son,
the Beloved,[d] with whom I am well
pleased."

The Temptation of Jesus

4 Then Jesus was led up by the
Spirit into the wilderness to be
tempted by the devil. 2 He fasted
forty days and forty nights, and
afterwards he was famished. 3 The
tempter came and said to him, "If
you are the Son of God, command
these stones to become loaves of
bread." 4 But he answered, "It is
written,

'One does not live by bread
alone,
but by every word that comes
from the mouth of God.' "

5 Then the devil took him to the
holy city and placed him on the pin-
nacle of the temple, 6 saying to him,
"If you are the Son of God, throw
yourself down; for it is written,

'He will command his angels
concerning you,'
and 'On their hands they will
bear you up,
so that you will not dash your
foot against a stone.' "

7 Jesus said to him, "Again it is written, 'Do not put the Lord your God
to the test.' "
8 Again, the devil took him to
a very high mountain and showed
him all the kingdoms of the world
and their splendor; 9 and he said
to him, "All these I will give you,
if you will fall down and worship
me." 10 Jesus said to him, "Away
with you, Satan! for it is written,

'Worship the Lord your God,
and serve only him.' "

11 Then the devil left him, and suddenly angels came and waited on
him.

Jesus Begins His Ministry in Galilee

12 Now when Jesus[a] heard that
John had been arrested, he withdrew to Galilee. 13 He left Nazareth
and made his home in Capernaum
by the sea, in the territory of Zebulun and Naphtali, 14 so that what had
been spoken through the prophet
Isaiah might be fulfilled:

b Or *in* *c* Or *in* *d* Or *my beloved Son*
a Gk *he*

15 "Land of Zebulun, land of
Naphtali,
on the road by the sea, across
the Jordan, Galilee of the
Gentiles—
16 the people who sat in darkness
have seen a great light,
and for those who sat in the
region and shadow of
death
light has dawned."
17 From that time Jesus began to
proclaim, "Repent, for the kingdom
of heaven has come near."[b]

Jesus Calls the First Disciples

18 As he walked by the Sea of
Galilee, he saw two brothers, Simon, who is called Peter, and Andrew his brother, casting a net into
the sea—for they were fishermen.
19 And he said to them, "Follow me,
and I will make you fish for people." 20 Immediately they left their
nets and followed him. 21 As he
went from there, he saw two other
brothers, James son of Zebedee and
his brother John, in the boat with
their father Zebedee, mending their
nets, and he called them. 22 Immediately they left the boat and their
father, and followed him.

Jesus Ministers to Crowds of People

23 Jesus[c] went throughout Galilee, teaching in their synagogues
and proclaiming the good news[d]
of the kingdom and curing every
disease and every sickness among
the people. 24 So his fame spread
throughout all Syria, and they
brought to him all the sick, those
who were afflicted with various
diseases and pains, demoniacs, epi-
leptics, and paralytics, and he cured
them. 25 And great crowds followed
him from Galilee, the Decapolis,
Jerusalem, Judea, and from beyond
the Jordan.

The Beatitudes

5 When Jesus[a] saw the crowds, he
went up the mountain; and after
he sat down, his disciples came to
him. 2 Then he began to speak, and
taught them, saying:
3 "Blessed are the poor in spirit,
for theirs is the kingdom of heaven.
4 "Blessed are those who mourn,
for they will be comforted.
5 "Blessed are the meek, for they
will inherit the earth.
6 "Blessed are those who hunger
and thirst for righteousness, for
they will be filled.
7 "Blessed are the merciful, for
they will receive mercy.
8 "Blessed are the pure in heart,
for they will see God.
9 "Blessed are the peacemakers,
for they will be called children of
God.
10 "Blessed are those who are
persecuted for righteousness' sake,
for theirs is the kingdom of heaven.
11 "Blessed are you when people revile you and persecute you
and utter all kinds of evil against
you falsely[b] on my account. 12 Rejoice and be glad, for your reward
is great in heaven, for in the same
way they persecuted the prophets
who were before you.

---

b Or *is at hand* *c* Gk *He* *d* Gk *gospel*
a Gk *he* *b* Other ancient authorities lack *falsely*

Salt and Light
13 "You are the salt of the earth;
but if salt has lost its taste, how
can its saltiness be restored? It is
no longer good for anything, but
is thrown out and trampled under
foot.
14 "You are the light of the
world. A city built on a hill cannot
be hid. 15 No one after lighting a
lamp puts it under the bushel basket, but on the lampstand, and it
gives light to all in the house. 16 In
the same way, let your light shine
before others, so that they may see
your good works and give glory to
your Father in heaven.

The Law and the Prophets
17 "Do not think that I have come
to abolish the law or the prophets; I
have come not to abolish but to fulfill. 18 For truly I tell you, until heav-
en and earth pass away, not one
letter,[c] not one stroke of a letter,
will pass from the law until all is
accomplished. 19 Therefore, whoever breaks[d] one of the least of these
commandments, and teaches others
to do the same, will be called least
in the kingdom of heaven; but whoever does them and teaches them
will be called great in the kingdom
of heaven. 20 For I tell you, unless
your righteousness exceeds that of
the scribes and Pharisees, you will
never enter the kingdom of heaven.

Concerning Anger
21 "You have heard that it was
said to those of ancient times, 'You
shall not murder'; and 'whoever
murders shall be liable to judgment.' 22 But I say to you that if you
are angry with a brother or sister,[e]
you will be liable to judgment; and
if you insult[f] a brother or sister,[g]
you will be liable to the council;
and if you say, 'You fool,' you will
be liable to the hell[h] of fire. 23 So
when you are offering your gift at
the altar, if you remember that your
brother or sister[i] has something
against you, 24 leave your gift there
before the altar and go; first be rec-
onciled to your brother or sister,[j]
and then come and offer your gift.
25 Come to terms quickly with your
accuser while you are on the way
to court[k] with him, or your accuser
may hand you over to the judge,
and the judge to the guard, and you
will be thrown into prison. 26 Truly I
tell you, you will never get out until
you have paid the last penny.

Concerning Adultery
27 "You have heard that it was
said, 'You shall not commit adultery.' 28 But I say to you that everyone who looks at a woman with
lust has already committed adultery
with her in his heart. 29 If your right
eye causes you to sin, tear it out and
throw it away; it is better for you to
lose one of your members than for
your whole body to be thrown into
hell.[l] 30 And if your right hand causes you to sin, cut it off and throw
it away; it is better for you to lose
one of your members than for your
whole body to go into hell.[m]

---

c Gk *one iota* d Or *annuls* e Gk *a brother*; other ancient authorities add *without cause* f Gk *say Raca to* (an obscure term of abuse) g Gk *a brother* h Gk *Gehenna* i Gk *your brother* j Gk *your brother* k Gk lacks *to court* l Gk *Gehenna* m Gk *Gehenna*

Concerning Divorce

31 "It was also said, 'Whoever
divorces his wife, let him give her
a certificate of divorce.' 32 But I say
to you that anyone who divorces
his wife, except on the ground of
unchastity, causes her to commit
adultery; and whoever marries a
divorced woman commits adultery.

Concerning Oaths

33 "Again, you have heard that it
was said to those of ancient times,
'You shall not swear falsely, but
carry out the vows you have made
to the Lord.' 34 But I say to you, Do
not swear at all, either by heaven,
for it is the throne of God, 35 or by
the earth, for it is his footstool, or
by Jerusalem, for it is the city of the
great King. 36 And do not swear by
your head, for you cannot make one
hair white or black. 37 Let your word
be 'Yes, Yes' or 'No, No'; anything
more than this comes from the evil
one.[n]

Concerning Retaliation

38 "You have heard that it was
said, 'An eye for an eye and a tooth
for a tooth.' 39 But I say to you, Do
not resist an evildoer. But if anyone strikes you on the right cheek,
turn the other also; 40 and if anyone
wants to sue you and take your
coat, give your cloak as well; 41 and
if anyone forces you to go one mile,
go also the second mile. 42 Give to
everyone who begs from you, and
do not refuse anyone who wants to
borrow from you.

Love for Enemies

43 "You have heard that it was
said, 'You shall love your neighbor and hate your enemy.' 44 But I
say to you, Love your enemies and
pray for those who persecute you,
45 so that you may be children of
your Father in heaven; for he makes
his sun rise on the evil and on the
good, and sends rain on the righteous and on the unrighteous. 46 For
if you love those who love you,
what reward do you have? Do not
even the tax collectors do the same?
47 And if you greet only your brothers and sisters,[o] what more are you
doing than others? Do not even the
Gentiles do the same? 48 Be perfect,
therefore, as your heavenly Father
is perfect.

Concerning Almsgiving

6 "Beware of practicing your piety
before others in order to be seen
by them; for then you have no reward from your Father in heaven.
2 "So whenever you give alms, do
not sound a trumpet before you, as
the hypocrites do in the synagogues
and in the streets, so that they may
be praised by others. Truly I tell
you, they have received their reward. 3 But when you give alms, do
not let your left hand know what
your right hand is doing, 4 so that
your alms may be done in secret;
and your Father who sees in secret
will reward you.[a]

Concerning Prayer

5 "And whenever you pray, do
not be like the hypocrites; for they
love to stand and pray in the synagogues and at the street corners,

---

n Or *evil* *o* Gk *your brothers* *a* Other
ancient authorities add *openly*

so that they may be seen by others. Truly I tell you, they have received their reward. [6]But whenever you pray, go into your room and shut the door and pray to your Father who is in secret; and your Father who sees in secret will reward you.[b]

7 "When you are praying, do not heap up empty phrases as the Gentiles do; for they think that they will be heard because of their many words. [8]Do not be like them, for your Father knows what you need before you ask him.

9 "Pray then in this way:

Our Father in heaven,
hallowed be your name.
10 Your kingdom come.
Your will be done,
on earth as it is in heaven.
11 Give us this day our daily bread.[c]
12 And forgive us our debts,
as we also have forgiven our debtors.
13 And do not bring us to the time of trial,[d]
but rescue us from the evil one.[e]

[14]For if you forgive others their trespasses, your heavenly Father will also forgive you; [15]but if you do not forgive others, neither will your Father forgive your trespasses.

Concerning Fasting

16 "And whenever you fast, do not look dismal, like the hypocrites, for they disfigure their faces so as to show others that they are fasting. Truly I tell you, they have received their reward. [17]But when you fast, put oil on your head and wash your face, [18]so that your fasting may be seen not by others but by your Father who is in secret; and your Father who sees in secret will reward you.[f]

Concerning Treasures

19 "Do not store up for yourselves treasures on earth, where moth and rust[g] consume and where thieves break in and steal; [20]but store up for yourselves treasures in heaven, where neither moth nor rust[h] consumes and where thieves do not break in and steal. [21]For where your treasure is, there your heart will be also.

The Sound Eye

22 "The eye is the lamp of the body. So, if your eye is healthy, your whole body will be full of light; [23]but if your eye is unhealthy, your whole body will be full of darkness. If then the light in you is darkness, how great is the darkness!

Serving Two Masters

24 "No one can serve two masters; for a slave will either hate the one and love the other, or be devoted to the one and despise the other. You cannot serve God and wealth.[i]

Do Not Worry

25 "Therefore I tell you, do not worry about your life, what you

b Other ancient authorities add *openly*
c Or *our bread for tomorrow* *d* Or *us into temptation* *e* Or *from evil.* Other ancient authorities add, in some form, *For the kingdom and the power and the glory are yours forever. Amen.* *f* Other ancient authorities add *openly*
g Gk *eating* *h* Gk *eating* *i* Gk *mammon*

will eat or what you will drink,[j]
or about your body, what you will
wear. Is not life more than food,
and the body more than clothing?
26 Look at the birds of the air; they
neither sow nor reap nor gather into
barns, and yet your heavenly Father
feeds them. Are you not of more
value than they? 27 And can any of
you by worrying add a single hour
to your span of life?[k] 28 And why do
you worry about clothing? Consider the lilies of the field, how they
grow; they neither toil nor spin,
29 yet I tell you, even Solomon in all
his glory was not clothed like one
of these. 30 But if God so clothes
the grass of the field, which is alive
today and tomorrow is thrown into
the oven, will he not much more
clothe you—you of little faith?
31 Therefore do not worry, saying,
'What will we eat?' or 'What will
we drink?' or 'What will we wear?'
32 For it is the Gentiles who strive
for all these things; and indeed your
heavenly Father knows that you
need all these things. 33 But strive
first for the kingdom of God[l] and
his[m] righteousness, and all these
things will be given to you as well.
34 "So do not worry about tomorrow, for tomorrow will bring
worries of its own. Today's trouble
is enough for today.

Judging Others

7 "Do not judge, so that you may
not be judged. 2 For with the
judgment you make you will be
judged, and the measure you give
will be the measure you get. 3 Why
do you see the speck in your neighbor's[a] eye, but do not notice the log
in your own eye? 4 Or how can you
say to your neighbor,[b] 'Let me take
the speck out of your eye,' while
the log is in your own eye? 5 You
hypocrite, first take the log out of
your own eye, and then you will see
clearly to take the speck out of your
neighbor's[c] eye.

Profaning the Holy

6 "Do not give what is holy to
dogs; and do not throw your pearls
before swine, or they will trample
them under foot and turn and maul
you.

Ask, Search, Knock

7 "Ask, and it will be given you;
search, and you will find; knock,
and the door will be opened for
you. 8 For everyone who asks receives, and everyone who searches finds, and for everyone who
knocks, the door will be opened.
9 Is there anyone among you who, if
your child asks for bread, will give
a stone? 10 Or if the child asks for
a fish, will give a snake? 11 If you
then, who are evil, know how to
give good gifts to your children,
how much more will your Father
in heaven give good things to those
who ask him!

The Golden Rule

12 "In everything do to others as
you would have them do to you; for
this is the law and the prophets.

---

j Other ancient authorities lack *or what you will drink* *k* Or *add one cubit to your height* *l* Other ancient authorities lack *of God* *m* Or *its* *a* Gk *brother's* *b* Gk *brother* *c* Gk *brother's*

The Narrow Gate
13 "Enter through the narrow
gate; for the gate is wide and the
road is easy[d] that leads to destruction, and there are many who take
it. [14]For the gate is narrow and the
road is hard that leads to life, and
there are few who find it.

A Tree and Its Fruit
15 "Beware of false prophets,
who come to you in sheep's clothing but inwardly are ravenous
wolves. [16]You will know them by
their fruits. Are grapes gathered
from thorns, or figs from thistles?
[17]In the same way, every good tree
bears good fruit, but the bad tree
bears bad fruit. [18]A good tree cannot bear bad fruit, nor can a bad tree
bear good fruit. [19]Every tree that
does not bear good fruit is cut down
and thrown into the fire. [20]Thus you
will know them by their fruits.

Concerning Self-Deception
21 "Not everyone who says to
me, 'Lord, Lord,' will enter the
kingdom of heaven, but only the
one who does the will of my Father
in heaven. [22]On that day many will
say to me, 'Lord, Lord, did we not
prophesy in your name, and cast
out demons in your name, and
do many deeds of power in your
name?' [23]Then I will declare to
them, 'I never knew you; go away
from me, you evildoers.'

Hearers and Doers
24 "Everyone then who hears
these words of mine and acts on
them will be like a wise man who
built his house on rock. [25]The rain
fell, the floods came, and the winds
blew and beat on that house, but
it did not fall, because it had been
founded on rock. [26]And everyone
who hears these words of mine and
does not act on them will be like a
foolish man who built his house on
sand. [27]The rain fell, and the floods
came, and the winds blew and beat
against that house, and it fell—and
great was its fall!"
28 Now when Jesus had finished
saying these things, the crowds
were astounded at his teaching,
[29]for he taught them as one having
authority, and not as their scribes.

Jesus Cleanses a Leper
8 When Jesus[a] had come down
from the mountain, great crowds
followed him; [2]and there was a
leper[b] who came to him and knelt
before him, saying, "Lord, if you
choose, you can make me clean."
[3]He stretched out his hand and
touched him, saying, "I do choose.
Be made clean!" Immediately his
leprosy[c] was cleansed. [4]Then Jesus said to him, "See that you say
nothing to anyone; but go, show
yourself to the priest, and offer the
gift that Moses commanded, as a
testimony to them."

Jesus Heals a Centurion's Servant
5 When he entered Capernaum, a
centurion came to him, appealing to
him [6]and saying, "Lord, my servant
is lying at home paralyzed, in terri-

---

d Other ancient authorities read *for the road is wide and easy* *a* Gk *he* *b* The terms *leper* and *leprosy* can refer to several diseases
c The terms *leper* and *leprosy* can refer to several diseases

ble distress." [7]And he said to him, "I will come and cure him." [8]The centurion answered, "Lord, I am not worthy to have you come under my roof; but only speak the word, and my servant will be healed. [9]For I also am a man under authority, with soldiers under me; and I say to one, 'Go,' and he goes, and to another, 'Come,' and he comes, and to my slave, 'Do this,' and the slave does it." [10]When Jesus heard him, he was amazed and said to those who followed him, "Truly I tell you, in no one[d] in Israel have I found such faith. [11]I tell you, many will come from east and west and will eat with Abraham and Isaac and Jacob in the kingdom of heaven, [12]while the heirs of the kingdom will be thrown into the outer darkness, where there will be weeping and gnashing of teeth." [13]And to the centurion Jesus said, "Go; let it be done for you according to your faith." And the servant was healed in that hour.

Jesus Heals Many at Peter's House

14 When Jesus entered Peter's house, he saw his mother-in-law lying in bed with a fever; [15]he touched her hand, and the fever left her, and she got up and began to serve him. [16]That evening they brought to him many who were possessed with demons; and he cast out the spirits with a word, and cured all who were sick. [17]This was to fulfill what had been spoken through the prophet Isaiah, "He took our infirmities and bore our diseases."

Would-Be Followers of Jesus

18 Now when Jesus saw great crowds around him, he gave orders to go over to the other side. [19]A scribe then approached and said, "Teacher, I will follow you wherever you go." [20]And Jesus said to him, "Foxes have holes, and birds of the air have nests; but the Son of Man has nowhere to lay his head." [21]Another of his disciples said to him, "Lord, first let me go and bury my father." [22]But Jesus said to him, "Follow me, and let the dead bury their own dead."

Jesus Stills the Storm

23 And when he got into the boat, his disciples followed him. [24]A windstorm arose on the sea, so great that the boat was being swamped by the waves; but he was asleep. [25]And they went and woke him up, saying, "Lord, save us! We are perishing!" [26]And he said to them, "Why are you afraid, you of little faith?" Then he got up and rebuked the winds and the sea; and there was a dead calm. [27]They were amazed, saying, "What sort of man is this, that even the winds and the sea obey him?"

Jesus Heals the Gadarene Demoniacs

28 When he came to the other side, to the country of the Gadarenes,[e] two demoniacs coming out of the tombs met him. They were so fierce that no one could pass that way. [29]Suddenly

---

d Other ancient authorities read *Truly I tell you, not even* *e* Other ancient authorities read *Gergesenes*; others, *Gerasenes*

they shouted, "What have you to
do with us, Son of God? Have you
come here to torment us before the
time?" 30 Now a large herd of swine
was feeding at some distance from
them. 31 The demons begged him,
"If you cast us out, send us into
the herd of swine." 32 And he said
to them, "Go!" So they came out
and entered the swine; and suddenly, the whole herd rushed down the
steep bank into the sea and perished
in the water. 33 The swineherds ran
off, and on going into the town,
they told the whole story about
what had happened to the demoniacs. 34 Then the whole town came
out to meet Jesus; and when they
saw him, they begged him to leave
their neighborhood.

9 1 And after getting into a boat he
crossed the sea and came to his
own town.

Jesus Heals a Paralytic

2 And just then some people were
carrying a paralyzed man lying on a
bed. When Jesus saw their faith, he
said to the paralytic, "Take heart,
son; your sins are forgiven." 3 Then
some of the scribes said to themselves, "This man is blaspheming." 4 But Jesus, perceiving their
thoughts, said, "Why do you think
evil in your hearts? 5 For which is
easier, to say, 'Your sins are forgiv-
en,' or to say, 'Stand up and walk'?
6 But so that you may know that the
Son of Man has authority on earth
to forgive sins"—he then said to
the paralytic—"Stand up, take your
bed and go to your home." 7 And
he stood up and went to his home.
8 When the crowds saw it, they were
filled with awe, and they glorified
God, who had given such authority
to human beings.

The Call of Matthew

9 As Jesus was walking along, he
saw a man called Matthew sitting
at the tax booth; and he said to him,
"Follow me." And he got up and
followed him.

10 And as he sat at dinner[a] in
the house, many tax collectors and
sinners came and were sitting[b] with
him and his disciples. 11 When the
Pharisees saw this, they said to his
disciples, "Why does your teacher
eat with tax collectors and sinners?" 12 But when he heard this, he
said, "Those who are well have no
need of a physician, but those who
are sick. 13 Go and learn what this
means, 'I desire mercy, not sacrifice.' For I have come to call not
the righteous but sinners."

The Question about Fasting

14 Then the disciples of John
came to him, saying, "Why do we
and the Pharisees fast often,[c] but
your disciples do not fast?" 15 And
Jesus said to them, "The wedding
guests cannot mourn as long as
the bridegroom is with them, can
they? The days will come when
the bridegroom is taken away from
them, and then they will fast. 16 No
one sews a piece of unshrunk cloth
on an old cloak, for the patch pulls
away from the cloak, and a worse
tear is made. 17 Neither is new wine
put into old wineskins; otherwise,
the skins burst, and the wine is

a Gk *reclined* *b* Gk *were reclining* *c* Other ancient authorities lack *often* spilled, and the skins are destroyed; but new wine is put into fresh wineskins, and so both are preserved."

A Girl Restored to Life and a Woman Healed

18 While he was saying these things to them, suddenly a leader of the synagogue[d] came in and knelt before him, saying, "My daughter has just died; but come and lay your hand on her, and she will live." 19 And Jesus got up and followed him, with his disciples. 20 Then suddenly a woman who had been suffering from hemorrhages for twelve years came up behind him and touched the fringe of his cloak, 21 for she said to herself, "If I only touch his cloak, I will be made well." 22 Jesus turned, and seeing her he said, "Take heart, daughter; your faith has made you well." And instantly the woman was made well. 23 When Jesus came to the leader's house and saw the flute players and the crowd making a commotion, 24 he said, "Go away; for the girl is not dead but sleeping." And they laughed at him. 25 But when the crowd had been put outside, he went in and took her by the hand, and the girl got up. 26 And the report of this spread throughout that district.

Jesus Heals Two Blind Men

27 As Jesus went on from there, two blind men followed him, crying loudly, "Have mercy on us, Son of David!" 28 When he entered the house, the blind men came to him; and Jesus said to them, "Do you believe that I am able to do this?" They said to him, "Yes, Lord." 29 Then he touched their eyes and said, "According to your faith let it be done to you." 30 And their eyes were opened. Then Jesus sternly ordered them, "See that no one knows of this." 31 But they went away and spread the news about him throughout that district.

Jesus Heals One Who Was Mute

32 After they had gone away, a demoniac who was mute was brought to him. 33 And when the demon had been cast out, the one who had been mute spoke; and the crowds were amazed and said, "Never has anything like this been seen in Israel." 34 But the Pharisees said, "By the ruler of the demons he casts out the demons."[e]

The Harvest Is Great, the Laborers Few

35 Then Jesus went about all the cities and villages, teaching in their synagogues, and proclaiming the good news of the kingdom, and curing every disease and every sickness. 36 When he saw the crowds, he had compassion for them, because they were harassed and helpless, like sheep without a shepherd. 37 Then he said to his disciples, "The harvest is plentiful, but the laborers are few; 38 therefore ask the Lord of the harvest to send out laborers into his harvest."

The Twelve Apostles

10 Then Jesus[a] summoned his twelve disciples and gave

d Gk lacks *of the synagogue* *e* Other ancient authorities lack this verse *a* Gk *he*

them authority over unclean spirits,
to cast them out, and to cure every
disease and every sickness. 2 These
are the names of the twelve apostles: first, Simon, also known as Peter, and his brother Andrew; James
son of Zebedee, and his brother
John; 3 Philip and Bartholomew;
Thomas and Matthew the tax collector; James son of Alphaeus, and
Thaddaeus;[b] 4 Simon the Cananaean, and Judas Iscariot, the one who
betrayed him.

The Mission of the Twelve

5 These twelve Jesus sent out
with the following instructions:
"Go nowhere among the Gentiles,
and enter no town of the Samaritans, 6 but go rather to the lost
sheep of the house of Israel. 7 As
you go, proclaim the good news,
'The kingdom of heaven has come
near.'[c] 8 Cure the sick, raise the
dead, cleanse the lepers,[d] cast out
demons. You received without payment; give without payment. 9 Take
no gold, or silver, or copper in your
belts, 10 no bag for your journey, or
two tunics, or sandals, or a staff; for
laborers deserve their food. 11 Whatever town or village you enter, find
out who in it is worthy, and stay
there until you leave. 12 As you enter the house, greet it. 13 If the house
is worthy, let your peace come
upon it; but if it is not worthy, let
your peace return to you. 14 If anyone will not welcome you or listen
to your words, shake off the dust
from your feet as you leave that
house or town. 15 Truly I tell you, it
will be more tolerable for the land
of Sodom and Gomorrah on the day
of judgment than for that town.

Coming Persecutions

16 "See, I am sending you out like
sheep into the midst of wolves; so
be wise as serpents and innocent as
doves. 17 Beware of them, for they
will hand you over to councils and
flog you in their synagogues; 18 and
you will be dragged before governors and kings because of me, as a
testimony to them and the Gentiles.
19 When they hand you over, do not
worry about how you are to speak
or what you are to say; for what
you are to say will be given to you
at that time; 20 for it is not you who
speak, but the Spirit of your Father
speaking through you. 21 Brother
will betray brother to death, and a
father his child, and children will
rise against parents and have them
put to death; 22 and you will be hated
by all because of my name. But the
one who endures to the end will be
saved. 23 When they persecute you
in one town, flee to the next; for
truly I tell you, you will not have
gone through all the towns of Israel
before the Son of Man comes.

24 "A disciple is not above the
teacher, nor a slave above the master; 25 it is enough for the disciple
to be like the teacher, and the slave
like the master. If they have called
the master of the house Beelzebul,
how much more will they malign
those of his household!

---

b Other ancient authorities read *Lebbaeus*, or *Lebbaeus called Thaddaeus* *c* Or *is at hand*
d The terms *leper* and *leprosy* can refer to several diseases

Whom to Fear

26 “So have no fear of them;
for nothing is covered up that will
not be uncovered, and nothing secret that will not become known.
27 What I say to you in the dark,
tell in the light; and what you
hear whispered, proclaim from the
housetops. 28 Do not fear those who
kill the body but cannot kill the
soul; rather fear him who can destroy both soul and body in hell.[e]
29 Are not two sparrows sold for a
penny? Yet not one of them will
fall to the ground apart from your
Father. 30 And even the hairs of your
head are all counted. 31 So do not be
afraid; you are of more value than
many sparrows.

32 “Everyone therefore who
acknowledges me before others, I
also will acknowledge before my
Father in heaven; 33 but whoever
denies me before others, I also will
deny before my Father in heaven.

Not Peace, but a Sword

34 “Do not think that I have
come to bring peace to the earth; I
have not come to bring peace, but
a sword.

35 For I have come to set a man
against his father,
and a daughter against her
mother,
and a daughter-in-law against
her mother-in-law;
36 and one’s foes will be members
of one’s own household.

37 Whoever loves father or mother
more than me is not worthy of me;
and whoever loves son or daughter
more than me is not worthy of me;
38 and whoever does not take up the
cross and follow me is not worthy
of me. 39 Those who find their life
will lose it, and those who lose their
life for my sake will find it.

Rewards

40 “Whoever welcomes you welcomes me, and whoever welcomes
me welcomes the one who sent me.
41 Whoever welcomes a prophet in
the name of a prophet will receive
a prophet’s reward; and whoever
welcomes a righteous person in the
name of a righteous person will receive the reward of the righteous;
42 and whoever gives even a cup
of cold water to one of these little
ones in the name of a disciple—truly I tell you, none of these will lose
their reward.”

11 Now when Jesus had finished
instructing his twelve disciples, he went on from there to teach
and proclaim his message in their
cities.

Messengers from John the Baptist

2 When John heard in prison
what the Messiah[a] was doing, he
sent word by his[b] disciples 3 and
said to him, “Are you the one who
is to come, or are we to wait for
another?” 4 Jesus answered them,
“Go and tell John what you hear
and see: 5 the blind receive their
sight, the lame walk, the lepers[c] are
cleansed, the deaf hear, the dead
are raised, and the poor have good
news brought to them. 6 And bless-

e Gk *Gehenna* a Or *the Christ* b Other ancient authorities read *two of his* c The terms *leper* and *leprosy* can refer to several diseases

ed is anyone who takes no offense
at me."

Jesus Praises John the Baptist

7 As they went away, Jesus began to speak to the crowds about
John: "What did you go out into
the wilderness to look at? A reed
shaken by the wind? [8] What then
did you go out to see? Someone[d]
dressed in soft robes? Look, those
who wear soft robes are in royal
palaces. [9] What then did you go out
to see? A prophet?[e] Yes, I tell you,
and more than a prophet. [10] This is
the one about whom it is written,

'See, I am sending my
messenger ahead of you,
who will prepare your way
before you.'

[11] Truly I tell you, among those born
of women no one has arisen greater
than John the Baptist; yet the least
in the kingdom of heaven is greater
than he. [12] From the days of John
the Baptist until now the kingdom
of heaven has suffered violence,[f]
and the violent take it by force.
[13] For all the prophets and the law
prophesied until John came; [14] and
if you are willing to accept it, he is
Elijah who is to come. [15] Let anyone
with ears[g] listen!

16 "But to what will I compare
this generation? It is like children
sitting in the marketplaces and calling to one another,

[17] 'We played the flute for you, and
you did not dance;
we wailed, and you did not
mourn.'

[18] For John came neither eating nor
drinking, and they say, 'He has a
demon'; [19] the Son of Man came
eating and drinking, and they say,
'Look, a glutton and a drunkard,
a friend of tax collectors and sinners!' Yet wisdom is vindicated by
her deeds."[h]

Woes to Unrepentant Cities

20 Then he began to reproach the
cities in which most of his deeds
of power had been done, because
they did not repent. [21] "Woe to you,
Chorazin! Woe to you, Bethsaida!
For if the deeds of power done in
you had been done in Tyre and
Sidon, they would have repented
long ago in sackcloth and ashes.
[22] But I tell you, on the day of judgment it will be more tolerable for
Tyre and Sidon than for you. [23] And
you, Capernaum,

will you be exalted to heaven?
No, you will be brought down
to Hades.

For if the deeds of power done in
you had been done in Sodom, it
would have remained until this day.
[24] But I tell you that on the day of
judgment it will be more tolerable
for the land of Sodom than for
you."

Jesus Thanks His Father

25 At that time Jesus said, "I
thank[i] you, Father, Lord of heaven
and earth, because you have hidden these things from the wise and
the intelligent and have revealed
them to infants; [26] yes, Father, for

---

d Or *Why then did you go out? To see someone* *e* Other ancient authorities read *Why then did you go out? To see a prophet?* *f* Or *has been coming violently* *g* Other ancient authorities add *to hear* *h* Other ancient authorities read *children* *i* Or *praise*

such was your gracious will.[j] 27All
things have been handed over to me
by my Father; and no one knows
the Son except the Father, and no
one knows the Father except the
Son and anyone to whom the Son
chooses to reveal him.

28 "Come to me, all you that
are weary and are carrying heavy
burdens, and I will give you rest.
29Take my yoke upon you, and
learn from me; for I am gentle and
humble in heart, and you will find
rest for your souls. 30For my yoke is
easy, and my burden is light."

Plucking Grain on the Sabbath

12 At that time Jesus went
through the grainfields on the
sabbath; his disciples were hungry,
and they began to pluck heads of
grain and to eat. 2When the Pharisees saw it, they said to him, "Look,
your disciples are doing what is not
lawful to do on the sabbath." 3He
said to them, "Have you not read
what David did when he and his
companions were hungry? 4He entered the house of God and ate the
bread of the Presence, which it was
not lawful for him or his companions to eat, but only for the priests.
5Or have you not read in the law
that on the sabbath the priests in the
temple break the sabbath and yet
are guiltless? 6I tell you, something
greater than the temple is here. 7But
if you had known what this means,
'I desire mercy and not sacrifice,'
you would not have condemned the
guiltless. 8For the Son of Man is
lord of the sabbath."

The Man with a Withered Hand

9 He left that place and entered
their synagogue; 10a man was there
with a withered hand, and they
asked him, "Is it lawful to cure on
the sabbath?" so that they might accuse him. 11He said to them, "Suppose one of you has only one sheep
and it falls into a pit on the sabbath;
will you not lay hold of it and lift it
out? 12How much more valuable is
a human being than a sheep! So it is
lawful to do good on the sabbath."
13Then he said to the man, "Stretch
out your hand." He stretched it out,
and it was restored, as sound as the
other. 14But the Pharisees went out
and conspired against him, how to
destroy him.

God's Chosen Servant

15 When Jesus became aware of
this, he departed. Many crowds[a]
followed him, and he cured all of
them, 16and he ordered them not to
make him known. 17This was to fulfill what had been spoken through
the prophet Isaiah:

18 "Here is my servant, whom I
have chosen,
my beloved, with whom my
soul is well pleased.
I will put my Spirit upon him,
and he will proclaim justice to
the Gentiles.
19 He will not wrangle or cry
aloud,
nor will anyone hear his voice
in the streets.
20 He will not break a bruised reed
or quench a smoldering wick
until he brings justice to victory.

---

j Or *for so it was well-pleasing in your sight*

a Other ancient authorities lack *crowds*

21 And in his name the Gentiles
will hope."

Jesus and Beelzebul

22 Then they brought to him a
demoniac who was blind and mute;
and he cured him, so that the one
who had been mute could speak
and see. 23 All the crowds were
amazed and said, "Can this be the
Son of David?" 24 But when the
Pharisees heard it, they said, "It is
only by Beelzebul, the ruler of the
demons, that this fellow casts out
the demons." 25 He knew what they
were thinking and said to them,
"Every kingdom divided against
itself is laid waste, and no city or
house divided against itself will
stand. 26 If Satan casts out Satan,
he is divided against himself; how
then will his kingdom stand? 27 If
I cast out demons by Beelzebul,
by whom do your own exorcists[b]
cast them out? Therefore they will
be your judges. 28 But if it is by the
Spirit of God that I cast out demons,
then the kingdom of God has come
to you. 29 Or how can one enter a
strong man's house and plunder his
property, without first tying up the
strong man? Then indeed the house
can be plundered. 30 Whoever is not
with me is against me, and whoever
does not gather with me scatters.
31 Therefore I tell you, people will
be forgiven for every sin and blasphemy, but blasphemy against the
Spirit will not be forgiven. 32 Whoever speaks a word against the Son
of Man will be forgiven, but whoever speaks against the Holy Spirit
will not be forgiven, either in this
age or in the age to come.

A Tree and Its Fruit

33 "Either make the tree good,
and its fruit good; or make the tree
bad, and its fruit bad; for the tree
is known by its fruit. 34 You brood
of vipers! How can you speak good
things, when you are evil? For out
of the abundance of the heart the
mouth speaks. 35 The good person
brings good things out of a good
treasure, and the evil person brings
evil things out of an evil treasure.
36 I tell you, on the day of judgment
you will have to give an account for
every careless word you utter; 37 for
by your words you will be justified,
and by your words you will be condemned."

The Sign of Jonah

38 Then some of the scribes and
Pharisees said to him, "Teacher,
we wish to see a sign from you."
39 But he answered them, "An evil
and adulterous generation asks for
a sign, but no sign will be given to
it except the sign of the prophet Jonah. 40 For just as Jonah was three
days and three nights in the belly of
the sea monster, so for three days
and three nights the Son of Man
will be in the heart of the earth.
41 The people of Nineveh will rise
up at the judgment with this generation and condemn it, because
they repented at the proclamation of Jonah, and see, something
greater than Jonah is here! 42 The
queen of the South will rise up at
the judgment with this generation
and condemn it, because she came
from the ends of the earth to listen

---

b Gk *sons*

to the wisdom of Solomon, and see,
something greater than Solomon is
here!

The Return of the Unclean Spirit

43 "When the unclean spirit has
gone out of a person, it wanders
through waterless regions looking
for a resting place, but it finds none.
44 Then it says, 'I will return to my
house from which I came.' When
it comes, it finds it empty, swept,
and put in order. 45 Then it goes
and brings along seven other spirits
more evil than itself, and they enter
and live there; and the last state of
that person is worse than the first.
So will it be also with this evil generation."

The True Kindred of Jesus

46 While he was still speaking
to the crowds, his mother and his
brothers were standing outside,
wanting to speak to him. 47 Someone told him, "Look, your mother
and your brothers are standing
outside, wanting to speak to you."[c]
48 But to the one who had told him
this, Jesus[d] replied, "Who is my
mother, and who are my brothers?"
49 And pointing to his disciples, he
said, "Here are my mother and my
brothers! 50 For whoever does the
will of my Father in heaven is my
brother and sister and mother."

The Parable of the Sower

13 That same day Jesus went
out of the house and sat beside the sea. 2 Such great crowds
gathered around him that he got
into a boat and sat there, while the
whole crowd stood on the beach.
3 And he told them many things in
parables, saying: "Listen! A sower
went out to sow. 4 And as he sowed,
some seeds fell on the path, and the
birds came and ate them up. 5 Other
seeds fell on rocky ground, where
they did not have much soil, and
they sprang up quickly, since they
had no depth of soil. 6 But when the
sun rose, they were scorched; and
since they had no root, they withered away. 7 Other seeds fell among
thorns, and the thorns grew up and
choked them. 8 Other seeds fell on
good soil and brought forth grain,
some a hundredfold, some sixty,
some thirty. 9 Let anyone with ears[a]
listen!"

The Purpose of the Parables

10 Then the disciples came and
asked him, "Why do you speak to
them in parables?" 11 He answered,
"To you it has been given to know
the secrets[b] of the kingdom of
heaven, but to them it has not been
given. 12 For to those who have,
more will be given, and they will
have an abundance; but from those
who have nothing, even what they
have will be taken away. 13 The reason I speak to them in parables is
that 'seeing they do not perceive,
and hearing they do not listen, nor
do they understand.' 14 With them
indeed is fulfilled the prophecy of
Isaiah that says:

'You will indeed listen, but
never understand,
and you will indeed look, but
never perceive.

---

c Other ancient authorities lack verse 47
d Gk *he* a Other ancient authorities add *to hear* b Or *mysteries*

15 For this people's heart has
grown dull,
and their ears are hard of
hearing,
and they have shut their eyes;
so that they might not look
with their eyes,
and listen with their ears,
and understand with their heart
and turn—
and I would heal them.'
16 But blessed are your eyes, for they
see, and your ears, for they hear.
17 Truly I tell you, many prophets
and righteous people longed to see
what you see, but did not see it, and
to hear what you hear, but did not
hear it.

The Parable of the Sower Explained

18 "Hear then the parable of the
sower. 19 When anyone hears the
word of the kingdom and does not
understand it, the evil one comes
and snatches away what is sown in
the heart; this is what was sown on
the path. 20 As for what was sown
on rocky ground, this is the one
who hears the word and immediately receives it with joy; 21 yet such
a person has no root, but endures
only for a while, and when trouble
or persecution arises on account of
the word, that person immediately falls away.[c] 22 As for what was
sown among thorns, this is the one
who hears the word, but the cares
of the world and the lure of wealth
choke the word, and it yields nothing. 23 But as for what was sown on
good soil, this is the one who hears
the word and understands it, who
indeed bears fruit and yields, in one
case a hundredfold, in another sixty, and in another thirty."

The Parable of Weeds among the Wheat

24 He put before them another
parable: "The kingdom of heav-
en may be compared to someone
who sowed good seed in his field;
25 but while everybody was asleep,
an enemy came and sowed weeds
among the wheat, and then went
away. 26 So when the plants came
up and bore grain, then the weeds
appeared as well. 27 And the slaves
of the householder came and said to
him, 'Master, did you not sow good
seed in your field? Where, then,
did these weeds come from?' 28 He
answered, 'An enemy has done
this.' The slaves said to him, 'Then
do you want us to go and gather
them?' 29 But he replied, 'No; for
in gathering the weeds you would
uproot the wheat along with them.
30 Let both of them grow together
until the harvest; and at harvest
time I will tell the reapers, Collect
the weeds first and bind them in
bundles to be burned, but gather the
wheat into my barn.' "

The Parable of the Mustard Seed

31 He put before them another
parable: "The kingdom of heaven
is like a mustard seed that someone
took and sowed in his field; 32 it is
the smallest of all the seeds, but
when it has grown it is the greatest
of shrubs and becomes a tree, so
that the birds of the air come and
make nests in its branches."

---

c Gk *stumbles*

The Parable of the Yeast
33 He told them another parable:
"The kingdom of heaven is like
yeast that a woman took and mixed
in with[d] three measures of flour until all of it was leavened."

The Use of Parables
34 Jesus told the crowds all these
things in parables; without a parable he told them nothing. 35 This
was to fulfill what had been spoken
through the prophet:[e]

"I will open my mouth to speak
in parables;
I will proclaim what has
been hidden from the
foundation of the world."[f]

Jesus Explains the Parable of the Weeds
36 Then he left the crowds and
went into the house. And his disciples approached him, saying, "Ex-
plain to us the parable of the weeds
of the field." 37 He answered, "The
one who sows the good seed is the
Son of Man; 38 the field is the world,
and the good seed are the children
of the kingdom; the weeds are the
children of the evil one, 39 and the
enemy who sowed them is the devil; the harvest is the end of the age,
and the reapers are angels. 40 Just as
the weeds are collected and burned
up with fire, so will it be at the end
of the age. 41 The Son of Man will
send his angels, and they will collect out of his kingdom all causes
of sin and all evildoers, 42 and they
will throw them into the furnace of
fire, where there will be weeping
and gnashing of teeth. 43 Then the
righteous will shine like the sun
in the kingdom of their Father. Let
anyone with ears[g] listen!

Three Parables
44 "The kingdom of heaven
is like treasure hidden in a field,
which someone found and hid; then
in his joy he goes and sells all that
he has and buys that field.
45 "Again, the kingdom of heav-
en is like a merchant in search of
fine pearls; 46 on finding one pearl
of great value, he went and sold all
that he had and bought it.
47 "Again, the kingdom of heav-
en is like a net that was thrown into
the sea and caught fish of every
kind; 48 when it was full, they drew
it ashore, sat down, and put the
good into baskets but threw out the
bad. 49 So it will be at the end of the
age. The angels will come out and
separate the evil from the righteous
50 and throw them into the furnace
of fire, where there will be weeping
and gnashing of teeth.

Treasures New and Old
51 "Have you understood all
this?" They answered, "Yes."
52 And he said to them, "Therefore
every scribe who has been trained
for the kingdom of heaven is like
the master of a household who
brings out of his treasure what is
new and what is old." 53 When Jesus
had finished these parables, he left
that place.

---

d Gk *hid in* *e* Other ancient authorities read *the prophet Isaiah* *f* Other ancient authorities lack *of the world* *g* Other ancient authorities add *to hear*

The Rejection of Jesus at Nazareth

54 He came to his hometown
and began to teach the people[h] in
their synagogue, so that they were
astounded and said, "Where did
this man get this wisdom and these
deeds of power? 55 Is not this the
carpenter's son? Is not his mother called Mary? And are not his
brothers James and Joseph and Simon and Judas? 56 And are not all
his sisters with us? Where then did
this man get all this?" 57 And they
took offense at him. But Jesus said
to them, "Prophets are not without
honor except in their own country
and in their own house." 58 And he
did not do many deeds of power
there, because of their unbelief.

The Death of John the Baptist

14 At that time Herod the ruler[a]
heard reports about Jesus;
2 and he said to his servants, "This
is John the Baptist; he has been
raised from the dead, and for this
reason these powers are at work
in him." 3 For Herod had arrested
John, bound him, and put him in
prison on account of Herodias, his
brother Philip's wife,[b] 4 because
John had been telling him, "It is
not lawful for you to have her."
5 Though Herod[c] wanted to put
him to death, he feared the crowd,
because they regarded him as a
prophet. 6 But when Herod's birthday came, the daughter of Herodias
danced before the company, and
she pleased Herod 7 so much that
he promised on oath to grant her
whatever she might ask. 8 Prompted
by her mother, she said, "Give me
the head of John the Baptist here on
a platter." 9 The king was grieved,
yet out of regard for his oaths and
for the guests, he commanded it to
be given; 10 he sent and had John
beheaded in the prison. 11 The head
was brought on a platter and given
to the girl, who brought it to her
mother. 12 His disciples came and
took the body and buried it; then
they went and told Jesus.

Feeding the Five Thousand

13 Now when Jesus heard this,
he withdrew from there in a boat
to a deserted place by himself. But
when the crowds heard it, they
followed him on foot from the
towns. 14 When he went ashore,
he saw a great crowd; and he had
compassion for them and cured
their sick. 15 When it was evening,
the disciples came to him and said,
"This is a deserted place, and the
hour is now late; send the crowds
away so that they may go into the
villages and buy food for themselves." 16 Jesus said to them, "They
need not go away; you give them
something to eat." 17 They replied,
"We have nothing here but five
loaves and two fish." 18 And he said,
"Bring them here to me." 19 Then
he ordered the crowds to sit down
on the grass. Taking the five loaves
and the two fish, he looked up to
heaven, and blessed and broke the
loaves, and gave them to the disciples, and the disciples gave them
to the crowds. 20 And all ate and
were filled; and they took up what
was left over of the broken pieces,
twelve baskets full. 21 And those

---

h Gk *them* *a* Gk *tetrarch* *b* Other ancient authorities read *his brother's wife* *c* Gk *he*

who ate were about five thousand
men, besides women and children.

Jesus Walks on the Water

22 Immediately he made the disciples get into the boat and go on
ahead to the other side, while he
dismissed the crowds. 23 And after
he had dismissed the crowds, he
went up the mountain by himself to
pray. When evening came, he was
there alone, 24 but by this time the
boat, battered by the waves, was
far from the land,[d] for the wind was
against them. 25 And early in the
morning he came walking toward
them on the sea. 26 But when the
disciples saw him walking on the
sea, they were terrified, saying, "It
is a ghost!" And they cried out in
fear. 27 But immediately Jesus spoke
to them and said, "Take heart, it is I;
do not be afraid."

28 Peter answered him, "Lord,
if it is you, command me to come
to you on the water." 29 He said,
"Come." So Peter got out of the
boat, started walking on the water,
and came toward Jesus. 30 But when
he noticed the strong wind,[e] he became frightened, and beginning to
sink, he cried out, "Lord, save me!"
31 Jesus immediately reached out
his hand and caught him, saying to
him, "You of little faith, why did
you doubt?" 32 When they got into
the boat, the wind ceased. 33 And
those in the boat worshiped him,
saying, "Truly you are the Son of
God."

Jesus Heals the Sick in Gennesaret

34 When they had crossed over,
they came to land at Gennesaret.
35 After the people of that place
recognized him, they sent word
throughout the region and brought
all who were sick to him, 36 and
begged him that they might touch
even the fringe of his cloak; and all
who touched it were healed.

The Tradition of the Elders

15 Then Pharisees and scribes
came to Jesus from Jerusalem
and said, 2 "Why do your disciples
break the tradition of the elders?
For they do not wash their hands
before they eat." 3 He answered
them, "And why do you break the
commandment of God for the sake
of your tradition? 4 For God said,[a]
'Honor your father and your mother,' and, 'Whoever speaks evil of
father or mother must surely die.'
5 But you say that whoever tells father or mother, 'Whatever support
you might have had from me is giv-
en to God,'[b] then that person need
not honor the father.[c] 6 So, for the
sake of your tradition, you make
void the word[d] of God. 7 You hypocrites! Isaiah prophesied rightly
about you when he said:

8 'This people honors me with
their lips,
but their hearts are far from
me;
9 in vain do they worship me,
teaching human precepts as
doctrines.' "

---

d Other ancient authorities read *was out on the sea* *e* Other ancient authorities read *the wind*
a Other ancient authorities read *commanded, saying* *b* Or *is an offering* *c* Other ancient authorities add *or the mother* *d* Other ancient authorities read *law*; others, *commandment*

Things That Defile

10 Then he called the crowd to
him and said to them, "Listen and
understand: 11 it is not what goes
into the mouth that defiles a person, but it is what comes out of the
mouth that defiles." 12 Then the disciples approached and said to him,
"Do you know that the Pharisees
took offense when they heard what
you said?" 13 He answered, "Every
plant that my heavenly Father has
not planted will be uprooted. 14 Let
them alone; they are blind guides of
the blind.[e] And if one blind person
guides another, both will fall into a
pit." 15 But Peter said to him, "Ex-
plain this parable to us." 16 Then he
said, "Are you also still without understanding? 17 Do you not see that
whatever goes into the mouth enters the stomach, and goes out into
the sewer? 18 But what comes out of
the mouth proceeds from the heart,
and this is what defiles. 19 For out
of the heart come evil intentions,
murder, adultery, fornication, theft,
false witness, slander. 20 These are
what defile a person, but to eat with
unwashed hands does not defile."

The Canaanite Woman's Faith

21 Jesus left that place and
went away to the district of Tyre
and Sidon. 22 Just then a Canaanite
woman from that region came out
and started shouting, "Have mercy
on me, Lord, Son of David; my
daughter is tormented by a demon."
23 But he did not answer her at all.
And his disciples came and urged
him, saying, "Send her away, for
she keeps shouting after us." 24 He
answered, "I was sent only to the
lost sheep of the house of Israel."
25 But she came and knelt before
him, saying, "Lord, help me." 26 He
answered, "It is not fair to take the
children's food and throw it to the
dogs." 27 She said, "Yes, Lord, yet
even the dogs eat the crumbs that
fall from their masters' table."
28 Then Jesus answered her, "Woman, great is your faith! Let it be
done for you as you wish." And her
daughter was healed instantly.

Jesus Cures Many People

29 After Jesus had left that place,
he passed along the Sea of Galilee, and he went up the mountain,
where he sat down. 30 Great crowds
came to him, bringing with them
the lame, the maimed, the blind, the
mute, and many others. They put
them at his feet, and he cured them,
31 so that the crowd was amazed
when they saw the mute speaking,
the maimed whole, the lame walking, and the blind seeing. And they
praised the God of Israel.

Feeding the Four Thousand

32 Then Jesus called his disciples to him and said, "I have compassion for the crowd, because they
have been with me now for three
days and have nothing to eat; and
I do not want to send them away
hungry, for they might faint on
the way." 33 The disciples said to
him, "Where are we to get enough
bread in the desert to feed so great a
crowd?" 34 Jesus asked them, "How
many loaves have you?" They said,
"Seven, and a few small fish."

---

e Other ancient authorities lack *of the blind*

35 Then ordering the crowd to sit
down on the ground, 36 he took the
seven loaves and the fish; and after
giving thanks he broke them and
gave them to the disciples, and the
disciples gave them to the crowds.
37 And all of them ate and were
filled; and they took up the broken
pieces left over, seven baskets full.
38 Those who had eaten were four
thousand men, besides women and
children. 39 After sending away the
crowds, he got into the boat and
went to the region of Magadan.[f]

The Demand for a Sign

16 The Pharisees and Sadducees
came, and to test Jesus[a] they
asked him to show them a sign
from heaven. 2 He answered them,
"When it is evening, you say, 'It
will be fair weather, for the sky is
red.' 3 And in the morning, 'It will
be stormy today, for the sky is red
and threatening.' You know how to
interpret the appearance of the sky,
but you cannot interpret the signs of
the times.[b] 4 An evil and adulterous
generation asks for a sign, but no
sign will be given to it except the
sign of Jonah." Then he left them
and went away.

The Yeast of the Pharisees and Sadducees

5 When the disciples reached
the other side, they had forgotten
to bring any bread. 6 Jesus said to
them, "Watch out, and beware of
the yeast of the Pharisees and Sadducees." 7 They said to one another,
"It is because we have brought no
bread." 8 And becoming aware of it,
Jesus said, "You of little faith, why
are you talking about having no
bread? 9 Do you still not perceive?
Do you not remember the five
loaves for the five thousand, and
how many baskets you gathered?
10 Or the seven loaves for the four
thousand, and how many baskets
you gathered? 11 How could you fail
to perceive that I was not speaking
about bread? Beware of the yeast
of the Pharisees and Sadducees!"
12 Then they understood that he had
not told them to beware of the yeast
of bread, but of the teaching of the
Pharisees and Sadducees.

Peter's Declaration about Jesus

13 Now when Jesus came into
the district of Caesarea Philippi,
he asked his disciples, "Who do
people say that the Son of Man
is?" 14 And they said, "Some say
John the Baptist, but others Elijah,
and still others Jeremiah or one of
the prophets." 15 He said to them,
"But who do you say that I am?"
16 Simon Peter answered, "You are
the Messiah,[c] the Son of the living
God." 17 And Jesus answered him,
"Blessed are you, Simon son of
Jonah! For flesh and blood has not
revealed this to you, but my Father
in heaven. 18 And I tell you, you are
Peter,[d] and on this rock[e] I will build
my church, and the gates of Hades
will not prevail against it. 19 I will
give you the keys of the kingdom of
heaven, and whatever you bind on
earth will be bound in heaven, and
whatever you loose on earth will be

---

f Other ancient authorities read *Magdala* or *Magdalan* *a* Gk *him* *b* Other ancient authorities lack [2]*When it is . . . of the times* *c* Or *the Christ* *d* Gk *Petros* *e* Gk *petra*

loosed in heaven." 20 Then he sternly ordered the disciples not to tell
anyone that he was[f] the Messiah.[g]

Jesus Foretells His Death and Resurrection

21 From that time on, Jesus began to show his disciples that he
must go to Jerusalem and undergo
great suffering at the hands of the
elders and chief priests and scribes,
and be killed, and on the third day
be raised. 22 And Peter took him
aside and began to rebuke him,
saying, "God forbid it, Lord! This
must never happen to you." 23 But
he turned and said to Peter, "Get
behind me, Satan! You are a stumbling block to me; for you are setting your mind not on divine things
but on human things."

The Cross and Self-Denial

24 Then Jesus told his disciples,
"If any want to become my followers, let them deny themselves and
take up their cross and follow me.
25 For those who want to save their
life will lose it, and those who lose
their life for my sake will find it.
26 For what will it profit them if they
gain the whole world but forfeit
their life? Or what will they give in
return for their life?

27 "For the Son of Man is to
come with his angels in the glory
of his Father, and then he will repay
everyone for what has been done.
28 Truly I tell you, there are some
standing here who will not taste
death before they see the Son of
Man coming in his kingdom."

The Transfiguration

17 Six days later, Jesus took with
him Peter and James and his
brother John and led them up a high
mountain, by themselves. 2 And he
was transfigured before them, and
his face shone like the sun, and his
clothes became dazzling white.
3 Suddenly there appeared to them
Moses and Elijah, talking with him.
4 Then Peter said to Jesus, "Lord,
it is good for us to be here; if you
wish, I[a] will make three dwellings[b]
here, one for you, one for Moses,
and one for Elijah." 5 While he was
still speaking, suddenly a bright
cloud overshadowed them, and
from the cloud a voice said, "This
is my Son, the Beloved;[c] with him
I am well pleased; listen to him!"
6 When the disciples heard this, they
fell to the ground and were overcome by fear. 7 But Jesus came and
touched them, saying, "Get up and
do not be afraid." 8 And when they
looked up, they saw no one except
Jesus himself alone.

9 As they were coming down
the mountain, Jesus ordered them,
"Tell no one about the vision until after the Son of Man has been
raised from the dead." 10 And the
disciples asked him, "Why, then,
do the scribes say that Elijah must
come first?" 11 He replied, "Elijah
is indeed coming and will restore
all things; 12 but I tell you that Elijah has already come, and they did
not recognize him, but they did to
him whatever they pleased. So also
the Son of Man is about to suffer

f Other ancient authorities add *Jesus* *g* Or *the Christ* *a* Other ancient authorities read *we* *b* Or *tents* *c* Or *my beloved Son*

at their hands." 13 Then the disciples
understood that he was speaking to
them about John the Baptist.

Jesus Cures a Boy with a Demon

14 When they came to the crowd,
a man came to him, knelt before
him, 15 and said, "Lord, have mercy on my son, for he is an epilep-
tic and he suffers terribly; he often
falls into the fire and often into the
water. 16 And I brought him to your
disciples, but they could not cure
him." 17 Jesus answered, "You faithless and perverse generation, how
much longer must I be with you?
How much longer must I put up
with you? Bring him here to me."
18 And Jesus rebuked the demon,[d]
and it[e] came out of him, and the
boy was cured instantly. 19 Then the
disciples came to Jesus privately
and said, "Why could we not cast it
out?" 20 He said to them, "Because
of your little faith. For truly I tell
you, if you have faith the size of
a[f] mustard seed, you will say to
this mountain, 'Move from here to
there,' and it will move; and nothing will be impossible for you."[g]

Jesus Again Foretells His Death and Resurrection

22 As they were gathering[h] in
Galilee, Jesus said to them, "The
Son of Man is going to be betrayed
into human hands, 23 and they will
kill him, and on the third day he
will be raised." And they were
greatly distressed.

Jesus and the Temple Tax

24 When they reached Capernaum, the collectors of the temple
tax[i] came to Peter and said, "Does
your teacher not pay the temple
tax?"[j] 25 He said, "Yes, he does."
And when he came home, Jesus
spoke of it first, asking, "What do
you think, Simon? From whom do
kings of the earth take toll or tribute? From their children or from
others?" 26 When Peter[k] said, "From
others," Jesus said to him, "Then
the children are free. 27 However,
so that we do not give offense to
them, go to the sea and cast a hook;
take the first fish that comes up; and
when you open its mouth, you will
find a coin;[l] take that and give it to
them for you and me."

True Greatness

18 At that time the disciples
came to Jesus and asked,
"Who is the greatest in the kingdom of heaven?" 2 He called a
child, whom he put among them,
3 and said, "Truly I tell you, unless
you change and become like children, you will never enter the kingdom of heaven. 4 Whoever becomes
humble like this child is the greatest
in the kingdom of heaven. 5 Whoever welcomes one such child in my
name welcomes me.

Temptations to Sin

6 "If any of you put a stumbling
block before one of these little ones
who believe in me, it would be better for you if a great millstone were

---

d Gk *it* or *him* *e* Gk *the demon* *f* Gk *faith as a grain of* *g* Other ancient authorities add verse 21, *But this kind does not come out except by prayer and fasting* *h* Other ancient authorities read *living* *i* Gk *didrachma* *j* Gk *didrachma* *k* Gk *he* *l* Gk *stater*; the stater was worth two didrachmas

fastened around your neck and you were drowned in the depth of the sea. 7 Woe to the world because of stumbling blocks! Occasions for stumbling are bound to come, but woe to the one by whom the stumbling block comes!

8 "If your hand or your foot causes you to stumble, cut it off and throw it away; it is better for you to enter life maimed or lame than to have two hands or two feet and to be thrown into the eternal fire. 9 And if your eye causes you to stumble, tear it out and throw it away; it is better for you to enter life with one eye than to have two eyes and to be thrown into the hell[a] of fire.

The Parable of the Lost Sheep

10 "Take care that you do not despise one of these little ones; for, I tell you, in heaven their angels continually see the face of my Father in heaven.[b] 12 What do you think? If a shepherd has a hundred sheep, and one of them has gone astray, does he not leave the ninety-nine on the mountains and go in search of the one that went astray? 13 And if he finds it, truly I tell you, he rejoices over it more than over the ninety-nine that never went astray. 14 So it is not the will of your[c] Father in heaven that one of these little ones should be lost.

Reproving Another Who Sins

15 "If another member of the church[d] sins against you,[e] go and point out the fault when the two of you are alone. If the member listens to you, you have regained that one.[f] 16 But if you are not listened to, take one or two others along with you, so that every word may be confirmed by the evidence of two or three witnesses. 17 If the member refuses to listen to them, tell it to the church; and if the offender refuses to listen even to the church, let such a one be to you as a Gentile and a tax collector. 18 Truly I tell you, whatever you bind on earth will be bound in heaven, and whatever you loose on earth will be loosed in heaven. 19 Again, truly I tell you, if two of you agree on earth about anything you ask, it will be done for you by my Father in heaven. 20 For where two or three are gathered in my name, I am there among them."

Forgiveness

21 Then Peter came and said to him, "Lord, if another member of the church[g] sins against me, how often should I forgive? As many as seven times?" 22 Jesus said to him, "Not seven times, but, I tell you, seventy-seven[h] times.

The Parable of the Unforgiving Servant

23 "For this reason the kingdom of heaven may be compared to a king who wished to settle accounts with his slaves. 24 When he began the reckoning, one who owed him ten thousand talents[i] was brought

a Gk *Gehenna* *b* Other ancient authorities add verse 11, *For the Son of Man came to save the lost* *c* Other ancient authorities read *my* *d* Gk *If your brother* *e* Other ancient authorities lack *against you* *f* Gk *the brother* *g* Gk *if my brother* *h* Or *seventy times seven* *i* A talent was worth more than fifteen years' wages of a laborer

to him; [25]and, as he could not pay,
his lord ordered him to be sold, together with his wife and children
and all his possessions, and payment to be made. [26]So the slave
fell on his knees before him, saying, 'Have patience with me, and
I will pay you everything.' [27]And
out of pity for him, the lord of that
slave released him and forgave him
the debt. [28]But that same slave,
as he went out, came upon one of
his fellow slaves who owed him a
hundred denarii;[j] and seizing him
by the throat, he said, 'Pay what
you owe.' [29]Then his fellow slave
fell down and pleaded with him,
'Have patience with me, and I will
pay you.' [30]But he refused; then he
went and threw him into prison until he would pay the debt. [31]When
his fellow slaves saw what had happened, they were greatly distressed,
and they went and reported to their
lord all that had taken place. [32]Then
his lord summoned him and said to
him, 'You wicked slave! I forgave
you all that debt because you pleaded with me. [33]Should you not have
had mercy on your fellow slave, as
I had mercy on you?' [34]And in anger his lord handed him over to be
tortured until he would pay his entire debt. [35]So my heavenly Father
will also do to every one of you, if
you do not forgive your brother or
sister[k] from your heart."

Teaching about Divorce

19 When Jesus had finished
saying these things, he left
Galilee and went to the region of
Judea beyond the Jordan. [2]Large
crowds followed him, and he cured
them there.
3 Some Pharisees came to him,
and to test him they asked, "Is
it lawful for a man to divorce his
wife for any cause?" [4]He answered,
"Have you not read that the one
who made them at the beginning
'made them male and female,' [5]and
said, 'For this reason a man shall
leave his father and mother and
be joined to his wife, and the two
shall become one flesh'? [6]So they
are no longer two, but one flesh.
Therefore what God has joined together, let no one separate." [7]They
said to him, "Why then did Moses
command us to give a certificate of
dismissal and to divorce her?" [8]He
said to them, "It was because you
were so hard-hearted that Moses
allowed you to divorce your wives,
but from the beginning it was not
so. [9]And I say to you, whoever divorces his wife, except for unchastity, and marries another commits
adultery."[a]
10 His disciples said to him, "If
such is the case of a man with his
wife, it is better not to marry." [11]But
he said to them, "Not everyone can
accept this teaching, but only those
to whom it is given. [12]For there are
eunuchs who have been so from
birth, and there are eunuchs who
have been made eunuchs by others,
and there are eunuchs who have
made themselves eunuchs for the
sake of the kingdom of heaven. Let
anyone accept this who can."

---

j The denarius was the usual day's wage for a laborer *k* Gk *brother* *a* Other ancient authorities read *except on the ground of unchastity, causes her to commit adultery*; others add at the end of the verse *and he who marries a divorced woman commits adultery*

Jesus Blesses Little Children

13 Then little children were being brought to him in order that he
might lay his hands on them and
pray. The disciples spoke sternly
to those who brought them; 14 but
Jesus said, "Let the little children come to me, and do not stop
them; for it is to such as these that
the kingdom of heaven belongs."
15 And he laid his hands on them
and went on his way.

The Rich Young Man

16 Then someone came to him
and said, "Teacher, what good deed
must I do to have eternal life?"
17 And he said to him, "Why do
you ask me about what is good?
There is only one who is good. If
you wish to enter into life, keep the
commandments." 18 He said to him,
"Which ones?" And Jesus said,
"You shall not murder; You shall
not commit adultery; You shall
not steal; You shall not bear false
witness; 19 Honor your father and
mother; also, You shall love your
neighbor as yourself." 20 The young
man said to him, "I have kept all
these;[b] what do I still lack?" 21 Jesus said to him, "If you wish to be
perfect, go, sell your possessions,
and give the money[c] to the poor,
and you will have treasure in heav-
en; then come, follow me." 22 When
the young man heard this word,
he went away grieving, for he had
many possessions.

23 Then Jesus said to his disciples, "Truly I tell you, it will be
hard for a rich person to enter the
kingdom of heaven. 24 Again I tell
you, it is easier for a camel to go
through the eye of a needle than for
someone who is rich to enter the
kingdom of God." 25 When the disciples heard this, they were greatly
astounded and said, "Then who
can be saved?" 26 But Jesus looked
at them and said, "For mortals it is
impossible, but for God all things
are possible."

27 Then Peter said in reply,
"Look, we have left everything
and followed you. What then will
we have?" 28 Jesus said to them,
"Truly I tell you, at the renewal of
all things, when the Son of Man is
seated on the throne of his glory,
you who have followed me will
also sit on twelve thrones, judging
the twelve tribes of Israel. 29 And
everyone who has left houses or
brothers or sisters or father or
mother or children or fields, for my
name's sake, will receive a hundredfold,[d] and will inherit eternal
life. 30 But many who are first will
be last, and the last will be first.

The Laborers in the Vineyard

20 "For the kingdom of heaven
is like a landowner who went
out early in the morning to hire
laborers for his vineyard. 2 After
agreeing with the laborers for the
usual daily wage,[a] he sent them
into his vineyard. 3 When he went
out about nine o'clock, he saw
others standing idle in the marketplace; 4 and he said to them, 'You
also go into the vineyard, and I will
pay you whatever is right.' So they
went. 5 When he went out again

---

b Other ancient authorities add *from my youth*
c Gk lacks *the money* *d* Other ancient authorities read *manifold* *a* Gk *a denarius*

about noon and about three o'clock, he did the same. 6 And about five o'clock he went out and found others standing around; and he said to them, 'Why are you standing here idle all day?' 7 They said to him, 'Because no one has hired us.' He said to them, 'You also go into the vineyard.' 8 When evening came, the owner of the vineyard said to his manager, 'Call the laborers and give them their pay, beginning with the last and then going to the first.' 9 When those hired about five o'clock came, each of them received the usual daily wage.[b] 10 Now when the first came, they thought they would receive more; but each of them also received the usual daily wage.[c] 11 And when they received it, they grumbled against the landowner, 12 saying, 'These last worked only one hour, and you have made them equal to us who have borne the burden of the day and the scorching heat.' 13 But he replied to one of them, 'Friend, I am doing you no wrong; did you not agree with me for the usual daily wage?[d] 14 Take what belongs to you and go; I choose to give to this last the same as I give to you. 15 Am I not allowed to do what I choose with what belongs to me? Or are you envious because I am generous?'[e] 16 So the last will be first, and the first will be last."[f]

A Third Time Jesus Foretells His Death and Resurrection

17 While Jesus was going up to Jerusalem, he took the twelve disciples aside by themselves, and said to them on the way, 18 "See, we are going up to Jerusalem, and the Son of Man will be handed over to the chief priests and scribes, and they will condemn him to death; 19 then they will hand him over to the Gentiles to be mocked and flogged and crucified; and on the third day he will be raised."

The Request of the Mother of James and John

20 Then the mother of the sons of Zebedee came to him with her sons, and kneeling before him, she asked a favor of him. 21 And he said to her, "What do you want?" She said to him, "Declare that these two sons of mine will sit, one at your right hand and one at your left, in your kingdom." 22 But Jesus answered, "You do not know what you are asking. Are you able to drink the cup that I am about to drink?"[g] They said to him, "We are able." 23 He said to them, "You will indeed drink my cup, but to sit at my right hand and at my left, this is not mine to grant, but it is for those for whom it has been prepared by my Father."

24 When the ten heard it, they were angry with the two brothers. 25 But Jesus called them to him and said, "You know that the rulers of the Gentiles lord it over them, and their great ones are tyrants over them. 26 It will not be so among you; but whoever wishes to be great among you must be your servant, 27 and whoever wishes to be

---

b Gk *a denarius* *c* Gk *a denarius* *d* Gk *a denarius* *e* Gk *is your eye evil because I am good?* *f* Other ancient authorities add *for many are called but few are chosen* *g* Other ancient authorities add *or to be baptized with the baptism that I am baptized with?*

first among you must be your slave;
28 just as the Son of Man came not
to be served but to serve, and to
give his life a ransom for many."

Jesus Heals Two Blind Men

29 As they were leaving Jericho, a large crowd followed him.
30 There were two blind men sitting
by the roadside. When they heard
that Jesus was passing by, they
shouted, "Lord,[h] have mercy on us,
Son of David!" 31 The crowd sternly
ordered them to be quiet; but they
shouted even more loudly, "Have
mercy on us, Lord, Son of David!"
32 Jesus stood still and called them,
saying, "What do you want me to
do for you?" 33 They said to him,
"Lord, let our eyes be opened."
34 Moved with compassion, Jesus
touched their eyes. Immediately
they regained their sight and followed him.

Jesus' Triumphal Entry into Jerusalem

21 When they had come near
Jerusalem and had reached
Bethphage, at the Mount of Olives,
Jesus sent two disciples, 2 saying to
them, "Go into the village ahead
of you, and immediately you will
find a donkey tied, and a colt with
her; untie them and bring them to
me. 3 If anyone says anything to
you, just say this, 'The Lord needs
them.' And he will send them
immediately.[a]" 4 This took place
to fulfill what had been spoken
through the prophet, saying,
5 "Tell the daughter of Zion,
Look, your king is coming to
you,
humble, and mounted on a
donkey,
and on a colt, the foal of a
donkey."
6 The disciples went and did as
Jesus had directed them; 7 they
brought the donkey and the colt,
and put their cloaks on them, and he
sat on them. 8 A very large crowd[b]
spread their cloaks on the road, and
others cut branches from the trees
and spread them on the road. 9 The
crowds that went ahead of him and
that followed were shouting,
"Hosanna to the Son of David!
Blessed is the one who comes
in the name of the Lord!
Hosanna in the highest heaven!"
10 When he entered Jerusalem, the
whole city was in turmoil, asking,
"Who is this?" 11 The crowds were
saying, "This is the prophet Jesus
from Nazareth in Galilee."

Jesus Cleanses the Temple

12 Then Jesus entered the temple[c] and drove out all who were
selling and buying in the temple,
and he overturned the tables of the
money changers and the seats of
those who sold doves. 13 He said to
them, "It is written,
'My house shall be called a
house of prayer';
but you are making it a den of
robbers."

14 The blind and the lame came
to him in the temple, and he cured
them. 15 But when the chief priests
and the scribes saw the amazing

---

h Other ancient authorities lack *Lord*
a Or *'The Lord needs them and will send them back immediately.'* *b* Or *Most of the crowd*
c Other ancient authorities add *of God*

things that he did, and heard[d] the
children crying out in the temple,
"Hosanna to the Son of David,"
they became angry [16]and said to
him, "Do you hear what these are
saying?" Jesus said to them, "Yes;
have you never read,

'Out of the mouths of infants
and nursing babies
you have prepared praise for
yourself'?"

[17]He left them, went out of the city
to Bethany, and spent the night
there.

Jesus Curses the Fig Tree

18 In the morning, when he returned to the city, he was hungry.
[19]And seeing a fig tree by the side
of the road, he went to it and found
nothing at all on it but leaves. Then
he said to it, "May no fruit ever
come from you again!" And the fig
tree withered at once. [20]When the
disciples saw it, they were amazed,
saying, "How did the fig tree wither
at once?" [21]Jesus answered them,
"Truly I tell you, if you have faith
and do not doubt, not only will
you do what has been done to the
fig tree, but even if you say to
this mountain, 'Be lifted up and
thrown into the sea,' it will be done.
[22]Whatever you ask for in prayer
with faith, you will receive."

The Authority of Jesus Questioned

23 When he entered the temple,
the chief priests and the elders of
the people came to him as he was
teaching, and said, "By what authority are you doing these things,
and who gave you this authority?"
[24]Jesus said to them, "I will also ask
you one question; if you tell me the
answer, then I will also tell you by
what authority I do these things.
[25]Did the baptism of John come
from heaven, or was it of human
origin?" And they argued with one
another, "If we say, 'From heaven,'
he will say to us, 'Why then did you
not believe him?' [26]But if we say,
'Of human origin,' we are afraid
of the crowd; for all regard John
as a prophet." [27]So they answered
Jesus, "We do not know." And he
said to them, "Neither will I tell
you by what authority I am doing
these things.

The Parable of the Two Sons

28 "What do you think? A man
had two sons; he went to the first
and said, 'Son, go and work in the
vineyard today.' [29]He answered, 'I
will not'; but later he changed his
mind and went. [30]The father[e] went
to the second and said the same;
and he answered, 'I go, sir'; but he
did not go. [31]Which of the two did
the will of his father?" They said,
"The first." Jesus said to them,
"Truly I tell you, the tax collectors
and the prostitutes are going into
the kingdom of God ahead of you.
[32]For John came to you in the way
of righteousness and you did not
believe him, but the tax collectors
and the prostitutes believed him;
and even after you saw it, you did
not change your minds and believe
him.

The Parable of the Wicked Tenants

33 "Listen to another parable.

---

d Gk lacks *heard* *e* Gk *He*

There was a landowner who planted a vineyard, put a fence around
it, dug a wine press in it, and built
a watchtower. Then he leased it
to tenants and went to another
country. 34 When the harvest time
had come, he sent his slaves to
the tenants to collect his produce.
35 But the tenants seized his slaves
and beat one, killed another, and
stoned another. 36 Again he sent other slaves, more than the first; and
they treated them in the same way.
37 Finally he sent his son to them,
saying, 'They will respect my son.'
38 But when the tenants saw the son,
they said to themselves, 'This is the
heir; come, let us kill him and get
his inheritance.' 39 So they seized
him, threw him out of the vineyard,
and killed him. 40 Now when the
owner of the vineyard comes, what
will he do to those tenants?" 41 They
said to him, "He will put those
wretches to a miserable death, and
lease the vineyard to other tenants
who will give him the produce at
the harvest time."

42 Jesus said to them, "Have you
never read in the scriptures:

'The stone that the builders
rejected
has become the cornerstone;[f]
this was the Lord's doing,
and it is amazing in our eyes'?

43 Therefore I tell you, the kingdom
of God will be taken away from
you and given to a people that produces the fruits of the kingdom.[g]
44 The one who falls on this stone
will be broken to pieces; and it will
crush anyone on whom it falls."[h]

45 When the chief priests and the
Pharisees heard his parables, they
realized that he was speaking about
them. 46 They wanted to arrest him,
but they feared the crowds, because
they regarded him as a prophet.

The Parable of the Wedding Banquet

22 Once more Jesus spoke to
them in parables, saying:
2 "The kingdom of heaven may be
compared to a king who gave a
wedding banquet for his son. 3 He
sent his slaves to call those who
had been invited to the wedding
banquet, but they would not come.
4 Again he sent other slaves, saying,
'Tell those who have been invited:
Look, I have prepared my dinner,
my oxen and my fat calves have
been slaughtered, and everything
is ready; come to the wedding
banquet.' 5 But they made light of
it and went away, one to his farm,
another to his business, 6 while the
rest seized his slaves, mistreated
them, and killed them. 7 The king
was enraged. He sent his troops,
destroyed those murderers, and
burned their city. 8 Then he said to
his slaves, 'The wedding is ready,
but those invited were not worthy.
9 Go therefore into the main streets,
and invite everyone you find to the
wedding banquet.' 10 Those slaves
went out into the streets and gathered all whom they found, both
good and bad; so the wedding hall
was filled with guests.

11 "But when the king came
in to see the guests, he noticed a
man there who was not wearing a
wedding robe, 12 and he said to him,

f Or *keystone* *g* Gk *the fruits of it* *h* Other ancient authorities lack verse 44

'Friend, how did you get in here
without a wedding robe?' And he
was speechless. 13 Then the king
said to the attendants, 'Bind him
hand and foot, and throw him into
the outer darkness, where there will
be weeping and gnashing of teeth.'
14 For many are called, but few are
chosen."

The Question about Paying Taxes

15 Then the Pharisees went and
plotted to entrap him in what he
said. 16 So they sent their disciples
to him, along with the Herodians,
saying, "Teacher, we know that you
are sincere, and teach the way of
God in accordance with truth, and
show deference to no one; for you
do not regard people with partiality.
17 Tell us, then, what you think. Is
it lawful to pay taxes to the emperor, or not?" 18 But Jesus, aware
of their malice, said, "Why are you
putting me to the test, you hypocrites? 19 Show me the coin used
for the tax." And they brought him
a denarius. 20 Then he said to them,
"Whose head is this, and whose
title?" 21 They answered, "The
emperor's." Then he said to them,
"Give therefore to the emperor the
things that are the emperor's, and
to God the things that are God's."
22 When they heard this, they were
amazed; and they left him and went
away.

The Question about the Resurrection

23 The same day some Sadducees came to him, saying there is no
resurrection;[a] and they asked him a
question, saying, 24 "Teacher, Moses said, 'If a man dies childless,
his brother shall marry the widow,
and raise up children for his brother.' 25 Now there were seven brothers among us; the first married, and
died childless, leaving the widow
to his brother. 26 The second did the
same, so also the third, down to the
seventh. 27 Last of all, the woman
herself died. 28 In the resurrection,
then, whose wife of the seven will
she be? For all of them had married
her."

29 Jesus answered them, "You
are wrong, because you know neither the scriptures nor the power
of God. 30 For in the resurrection
they neither marry nor are given
in marriage, but are like angels[b] in
heaven. 31 And as for the resurrection of the dead, have you not read
what was said to you by God, 32 'I
am the God of Abraham, the God
of Isaac, and the God of Jacob'?
He is God not of the dead, but of
the living." 33 And when the crowd
heard it, they were astounded at his
teaching.

The Greatest Commandment

34 When the Pharisees heard
that he had silenced the Sadducees,
they gathered together, 35 and one of
them, a lawyer, asked him a question to test him. 36 "Teacher, which
commandment in the law is the
greatest?" 37 He said to him, " 'You
shall love the Lord your God with
all your heart, and with all your
soul, and with all your mind.'
38 This is the greatest and first com-

---

a Other ancient authorities read *who say that there is no resurrection* b Other ancient authorities add *of God*

mandment. 39And a second is like
it: 'You shall love your neighbor
as yourself.' 40On these two commandments hang all the law and
the prophets."

The Question about David's Son

41 Now while the Pharisees were
gathered together, Jesus asked them
this question: 42"What do you think
of the Messiah?[c] Whose son is he?"
They said to him, "The son of David." 43He said to them, "How is it
then that David by the Spirit[d] calls
him Lord, saying,
44 'The Lord said to my Lord,
"Sit at my right hand,
until I put your enemies under
your feet" '?
45If David thus calls him Lord, how
can he be his son?" 46No one was
able to give him an answer, nor
from that day did anyone dare to
ask him any more questions.

Jesus Denounces Scribes and Pharisees

23 Then Jesus said to the crowds
and to his disciples, 2"The
scribes and the Pharisees sit on
Moses' seat; 3therefore, do whatever they teach you and follow it; but
do not do as they do, for they do
not practice what they teach. 4They
tie up heavy burdens, hard to bear,[a]
and lay them on the shoulders of
others; but they themselves are
unwilling to lift a finger to move
them. 5They do all their deeds to
be seen by others; for they make
their phylacteries broad and their
fringes long. 6They love to have the
place of honor at banquets and the
best seats in the synagogues, 7and
to be greeted with respect in the
marketplaces, and to have people
call them rabbi. 8But you are not
to be called rabbi, for you have one
teacher, and you are all students.[b]
9And call no one your father on
earth, for you have one Father—
the one in heaven. 10Nor are you to
be called instructors, for you have
one instructor, the Messiah.[c] 11The
greatest among you will be your
servant. 12All who exalt themselves
will be humbled, and all who humble themselves will be exalted.
13 "But woe to you, scribes and
Pharisees, hypocrites! For you
lock people out of the kingdom of
heaven. For you do not go in yourselves, and when others are going
in, you stop them.[d] 15Woe to you,
scribes and Pharisees, hypocrites!
For you cross sea and land to make
a single convert, and you make the
new convert twice as much a child
of hell[e] as yourselves.
16 "Woe to you, blind guides,
who say, 'Whoever swears by the
sanctuary is bound by nothing, but
whoever swears by the gold of the
sanctuary is bound by the oath.'
17You blind fools! For which is
greater, the gold or the sanctuary
that has made the gold sacred?
18And you say, 'Whoever swears
by the altar is bound by nothing,
but whoever swears by the gift that
is on the altar is bound by the oath.'

---

c Or *Christ* d Gk *in spirit* a Other ancient authorities lack *hard to bear* b Gk *brothers* c Or *the Christ* d Other authorities add here (or after verse 12) verse 14, *Woe to you, scribes and Pharisees, hypocrites! For you devour widows' houses and for the sake of appearance you make long prayers; therefore you will receive the greater condemnation* e Gk *Gehenna*

19 How blind you are! For which is greater, the gift or the altar that makes the gift sacred? 20 So whoever swears by the altar, swears by it and by everything on it; 21 and whoever swears by the sanctuary, swears by it and by the one who dwells in it; 22 and whoever swears by heaven, swears by the throne of God and by the one who is seated upon it.

23 "Woe to you, scribes and Pharisees, hypocrites! For you tithe mint, dill, and cummin, and have neglected the weightier matters of the law: justice and mercy and faith. It is these you ought to have practiced without neglecting the others. 24 You blind guides! You strain out a gnat but swallow a camel!

25 "Woe to you, scribes and Pharisees, hypocrites! For you clean the outside of the cup and of the plate, but inside they are full of greed and self-indulgence. 26 You blind Pharisee! First clean the inside of the cup,[f] so that the outside also may become clean.

27 "Woe to you, scribes and Pharisees, hypocrites! For you are like whitewashed tombs, which on the outside look beautiful, but inside they are full of the bones of the dead and of all kinds of filth. 28 So you also on the outside look righteous to others, but inside you are full of hypocrisy and lawlessness.

29 "Woe to you, scribes and Pharisees, hypocrites! For you build the tombs of the prophets and decorate the graves of the righteous, 30 and you say, 'If we had lived in the days of our ancestors, we would not have taken part with them in shedding the blood of the prophets.' 31 Thus you testify against yourselves that you are descendants of those who murdered the prophets. 32 Fill up, then, the measure of your ancestors. 33 You snakes, you brood of vipers! How can you escape being sentenced to hell?[g] 34 Therefore I send you prophets, sages, and scribes, some of whom you will kill and crucify, and some you will flog in your synagogues and pursue from town to town, 35 so that upon you may come all the righteous blood shed on earth, from the blood of righteous Abel to the blood of Zechariah son of Barachiah, whom you murdered between the sanctuary and the altar. 36 Truly I tell you, all this will come upon this generation.

The Lament over Jerusalem

37 "Jerusalem, Jerusalem, the city that kills the prophets and stones those who are sent to it! How often have I desired to gather your children together as a hen gathers her brood under her wings, and you were not willing! 38 See, your house is left to you, desolate.[h] 39 For I tell you, you will not see me again until you say, 'Blessed is the one who comes in the name of the Lord.' "

The Destruction of the Temple Foretold

24 As Jesus came out of the temple and was going away,

---

f Other ancient authorities add *and of the plate*
g Gk *Gehenna* *h* Other ancient authorities lack *desolate*

his disciples came to point out to
him the buildings of the temple.
2 Then he asked them, "You see all
these, do you not? Truly I tell you,
not one stone will be left here upon
another; all will be thrown down."

Signs of the End of the Age

3 When he was sitting on the
Mount of Olives, the disciples
came to him privately, saying, "Tell
us, when will this be, and what will
be the sign of your coming and
of the end of the age?" 4 Jesus answered them, "Beware that no one
leads you astray. 5 For many will
come in my name, saying, 'I am
the Messiah!'[a] and they will lead
many astray. 6 And you will hear of
wars and rumors of wars; see that
you are not alarmed; for this must
take place, but the end is not yet.
7 For nation will rise against nation,
and kingdom against kingdom, and
there will be famines[b] and earthquakes in various places: 8 all this
is but the beginning of the birth
pangs.

Persecutions Foretold

9 "Then they will hand you over
to be tortured and will put you to
death, and you will be hated by
all nations because of my name.
10 Then many will fall away,[c] and
they will betray one another and
hate one another. 11 And many
false prophets will arise and lead
many astray. 12 And because of the
increase of lawlessness, the love
of many will grow cold. 13 But the
one who endures to the end will
be saved. 14 And this good news[d]
of the kingdom will be proclaimed
throughout the world, as a testimony to all the nations; and then the
end will come.

The Desolating Sacrilege

15 "So when you see the desolating sacrilege standing in the
holy place, as was spoken of by
the prophet Daniel (let the reader
understand), 16 then those in Judea
must flee to the mountains; 17 the
one on the housetop must not go
down to take what is in the house;
18 the one in the field must not turn
back to get a coat. 19 Woe to those
who are pregnant and to those who
are nursing infants in those days!
20 Pray that your flight may not be
in winter or on a sabbath. 21 For at
that time there will be great suffering, such as has not been from
the beginning of the world until
now, no, and never will be. 22 And
if those days had not been cut short,
no one would be saved; but for the
sake of the elect those days will be
cut short. 23 Then if anyone says to
you, 'Look! Here is the Messiah!'[e]
or 'There he is!'—do not believe
it. 24 For false messiahs[f] and false
prophets will appear and produce
great signs and omens, to lead
astray, if possible, even the elect.
25 Take note, I have told you beforehand. 26 So, if they say to you,
'Look! He is in the wilderness,' do
not go out. If they say, 'Look! He is
in the inner rooms,' do not believe
it. 27 For as the lightning comes
from the east and flashes as far as
the west, so will be the coming of

---

a Or *the Christ* *b* Other ancient authorities add *and pestilences* *c* Or *stumble* *d* Or *gospel* *e* Or *the Christ* *f* Or *christs*

the Son of Man. 28 Wherever the
corpse is, there the vultures will
gather.

The Coming of the Son of Man

29 "Immediately after the suffering of those days
the sun will be darkened,
and the moon will not give its
light;
the stars will fall from heaven,
and the powers of heaven will
be shaken.
30 Then the sign of the Son of Man
will appear in heaven, and then all
the tribes of the earth will mourn,
and they will see 'the Son of Man
coming on the clouds of heav-
en' with power and great glory.
31 And he will send out his angels
with a loud trumpet call, and they
will gather his elect from the four
winds, from one end of heaven to
the other.

The Lesson of the Fig Tree

32 "From the fig tree learn its lesson: as soon as its branch becomes
tender and puts forth its leaves, you
know that summer is near. 33 So
also, when you see all these things,
you know that he[g] is near, at the
very gates. 34 Truly I tell you, this
generation will not pass away until
all these things have taken place.
35 Heaven and earth will pass away,
but my words will not pass away.

The Necessity for Watchfulness

36 "But about that day and hour
no one knows, neither the angels of
heaven, nor the Son,[h] but only the
Father. 37 For as the days of Noah
were, so will be the coming of the
Son of Man. 38 For as in those days
before the flood they were eating
and drinking, marrying and giving
in marriage, until the day Noah
entered the ark, 39 and they knew
nothing until the flood came and
swept them all away, so too will
be the coming of the Son of Man.
40 Then two will be in the field; one
will be taken and one will be left.
41 Two women will be grinding
meal together; one will be taken
and one will be left. 42 Keep awake
therefore, for you do not know on
what day[i] your Lord is coming.
43 But understand this: if the owner
of the house had known in what
part of the night the thief was coming, he would have stayed awake
and would not have let his house be
broken into. 44 Therefore you also
must be ready, for the Son of Man
is coming at an unexpected hour.

The Faithful or the Unfaithful Slave

45 "Who then is the faithful and
wise slave, whom his master has
put in charge of his household, to
give the other slaves[j] their allowance of food at the proper time?
46 Blessed is that slave whom his
master will find at work when he
arrives. 47 Truly I tell you, he will
put that one in charge of all his possessions. 48 But if that wicked slave
says to himself, 'My master is delayed,' 49 and he begins to beat his
fellow slaves, and eats and drinks
with drunkards, 50 the master of that
slave will come on a day when he

---

g Or *it* *h* Other ancient authorities lack *nor the Son* *i* Other ancient authorities read *at what hour* *j* Gk *to give them*

does not expect him and at an hour that he does not know. 51 He will cut him in pieces[k] and put him with the hypocrites, where there will be weeping and gnashing of teeth.

The Parable of the Ten Bridesmaids

25 "Then the kingdom of heaven will be like this. Ten bridesmaids[a] took their lamps and went to meet the bridegroom.[b] 2 Five of them were foolish, and five were wise. 3 When the foolish took their lamps, they took no oil with them; 4 but the wise took flasks of oil with their lamps. 5 As the bridegroom was delayed, all of them became drowsy and slept. 6 But at midnight there was a shout, 'Look! Here is the bridegroom! Come out to meet him.' 7 Then all those bridesmaids[c] got up and trimmed their lamps. 8 The foolish said to the wise, 'Give us some of your oil, for our lamps are going out.' 9 But the wise replied, 'No! there will not be enough for you and for us; you had better go to the dealers and buy some for yourselves.' 10 And while they went to buy it, the bridegroom came, and those who were ready went with him into the wedding banquet; and the door was shut. 11 Later the other bridesmaids[d] came also, saying, 'Lord, lord, open to us.' 12 But he replied, 'Truly I tell you, I do not know you.' 13 Keep awake therefore, for you know neither the day nor the hour.[e]

The Parable of the Talents

14 "For it is as if a man, going on a journey, summoned his slaves and entrusted his property to them; 15 to one he gave five talents,[f] to another two, to another one, to each according to his ability. Then he went away. 16 The one who had received the five talents went off at once and traded with them, and made five more talents. 17 In the same way, the one who had the two talents made two more talents. 18 But the one who had received the one talent went off and dug a hole in the ground and hid his master's money. 19 After a long time the master of those slaves came and settled accounts with them. 20 Then the one who had received the five talents came forward, bringing five more talents, saying, 'Master, you handed over to me five talents; see, I have made five more talents.' 21 His master said to him, 'Well done, good and trustworthy slave; you have been trustworthy in a few things, I will put you in charge of many things; enter into the joy of your master.' 22 And the one with the two talents also came forward, saying, 'Master, you handed over to me two talents; see, I have made two more talents.' 23 His master said to him, 'Well done, good and trustworthy slave; you have been trustworthy in a few things, I will put you in charge of many things; enter into the joy of your master.' 24 Then the one who had received the one talent also came forward, saying, 'Master, I knew that you were a harsh man, reaping where you did not sow, and

k Or *cut him off* *a* Gk *virgins* *b* Other ancient authorities add *and the bride* *c* Gk *virgins* *d* Gk *virgins* *e* Other ancient authorities add *in which the Son of Man is coming* *f* A talent was worth more than fifteen years' wages of a laborer

gathering where you did not scatter
seed; 25so I was afraid, and I went
and hid your talent in the ground.
Here you have what is yours.' 26But
his master replied, 'You wicked
and lazy slave! You knew, did you,
that I reap where I did not sow,
and gather where I did not scatter?
27Then you ought to have invested
my money with the bankers, and on
my return I would have received
what was my own with interest.
28So take the talent from him, and
give it to the one with the ten talents. 29For to all those who have,
more will be given, and they will
have an abundance; but from those
who have nothing, even what they
have will be taken away. 30As for
this worthless slave, throw him into
the outer darkness, where there will
be weeping and gnashing of teeth.'

The Judgment of the Nations

31 "When the Son of Man comes
in his glory, and all the angels with
him, then he will sit on the throne
of his glory. 32All the nations will
be gathered before him, and he will
separate people one from another
as a shepherd separates the sheep
from the goats, 33and he will put
the sheep at his right hand and the
goats at the left. 34Then the king
will say to those at his right hand,
'Come, you that are blessed by my
Father, inherit the kingdom prepared for you from the foundation
of the world; 35for I was hungry and
you gave me food, I was thirsty and
you gave me something to drink, I
was a stranger and you welcomed
me, 36I was naked and you gave me
clothing, I was sick and you took
care of me, I was in prison and you
visited me.' 37Then the righteous
will answer him, 'Lord, when was
it that we saw you hungry and gave
you food, or thirsty and gave you
something to drink? 38And when
was it that we saw you a stranger
and welcomed you, or naked and
gave you clothing? 39And when
was it that we saw you sick or in
prison and visited you?' 40And the
king will answer them, 'Truly I tell
you, just as you did it to one of the
least of these who are members
of my family,[g] you did it to me.'
41Then he will say to those at his
left hand, 'You that are accursed,
depart from me into the eternal
fire prepared for the devil and his
angels; 42for I was hungry and you
gave me no food, I was thirsty and
you gave me nothing to drink, 43I
was a stranger and you did not welcome me, naked and you did not
give me clothing, sick and in prison
and you did not visit me.' 44Then
they also will answer, 'Lord, when
was it that we saw you hungry or
thirsty or a stranger or naked or sick
or in prison, and did not take care of
you?' 45Then he will answer them,
'Truly I tell you, just as you did not
do it to one of the least of these,
you did not do it to me.' 46And
these will go away into eternal
punishment, but the righteous into
eternal life."

The Plot to Kill Jesus

26 When Jesus had finished saying all these things, he said to
his disciples, 2"You know that after

g Gk *these my brothers*

two days the Passover is coming, and the Son of Man will be handed over to be crucified."

3 Then the chief priests and the elders of the people gathered in the palace of the high priest, who was called Caiaphas, [4]and they conspired to arrest Jesus by stealth and kill him. [5]But they said, "Not during the festival, or there may be a riot among the people."

The Anointing at Bethany

6 Now while Jesus was at Bethany in the house of Simon the leper,[a] [7]a woman came to him with an alabaster jar of very costly ointment, and she poured it on his head as he sat at the table. [8]But when the disciples saw it, they were angry and said, "Why this waste? [9]For this ointment could have been sold for a large sum, and the money given to the poor." [10]But Jesus, aware of this, said to them, "Why do you trouble the woman? She has performed a good service for me. [11]For you always have the poor with you, but you will not always have me. [12]By pouring this ointment on my body she has prepared me for burial. [13]Truly I tell you, wherever this good news[b] is proclaimed in the whole world, what she has done will be told in remembrance of her."

Judas Agrees to Betray Jesus

14 Then one of the twelve, who was called Judas Iscariot, went to the chief priests [15]and said, "What will you give me if I betray him to you?" They paid him thirty pieces of silver. [16]And from that moment he began to look for an opportunity to betray him.

The Passover with the Disciples

17 On the first day of Unleavened Bread the disciples came to Jesus, saying, "Where do you want us to make the preparations for you to eat the Passover?" [18]He said, "Go into the city to a certain man, and say to him, 'The Teacher says, My time is near; I will keep the Passover at your house with my disciples.' " [19]So the disciples did as Jesus had directed them, and they prepared the Passover meal.

20 When it was evening, he took his place with the twelve;[c] [21]and while they were eating, he said, "Truly I tell you, one of you will betray me." [22]And they became greatly distressed and began to say to him one after another, "Surely not I, Lord?" [23]He answered, "The one who has dipped his hand into the bowl with me will betray me. [24]The Son of Man goes as it is written of him, but woe to that one by whom the Son of Man is betrayed! It would have been better for that one not to have been born." [25]Judas, who betrayed him, said, "Surely not I, Rabbi?" He replied, "You have said so."

The Institution of the Lord's Supper

26 While they were eating, Jesus took a loaf of bread, and after blessing it he broke it, gave it to the disciples, and said, "Take, eat; this

---

a The terms *leper* and *leprosy* can refer to several diseases *b* Or *gospel* *c* Other ancient authorities add *disciples*

is my body." 27 Then he took a cup,
and after giving thanks he gave it to
them, saying, "Drink from it, all of
you; 28 for this is my blood of the[d]
covenant, which is poured out for
many for the forgiveness of sins. 29 I
tell you, I will never again drink of
this fruit of the vine until that day
when I drink it new with you in my
Father's kingdom."

30 When they had sung the
hymn, they went out to the Mount
of Olives.

Peter's Denial Foretold

31 Then Jesus said to them, "You
will all become deserters because
of me this night; for it is written,
'I will strike the shepherd,
and the sheep of the flock will
be scattered.'
32 But after I am raised up, I will go
ahead of you to Galilee." 33 Peter
said to him, "Though all become
deserters because of you, I will
never desert you." 34 Jesus said to
him, "Truly I tell you, this very
night, before the cock crows, you
will deny me three times." 35 Peter
said to him, "Even though I must
die with you, I will not deny you."
And so said all the disciples.

Jesus Prays in Gethsemane

36 Then Jesus went with them
to a place called Gethsemane; and
he said to his disciples, "Sit here
while I go over there and pray."
37 He took with him Peter and the
two sons of Zebedee, and began to
be grieved and agitated. 38 Then he
said to them, "I am deeply grieved,
even to death; remain here, and stay
awake with me." 39 And going a little farther, he threw himself on the
ground and prayed, "My Father, if
it is possible, let this cup pass from
me; yet not what I want but what
you want." 40 Then he came to the
disciples and found them sleeping;
and he said to Peter, "So, could
you not stay awake with me one
hour? 41 Stay awake and pray that
you may not come into the time of
trial;[e] the spirit indeed is willing,
but the flesh is weak." 42 Again he
went away for the second time and
prayed, "My Father, if this cannot
pass unless I drink it, your will be
done." 43 Again he came and found
them sleeping, for their eyes were
heavy. 44 So leaving them again,
he went away and prayed for the
third time, saying the same words.
45 Then he came to the disciples and
said to them, "Are you still sleeping
and taking your rest? See, the hour
is at hand, and the Son of Man is
betrayed into the hands of sinners.
46 Get up, let us be going. See, my
betrayer is at hand."

The Betrayal and Arrest of Jesus

47 While he was still speaking,
Judas, one of the twelve, arrived;
with him was a large crowd with
swords and clubs, from the chief
priests and the elders of the people. 48 Now the betrayer had given
them a sign, saying, "The one I will
kiss is the man; arrest him." 49 At
once he came up to Jesus and said,
"Greetings, Rabbi!" and kissed
him. 50 Jesus said to him, "Friend,
do what you are here to do." Then
they came and laid hands on Jesus

d Other ancient authorities add *new* *e* Or *into temptation*

and arrested him. 51 Suddenly, one
of those with Jesus put his hand on
his sword, drew it, and struck the
slave of the high priest, cutting off
his ear. 52 Then Jesus said to him,
"Put your sword back into its place;
for all who take the sword will perish by the sword. 53 Do you think
that I cannot appeal to my Father,
and he will at once send me more
than twelve legions of angels?
54 But how then would the scriptures be fulfilled, which say it must
happen in this way?" 55 At that hour
Jesus said to the crowds, "Have you
come out with swords and clubs to
arrest me as though I were a bandit? Day after day I sat in the temple teaching, and you did not arrest
me. 56 But all this has taken place,
so that the scriptures of the prophets may be fulfilled." Then all the
disciples deserted him and fled.

Jesus before the High Priest

57 Those who had arrested Jesus took him to Caiaphas the high
priest, in whose house the scribes
and the elders had gathered. 58 But
Peter was following him at a distance, as far as the courtyard of
the high priest; and going inside,
he sat with the guards in order to
see how this would end. 59 Now the
chief priests and the whole council
were looking for false testimony
against Jesus so that they might put
him to death, 60 but they found none,
though many false witnesses came
forward. At last two came forward
61 and said, "This fellow said, 'I am
able to destroy the temple of God
and to build it in three days.' "
62 The high priest stood up and said,
"Have you no answer? What is it
that they testify against you?" 63 But
Jesus was silent. Then the high
priest said to him, "I put you under
oath before the living God, tell us
if you are the Messiah,[f] the Son of
God." 64 Jesus said to him, "You
have said so. But I tell you,

From now on you will see the
Son of Man
seated at the right hand of
Power
and coming on the clouds of
heaven."

65 Then the high priest tore his
clothes and said, "He has blasphemed! Why do we still need
witnesses? You have now heard
his blasphemy. 66 What is your
verdict?" They answered, "He deserves death." 67 Then they spat in
his face and struck him; and some
slapped him, 68 saying, "Prophesy
to us, you Messiah![g] Who is it that
struck you?"

Peter's Denial of Jesus

69 Now Peter was sitting outside
in the courtyard. A servant-girl
came to him and said, "You also
were with Jesus the Galilean."
70 But he denied it before all of
them, saying, "I do not know what
you are talking about." 71 When he
went out to the porch, another servant-girl saw him, and she said to
the bystanders, "This man was with
Jesus of Nazareth."[h] 72 Again he denied it with an oath, "I do not know
the man." 73 After a little while the
bystanders came up and said to
Peter, "Certainly you are also one

f Or *Christ* *g* Or *Christ* *h* Gk *the Nazorean*

of them, for your accent betrays
you." 74 Then he began to curse, and
he swore an oath, "I do not know
the man!" At that moment the cock
crowed. 75 Then Peter remembered
what Jesus had said: "Before the
cock crows, you will deny me three
times." And he went out and wept
bitterly.

Jesus Brought before Pilate

27 When morning came, all the
chief priests and the elders
of the people conferred together against Jesus in order to bring
about his death. 2 They bound him,
led him away, and handed him over
to Pilate the governor.

The Suicide of Judas

3 When Judas, his betrayer,
saw that Jesus[a] was condemned,
he repented and brought back the
thirty pieces of silver to the chief
priests and the elders. 4 He said, "I
have sinned by betraying innocent[b]
blood." But they said, "What is that
to us? See to it yourself." 5 Throwing down the pieces of silver in the
temple, he departed; and he went
and hanged himself. 6 But the chief
priests, taking the pieces of silver,
said, "It is not lawful to put them
into the treasury, since they are
blood money." 7 After conferring
together, they used them to buy the
potter's field as a place to bury foreigners. 8 For this reason that field
has been called the Field of Blood
to this day. 9 Then was fulfilled
what had been spoken through
the prophet Jeremiah,[c] "And they
took[d] the thirty pieces of silver, the
price of the one on whom a price
had been set,[e] on whom some of
the people of Israel had set a price,
10 and they gave[f] them for the potter's field, as the Lord commanded
me."

Pilate Questions Jesus

11 Now Jesus stood before the
governor; and the governor asked
him, "Are you the King of the
Jews?" Jesus said, "You say so."
12 But when he was accused by the
chief priests and elders, he did not
answer. 13 Then Pilate said to him,
"Do you not hear how many accu-
sations they make against you?"
14 But he gave him no answer, not
even to a single charge, so that the
governor was greatly amazed.

Barabbas or Jesus?

15 Now at the festival the governor was accustomed to release
a prisoner for the crowd, anyone
whom they wanted. 16 At that time
they had a notorious prisoner,
called Jesus[g] Barabbas. 17 So after
they had gathered, Pilate said to
them, "Whom do you want me to
release for you, Jesus[h] Barabbas or
Jesus who is called the Messiah?"[i]
18 For he realized that it was out of
jealousy that they had handed him
over. 19 While he was sitting on the
judgment seat, his wife sent word
to him, "Have nothing to do with
that innocent man, for today I have
suffered a great deal because of a

---

a Gk *he* *b* Other ancient authorities read *righteous* *c* Other ancient authorities read *Zechariah* or *Isaiah* *d* Or *I took* *e* Or *the price of the precious One* *f* Other ancient authorities read *I gave* *g* Other ancient authorities lack *Jesus* *h* Other ancient authorities lack *Jesus* *i* Or *the Christ*

dream about him." 20 Now the chief
priests and the elders persuaded the
crowds to ask for Barabbas and to
have Jesus killed. 21 The governor
again said to them, "Which of the
two do you want me to release for
you?" And they said, "Barabbas."
22 Pilate said to them, "Then what
should I do with Jesus who is
called the Messiah?"[j] All of them
said, "Let him be crucified!" 23 Then
he asked, "Why, what evil has he
done?" But they shouted all the
more, "Let him be crucified!"

Pilate Hands Jesus over to Be Crucified

24 So when Pilate saw that he
could do nothing, but rather that a
riot was beginning, he took some
water and washed his hands before
the crowd, saying, "I am innocent
of this man's blood;[k] see to it yourselves." 25 Then the people as a
whole answered, "His blood be on
us and on our children!" 26 So he released Barabbas for them; and after
flogging Jesus, he handed him over
to be crucified.

The Soldiers Mock Jesus

27 Then the soldiers of the governor took Jesus into the governor's headquarters,[l] and they gathered the whole cohort around him.
28 They stripped him and put a scar-
let robe on him, 29 and after twisting
some thorns into a crown, they put
it on his head. They put a reed in his
right hand and knelt before him and
mocked him, saying, "Hail, King of
the Jews!" 30 They spat on him, and
took the reed and struck him on the
head. 31 After mocking him, they
stripped him of the robe and put his
own clothes on him. Then they led
him away to crucify him.

The Crucifixion of Jesus

32 As they went out, they came
upon a man from Cyrene named
Simon; they compelled this man
to carry his cross. 33 And when they
came to a place called Golgotha
(which means Place of a Skull),
34 they offered him wine to drink,
mixed with gall; but when he tasted it, he would not drink it. 35 And
when they had crucified him, they
divided his clothes among themselves by casting lots;[m] 36 then they
sat down there and kept watch over
him. 37 Over his head they put the
charge against him, which read,
"This is Jesus, the King of the
Jews."

38 Then two bandits were crucified with him, one on his right
and one on his left. 39 Those who
passed by derided[n] him, shaking
their heads 40 and saying, "You who
would destroy the temple and build
it in three days, save yourself! If
you are the Son of God, come down
from the cross." 41 In the same way
the chief priests also, along with the
scribes and elders, were mocking
him, saying, 42 "He saved others;
he cannot save himself.[o] He is the
King of Israel; let him come down
from the cross now, and we will be-

j Or *the Christ* *k* Other ancient authorities read *this righteous blood,* or *this righteous man's blood* *l* Gk *the praetorium* *m* Other ancient authorities add *in order that what had been spoken through the prophet might be fulfilled, "They divided my clothes among themselves, and for my clothing they cast lots."* *n* Or *blasphemed* *o* Or *is he unable to save himself?*

lieve in him. 43 He trusts in God; let
God deliver him now, if he wants
to; for he said, 'I am God's Son.' "
44 The bandits who were crucified
with him also taunted him in the
same way.

The Death of Jesus

45 From noon on, darkness came
over the whole land[p] until three in
the afternoon. 46 And about three
o'clock Jesus cried with a loud
voice, "Eli, Eli, lema sabachthani?"
that is, "My God, my God, why
have you forsaken me?" 47 When
some of the bystanders heard it,
they said, "This man is calling for
Elijah." 48 At once one of them ran
and got a sponge, filled it with sour
wine, put it on a stick, and gave it to
him to drink. 49 But the others said,
"Wait, let us see whether Elijah will
come to save him."[q] 50 Then Jesus
cried again with a loud voice and
breathed his last.[r] 51 At that moment
the curtain of the temple was torn in
two, from top to bottom. The earth
shook, and the rocks were split.
52 The tombs also were opened, and
many bodies of the saints who had
fallen asleep were raised. 53 After
his resurrection they came out of
the tombs and entered the holy
city and appeared to many. 54 Now
when the centurion and those with
him, who were keeping watch over
Jesus, saw the earthquake and what
took place, they were terrified and
said, "Truly this man was God's
Son!"[s]

55 Many women were also there,
looking on from a distance; they
had followed Jesus from Galilee
and had provided for him. 56 Among
them were Mary Magdalene, and
Mary the mother of James and Joseph, and the mother of the sons of
Zebedee.

The Burial of Jesus

57 When it was evening, there
came a rich man from Arimathea,
named Joseph, who was also a disciple of Jesus. 58 He went to Pilate
and asked for the body of Jesus;
then Pilate ordered it to be given to
him. 59 So Joseph took the body and
wrapped it in a clean linen cloth
60 and laid it in his own new tomb,
which he had hewn in the rock.
He then rolled a great stone to the
door of the tomb and went away.
61 Mary Magdalene and the other
Mary were there, sitting opposite
the tomb.

The Guard at the Tomb

62 The next day, that is, after
the day of Preparation, the chief
priests and the Pharisees gathered
before Pilate 63 and said, "Sir, we
remember what that impostor said
while he was still alive, 'After three
days I will rise again.' 64 Therefore
command the tomb to be made secure until the third day; otherwise
his disciples may go and steal him
away, and tell the people, 'He has
been raised from the dead,' and
the last deception would be worse
than the first." 65 Pilate said to them,
"You have a guard[t] of soldiers; go,
make it as secure as you can."[u]

---

p Or *earth* *q* Other ancient authorities add *And another took a spear and pierced his side, and out came water and blood* *r* Or *gave up his spirit* *s* Or *a son of God* *t* Or *Take a guard* *u* Gk *you know how*

66So they went with the guard and made the tomb secure by sealing the stone.

The Resurrection of Jesus

28 After the sabbath, as the first day of the week was dawning, Mary Magdalene and the other Mary went to see the tomb. 2And suddenly there was a great earthquake; for an angel of the Lord, descending from heaven, came and rolled back the stone and sat on it. 3His appearance was like lightning, and his clothing white as snow. 4For fear of him the guards shook and became like dead men. 5But the angel said to the women, "Do not be afraid; I know that you are looking for Jesus who was crucified. 6He is not here; for he has been raised, as he said. Come, see the place where he[a] lay. 7Then go quickly and tell his disciples, 'He has been raised from the dead,[b] and indeed he is going ahead of you to Galilee; there you will see him.' This is my message for you." 8So they left the tomb quickly with fear and great joy, and ran to tell his disciples. 9Suddenly Jesus met them and said, "Greetings!" And they came to him, took hold of his feet, and worshiped him. 10Then Jesus said to them, "Do not be afraid; go and tell my brothers to go to Galilee; there they will see me."

The Report of the Guard

11 While they were going, some of the guard went into the city and told the chief priests everything that had happened. 12After the priests[c] had assembled with the elders, they devised a plan to give a large sum of money to the soldiers, 13telling them, "You must say, 'His disciples came by night and stole him away while we were asleep.' 14If this comes to the governor's ears, we will satisfy him and keep you out of trouble." 15So they took the money and did as they were directed. And this story is still told among the Jews to this day.

The Commissioning of the Disciples

16 Now the eleven disciples went to Galilee, to the mountain to which Jesus had directed them. 17When they saw him, they worshiped him; but some doubted. 18And Jesus came and said to them, "All authority in heaven and on earth has been given to me. 19Go therefore and make disciples of all nations, baptizing them in the name of the Father and of the Son and of the Holy Spirit, 20and teaching them to obey everything that I have commanded you. And remember, I am with you always, to the end of the age."[d]

---

a Other ancient authorities read *the Lord*
b Other ancient authorities lack *from the dead* *c* Gk *they* *d* Other ancient authorities add *Amen*

The Gospel According to MARK

The Proclamation of John the Baptist

1 The beginning of the good news[a]
of Jesus Christ, the Son of God.[b]
2 As it is written in the prophet
Isaiah,[c]

"See, I am sending my
messenger ahead of you,[d]
who will prepare your way;
3 the voice of one crying out in
the wilderness:
'Prepare the way of the Lord,
make his paths straight,' "

4 John the baptizer appeared[e] in the
wilderness, proclaiming a baptism
of repentance for the forgiveness of
sins. 5 And people from the whole
Judean countryside and all the people of Jerusalem were going out to
him, and were baptized by him in
the river Jordan, confessing their
sins. 6 Now John was clothed with
camel's hair, with a leather belt
around his waist, and he ate locusts
and wild honey. 7 He proclaimed,
"The one who is more powerful
than I is coming after me; I am not
worthy to stoop down and untie the
thong of his sandals. 8 I have baptized you with[f] water; but he will
baptize you with[g] the Holy Spirit."

The Baptism of Jesus

9 In those days Jesus came from
Nazareth of Galilee and was baptized by John in the Jordan. 10 And
just as he was coming up out of
the water, he saw the heavens torn
apart and the Spirit descending like
a dove on him. 11 And a voice came
from heaven, "You are my Son,
the Beloved;[h] with you I am well
pleased."

The Temptation of Jesus

12 And the Spirit immediately
drove him out into the wilderness.
13 He was in the wilderness forty
days, tempted by Satan; and he was
with the wild beasts; and the angels
waited on him.

The Beginning of the Galilean Ministry

14 Now after John was arrested,
Jesus came to Galilee, proclaiming
the good news[i] of God,[j] 15 and saying, "The time is fulfilled, and the
kingdom of God has come near;[k]
repent, and believe in the good
news."[l]

Jesus Calls the First Disciples

16 As Jesus passed along the Sea
of Galilee, he saw Simon and his
brother Andrew casting a net into
the sea—for they were fishermen.
17 And Jesus said to them, "Follow me and I will make you fish

---

a Or *gospel* *b* Other ancient authorities lack *the Son of God* *c* Other ancient authorities read *in the prophets* *d* Gk *before your face* *e* Other ancient authorities read *John was baptizing* *f* Or *in* *g* Or *in* *h* Or *my beloved Son* *i* Or *gospel* *j* Other ancient authorities read *of the kingdom* *k* Or *is at hand* *l* Or *gospel*

for people." [18]And immediately
they left their nets and followed
him. [19]As he went a little farther,
he saw James son of Zebedee and
his brother John, who were in their
boat mending the nets. [20]Immedi-
ately he called them; and they left
their father Zebedee in the boat
with the hired men, and followed
him.

The Man with an Unclean Spirit

21 They went to Capernaum; and
when the sabbath came, he entered
the synagogue and taught. [22]They
were astounded at his teaching,
for he taught them as one having
authority, and not as the scribes.
[23]Just then there was in their synagogue a man with an unclean spirit,
[24]and he cried out, "What have you
to do with us, Jesus of Nazareth?
Have you come to destroy us? I
know who you are, the Holy One
of God." [25]But Jesus rebuked him,
saying, "Be silent, and come out
of him!" [26]And the unclean spirit,
convulsing him and crying with a
loud voice, came out of him. [27]They
were all amazed, and they kept on
asking one another, "What is this?
A new teaching—with authority!
He[m] commands even the unclean
spirits, and they obey him." [28]At
once his fame began to spread
throughout the surrounding region
of Galilee.

Jesus Heals Many at Simon's House

29 As soon as they[n] left the synagogue, they entered the house of
Simon and Andrew, with James
and John. [30]Now Simon's mother-
in-law was in bed with a fever, and
they told him about her at once.
[31]He came and took her by the hand
and lifted her up. Then the fever left
her, and she began to serve them.

32 That evening, at sunset, they
brought to him all who were sick
or possessed with demons. [33]And
the whole city was gathered around
the door. [34]And he cured many who
were sick with various diseases,
and cast out many demons; and he
would not permit the demons to
speak, because they knew him.

A Preaching Tour in Galilee

35 In the morning, while it was
still very dark, he got up and went
out to a deserted place, and there he
prayed. [36]And Simon and his companions hunted for him. [37]When
they found him, they said to him,
"Everyone is searching for you."
[38]He answered, "Let us go on to
the neighboring towns, so that I
may proclaim the message there
also; for that is what I came out
to do." [39]And he went throughout
Galilee, proclaiming the message
in their synagogues and casting out
demons.

Jesus Cleanses a Leper

40 A leper[o] came to him begging
him, and kneeling[p] he said to him,
"If you choose, you can make me
clean." [41]Moved with pity,[q] Jesus[r]
stretched out his hand and touched
him, and said to him, "I do choose.

---

m Or *A new teaching! With authority he* *n* Other ancient authorities read *he* *o* The terms *leper* and *leprosy* can refer to several diseases *p* Other ancient authorities lack *kneeling* *q* Other ancient authorities read *anger* *r* Gk *he*

Be made clean!" 42 Immediately the
leprosy[s] left him, and he was made
clean. 43 After sternly warning him
he sent him away at once, 44 saying
to him, "See that you say nothing
to anyone; but go, show yourself to
the priest, and offer for your cleansing what Moses commanded, as a
testimony to them." 45 But he went
out and began to proclaim it freely,
and to spread the word, so that Jesus[t] could no longer go into a town
openly, but stayed out in the country; and people came to him from
every quarter.

Jesus Heals a Paralytic

2 When he returned to Capernaum
after some days, it was reported that he was at home. 2 So many
gathered around that there was no
longer room for them, not even in
front of the door; and he was speaking the word to them. 3 Then some
people[a] came, bringing to him a
paralyzed man, carried by four
of them. 4 And when they could
not bring him to Jesus because of
the crowd, they removed the roof
above him; and after having dug
through it, they let down the mat
on which the paralytic lay. 5 When
Jesus saw their faith, he said to the
paralytic, "Son, your sins are forgiven." 6 Now some of the scribes
were sitting there, questioning in
their hearts, 7 "Why does this fellow
speak in this way? It is blasphemy! Who can forgive sins but God
alone?" 8 At once Jesus perceived in
his spirit that they were discussing
these questions among themselves;
and he said to them, "Why do you
raise such questions in your hearts?
9 Which is easier, to say to the paralytic, 'Your sins are forgiven,' or
to say, 'Stand up and take your mat
and walk'? 10 But so that you may
know that the Son of Man has authority on earth to forgive sins"—
he said to the paralytic— 11 "I say to
you, stand up, take your mat and go
to your home." 12 And he stood up,
and immediately took the mat and
went out before all of them; so that
they were all amazed and glorified
God, saying, "We have never seen
anything like this!"

Jesus Calls Levi

13 Jesus[b] went out again beside
the sea; the whole crowd gathered
around him, and he taught them.
14 As he was walking along, he
saw Levi son of Alphaeus sitting at
the tax booth, and he said to him,
"Follow me." And he got up and
followed him.

15 And as he sat at dinner[c] in
Levi's[d] house, many tax collectors
and sinners were also sitting[e] with
Jesus and his disciples—for there
were many who followed him.
16 When the scribes of[f] the Pharisees saw that he was eating with
sinners and tax collectors, they said
to his disciples, "Why does he eat[g]
with tax collectors and sinners?"
17 When Jesus heard this, he said to
them, "Those who are well have no
need of a physician, but those who
are sick; I have come to call not the
righteous but sinners."

---

s The terms *leper* and *leprosy* can refer to several diseases *t* Gk *he* *a* Gk *they* *b* Gk *He* *c* Gk *reclined* *d* Gk *his* *e* Gk *reclining* *f* Other ancient authorities read *and* *g* Other ancient authorities add *and drink*

The Question about Fasting

18 Now John's disciples and the Pharisees were fasting; and people[h] came and said to him, "Why do John's disciples and the disciples of the Pharisees fast, but your disciples do not fast?" 19 Jesus said to them, "The wedding guests cannot fast while the bridegroom is with them, can they? As long as they have the bridegroom with them, they cannot fast. 20 The days will come when the bridegroom is taken away from them, and then they will fast on that day.

21 "No one sews a piece of unshrunk cloth on an old cloak; otherwise, the patch pulls away from it, the new from the old, and a worse tear is made. 22 And no one puts new wine into old wineskins; otherwise, the wine will burst the skins, and the wine is lost, and so are the skins; but one puts new wine into fresh wineskins."[i]

Pronouncement about the Sabbath

23 One sabbath he was going through the grainfields; and as they made their way his disciples began to pluck heads of grain. 24 The Pharisees said to him, "Look, why are they doing what is not lawful on the sabbath?" 25 And he said to them, "Have you never read what David did when he and his companions were hungry and in need of food? 26 He entered the house of God, when Abiathar was high priest, and ate the bread of the Presence, which it is not lawful for any but the priests to eat, and he gave some to his companions." 27 Then he said to them, "The sabbath was made for humankind, and not humankind for the sabbath; 28 so the Son of Man is lord even of the sabbath."

The Man with a Withered Hand

3 Again he entered the synagogue, and a man was there who had a withered hand. 2 They watched him to see whether he would cure him on the sabbath, so that they might accuse him. 3 And he said to the man who had the withered hand, "Come forward." 4 Then he said to them, "Is it lawful to do good or to do harm on the sabbath, to save life or to kill?" But they were silent. 5 He looked around at them with anger; he was grieved at their hardness of heart and said to the man, "Stretch out your hand." He stretched it out, and his hand was restored. 6 The Pharisees went out and immediately conspired with the Herodians against him, how to destroy him.

A Multitude at the Seaside

7 Jesus departed with his disciples to the sea, and a great multitude from Galilee followed him; 8 hearing all that he was doing, they came to him in great numbers from Judea, Jerusalem, Idumea, beyond the Jordan, and the region around Tyre and Sidon. 9 He told his disciples to have a boat ready for him because of the crowd, so that they would not crush him; 10 for he had cured many, so that all who had diseases pressed upon him to touch him. 11 Whenever the unclean spirits saw him, they fell down before

---

h Gk *they* *i* Other ancient authorities lack *but one puts new wine into fresh wineskins*

him and shouted, "You are the Son
of God!" 12 But he sternly ordered
them not to make him known.

Jesus Appoints the Twelve

13 He went up the mountain and
called to him those whom he wanted, and they came to him. 14 And he
appointed twelve, whom he also
named apostles,[a] to be with him,
and to be sent out to proclaim the
message, 15 and to have authority to
cast out demons. 16 So he appointed
the twelve:[b] Simon (to whom he
gave the name Peter); 17 James son
of Zebedee and John the brother of
James (to whom he gave the name
Boanerges, that is, Sons of Thunder); 18 and Andrew, and Philip, and
Bartholomew, and Matthew, and
Thomas, and James son of Alphaeus, and Thaddaeus, and Simon the
Cananaean, 19 and Judas Iscariot,
who betrayed him.

Jesus and Beelzebul

Then he went home; 20 and the
crowd came together again, so that
they could not even eat. 21 When his
family heard it, they went out to
restrain him, for people were saying, "He has gone out of his mind."
22 And the scribes who came down
from Jerusalem said, "He has Beelzebul, and by the ruler of the demons he casts out demons." 23 And
he called them to him, and spoke to
them in parables, "How can Satan
cast out Satan? 24 If a kingdom is
divided against itself, that kingdom
cannot stand. 25 And if a house is divided against itself, that house will
not be able to stand. 26 And if Satan
has risen up against himself and is
divided, he cannot stand, but his
end has come. 27 But no one can enter a strong man's house and plunder his property without first tying
up the strong man; then indeed the
house can be plundered.

28 "Truly I tell you, people will
be forgiven for their sins and whatever blasphemies they utter; 29 but
whoever blasphemes against the
Holy Spirit can never have forgiveness, but is guilty of an eternal
sin"— 30 for they had said, "He has
an unclean spirit."

The True Kindred of Jesus

31 Then his mother and his
brothers came; and standing outside, they sent to him and called
him. 32 A crowd was sitting around
him; and they said to him, "Your
mother and your brothers and sisters[c] are outside, asking for you."
33 And he replied, "Who are my
mother and my brothers?" 34 And
looking at those who sat around
him, he said, "Here are my mother
and my brothers! 35 Whoever does
the will of God is my brother and
sister and mother."

The Parable of the Sower

4 Again he began to teach beside
the sea. Such a very large crowd
gathered around him that he got
into a boat on the sea and sat there,
while the whole crowd was beside
the sea on the land. 2 He began to
teach them many things in parables,
and in his teaching he said to them:

---

a Other ancient authorities lack *whom he also named apostles* *b* Other ancient authorities lack *So he appointed the twelve* *c* Other ancient authorities lack *and sisters*

3 "Listen! A sower went out to sow.
4 And as he sowed, some seed fell
on the path, and the birds came and
ate it up. 5 Other seed fell on rocky
ground, where it did not have much
soil, and it sprang up quickly, since
it had no depth of soil. 6 And when
the sun rose, it was scorched; and
since it had no root, it withered
away. 7 Other seed fell among
thorns, and the thorns grew up and
choked it, and it yielded no grain.
8 Other seed fell into good soil and
brought forth grain, growing up and
increasing and yielding thirty and
sixty and a hundredfold." 9 And he
said, "Let anyone with ears to hear
listen!"

The Purpose of the Parables

10 When he was alone, those
who were around him along with
the twelve asked him about the parables. 11 And he said to them, "To
you has been given the secret[a] of
the kingdom of God, but for those
outside, everything comes in parables; 12 in order that

'they may indeed look, but not
perceive,
and may indeed listen, but not
understand;
so that they may not turn again
and be forgiven.' "

13 And he said to them, "Do
you not understand this parable?
Then how will you understand all
the parables? 14 The sower sows
the word. 15 These are the ones on
the path where the word is sown:
when they hear, Satan immediately comes and takes away the word
that is sown in them. 16 And these
are the ones sown on rocky ground:
when they hear the word, they immediately receive it with joy. 17 But
they have no root, and endure only
for a while; then, when trouble or
persecution arises on account of the
word, immediately they fall away.[b]
18 And others are those sown among
the thorns: these are the ones who
hear the word, 19 but the cares of the
world, and the lure of wealth, and
the desire for other things come in
and choke the word, and it yields
nothing. 20 And these are the ones
sown on the good soil: they hear the
word and accept it and bear fruit,
thirty and sixty and a hundredfold."

A Lamp under a Bushel Basket

21 He said to them, "Is a lamp
brought in to be put under the
bushel basket, or under the bed,
and not on the lampstand? 22 For
there is nothing hidden, except to
be disclosed; nor is anything secret,
except to come to light. 23 Let anyone with ears to hear listen!" 24 And
he said to them, "Pay attention to
what you hear; the measure you
give will be the measure you get,
and still more will be given you.
25 For to those who have, more will
be given; and from those who have
nothing, even what they have will
be taken away."

The Parable of the Growing Seed

26 He also said, "The kingdom
of God is as if someone would
scatter seed on the ground, 27 and
would sleep and rise night and
day, and the seed would sprout
and grow, he does not know how.

---

a Or *mystery* b Or *stumble*

[28]The earth produces of itself, first the stalk, then the head, then the full grain in the head. [29]But when the grain is ripe, at once he goes in with his sickle, because the harvest has come."

The Parable of the Mustard Seed

30 He also said, "With what can we compare the kingdom of God, or what parable will we use for it? [31]It is like a mustard seed, which, when sown upon the ground, is the smallest of all the seeds on earth; [32]yet when it is sown it grows up and becomes the greatest of all shrubs, and puts forth large branches, so that the birds of the air can make nests in its shade."

The Use of Parables

33 With many such parables he spoke the word to them, as they were able to hear it; [34]he did not speak to them except in parables, but he explained everything in private to his disciples.

Jesus Stills a Storm

35 On that day, when evening had come, he said to them, "Let us go across to the other side." [36]And leaving the crowd behind, they took him with them in the boat, just as he was. Other boats were with him. [37]A great windstorm arose, and the waves beat into the boat, so that the boat was already being swamped. [38]But he was in the stern, asleep on the cushion; and they woke him up and said to him, "Teacher, do you not care that we are perishing?" [39]He woke up and rebuked the wind, and said to the sea, "Peace! Be still!" Then the wind ceased, and there was a dead calm. [40]He said to them, "Why are you afraid? Have you still no faith?" [41]And they were filled with great awe and said to one another, "Who then is this, that even the wind and the sea obey him?"

Jesus Heals the Gerasene Demoniac

5 They came to the other side of the sea, to the country of the Gerasenes.[a] [2]And when he had stepped out of the boat, immediately a man out of the tombs with an unclean spirit met him. [3]He lived among the tombs; and no one could restrain him any more, even with a chain; [4]for he had often been restrained with shackles and chains, but the chains he wrenched apart, and the shackles he broke in pieces; and no one had the strength to subdue him. [5]Night and day among the tombs and on the mountains he was always howling and bruising himself with stones. [6]When he saw Jesus from a distance, he ran and bowed down before him; [7]and he shouted at the top of his voice, "What have you to do with me, Jesus, Son of the Most High God? I adjure you by God, do not torment me." [8]For he had said to him, "Come out of the man, you unclean spirit!" [9]Then Jesus[b] asked him, "What is your name?" He replied, "My name is Legion; for we are many." [10]He begged him earnestly not to send them out of the country. [11]Now there on the hillside a great

a Other ancient authorities read *Gergesenes*; others, *Gadarenes* *b* Gk *he*

herd of swine was feeding; [12]and
the unclean spirits[c] begged him,
"Send us into the swine; let us enter
them." [13]So he gave them permission. And the unclean spirits came
out and entered the swine; and the
herd, numbering about two thousand, rushed down the steep bank
into the sea, and were drowned in
the sea.

14 The swineherds ran off and
told it in the city and in the country. Then people came to see what
it was that had happened. [15]They
came to Jesus and saw the demoniac sitting there, clothed and in
his right mind, the very man who
had had the legion; and they were
afraid. [16]Those who had seen what
had happened to the demoniac and
to the swine reported it. [17]Then
they began to beg Jesus[d] to leave
their neighborhood. [18]As he was
getting into the boat, the man who
had been possessed by demons
begged him that he might be with
him. [19]But Jesus[e] refused, and said
to him, "Go home to your friends,
and tell them how much the Lord
has done for you, and what mercy
he has shown you." [20]And he went
away and began to proclaim in the
Decapolis how much Jesus had
done for him; and everyone was
amazed.

A Girl Restored to Life and a Woman Healed

21 When Jesus had crossed again
in the boat[f] to the other side, a great
crowd gathered around him; and he
was by the sea. [22]Then one of the
leaders of the synagogue named
Jairus came and, when he saw him,
fell at his feet [23]and begged him
repeatedly, "My little daughter is
at the point of death. Come and lay
your hands on her, so that she may
be made well, and live." [24]So he
went with him.

And a large crowd followed him
and pressed in on him. [25]Now there
was a woman who had been suffering from hemorrhages for twelve
years. [26]She had endured much
under many physicians, and had
spent all that she had; and she was
no better, but rather grew worse.
[27]She had heard about Jesus, and
came up behind him in the crowd
and touched his cloak, [28]for she
said, "If I but touch his clothes, I
will be made well." [29]Immediate-
ly her hemorrhage stopped; and
she felt in her body that she was
healed of her disease. [30]Immediate-
ly aware that power had gone forth
from him, Jesus turned about in the
crowd and said, "Who touched my
clothes?" [31]And his disciples said
to him, "You see the crowd pressing in on you; how can you say,
'Who touched me?'" [32]He looked
all around to see who had done it.
[33]But the woman, knowing what
had happened to her, came in fear
and trembling, fell down before
him, and told him the whole truth.
[34]He said to her, "Daughter, your
faith has made you well; go in
peace, and be healed of your disease."

35 While he was still speaking,
some people came from the leader's house to say, "Your daughter is

---

c Gk *they* *d* Gk *him* *e* Gk *he* *f* Other ancient authorities lack *in the boat*

dead. Why trouble the teacher any
further?" 36 But overhearing[g] what
they said, Jesus said to the leader
of the synagogue, "Do not fear,
only believe." 37 He allowed no one
to follow him except Peter, James,
and John, the brother of James.
38 When they came to the house
of the leader of the synagogue, he
saw a commotion, people weeping
and wailing loudly. 39 When he had
entered, he said to them, "Why do
you make a commotion and weep?
The child is not dead but sleeping."
40 And they laughed at him. Then he
put them all outside, and took the
child's father and mother and those
who were with him, and went in
where the child was. 41 He took her
by the hand and said to her, "Talitha
cum," which means, "Little girl, get
up!" 42 And immediately the girl got
up and began to walk about (she
was twelve years of age). At this
they were overcome with amazement. 43 He strictly ordered them
that no one should know this, and
told them to give her something to
eat.

The Rejection of Jesus at Nazareth

6 He left that place and came to
his hometown, and his disciples
followed him. 2 On the sabbath he
began to teach in the synagogue,
and many who heard him were
astounded. They said, "Where did
this man get all this? What is this
wisdom that has been given to
him? What deeds of power are being done by his hands! 3 Is not this
the carpenter, the son of Mary[a] and
brother of James and Joses and Judas and Simon, and are not his sisters here with us?" And they took
offense[b] at him. 4 Then Jesus said
to them, "Prophets are not without
honor, except in their hometown,
and among their own kin, and in
their own house." 5 And he could do
no deed of power there, except that
he laid his hands on a few sick people and cured them. 6 And he was
amazed at their unbelief.

The Mission of the Twelve

Then he went about among the
villages teaching. 7 He called the
twelve and began to send them out
two by two, and gave them authority over the unclean spirits. 8 He ordered them to take nothing for their
journey except a staff; no bread,
no bag, no money in their belts;
9 but to wear sandals and not to put
on two tunics. 10 He said to them,
"Wherever you enter a house, stay
there until you leave the place. 11 If
any place will not welcome you
and they refuse to hear you, as you
leave, shake off the dust that is on
your feet as a testimony against
them." 12 So they went out and
proclaimed that all should repent.
13 They cast out many demons, and
anointed with oil many who were
sick and cured them.

The Death of John the Baptist

14 King Herod heard of it, for
Jesus'[c] name had become known.
Some were[d] saying, "John the baptizer has been raised from the dead;
and for this reason these powers are

g Or *ignoring* ; other ancient authorities read *hearing* *a* Other ancient authorities read *son of the carpenter and of Mary* *b* Or *stumbled* *c* Gk *his* *d* Other ancient authorities read *He was*

at work in him." 15 But others said, "It is Elijah." And others said, "It is a prophet, like one of the prophets of old." 16 But when Herod heard of it, he said, "John, whom I beheaded, has been raised."

17 For Herod himself had sent men who arrested John, bound him, and put him in prison on account of Herodias, his brother Philip's wife, because Herod[e] had married her. 18 For John had been telling Herod, "It is not lawful for you to have your brother's wife." 19 And Herodias had a grudge against him, and wanted to kill him. But she could not, 20 for Herod feared John, knowing that he was a righteous and holy man, and he protected him. When he heard him, he was greatly perplexed;[f] and yet he liked to listen to him. 21 But an opportunity came when Herod on his birthday gave a banquet for his courtiers and officers and for the leaders of Galilee. 22 When his daughter Herodias[g] came in and danced, she pleased Herod and his guests; and the king said to the girl, "Ask me for whatever you wish, and I will give it." 23 And he solemnly swore to her, "Whatever you ask me, I will give you, even half of my kingdom." 24 She went out and said to her mother, "What should I ask for?" She replied, "The head of John the baptizer." 25 Immediately she rushed back to the king and requested, "I want you to give me at once the head of John the Baptist on a platter." 26 The king was deeply grieved; yet out of regard for his oaths and for the guests, he did not want to refuse her. 27 Immediately the king sent a soldier of the guard with orders to bring John's[h] head. He went and beheaded him in the prison, 28 brought his head on a platter, and gave it to the girl. Then the girl gave it to her mother. 29 When his disciples heard about it, they came and took his body, and laid it in a tomb.

Feeding the Five Thousand

30 The apostles gathered around Jesus, and told him all that they had done and taught. 31 He said to them, "Come away to a deserted place all by yourselves and rest a while." For many were coming and going, and they had no leisure even to eat. 32 And they went away in the boat to a deserted place by themselves. 33 Now many saw them going and recognized them, and they hurried there on foot from all the towns and arrived ahead of them. 34 As he went ashore, he saw a great crowd; and he had compassion for them, because they were like sheep without a shepherd; and he began to teach them many things. 35 When it grew late, his disciples came to him and said, "This is a deserted place, and the hour is now very late; 36 send them away so that they may go into the surrounding country and villages and buy something for themselves to eat." 37 But he answered them, "You give them something to eat." They said to him, "Are we to go and buy two hundred denarii[i] worth of bread, and give it to them

e Gk *he* *f* Other ancient authorities read *he did many things* *g* Other ancient authorities read *the daughter of Herodias herself* *h* Gk *his* *i* The denarius was the usual day's wage for a laborer

to eat?" 38 And he said to them, "How many loaves have you? Go and see." When they had found out, they said, "Five, and two fish." 39 Then he ordered them to get all the people to sit down in groups on the green grass. 40 So they sat down in groups of hundreds and of fifties. 41 Taking the five loaves and the two fish, he looked up to heaven, and blessed and broke the loaves, and gave them to his disciples to set before the people; and he divided the two fish among them all. 42 And all ate and were filled; 43 and they took up twelve baskets full of broken pieces and of the fish. 44 Those who had eaten the loaves numbered five thousand men.

Jesus Walks on the Water

45 Immediately he made his disciples get into the boat and go on ahead to the other side, to Bethsaida, while he dismissed the crowd. 46 After saying farewell to them, he went up on the mountain to pray.

47 When evening came, the boat was out on the sea, and he was alone on the land. 48 When he saw that they were straining at the oars against an adverse wind, he came towards them early in the morning, walking on the sea. He intended to pass them by. 49 But when they saw him walking on the sea, they thought it was a ghost and cried out; 50 for they all saw him and were terrified. But immediately he spoke to them and said, "Take heart, it is I; do not be afraid." 51 Then he got into the boat with them and the wind ceased. And they were utterly astounded, 52 for they did not understand about the loaves, but their hearts were hardened.

Healing the Sick in Gennesaret

53 When they had crossed over, they came to land at Gennesaret and moored the boat. 54 When they got out of the boat, people at once recognized him, 55 and rushed about that whole region and began to bring the sick on mats to wherever they heard he was. 56 And wherever he went, into villages or cities or farms, they laid the sick in the marketplaces, and begged him that they might touch even the fringe of his cloak; and all who touched it were healed.

The Tradition of the Elders

7 Now when the Pharisees and some of the scribes who had come from Jerusalem gathered around him, 2 they noticed that some of his disciples were eating with defiled hands, that is, without washing them. 3 (For the Pharisees, and all the Jews, do not eat unless they thoroughly wash their hands,[a] thus observing the tradition of the elders; 4 and they do not eat anything from the market unless they wash it;[b] and there are also many other traditions that they observe, the washing of cups, pots, and bronze kettles.[c]) 5 So the Pharisees and the scribes asked him, "Why do your disciples not live[d] according to the tradition of the elders,

a Meaning of Gk uncertain *b* Other ancient authorities read *and when they come from the marketplace, they do not eat unless they purify themselves* *c* Other ancient authorities add *and beds* *d* Gk *walk*

but eat with defiled hands?" 6 He
said to them, "Isaiah prophesied
rightly about you hypocrites, as it
is written,

'This people honors me with
their lips,
but their hearts are far from
me;
7 in vain do they worship me,
teaching human precepts as
doctrines.'

8 You abandon the commandment
of God and hold to human tradition."

9 Then he said to them, "You
have a fine way of rejecting the
commandment of God in order to
keep your tradition! 10 For Moses
said, 'Honor your father and your
mother'; and, 'Whoever speaks
evil of father or mother must surely
die.' 11 But you say that if anyone
tells father or mother, 'Whatever
support you might have had from
me is Corban' (that is, an offering
to God[e])— 12 then you no longer
permit doing anything for a father
or mother, 13 thus making void the
word of God through your tradition
that you have handed on. And you
do many things like this."

14 Then he called the crowd
again and said to them, "Listen
to me, all of you, and understand:
15 there is nothing outside a person
that by going in can defile, but the
things that come out are what defile."[f]

17 When he had left the crowd
and entered the house, his disciples
asked him about the parable. 18 He
said to them, "Then do you also fail
to understand? Do you not see that
whatever goes into a person from
outside cannot defile, 19 since it enters, not the heart but the stomach,
and goes out into the sewer?" (Thus
he declared all foods clean.) 20 And
he said, "It is what comes out of a
person that defiles. 21 For it is from
within, from the human heart, that
evil intentions come: fornication,
theft, murder, 22 adultery, avarice,
wickedness, deceit, licentiousness,
envy, slander, pride, folly. 23 All
these evil things come from within,
and they defile a person."

The Syrophoenician Woman's Faith

24 From there he set out and
went away to the region of Tyre.[g]
He entered a house and did not want
anyone to know he was there. Yet
he could not escape notice, 25 but
a woman whose little daughter
had an unclean spirit immediately
heard about him, and she came and
bowed down at his feet. 26 Now the
woman was a Gentile, of Syrophoenician origin. She begged him to
cast the demon out of her daughter.
27 He said to her, "Let the children
be fed first, for it is not fair to take
the children's food and throw it to
the dogs." 28 But she answered him,
"Sir,[h] even the dogs under the table
eat the children's crumbs." 29 Then
he said to her, "For saying that, you
may go—the demon has left your
daughter." 30 So she went home,
found the child lying on the bed,
and the demon gone.

---

e Gk lacks *to God* *f* Other ancient authorities add verse 16, *"Let anyone with ears to hear listen"* *g* Other ancient authorities add *and Sidon* *h* Or *Lord*; other ancient authorities prefix *Yes*

Jesus Cures a Deaf Man

31 Then he returned from the region of Tyre, and went by way of Sidon towards the Sea of Galilee, in the region of the Decapolis. 32 They brought to him a deaf man who had an impediment in his speech; and they begged him to lay his hand on him. 33 He took him aside in private, away from the crowd, and put his fingers into his ears, and he spat and touched his tongue. 34 Then looking up to heaven, he sighed and said to him, "Ephphatha," that is, "Be opened." 35 And immediately his ears were opened, his tongue was released, and he spoke plainly. 36 Then Jesus[i] ordered them to tell no one; but the more he ordered them, the more zealously they proclaimed it. 37 They were astounded beyond measure, saying, "He has done everything well; he even makes the deaf to hear and the mute to speak."

Feeding the Four Thousand

8 In those days when there was again a great crowd without anything to eat, he called his disciples and said to them, 2 "I have compassion for the crowd, because they have been with me now for three days and have nothing to eat. 3 If I send them away hungry to their homes, they will faint on the way—and some of them have come from a great distance." 4 His disciples replied, "How can one feed these people with bread here in the desert?" 5 He asked them, "How many loaves do you have?" They said, "Seven." 6 Then he ordered the crowd to sit down on the ground; and he took the seven loaves, and after giving thanks he broke them and gave them to his disciples to distribute; and they distributed them to the crowd. 7 They had also a few small fish; and after blessing them, he ordered that these too should be distributed. 8 They ate and were filled; and they took up the broken pieces left over, seven baskets full. 9 Now there were about four thousand people. And he sent them away. 10 And immediately he got into the boat with his disciples and went to the district of Dalmanutha.[a]

The Demand for a Sign

11 The Pharisees came and began to argue with him, asking him for a sign from heaven, to test him. 12 And he sighed deeply in his spirit and said, "Why does this generation ask for a sign? Truly I tell you, no sign will be given to this generation." 13 And he left them, and getting into the boat again, he went across to the other side.

The Yeast of the Pharisees and of Herod

14 Now the disciples[b] had forgotten to bring any bread; and they had only one loaf with them in the boat. 15 And he cautioned them, saying, "Watch out—beware of the yeast of the Pharisees and the yeast of Herod."[c] 16 They said to one another, "It is because we have no bread." 17 And becoming aware of it, Jesus said to them, "Why are

---

i Gk *he* *a* Other ancient authorities read *Mageda* or *Magdala* *b* Gk *they* *c* Other ancient authorities read *the Herodians*

you talking about having no bread? Do you still not perceive or understand? Are your hearts hardened?
18 Do you have eyes, and fail to see? Do you have ears, and fail to hear? And do you not remember?
19 When I broke the five loaves for the five thousand, how many baskets full of broken pieces did you collect?" They said to him, "Twelve."
20 "And the seven for the four thousand, how many baskets full of broken pieces did you collect?" And they said to him, "Seven."
21 Then he said to them, "Do you not yet understand?"

Jesus Cures a Blind Man at Bethsaida

22 They came to Bethsaida. Some people[d] brought a blind man to him and begged him to touch him.
23 He took the blind man by the hand and led him out of the village; and when he had put saliva on his eyes and laid his hands on him, he asked him, "Can you see anything?"
24 And the man[e] looked up and said, "I can see people, but they look like trees, walking."
25 Then Jesus[f] laid his hands on his eyes again; and he looked intently and his sight was restored, and he saw everything clearly.
26 Then he sent him away to his home, saying, "Do not even go into the village."[g]

Peter's Declaration about Jesus

27 Jesus went on with his disciples to the villages of Caesarea Philippi; and on the way he asked his disciples, "Who do people say that I am?"
28 And they answered him, "John the Baptist; and others, Elijah; and still others, one of the prophets."
29 He asked them, "But who do you say that I am?" Peter answered him, "You are the Messiah."[h]
30 And he sternly ordered them not to tell anyone about him.

Jesus Foretells His Death and Resurrection

31 Then he began to teach them that the Son of Man must undergo great suffering, and be rejected by the elders, the chief priests, and the scribes, and be killed, and after three days rise again.
32 He said all this quite openly. And Peter took him aside and began to rebuke him.
33 But turning and looking at his disciples, he rebuked Peter and said, "Get behind me, Satan! For you are setting your mind not on divine things but on human things."

34 He called the crowd with his disciples, and said to them, "If any want to become my followers, let them deny themselves and take up their cross and follow me.
35 For those who want to save their life will lose it, and those who lose their life for my sake, and for the sake of the gospel,[i] will save it.
36 For what will it profit them to gain the whole world and forfeit their life?
37 Indeed, what can they give in return for their life?
38 Those who are ashamed of me and of my words[j] in this adulterous and sinful generation, of them the Son of Man will also be ashamed when he comes in

d Gk *They* e Gk *he* f Gk *he* g Other ancient authorities add *or tell anyone in the village* h Or *the Christ* i Other ancient authorities read *lose their life for the sake of the gospel* j Other ancient authorities read *and of mine*

the glory of his Father with the holy
angels."

9 1 And he said to them, "Truly I
tell you, there are some standing
here who will not taste death until
they see that the kingdom of God
has come with[a] power."

The Transfiguration

2 Six days later, Jesus took with
him Peter and James and John, and
led them up a high mountain apart,
by themselves. And he was transfigured before them, 3 and his clothes
became dazzling white, such as no
one[b] on earth could bleach them.
4 And there appeared to them Elijah
with Moses, who were talking with
Jesus. 5 Then Peter said to Jesus,
"Rabbi, it is good for us to be here;
let us make three dwellings,[c] one
for you, one for Moses, and one for
Elijah." 6 He did not know what to
say, for they were terrified. 7 Then
a cloud overshadowed them, and
from the cloud there came a voice,
"This is my Son, the Beloved;[d] listen to him!" 8 Suddenly when they
looked around, they saw no one
with them any more, but only Jesus.

The Coming of Elijah

9 As they were coming down the
mountain, he ordered them to tell
no one about what they had seen,
until after the Son of Man had risen
from the dead. 10 So they kept the
matter to themselves, questioning what this rising from the dead
could mean. 11 Then they asked him,
"Why do the scribes say that Elijah must come first?" 12 He said to
them, "Elijah is indeed coming first
to restore all things. How then is it
written about the Son of Man, that
he is to go through many suffer-
ings and be treated with contempt?
13 But I tell you that Elijah has
come, and they did to him whatever
they pleased, as it is written about
him."

The Healing of a Boy with a Spirit

14 When they came to the disciples, they saw a great crowd
around them, and some scribes
arguing with them. 15 When the
whole crowd saw him, they were
immediately overcome with awe,
and they ran forward to greet him.
16 He asked them, "What are you
arguing about with them?" 17 Someone from the crowd answered him,
"Teacher, I brought you my son; he
has a spirit that makes him unable
to speak; 18 and whenever it seizes
him, it dashes him down; and he
foams and grinds his teeth and becomes rigid; and I asked your disciples to cast it out, but they could
not do so." 19 He answered them,
"You faithless generation, how
much longer must I be among you?
How much longer must I put up
with you? Bring him to me." 20 And
they brought the boy[e] to him. When
the spirit saw him, immediately it
convulsed the boy,[f] and he fell on
the ground and rolled about, foaming at the mouth. 21 Jesus[g] asked the
father, "How long has this been
happening to him?" And he said,
"From childhood. 22 It has often
cast him into the fire and into the
water, to destroy him; but if you
are able to do anything, have pity

a Or *in* *b* Gk *no fuller* *c* Or *tents* *d* Or *my beloved Son* *e* Gk *him* *f* Gk *him* *g* Gk *He*

on us and help us." 23 Jesus said to him, "If you are able!—All things can be done for the one who believes." 24 Immediately the father of the child cried out,[h] "I believe; help my unbelief!" 25 When Jesus saw that a crowd came running together, he rebuked the unclean spirit, saying to it, "You spirit that keeps this boy from speaking and hearing, I command you, come out of him, and never enter him again!" 26 After crying out and convulsing him terribly, it came out, and the boy was like a corpse, so that most of them said, "He is dead." 27 But Jesus took him by the hand and lifted him up, and he was able to stand. 28 When he had entered the house, his disciples asked him privately, "Why could we not cast it out?" 29 He said to them, "This kind can come out only through prayer."[i]

Jesus Again Foretells His Death and Resurrection

30 They went on from there and passed through Galilee. He did not want anyone to know it; 31 for he was teaching his disciples, saying to them, "The Son of Man is to be betrayed into human hands, and they will kill him, and three days after being killed, he will rise again." 32 But they did not understand what he was saying and were afraid to ask him.

Who Is the Greatest?

33 Then they came to Capernaum; and when he was in the house he asked them, "What were you arguing about on the way?" 34 But they were silent, for on the way they had argued with one another who was the greatest. 35 He sat down, called the twelve, and said to them, "Whoever wants to be first must be last of all and servant of all." 36 Then he took a little child and put it among them; and taking it in his arms, he said to them, 37 "Whoever welcomes one such child in my name welcomes me, and whoever welcomes me welcomes not me but the one who sent me."

Another Exorcist

38 John said to him, "Teacher, we saw someone[j] casting out demons in your name, and we tried to stop him, because he was not following us." 39 But Jesus said, "Do not stop him; for no one who does a deed of power in my name will be able soon afterward to speak evil of me. 40 Whoever is not against us is for us. 41 For truly I tell you, whoever gives you a cup of water to drink because you bear the name of Christ will by no means lose the reward.

Temptations to Sin

42 "If any of you put a stumbling block before one of these little ones who believe in me,[k] it would be better for you if a great millstone were hung around your neck and you were thrown into the sea. 43 If your hand causes you to stumble, cut it off; it is better for you to enter life maimed than to have two hands

---

h Other ancient authorities add *with tears*
i Other ancient authorities add *and fasting*
j Other ancient authorities add *who does not follow us* *k* Other ancient authorities lack *in me*

and to go to hell,[l] to the unquenchable fire.[m] 45 And if your foot causes
you to stumble, cut it off; it is better
for you to enter life lame than to
have two feet and to be thrown into
hell.[n,o] 47 And if your eye causes
you to stumble, tear it out; it is better for you to enter the kingdom of
God with one eye than to have two
eyes and to be thrown into hell,[p]
48 where their worm never dies, and
the fire is never quenched.
49 "For everyone will be salted
with fire.[q] 50 Salt is good; but if salt
has lost its saltiness, how can you
season it?[r] Have salt in yourselves,
and be at peace with one another."

Teaching about Divorce

10 He left that place and went to
the region of Judea and[a] beyond the Jordan. And crowds again
gathered around him; and, as was
his custom, he again taught them.
2 Some Pharisees came, and to
test him they asked, "Is it lawful
for a man to divorce his wife?"
3 He answered them, "What did
Moses command you?" 4 They
said, "Moses allowed a man to
write a certificate of dismissal and
to divorce her." 5 But Jesus said to
them, "Because of your hardness
of heart he wrote this commandment for you. 6 But from the beginning of creation, 'God made
them male and female.' 7 'For this
reason a man shall leave his father
and mother and be joined to his
wife,[b] 8 and the two shall become
one flesh.' So they are no longer
two, but one flesh. 9 Therefore what
God has joined together, let no one
separate."
10 Then in the house the disciples asked him again about this
matter. 11 He said to them, "Whoever divorces his wife and marries another commits adultery against her;
12 and if she divorces her husband
and marries another, she commits
adultery."

Jesus Blesses Little Children

13 People were bringing little
children to him in order that he
might touch them; and the disciples spoke sternly to them. 14 But
when Jesus saw this, he was indignant and said to them, "Let the
little children come to me; do not
stop them; for it is to such as these
that the kingdom of God belongs.
15 Truly I tell you, whoever does not
receive the kingdom of God as a little child will never enter it." 16 And
he took them up in his arms, laid his
hands on them, and blessed them.

The Rich Man

17 As he was setting out on a
journey, a man ran up and knelt
before him, and asked him, "Good
Teacher, what must I do to inherit
eternal life?" 18 Jesus said to him,
"Why do you call me good? No one
is good but God alone. 19 You know
the commandments: 'You shall not
murder; You shall not commit adul-

l Gk *Gehenna* *m* Verses 44 and 46 (which are identical with verse 48) are lacking in the best ancient authorities *n* Gk *Gehenna* *o* Verses 44 and 46 (which are identical with verse 48) are lacking in the best ancient authorities *p* Gk *Gehenna* *q* Other ancient authorities either add or substitute *and every sacrifice will be salted with salt* *r* Or *how can you restore its saltiness?* *a* Other ancient authorities lack *and* *b* Other ancient authorities lack *and be joined to his wife*

tery; You shall not steal; You shall
not bear false witness; You shall
not defraud; Honor your father
and mother.' " 20 He said to him,
"Teacher, I have kept all these since
my youth." 21 Jesus, looking at him,
loved him and said, "You lack one
thing; go, sell what you own, and
give the money[c] to the poor, and
you will have treasure in heaven;
then come, follow me." 22 When
he heard this, he was shocked and
went away grieving, for he had
many possessions.
23 Then Jesus looked around
and said to his disciples, "How
hard it will be for those who have
wealth to enter the kingdom of
God!" 24 And the disciples were
perplexed at these words. But Jesus said to them again, "Children,
how hard it is[d] to enter the kingdom
of God! 25 It is easier for a camel
to go through the eye of a needle
than for someone who is rich to
enter the kingdom of God." 26 They
were greatly astounded and said to
one another,[e] "Then who can be
saved?" 27 Jesus looked at them and
said, "For mortals it is impossible,
but not for God; for God all things
are possible."
28 Peter began to say to him,
"Look, we have left everything and
followed you." 29 Jesus said, "Truly I tell you, there is no one who
has left house or brothers or sisters
or mother or father or children or
fields, for my sake and for the sake
of the good news,[f] 30 who will not
receive a hundredfold now in this
age—houses, brothers and sisters,
mothers and children, and fields,
with persecutions—and in the age
to come eternal life. 31 But many
who are first will be last, and the
last will be first."

A Third Time Jesus Foretells His Death and Resurrection

32 They were on the road, going
up to Jerusalem, and Jesus was
walking ahead of them; they were
amazed, and those who followed
were afraid. He took the twelve
aside again and began to tell them
what was to happen to him, 33 saying, "See, we are going up to Jerusalem, and the Son of Man will be
handed over to the chief priests and
the scribes, and they will condemn
him to death; then they will hand
him over to the Gentiles; 34 they
will mock him, and spit upon him,
and flog him, and kill him; and after
three days he will rise again."

The Request of James and John

35 James and John, the sons of
Zebedee, came forward to him and
said to him, "Teacher, we want you
to do for us whatever we ask of
you." 36 And he said to them, "What
is it you want me to do for you?"
37 And they said to him, "Grant us to
sit, one at your right hand and one
at your left, in your glory." 38 But
Jesus said to them, "You do not
know what you are asking. Are you
able to drink the cup that I drink, or
be baptized with the baptism that I
am baptized with?" 39 They replied,
"We are able." Then Jesus said to
them, "The cup that I drink you

---

c Gk lacks *the money* d Other ancient authorities add *for those who trust in riches*
e Other ancient authorities read *to him*
f Or *gospel*

will drink; and with the baptism with which I am baptized, you will be baptized; [40]but to sit at my right hand or at my left is not mine to grant, but it is for those for whom it has been prepared."

41 When the ten heard this, they began to be angry with James and John. [42]So Jesus called them and said to them, "You know that among the Gentiles those whom they recognize as their rulers lord it over them, and their great ones are tyrants over them. [43]But it is not so among you; but whoever wishes to become great among you must be your servant, [44]and whoever wishes to be first among you must be slave of all. [45]For the Son of Man came not to be served but to serve, and to give his life a ransom for many."

The Healing of Blind Bartimaeus

46 They came to Jericho. As he and his disciples and a large crowd were leaving Jericho, Bartimaeus son of Timaeus, a blind beggar, was sitting by the roadside. [47]When he heard that it was Jesus of Nazareth, he began to shout out and say, "Jesus, Son of David, have mercy on me!" [48]Many sternly ordered him to be quiet, but he cried out even more loudly, "Son of David, have mercy on me!" [49]Jesus stood still and said, "Call him here." And they called the blind man, saying to him, "Take heart; get up, he is calling you." [50]So throwing off his cloak, he sprang up and came to Jesus. [51]Then Jesus said to him, "What do you want me to do for you?" The blind man said to him, "My teacher,[g] let me see again." [52]Jesus said to him, "Go; your faith has made you well." Immediately he regained his sight and followed him on the way.

Jesus' Triumphal Entry into Jerusalem

11 When they were approaching Jerusalem, at Bethphage and Bethany, near the Mount of Olives, he sent two of his disciples [2]and said to them, "Go into the village ahead of you, and immediately as you enter it, you will find tied there a colt that has never been ridden; untie it and bring it. [3]If anyone says to you, 'Why are you doing this?' just say this, 'The Lord needs it and will send it back here immediately.' " [4]They went away and found a colt tied near a door, outside in the street. As they were untying it, [5]some of the bystanders said to them, "What are you doing, untying the colt?" [6]They told them what Jesus had said; and they allowed them to take it. [7]Then they brought the colt to Jesus and threw their cloaks on it; and he sat on it. [8]Many people spread their cloaks on the road, and others spread leafy branches that they had cut in the fields. [9]Then those who went ahead and those who followed were shouting,

"Hosanna!
Blessed is the one who comes in
the name of the Lord!
[10] Blessed is the coming kingdom
of our ancestor David!
Hosanna in the highest heaven!"

11 Then he entered Jerusalem

g Aramaic *Rabbouni*

and went into the temple; and when he had looked around at everything, as it was already late, he went out to Bethany with the twelve.

Jesus Curses the Fig Tree

12 On the following day, when they came from Bethany, he was hungry. 13 Seeing in the distance a fig tree in leaf, he went to see whether perhaps he would find anything on it. When he came to it, he found nothing but leaves, for it was not the season for figs. 14 He said to it, "May no one ever eat fruit from you again." And his disciples heard it.

Jesus Cleanses the Temple

15 Then they came to Jerusalem. And he entered the temple and began to drive out those who were selling and those who were buying in the temple, and he overturned the tables of the money changers and the seats of those who sold doves; 16 and he would not allow anyone to carry anything through the temple. 17 He was teaching and saying, "Is it not written,

'My house shall be called a
    house of prayer for all the
    nations'?
  But you have made it a den of
    robbers."

18 And when the chief priests and the scribes heard it, they kept looking for a way to kill him; for they were afraid of him, because the whole crowd was spellbound by his teaching. 19 And when evening came, Jesus and his disciples[a] went out of the city.

The Lesson from the Withered Fig Tree

20 In the morning as they passed by, they saw the fig tree withered away to its roots. 21 Then Peter remembered and said to him, "Rabbi, look! The fig tree that you cursed has withered." 22 Jesus answered them, "Have[b] faith in God. 23 Truly I tell you, if you say to this mountain, 'Be taken up and thrown into the sea,' and if you do not doubt in your heart, but believe that what you say will come to pass, it will be done for you. 24 So I tell you, whatever you ask for in prayer, believe that you have received[c] it, and it will be yours.

25 "Whenever you stand praying, forgive, if you have anything against anyone; so that your Father in heaven may also forgive you your trespasses."[d]

Jesus' Authority Is Questioned

27 Again they came to Jerusalem. As he was walking in the temple, the chief priests, the scribes, and the elders came to him 28 and said, "By what authority are you doing these things? Who gave you this authority to do them?" 29 Jesus said to them, "I will ask you one question; answer me, and I will tell you by what authority I do these things. 30 Did the baptism of John come from heaven, or was it of human origin? Answer me." 31 They argued with one another,

---

a Gk *they*: other ancient authorities read *he*
b Other ancient authorities read *"If you have*
c Other ancient authorities read *are receiving*
d Other ancient authorities add verse 26, *"But if you do not forgive, neither will your Father in heaven forgive your trespasses."*

"If we say, 'From heaven,' he will
say, 'Why then did you not believe
him?' 32 But shall we say, 'Of human origin'?"—they were afraid of
the crowd, for all regarded John as
truly a prophet. 33 So they answered
Jesus, "We do not know." And Jesus said to them, "Neither will I tell
you by what authority I am doing
these things."

The Parable of the Wicked Tenants

12 Then he began to speak to
them in parables. "A man
planted a vineyard, put a fence
around it, dug a pit for the wine
press, and built a watchtower; then
he leased it to tenants and went to
another country. 2 When the season
came, he sent a slave to the tenants
to collect from them his share of the
produce of the vineyard. 3 But they
seized him, and beat him, and sent
him away empty-handed. 4 And
again he sent another slave to them;
this one they beat over the head and
insulted. 5 Then he sent another, and
that one they killed. And so it was
with many others; some they beat,
and others they killed. 6 He had still
one other, a beloved son. Finally
he sent him to them, saying, 'They
will respect my son.' 7 But those
tenants said to one another, 'This
is the heir; come, let us kill him,
and the inheritance will be ours.'
8 So they seized him, killed him,
and threw him out of the vineyard.
9 What then will the owner of the
vineyard do? He will come and destroy the tenants and give the vineyard to others. 10 Have you not read
this scripture:

'The stone that the builders
rejected
has become the cornerstone;[a]
11 this was the Lord's doing,
and it is amazing in our
eyes'?"

12 When they realized that he
had told this parable against them,
they wanted to arrest him, but they
feared the crowd. So they left him
and went away.

The Question about Paying Taxes

13 Then they sent to him some
Pharisees and some Herodians to
trap him in what he said. 14 And
they came and said to him, "Teacher, we know that you are sincere,
and show deference to no one; for
you do not regard people with partiality, but teach the way of God in
accordance with truth. Is it lawful
to pay taxes to the emperor, or not?
15 Should we pay them, or should
we not?" But knowing their hypocrisy, he said to them, "Why are you
putting me to the test? Bring me a
denarius and let me see it." 16 And
they brought one. Then he said to
them, "Whose head is this, and
whose title?" They answered, "The
emperor's." 17 Jesus said to them,
"Give to the emperor the things
that are the emperor's, and to God
the things that are God's." And they
were utterly amazed at him.

The Question about the Resurrection

18 Some Sadducees, who say
there is no resurrection, came to
him and asked him a question, say-

a Or *keystone*

ing, [19]"Teacher, Moses wrote for us
that if a man's brother dies, leaving
a wife but no child, the man[b] shall
marry the widow and raise up children for his brother. [20]There were
seven brothers; the first married
and, when he died, left no children;
[21]and the second married the widow[c] and died, leaving no children;
and the third likewise; [22]none of
the seven left children. Last of all
the woman herself died. [23]In the
resurrection[d] whose wife will she
be? For the seven had married her."
24 Jesus said to them, "Is not this
the reason you are wrong, that you
know neither the scriptures nor the
power of God? [25]For when they rise
from the dead, they neither marry
nor are given in marriage, but are
like angels in heaven. [26]And as for
the dead being raised, have you not
read in the book of Moses, in the
story about the bush, how God said
to him, 'I am the God of Abraham,
the God of Isaac, and the God of Jacob'? [27]He is God not of the dead,
but of the living; you are quite
wrong."

The First Commandment

28 One of the scribes came near
and heard them disputing with one
another, and seeing that he answered them well, he asked him,
"Which commandment is the first
of all?" [29]Jesus answered, "The first
is, 'Hear, O Israel: the Lord our
God, the Lord is one; [30]you shall
love the Lord your God with all
your heart, and with all your soul,
and with all your mind, and with
all your strength.' [31]The second is
this, 'You shall love your neighbor as yourself.' There is no other
commandment greater than these."
[32]Then the scribe said to him, "You
are right, Teacher; you have truly
said that 'he is one, and besides him
there is no other'; [33]and 'to love
him with all the heart, and with all
the understanding, and with all the
strength,' and 'to love one's neighbor as oneself,'—this is much more
important than all whole burnt offerings and sacrifices." [34]When Jesus saw that he answered wisely, he
said to him, "You are not far from
the kingdom of God." After that no
one dared to ask him any question.

The Question about David's Son

35 While Jesus was teaching in
the temple, he said, "How can the
scribes say that the Messiah[e] is the
son of David? [36]David himself, by
the Holy Spirit, declared,

'The Lord said to my Lord,
"Sit at my right hand,
until I put your enemies under
your feet." '

[37]David himself calls him Lord; so
how can he be his son?" And the
large crowd was listening to him
with delight.

Jesus Denounces the Scribes

38 As he taught, he said, "Beware of the scribes, who like to
walk around in long robes, and
to be greeted with respect in the
marketplaces, [39]and to have the
best seats in the synagogues and
places of honor at banquets! [40]They
devour widows' houses and for
the sake of appearance say long

---

b Gk *his brother* *c* Gk *her* *d* Other ancient authorities add *when they rise* *e* Or *the Christ*

prayers. They will receive the
greater condemnation."

The Widow's Offering

41 He sat down opposite the
treasury, and watched the crowd
putting money into the treasury.
Many rich people put in large sums.
42 A poor widow came and put in
two small copper coins, which are
worth a penny. 43 Then he called his
disciples and said to them, "Truly
I tell you, this poor widow has put
in more than all those who are con-
tributing to the treasury. 44 For all of
them have contributed out of their
abundance; but she out of her poverty has put in everything she had,
all she had to live on."

The Destruction of the Temple Foretold

13 As he came out of the temple, one of his disciples said
to him, "Look, Teacher, what large
stones and what large buildings!"
2 Then Jesus asked him, "Do you
see these great buildings? Not one
stone will be left here upon another;
all will be thrown down."

3 When he was sitting on the
Mount of Olives opposite the temple, Peter, James, John, and Andrew asked him privately, 4 "Tell
us, when will this be, and what will
be the sign that all these things are
about to be accomplished?" 5 Then
Jesus began to say to them, "Beware that no one leads you astray.
6 Many will come in my name and
say, 'I am he!'[a] and they will lead
many astray. 7 When you hear of
wars and rumors of wars, do not be
alarmed; this must take place, but
the end is still to come. 8 For nation
will rise against nation, and kingdom against kingdom; there will be
earthquakes in various places; there
will be famines. This is but the beginning of the birth pangs.

Persecution Foretold

9 "As for yourselves, beware; for
they will hand you over to councils; and you will be beaten in synagogues; and you will stand before
governors and kings because of
me, as a testimony to them. 10 And
the good news[b] must first be proclaimed to all nations. 11 When
they bring you to trial and hand
you over, do not worry beforehand
about what you are to say; but say
whatever is given you at that time,
for it is not you who speak, but the
Holy Spirit. 12 Brother will betray
brother to death, and a father his
child, and children will rise against
parents and have them put to death;
13 and you will be hated by all because of my name. But the one who
endures to the end will be saved.

The Desolating Sacrilege

14 "But when you see the desolating sacrilege set up where it
ought not to be (let the reader understand), then those in Judea must
flee to the mountains; 15 the one on
the housetop must not go down or
enter the house to take anything
away; 16 the one in the field must
not turn back to get a coat. 17 Woe
to those who are pregnant and to
those who are nursing infants in
those days! 18 Pray that it may not

a Gk *I am* b Gk *gospel*

be in winter. 19 For in those days
there will be suffering, such as has
not been from the beginning of the
creation that God created until now,
no, and never will be. 20 And if the
Lord had not cut short those days,
no one would be saved; but for the
sake of the elect, whom he chose,
he has cut short those days. 21 And
if anyone says to you at that time,
'Look! Here is the Messiah!'[c] or
'Look! There he is!'—do not believe it. 22 False messiahs[d] and false
prophets will appear and produce
signs and omens, to lead astray, if
possible, the elect. 23 But be alert; I
have already told you everything.

The Coming of the Son of Man

24 "But in those days, after that
suffering,

the sun will be darkened,
  and the moon will not give its
    light,
25 and the stars will be falling from
    heaven,
  and the powers in the heavens
    will be shaken.

26 Then they will see 'the Son of
Man coming in clouds' with great
power and glory. 27 Then he will
send out the angels, and gather his
elect from the four winds, from
the ends of the earth to the ends of
heaven.

The Lesson of the Fig Tree

28 "From the fig tree learn its lesson: as soon as its branch becomes
tender and puts forth its leaves, you
know that summer is near. 29 So
also, when you see these things taking place, you know that he[e] is near,
at the very gates. 30 Truly I tell you,
this generation will not pass away
until all these things have taken
place. 31 Heaven and earth will pass
away, but my words will not pass
away.

The Necessity for Watchfulness

32 "But about that day or hour
no one knows, neither the angels
in heaven, nor the Son, but only
the Father. 33 Beware, keep alert;[f]
for you do not know when the time
will come. 34 It is like a man going
on a journey, when he leaves home
and puts his slaves in charge, each
with his work, and commands the
doorkeeper to be on the watch.
35 Therefore, keep awake—for you
do not know when the master of the
house will come, in the evening,
or at midnight, or at cockcrow, or
at dawn, 36 or else he may find you
asleep when he comes suddenly.
37 And what I say to you I say to all:
Keep awake."

The Plot to Kill Jesus

14 It was two days before the
Passover and the festival
of Unleavened Bread. The chief
priests and the scribes were looking
for a way to arrest Jesus[a] by stealth
and kill him; 2 for they said, "Not
during the festival, or there may be
a riot among the people."

The Anointing at Bethany

3 While he was at Bethany in the
house of Simon the leper,[b] as he sat
at the table, a woman came with

---

c Or *the Christ* d Or *christs* e Or *it*
f Other ancient authorities add *and pray*
a Gk *him* b The terms *leper* and *leprosy* can refer to several diseases

an alabaster jar of very costly ointment of nard, and she broke open
the jar and poured the ointment on
his head. 4 But some were there who
said to one another in anger, "Why
was the ointment wasted in this
way? 5 For this ointment could have
been sold for more than three hundred denarii,[c] and the money given
to the poor." And they scolded her.
6 But Jesus said, "Let her alone;
why do you trouble her? She has
performed a good service for me.
7 For you always have the poor with
you, and you can show kindness
to them whenever you wish; but
you will not always have me. 8 She
has done what she could; she has
anointed my body beforehand for
its burial. 9 Truly I tell you, wherever the good news[d] is proclaimed
in the whole world, what she has
done will be told in remembrance
of her."

Judas Agrees to Betray Jesus

10 Then Judas Iscariot, who was
one of the twelve, went to the chief
priests in order to betray him to
them. 11 When they heard it, they
were greatly pleased, and promised
to give him money. So he began to
look for an opportunity to betray
him.

The Passover with the Disciples

12 On the first day of Unleavened Bread, when the Passover
lamb is sacrificed, his disciples said
to him, "Where do you want us to
go and make the preparations for
you to eat the Passover?" 13 So he
sent two of his disciples, saying to
them, "Go into the city, and a man
carrying a jar of water will meet
you; follow him, 14 and wherever
he enters, say to the owner of the
house, 'The Teacher asks, Where
is my guest room where I may eat
the Passover with my disciples?'
15 He will show you a large room
upstairs, furnished and ready. Make
preparations for us there." 16 So the
disciples set out and went to the
city, and found everything as he
had told them; and they prepared
the Passover meal.

17 When it was evening, he came
with the twelve. 18 And when they
had taken their places and were
eating, Jesus said, "Truly I tell you,
one of you will betray me, one who
is eating with me." 19 They began
to be distressed and to say to him
one after another, "Surely, not I?"
20 He said to them, "It is one of the
twelve, one who is dipping bread[e]
into the bowl[f] with me. 21 For the
Son of Man goes as it is written of
him, but woe to that one by whom
the Son of Man is betrayed! It
would have been better for that one
not to have been born."

The Institution of the Lord's Supper

22 While they were eating, he
took a loaf of bread, and after blessing it he broke it, gave it to them,
and said, "Take; this is my body."
23 Then he took a cup, and after giving thanks he gave it to them, and
all of them drank from it. 24 He said
to them, "This is my blood of the[g]
covenant, which is poured out for

c The denarius was the usual day's wage for a laborer *d* Or *gospel* *e* Gk lacks *bread*
f Other ancient authorities read *same bowl*
g Other ancient authorities add *new*

many. 25 Truly I tell you, I will never
again drink of the fruit of the vine
until that day when I drink it new in
the kingdom of God."

Peter's Denial Foretold

26 When they had sung the
hymn, they went out to the Mount
of Olives. 27 And Jesus said to them,
"You will all become deserters; for
it is written,

'I will strike the shepherd,
and the sheep will be
scattered.'

28 But after I am raised up, I will go
before you to Galilee." 29 Peter said
to him, "Even though all become
deserters, I will not." 30 Jesus said to
him, "Truly I tell you, this day, this
very night, before the cock crows
twice, you will deny me three
times." 31 But he said vehemently,
"Even though I must die with you, I
will not deny you." And all of them
said the same.

Jesus Prays in Gethsemane

32 They went to a place called
Gethsemane; and he said to his
disciples, "Sit here while I pray."
33 He took with him Peter and
James and John, and began to be
distressed and agitated. 34 And he
said to them, "I am deeply grieved,
even to death; remain here, and
keep awake." 35 And going a little
farther, he threw himself on the
ground and prayed that, if it were
possible, the hour might pass from
him. 36 He said, "Abba,[h] Father, for
you all things are possible; remove
this cup from me; yet, not what I
want, but what you want." 37 He
came and found them sleeping; and
he said to Peter, "Simon, are you
asleep? Could you not keep awake
one hour? 38 Keep awake and pray
that you may not come into the time
of trial;[i] the spirit indeed is willing,
but the flesh is weak." 39 And again
he went away and prayed, saying
the same words. 40 And once more
he came and found them sleeping,
for their eyes were very heavy; and
they did not know what to say to
him. 41 He came a third time and
said to them, "Are you still sleeping
and taking your rest? Enough! The
hour has come; the Son of Man is
betrayed into the hands of sinners.
42 Get up, let us be going. See, my
betrayer is at hand."

The Betrayal and Arrest of Jesus

43 Immediately, while he was
still speaking, Judas, one of the
twelve, arrived; and with him
there was a crowd with swords
and clubs, from the chief priests,
the scribes, and the elders. 44 Now
the betrayer had given them a sign,
saying, "The one I will kiss is the
man; arrest him and lead him away
under guard." 45 So when he came,
he went up to him at once and said,
"Rabbi!" and kissed him. 46 Then
they laid hands on him and arrested
him. 47 But one of those who stood
near drew his sword and struck the
slave of the high priest, cutting off
his ear. 48 Then Jesus said to them,
"Have you come out with swords
and clubs to arrest me as though
I were a bandit? 49 Day after day I
was with you in the temple teaching, and you did not arrest me. But

h Aramaic for *Father* *i* Or *into temptation*

let the scriptures be fulfilled." 50 All of them deserted him and fled.

51 A certain young man was following him, wearing nothing but a linen cloth. They caught hold of him, 52 but he left the linen cloth and ran off naked.

Jesus before the Council

53 They took Jesus to the high priest; and all the chief priests, the elders, and the scribes were assembled. 54 Peter had followed him at a distance, right into the courtyard of the high priest; and he was sitting with the guards, warming himself at the fire. 55 Now the chief priests and the whole council were looking for testimony against Jesus to put him to death; but they found none. 56 For many gave false testimony against him, and their testimony did not agree. 57 Some stood up and gave false testimony against him, saying, 58 "We heard him say, 'I will destroy this temple that is made with hands, and in three days I will build another, not made with hands.' " 59 But even on this point their testimony did not agree. 60 Then the high priest stood up before them and asked Jesus, "Have you no answer? What is it that they testify against you?" 61 But he was silent and did not answer. Again the high priest asked him, "Are you the Messiah,[j] the Son of the Blessed One?" 62 Jesus said, "I am; and

'you will see the Son of Man
seated at the right hand of the
Power,'
and 'coming with the clouds of
heaven.' "

63 Then the high priest tore his clothes and said, "Why do we still need witnesses? 64 You have heard his blasphemy! What is your decision?" All of them condemned him as deserving death. 65 Some began to spit on him, to blindfold him, and to strike him, saying to him, "Prophesy!" The guards also took him over and beat him.

Peter Denies Jesus

66 While Peter was below in the courtyard, one of the servant-girls of the high priest came by. 67 When she saw Peter warming himself, she stared at him and said, "You also were with Jesus, the man from Nazareth." 68 But he denied it, saying, "I do not know or understand what you are talking about." And he went out into the forecourt.[k] Then the cock crowed.[l] 69 And the servant-girl, on seeing him, began again to say to the bystanders, "This man is one of them." 70 But again he denied it. Then after a little while the bystanders again said to Peter, "Certainly you are one of them; for you are a Galilean." 71 But he began to curse, and he swore an oath, "I do not know this man you are talking about." 72 At that moment the cock crowed for the second time. Then Peter remembered that Jesus had said to him, "Before the cock crows twice, you will deny me three times." And he broke down and wept.

Jesus before Pilate

15 As soon as it was morning, the chief priests held a con-

j Or *the Christ* *k* Or *gateway* *l* Other ancient authorities lack *Then the cock crowed*

sultation with the elders and scribes
and the whole council. They bound
Jesus, led him away, and handed
him over to Pilate. 2 Pilate asked
him, "Are you the King of the
Jews?" He answered him, "You say
so." 3 Then the chief priests accused
him of many things. 4 Pilate asked
him again, "Have you no answer?
See how many charges they bring
against you." 5 But Jesus made no
further reply, so that Pilate was
amazed.

Pilate Hands Jesus over to Be Crucified

6 Now at the festival he used to
release a prisoner for them, anyone for whom they asked. 7 Now a
man called Barabbas was in prison
with the rebels who had committed
murder during the insurrection. 8 So
the crowd came and began to ask
Pilate to do for them according to
his custom. 9 Then he answered
them, "Do you want me to release
for you the King of the Jews?"
10 For he realized that it was out of
jealousy that the chief priests had
handed him over. 11 But the chief
priests stirred up the crowd to have
him release Barabbas for them instead. 12 Pilate spoke to them again,
"Then what do you wish me to do[a]
with the man you call[b] the King of
the Jews?" 13 They shouted back,
"Crucify him!" 14 Pilate asked them,
"Why, what evil has he done?" But
they shouted all the more, "Crucify
him!" 15 So Pilate, wishing to satisfy the crowd, released Barabbas for
them; and after flogging Jesus, he
handed him over to be crucified.

The Soldiers Mock Jesus

16 Then the soldiers led him into
the courtyard of the palace (that
is, the governor's headquarters[c]);
and they called together the whole
cohort. 17 And they clothed him in
a purple cloak; and after twisting
some thorns into a crown, they put
it on him. 18 And they began salut-
ing him, "Hail, King of the Jews!"
19 They struck his head with a reed,
spat upon him, and knelt down in
homage to him. 20 After mocking
him, they stripped him of the purple cloak and put his own clothes
on him. Then they led him out to
crucify him.

The Crucifixion of Jesus

21 They compelled a passer-by,
who was coming in from the country, to carry his cross; it was Simon
of Cyrene, the father of Alexander
and Rufus. 22 Then they brought
Jesus[d] to the place called Golgotha
(which means the place of a skull).
23 And they offered him wine mixed
with myrrh; but he did not take
it. 24 And they crucified him, and
divided his clothes among them,
casting lots to decide what each
should take.

25 It was nine o'clock in the
morning when they crucified him.
26 The inscription of the charge
against him read, "The King of the
Jews." 27 And with him they crucified two bandits, one on his right
and one on his left.[e] 29 Those who

---

a Other ancient authorities read *what should I do* *b* Other ancient authorities lack *the man you call* *c* Gk *the praetorium* *d* Gk *him*
e Other ancient authorities add verse 28, *And the scripture was fulfilled that says, "And he was counted among the lawless."*

passed by derided[f] him, shaking
their heads and saying, "Aha! You
who would destroy the temple
and build it in three days, 30 save
yourself, and come down from the
cross!" 31 In the same way the chief
priests, along with the scribes, were
also mocking him among themselves and saying, "He saved others; he cannot save himself. 32 Let
the Messiah,[g] the King of Israel,
come down from the cross now,
so that we may see and believe."
Those who were crucified with him
also taunted him.

The Death of Jesus

33 When it was noon, darkness
came over the whole land[h] until
three in the afternoon. 34 At three
o'clock Jesus cried out with a loud
voice, "Eloi, Eloi, lema sabachthani?" which means, "My God,
my God, why have you forsaken
me?"[i] 35 When some of the bystanders heard it, they said, "Listen, he
is calling for Elijah." 36 And someone ran, filled a sponge with sour
wine, put it on a stick, and gave it
to him to drink, saying, "Wait, let
us see whether Elijah will come to
take him down." 37 Then Jesus gave
a loud cry and breathed his last.
38 And the curtain of the temple was
torn in two, from top to bottom.
39 Now when the centurion, who
stood facing him, saw that in this
way he[j] breathed his last, he said,
"Truly this man was God's Son!"[k]

40 There were also women looking on from a distance; among them
were Mary Magdalene, and Mary
the mother of James the younger
and of Joses, and Salome. 41 These
used to follow him and provided
for him when he was in Galilee;
and there were many other wom-
en who had come up with him to
Jerusalem.

The Burial of Jesus

42 When evening had come, and
since it was the day of Preparation,
that is, the day before the sabbath,
43 Joseph of Arimathea, a respected
member of the council, who was
also himself waiting expectantly for the kingdom of God, went
boldly to Pilate and asked for the
body of Jesus. 44 Then Pilate won-
dered if he were already dead; and
summoning the centurion, he asked
him whether he had been dead for
some time. 45 When he learned from
the centurion that he was dead, he
granted the body to Joseph. 46 Then
Joseph[l] bought a linen cloth, and
taking down the body,[m] wrapped it
in the linen cloth, and laid it in a
tomb that had been hewn out of the
rock. He then rolled a stone against
the door of the tomb. 47 Mary Magdalene and Mary the mother of Joses saw where the body[n] was laid.

The Resurrection of Jesus

16 When the sabbath was over,
Mary Magdalene, and Mary
the mother of James, and Salome
bought spices, so that they might
go and anoint him. 2 And very early
on the first day of the week, when
the sun had risen, they went to the
tomb. 3 They had been saying to one

f Or *blasphemed* *g* Or *the Christ* *h* Or *earth*
i Other ancient authorities read *made me a reproach* *j* Other ancient authorities add *cried out and* *k* Or *a son of God* *l* Gk *he*
m Gk *it* *n* Gk *it*

another, "Who will roll away the
stone for us from the entrance to the
tomb?" [4] When they looked up, they
saw that the stone, which was very
large, had already been rolled back.
[5] As they entered the tomb, they saw
a young man, dressed in a white
robe, sitting on the right side; and
they were alarmed. [6] But he said to
them, "Do not be alarmed; you are
looking for Jesus of Nazareth, who
was crucified. He has been raised;
he is not here. Look, there is the
place they laid him. [7] But go, tell his
disciples and Peter that he is going
ahead of you to Galilee; there you
will see him, just as he told you."
[8] So they went out and fled from the
tomb, for terror and amazement had
seized them; and they said nothing
to anyone, for they were afraid.[a]

The Shorter Ending of Mark

[[And all that had been commanded them they told briefly to those around Peter. And afterward Jesus himself sent out through them, from east to west, the sacred and imperishable proclamation of eternal salvation.[b]]]

The Longer Ending of Mark

Jesus Appears to Mary Magdalene

9 [[Now after he rose early on the
first day of the week, he appeared
first to Mary Magdalene, from
whom he had cast out seven demons.
[10] She went out and told those
who had been with him, while they
were mourning and weeping. [11] But
when they heard that he was alive
and had been seen by her, they
would not believe it.

Jesus Appears to Two Disciples

12 After this he appeared in another
form to two of them, as they
were walking into the country.
[13] And they went back and told the
rest, but they did not believe them.

Jesus Commissions the Disciples

14 Later he appeared to the eleven
themselves as they were sitting
at the table; and he upbraided them
for their lack of faith and stubbornness,
because they had not believed
those who saw him after he had risen.[c]
[15] And he said to them, "Go into
all the world and proclaim the good
news[d] to the whole creation. [16] The
one who believes and is baptized
will be saved; but the one who does
not believe will be condemned.
[17] And these signs will accompany
those who believe: by using my
name they will cast out demons;

a Some of the most ancient authorities bring the book to a close at the end of verse 8. One authority concludes the book with the shorter ending; others include the shorter ending and then continue with verses 9-20. In most authorities verses 9-20 follow immediately after verse 8, though in some of these authorities the passage is marked as being doubtful. *b* Other ancient authorities add *Amen* *c* Other ancient authorities add, in whole or in part, *And they excused themselves, saying, "This age of lawlessness and unbelief is under Satan, who does not allow the truth and power of God to prevail over the unclean things of the spirits. Therefore reveal your righteousness now"--thus they spoke to Christ. And Christ replied to them, "The term of years of Satan's power has been fulfilled, but other terrible things draw near. And for those who have sinned I was handed over to death, that they may return to the truth and sin no more, that they may inherit the spiritual and imperishable glory of righteousness that is in heaven."* *d* Or gospel

they will speak in new tongues;
18 they will pick up snakes in their
hands,[e] and if they drink any deadly thing, it will not hurt them; they will lay their hands on the sick, and they will recover."

The Ascension of Jesus

19 So then the Lord Jesus, after he had spoken to them, was taken up into heaven and sat down at the
right hand of God. 20 And they went out and proclaimed the good news everywhere, while the Lord worked with them and confirmed the message by the signs that accompanied it.[f]]]

e Other ancient authorities lack *in their hands*
f Other ancient authorities add *Amen*

The Gospel According to LUKE

Dedication to Theophilus

1 Since many have undertaken to
set down an orderly account of
the events that have been fulfilled
among us, 2just as they were handed on to us by those who from the
beginning were eyewitnesses and
servants of the word, 3I too decided, after investigating everything
carefully from the very first,[a] to
write an orderly account for you,
most excellent Theophilus, 4so that
you may know the truth concerning
the things about which you have
been instructed.

The Birth of John the Baptist Foretold

5 In the days of King Herod of
Judea, there was a priest named
Zechariah, who belonged to the
priestly order of Abijah. His wife
was a descendant of Aaron, and her
name was Elizabeth. 6Both of them
were righteous before God, living
blamelessly according to all the
commandments and regulations of
the Lord. 7But they had no children,
because Elizabeth was barren, and
both were getting on in years.

8 Once when he was serving as
priest before God and his section
was on duty, 9he was chosen by
lot, according to the custom of the
priesthood, to enter the sanctuary of
the Lord and offer incense. 10Now
at the time of the incense offering,
the whole assembly of the people
was praying outside. 11Then there
appeared to him an angel of the
Lord, standing at the right side of
the altar of incense. 12When Zechariah saw him, he was terrified;
and fear overwhelmed him. 13But
the angel said to him, "Do not be
afraid, Zechariah, for your prayer
has been heard. Your wife Elizabeth will bear you a son, and you
will name him John. 14You will
have joy and gladness, and many
will rejoice at his birth, 15for he will
be great in the sight of the Lord. He
must never drink wine or strong
drink; even before his birth he will
be filled with the Holy Spirit. 16He
will turn many of the people of Israel to the Lord their God. 17With the
spirit and power of Elijah he will
go before him, to turn the hearts
of parents to their children, and the
disobedient to the wisdom of the
righteous, to make ready a people
prepared for the Lord." 18Zechariah
said to the angel, "How will I know
that this is so? For I am an old man,
and my wife is getting on in years."
19The angel replied, "I am Gabriel.
I stand in the presence of God, and
I have been sent to speak to you and
to bring you this good news. 20But
now, because you did not believe
my words, which will be fulfilled in
their time, you will become mute,
unable to speak, until the day these

a Or *for a long time*

things occur."
21 Meanwhile the people were
waiting for Zechariah, and won-
dered at his delay in the sanctuary.
22 When he did come out, he could
not speak to them, and they realized that he had seen a vision in
the sanctuary. He kept motioning
to them and remained unable to
speak. 23 When his time of service
was ended, he went to his home.
24 After those days his wife
Elizabeth conceived, and for five
months she remained in seclusion.
She said, 25 "This is what the Lord
has done for me when he looked
favorably on me and took away the
disgrace I have endured among my
people."

The Birth of Jesus Foretold

26 In the sixth month the angel
Gabriel was sent by God to a town
in Galilee called Nazareth, 27 to a
virgin engaged to a man whose
name was Joseph, of the house
of David. The virgin's name was
Mary. 28 And he came to her and
said, "Greetings, favored one! The
Lord is with you."[b] 29 But she was
much perplexed by his words and
pondered what sort of greeting this
might be. 30 The angel said to her,
"Do not be afraid, Mary, for you
have found favor with God. 31 And
now, you will conceive in your
womb and bear a son, and you will
name him Jesus. 32 He will be great,
and will be called the Son of the
Most High, and the Lord God will
give to him the throne of his ancestor David. 33 He will reign over
the house of Jacob forever, and of
his kingdom there will be no end."
34 Mary said to the angel, "How can
this be, since I am a virgin?"[c] 35 The
angel said to her, "The Holy Spirit
will come upon you, and the power
of the Most High will overshadow
you; therefore the child to be born[d]
will be holy; he will be called Son
of God. 36 And now, your relative
Elizabeth in her old age has also
conceived a son; and this is the
sixth month for her who was said to
be barren. 37 For nothing will be impossible with God." 38 Then Mary
said, "Here am I, the servant of the
Lord; let it be with me according to
your word." Then the angel departed from her.

Mary Visits Elizabeth

39 In those days Mary set out
and went with haste to a Judean
town in the hill country, 40 where
she entered the house of Zechariah and greeted Elizabeth. 41 When
Elizabeth heard Mary's greeting,
the child leaped in her womb.
And Elizabeth was filled with the
Holy Spirit 42 and exclaimed with a
loud cry, "Blessed are you among
women, and blessed is the fruit of
your womb. 43 And why has this
happened to me, that the mother
of my Lord comes to me? 44 For as
soon as I heard the sound of your
greeting, the child in my womb
leaped for joy. 45 And blessed is she
who believed that there would be[e]
a fulfillment of what was spoken to
her by the Lord."

---

b Other ancient authorities add *Blessed are you among women* *c* Gk *I do not know a man* *d* Other ancient authorities add *of you* *e* Or *believed, for there will be*

Mary's Song of Praise

46 And Mary[f] said,
"My soul magnifies the Lord,
47 and my spirit rejoices in God
my Savior,
48 for he has looked with favor
on the lowliness of his
servant.
Surely, from now on all
generations will call me
blessed;
49 for the Mighty One has done
great things for me,
and holy is his name.
50 His mercy is for those who fear
him
from generation to generation.
51 He has shown strength with his
arm;
he has scattered the proud
in the thoughts of their
hearts.
52 He has brought down the
powerful from their
thrones,
and lifted up the lowly;
53 he has filled the hungry with
good things,
and sent the rich away empty.
54 He has helped his servant Israel,
in remembrance of his mercy,
55 according to the promise he
made to our ancestors,
to Abraham and to his
descendants forever."

56 And Mary remained with her about three months and then returned to her home.

The Birth of John the Baptist

57 Now the time came for Elizabeth to give birth, and she bore a
son. 58 Her neighbors and relatives
heard that the Lord had shown his great mercy to her, and they rejoiced with her.

59 On the eighth day they came to circumcise the child, and they were going to name him Zechariah
after his father. 60 But his mother
said, "No; he is to be called John."
61 They said to her, "None of your
relatives has this name." 62 Then
they began motioning to his father to find out what name he wanted
to give him. 63 He asked for a writing tablet and wrote, "His name is John." And all of them were
amazed. 64 Immediately his mouth
was opened and his tongue freed, and he began to speak, praising
God. 65 Fear came over all their
neighbors, and all these things were talked about throughout the entire
hill country of Judea. 66 All who
heard them pondered them and said, "What then will this child become?" For, indeed, the hand of the Lord was with him.

Zechariah's Prophecy

67 Then his father Zechariah was filled with the Holy Spirit and spoke this prophecy:
68 "Blessed be the Lord God of
Israel,
for he has looked favorably on
his people and redeemed
them.
69 He has raised up a mighty
savior[g] for us
in the house of his servant
David,
70 as he spoke through the mouth
of his holy prophets from
of old,

f Other ancient authorities read *Elizabeth*
g Gk *a horn of salvation*

71 that we would be saved from
our enemies and from the
hand of all who hate us.
72 Thus he has shown the mercy
promised to our ancestors,
and has remembered his holy
covenant,
73 the oath that he swore to our
ancestor Abraham,
to grant us 74 that we, being
rescued from the hands of
our enemies,
might serve him without
fear, 75 in holiness and
righteousness
before him all our days.
76 And you, child, will be called
the prophet of the Most
High;
for you will go before the
Lord to prepare his ways,
77 to give knowledge of salvation
to his people
by the forgiveness of their sins.
78 By the tender mercy of our God,
the dawn from on high will
break upon[h] us,
79 to give light to those who sit
in darkness and in the
shadow of death,
to guide our feet into the way
of peace."

80 The child grew and became
strong in spirit, and he was in the
wilderness until the day he appeared publicly to Israel.

The Birth of Jesus

2 In those days a decree went out
from Emperor Augustus that
all the world should be registered.
2 This was the first registration and
was taken while Quirinius was
governor of Syria. 3 All went to
their own towns to be registered.
4 Joseph also went from the town
of Nazareth in Galilee to Judea,
to the city of David called Bethlehem, because he was descended
from the house and family of David. 5 He went to be registered with
Mary, to whom he was engaged and
who was expecting a child. 6 While
they were there, the time came for
her to deliver her child. 7 And she
gave birth to her firstborn son and
wrapped him in bands of cloth, and
laid him in a manger, because there
was no place for them in the inn.

The Shepherds and the Angels

8 In that region there were shepherds living in the fields, keeping
watch over their flock by night.
9 Then an angel of the Lord stood
before them, and the glory of the
Lord shone around them, and they
were terrified. 10 But the angel said
to them, "Do not be afraid; for
see—I am bringing you good news
of great joy for all the people: 11 to
you is born this day in the city of
David a Savior, who is the Messiah,[a] the Lord. 12 This will be a
sign for you: you will find a child
wrapped in bands of cloth and lying
in a manger." 13 And suddenly there
was with the angel a multitude of
the heavenly host,[b] praising God
and saying,
14 "Glory to God in the highest
heaven,
and on earth peace among
those whom he favors!"[c]

---

h Other ancient authorities read *has broken upon*
a Or *the Christ* *b* Gk *army* *c* Other ancient authorities read *peace, goodwill among people*

15 When the angels had left them and gone into heaven, the shepherds said to one another, “Let us go now to Bethlehem and see this thing that has taken place, which the Lord has made known to us.” 16 So they went with haste and found Mary and Joseph, and the child lying in the manger. 17 When they saw this, they made known what had been told them about this child; 18 and all who heard it were amazed at what the shepherds told them. 19 But Mary treasured all these words and pondered them in her heart. 20 The shepherds returned, glorifying and praising God for all they had heard and seen, as it had been told them.

Jesus Is Named

21 After eight days had passed, it was time to circumcise the child; and he was called Jesus, the name given by the angel before he was conceived in the womb.

Jesus Is Presented in the Temple

22 When the time came for their purification according to the law of Moses, they brought him up to Jerusalem to present him to the Lord 23 (as it is written in the law of the Lord, “Every firstborn male shall be designated as holy to the Lord”), 24 and they offered a sacrifice according to what is stated in the law of the Lord, “a pair of turtledoves or two young pigeons.”

25 Now there was a man in Jerusalem whose name was Simeon;[d] this man was righteous and devout, looking forward to the consolation of Israel, and the Holy Spirit rested on him. 26 It had been revealed to him by the Holy Spirit that he would not see death before he had seen the Lord’s Messiah.[e] 27 Guided by the Spirit, Simeon[f] came into the temple; and when the parents brought in the child Jesus, to do for him what was customary under the law, 28 Simeon[g] took him in his arms and praised God, saying,

29 “Master, now you are dismissing
your servant[h] in peace,
according to your word;
30 for my eyes have seen your
salvation,
31 which you have prepared in
the presence of all peoples,
32 a light for revelation to the
Gentiles
and for glory to your people
Israel.”

33 And the child’s father and mother were amazed at what was being said about him. 34 Then Simeon[i] blessed them and said to his mother Mary, “This child is destined for the falling and the rising of many in Israel, and to be a sign that will be opposed 35 so that the inner thoughts of many will be revealed—and a sword will pierce your own soul too.”

36 There was also a prophet, Anna[j] the daughter of Phanuel, of the tribe of Asher. She was of a great age, having lived with her husband seven years after her marriage, 37 then as a widow to the age of eighty-four. She never left the temple but worshiped there with fasting and prayer night and day.

---

d Gk *Symeon* *e* Or *the Lord’s Christ*
f Gk *In the Spirit, he* *g* Gk *he* *h* Gk *slave*
i Gk *Symeon* *j* Gk *Hanna*

38 At that moment she came, and
began to praise God and to speak
about the child[k] to all who were
looking for the redemption of Jerusalem.

The Return to Nazareth

39 When they had finished everything required by the law of the
Lord, they returned to Galilee, to
their own town of Nazareth. 40 The
child grew and became strong,
filled with wisdom; and the favor
of God was upon him.

The Boy Jesus in the Temple

41 Now every year his parents
went to Jerusalem for the festival
of the Passover. 42 And when he was
twelve years old, they went up as
usual for the festival. 43 When the
festival was ended and they started
to return, the boy Jesus stayed behind in Jerusalem, but his parents
did not know it. 44 Assuming that he
was in the group of travelers, they
went a day's journey. Then they
started to look for him among their
relatives and friends. 45 When they
did not find him, they returned to
Jerusalem to search for him. 46 After
three days they found him in the
temple, sitting among the teachers,
listening to them and asking them
questions. 47 And all who heard him
were amazed at his understanding
and his answers. 48 When his parents[l] saw him they were astonished;
and his mother said to him, "Child,
why have you treated us like this?
Look, your father and I have been
searching for you in great anxiety."
49 He said to them, "Why were you
searching for me? Did you not
know that I must be in my Father's
house?"[m] 50 But they did not understand what he said to them. 51 Then
he went down with them and came
to Nazareth, and was obedient to
them. His mother treasured all
these things in her heart.

52 And Jesus increased in wisdom and in years,[n] and in divine
and human favor.

The Proclamation of John the Baptist

3 In the fifteenth year of the reign
of Emperor Tiberius, when Pon-
tius Pilate was governor of Judea,
and Herod was ruler[a] of Galilee,
and his brother Philip ruler[b] of the
region of Ituraea and Trachonitis,
and Lysanias ruler[c] of Abilene,
2 during the high priesthood of Annas and Caiaphas, the word of God
came to John son of Zechariah in
the wilderness. 3 He went into all
the region around the Jordan, proclaiming a baptism of repentance
for the forgiveness of sins, 4 as it is
written in the book of the words of
the prophet Isaiah,

"The voice of one crying out in
the wilderness:
'Prepare the way of the Lord,
make his paths straight.
5 Every valley shall be filled,
and every mountain and hill
shall be made low,
and the crooked shall be made
straight,
and the rough ways made
smooth;

---

k Gk *him* *l* Gk *they* *m* Or *be about my Father's interests?* *n* Or *in stature*
a Gk *tetrarch* *b* Gk *tetrarch* *c* Gk *tetrarch*

6 and all flesh shall see the
salvation of God.' "

7 John said to the crowds that came out to be baptized by him, "You brood of vipers! Who warned you to flee from the wrath to come? 8 Bear fruits worthy of repentance. Do not begin to say to yourselves, 'We have Abraham as our ancestor'; for I tell you, God is able from these stones to raise up children to Abraham. 9 Even now the ax is lying at the root of the trees; every tree therefore that does not bear good fruit is cut down and thrown into the fire."

10 And the crowds asked him, "What then should we do?" 11 In reply he said to them, "Whoever has two coats must share with anyone who has none; and whoever has food must do likewise." 12 Even tax collectors came to be baptized, and they asked him, "Teacher, what should we do?" 13 He said to them, "Collect no more than the amount prescribed for you." 14 Soldiers also asked him, "And we, what should we do?" He said to them, "Do not extort money from anyone by threats or false accusation, and be satisfied with your wages."

15 As the people were filled with expectation, and all were questioning in their hearts concerning John, whether he might be the Messiah,[d] 16 John answered all of them by saying, "I baptize you with water; but one who is more powerful than I is coming; I am not worthy to untie the thong of his sandals. He will baptize you with[e] the Holy Spirit and fire. 17 His winnowing fork is in his hand, to clear his threshing floor and to gather the wheat into his granary; but the chaff he will burn with unquenchable fire."

18 So, with many other exhortations, he proclaimed the good news to the people. 19 But Herod the ruler,[f] who had been rebuked by him because of Herodias, his brother's wife, and because of all the evil things that Herod had done, 20 added to them all by shutting up John in prison.

The Baptism of Jesus

21 Now when all the people were baptized, and when Jesus also had been baptized and was praying, the heaven was opened, 22 and the Holy Spirit descended upon him in bodily form like a dove. And a voice came from heaven, "You are my Son, the Beloved;[g] with you I am well pleased."[h]

The Ancestors of Jesus

23 Jesus was about thirty years old when he began his work. He was the son (as was thought) of Joseph son of Heli, 24 son of Matthat, son of Levi, son of Melchi, son of Jannai, son of Joseph, 25 son of Mattathias, son of Amos, son of Nahum, son of Esli, son of Naggai, 26 son of Maath, son of Mattathias, son of Semein, son of Josech, son of Joda, 27 son of Joanan, son of Rhesa, son of Zerubbabel, son of Shealtiel,[i] son of Neri, 28 son of Melchi, son of Addi, son of Cosam, son of Elmadam, son of Er, 29 son

d Or *the Christ* e Or *in* f Gk *tetrarch* g Or *my beloved Son* h Other ancient authorities read *You are my Son, today I have begotten you* i Gk *Salathiel*

of Joshua, son of Eliezer, son of
Jorim, son of Matthat, son of Levi,
30 son of Simeon, son of Judah,
son of Joseph, son of Jonam, son
of Eliakim, 31 son of Melea, son
of Menna, son of Mattatha, son of
Nathan, son of David, 32 son of Jesse, son of Obed, son of Boaz, son
of Sala,[j] son of Nahshon, 33 son of
Amminadab, son of Admin, son of
Arni,[k] son of Hezron, son of Perez,
son of Judah, 34 son of Jacob, son of
Isaac, son of Abraham, son of Ter-
ah, son of Nahor, 35 son of Serug,
son of Reu, son of Peleg, son of
Eber, son of Shelah, 36 son of Cainan, son of Arphaxad, son of Shem,
son of Noah, son of Lamech, 37 son
of Methuselah, son of Enoch, son
of Jared, son of Mahalaleel, son of
Cainan, 38 son of Enos, son of Seth,
son of Adam, son of God.

The Temptation of Jesus

4 Jesus, full of the Holy Spirit, returned from the Jordan and was
led by the Spirit in the wilderness,
2 where for forty days he was tempted by the devil. He ate nothing at all
during those days, and when they
were over, he was famished. 3 The
devil said to him, "If you are the
Son of God, command this stone
to become a loaf of bread." 4 Jesus
answered him, "It is written, 'One
does not live by bread alone.' "
5 Then the devil[a] led him up and
showed him in an instant all the
kingdoms of the world. 6 And the
devil[b] said to him, "To you I will
give their glory and all this authority; for it has been given over to me,
and I give it to anyone I please. 7 If
you, then, will worship me, it will
all be yours." 8 Jesus answered him,
"It is written,
'Worship the Lord your God,
and serve only him.' "
9 Then the devil[c] took him to Jerusalem, and placed him on the pin-
nacle of the temple, saying to him,
"If you are the Son of God, throw
yourself down from here, 10 for it is
written,
'He will command his angels
concerning you,
to protect you,'
11 and
'On their hands they will bear
you up,
so that you will not dash your
foot against a stone.' "
12 Jesus answered him, "It is said,
'Do not put the Lord your God to
the test.' " 13 When the devil had finished every test, he departed from
him until an opportune time.

The Beginning of the Galilean Ministry

14 Then Jesus, filled with the
power of the Spirit, returned to
Galilee, and a report about him
spread through all the surrounding
country. 15 He began to teach in
their synagogues and was praised
by everyone.

The Rejection of Jesus at Nazareth

16 When he came to Nazareth,
where he had been brought up, he
went to the synagogue on the sabbath day, as was his custom. He
stood up to read, 17 and the scroll

j Other ancient authorities read *Salmon*
k Other ancient authorities read *Amminadab, son of Aram*; others vary widely *a* Gk *he*
b Gk *he* *c* Gk *he*

of the prophet Isaiah was given
to him. He unrolled the scroll and
found the place where it was written:

18 "The Spirit of the Lord is upon
me,
because he has anointed me
to bring good news to the
poor.
He has sent me to proclaim
release to the captives
and recovery of sight to the
blind,
to let the oppressed go free,
19 to proclaim the year of the
Lord's favor."

20 And he rolled up the scroll, gave
it back to the attendant, and sat
down. The eyes of all in the synagogue were fixed on him. 21 Then he
began to say to them, "Today this
scripture has been fulfilled in your
hearing." 22 All spoke well of him
and were amazed at the gracious
words that came from his mouth.
They said, "Is not this Joseph's
son?" 23 He said to them, "Doubt-
less you will quote to me this proverb, 'Doctor, cure yourself!' And
you will say, 'Do here also in your
hometown the things that we have
heard you did at Capernaum.' "
24 And he said, "Truly I tell you, no
prophet is accepted in the prophet's
hometown. 25 But the truth is, there
were many widows in Israel in the
time of Elijah, when the heaven was
shut up three years and six months,
and there was a severe famine over
all the land; 26 yet Elijah was sent
to none of them except to a widow at Zarephath in Sidon. 27 There
were also many lepers[d] in Israel in
the time of the prophet Elisha, and
none of them was cleansed except
Naaman the Syrian." 28 When they
heard this, all in the synagogue
were filled with rage. 29 They got
up, drove him out of the town, and
led him to the brow of the hill on
which their town was built, so that
they might hurl him off the cliff.
30 But he passed through the midst
of them and went on his way.

The Man with an Unclean Spirit

31 He went down to Capernaum,
a city in Galilee, and was teaching
them on the sabbath. 32 They were
astounded at his teaching, because
he spoke with authority. 33 In the
synagogue there was a man who
had the spirit of an unclean demon,
and he cried out with a loud voice,
34 "Let us alone! What have you
to do with us, Jesus of Nazareth?
Have you come to destroy us? I
know who you are, the Holy One
of God." 35 But Jesus rebuked him,
saying, "Be silent, and come out of
him!" When the demon had thrown
him down before them, he came out
of him without having done him
any harm. 36 They were all amazed
and kept saying to one another,
"What kind of utterance is this? For
with authority and power he commands the unclean spirits, and out
they come!" 37 And a report about
him began to reach every place in
the region.

Healings at Simon's House

38 After leaving the synagogue
he entered Simon's house. Now Simon's mother-in-law was suffering

d The terms *leper* and *leprosy* can refer to several diseases

from a high fever, and they asked
him about her. 39 Then he stood over
her and rebuked the fever, and it
left her. Immediately she got up and
began to serve them.
40 As the sun was setting, all
those who had any who were sick
with various kinds of diseases
brought them to him; and he laid
his hands on each of them and
cured them. 41 Demons also came
out of many, shouting, "You are the
Son of God!" But he rebuked them
and would not allow them to speak,
because they knew that he was the
Messiah.[e]

Jesus Preaches in the Synagogues

42 At daybreak he departed and
went into a deserted place. And
the crowds were looking for him;
and when they reached him, they
wanted to prevent him from leaving them. 43 But he said to them, "I
must proclaim the good news of the
kingdom of God to the other cities
also; for I was sent for this purpose." 44 So he continued proclaiming the message in the synagogues
of Judea.[f]

Jesus Calls the First Disciples

5 Once while Jesus[a] was standing
beside the lake of Gennesaret,
and the crowd was pressing in on
him to hear the word of God, 2 he
saw two boats there at the shore of
the lake; the fishermen had gone
out of them and were washing their
nets. 3 He got into one of the boats,
the one belonging to Simon, and
asked him to put out a little way
from the shore. Then he sat down
and taught the crowds from the
boat. 4 When he had finished speaking, he said to Simon, "Put out into
the deep water and let down your
nets for a catch." 5 Simon answered,
"Master, we have worked all night
long but have caught nothing. Yet
if you say so, I will let down the
nets." 6 When they had done this,
they caught so many fish that their
nets were beginning to break. 7 So
they signaled their partners in the
other boat to come and help them.
And they came and filled both
boats, so that they began to sink.
8 But when Simon Peter saw it, he
fell down at Jesus' knees, saying,
"Go away from me, Lord, for I am
a sinful man!" 9 For he and all who
were with him were amazed at the
catch of fish that they had taken;
10 and so also were James and John,
sons of Zebedee, who were partners with Simon. Then Jesus said
to Simon, "Do not be afraid; from
now on you will be catching people." 11 When they had brought their
boats to shore, they left everything
and followed him.

Jesus Cleanses a Leper

12 Once, when he was in one of
the cities, there was a man covered
with leprosy.[b] When he saw Jesus, he bowed with his face to the
ground and begged him, "Lord,
if you choose, you can make me
clean." 13 Then Jesus[c] stretched out
his hand, touched him, and said, "I

e Or *the Christ* *f* Other ancient authorities read *Galilee* *a* Gk *he* *b* The terms *leper* and *leprosy* can refer to several diseases *c* Gk *he*

do choose. Be made clean." Immediately the leprosy[d] left him. 14 And he ordered him to tell no one. "Go," he said, "and show yourself to the priest, and, as Moses commanded, make an offering for your cleansing, for a testimony to them." 15 But now more than ever the word about Jesus[e] spread abroad; many crowds would gather to hear him and to be cured of their diseases. 16 But he would withdraw to deserted places and pray.

Jesus Heals a Paralytic

17 One day, while he was teaching, Pharisees and teachers of the law were sitting near by (they had come from every village of Galilee and Judea and from Jerusalem); and the power of the Lord was with him to heal.[f] 18 Just then some men came, carrying a paralyzed man on a bed. They were trying to bring him in and lay him before Jesus;[g] 19 but finding no way to bring him in because of the crowd, they went up on the roof and let him down with his bed through the tiles into the middle of the crowd[h] in front of Jesus. 20 When he saw their faith, he said, "Friend,[i] your sins are forgiven you." 21 Then the scribes and the Pharisees began to question, "Who is this who is speaking blasphemies? Who can forgive sins but God alone?" 22 When Jesus perceived their questionings, he answered them, "Why do you raise such questions in your hearts? 23 Which is easier, to say, 'Your sins are forgiven you,' or to say, 'Stand up and walk'? 24 But so that you may know that the Son of Man has authority on earth to forgive sins"—he said to the one who was paralyzed—"I say to you, stand up and take your bed and go to your home." 25 Immediately he stood up before them, took what he had been lying on, and went to his home, glorifying God. 26 Amazement seized all of them, and they glorified God and were filled with awe, saying, "We have seen strange things today."

Jesus Calls Levi

27 After this he went out and saw a tax collector named Levi, sitting at the tax booth; and he said to him, "Follow me." 28 And he got up, left everything, and followed him.

29 Then Levi gave a great banquet for him in his house; and there was a large crowd of tax collectors and others sitting at the table[j] with them. 30 The Pharisees and their scribes were complaining to his disciples, saying, "Why do you eat and drink with tax collectors and sinners?" 31 Jesus answered, "Those who are well have no need of a physician, but those who are sick; 32 I have come to call not the righteous but sinners to repentance."

The Question about Fasting

33 Then they said to him, "John's disciples, like the disciples of the Pharisees, frequently fast and pray, but your disciples eat and drink." 34 Jesus said to them, "You cannot

---

d The terms *leper* and *leprosy* can refer to several diseases *e* Gk *him* *f* Other ancient authorities read *was present to heal them* *g* Gk *him* *h* Gk *into the midst* *i* Gk *Man* *j* Gk *reclining*

make wedding guests fast while the bridegroom is with them, can you? 35 The days will come when the bridegroom will be taken away from them, and then they will fast in those days." 36 He also told them a parable: "No one tears a piece from a new garment and sews it on an old garment; otherwise the new will be torn, and the piece from the new will not match the old. 37 And no one puts new wine into old wineskins; otherwise the new wine will burst the skins and will be spilled, and the skins will be destroyed. 38 But new wine must be put into fresh wineskins. 39 And no one after drinking old wine desires new wine, but says, 'The old is good.' "[k]

The Question about the Sabbath

6 One sabbath[a] while Jesus[b] was going through the grainfields, his disciples plucked some heads of grain, rubbed them in their hands, and ate them. 2 But some of the Pharisees said, "Why are you doing what is not lawful[c] on the sabbath?" 3 Jesus answered, "Have you not read what David did when he and his companions were hungry? 4 He entered the house of God and took and ate the bread of the Presence, which it is not lawful for any but the priests to eat, and gave some to his companions?" 5 Then he said to them, "The Son of Man is lord of the sabbath."

The Man with a Withered Hand

6 On another sabbath he entered the synagogue and taught, and there was a man there whose right hand was withered. 7 The scribes and the Pharisees watched him to see whether he would cure on the sabbath, so that they might find an accusation against him. 8 Even though he knew what they were thinking, he said to the man who had the withered hand, "Come and stand here." He got up and stood there. 9 Then Jesus said to them, "I ask you, is it lawful to do good or to do harm on the sabbath, to save life or to destroy it?" 10 After looking around at all of them, he said to him, "Stretch out your hand." He did so, and his hand was restored. 11 But they were filled with fury and discussed with one another what they might do to Jesus.

Jesus Chooses the Twelve Apostles

12 Now during those days he went out to the mountain to pray; and he spent the night in prayer to God. 13 And when day came, he called his disciples and chose twelve of them, whom he also named apostles: 14 Simon, whom he named Peter, and his brother Andrew, and James, and John, and Philip, and Bartholomew, 15 and Matthew, and Thomas, and James son of Alphaeus, and Simon, who was called the Zealot, 16 and Judas son of James, and Judas Iscariot, who became a traitor.

Jesus Teaches and Heals

17 He came down with them and stood on a level place, with a great

---

k Other ancient authorities read *better*; others lack verse 39 *a* Other ancient authorities read *On the second first sabbath* *b* Gk *he* *c* Other ancient authorities add *to do*

crowd of his disciples and a great
multitude of people from all Judea,
Jerusalem, and the coast of Tyre
and Sidon. 18 They had come to hear
him and to be healed of their diseases; and those who were troubled
with unclean spirits were cured.
19 And all in the crowd were trying
to touch him, for power came out
from him and healed all of them.

Blessings and Woes

20 Then he looked up at his disciples and said:

"Blessed are you who are poor,
for yours is the kingdom of
God.

21 "Blessed are you who are
hungry now,
for you will be filled.
"Blessed are you who weep
now,
for you will laugh.

22 "Blessed are you when people
hate you, and when they exclude
you, revile you, and defame you[d]
on account of the Son of Man.
23 Rejoice in that day and leap for
joy, for surely your reward is great
in heaven; for that is what their ancestors did to the prophets.

24 "But woe to you who are rich,
for you have received your
consolation.

25 "Woe to you who are full now,
for you will be hungry.
"Woe to you who are laughing
now,
for you will mourn and weep.

26 "Woe to you when all speak
well of you, for that is what their
ancestors did to the false prophets.

Love for Enemies

27 "But I say to you that listen,
Love your enemies, do good to
those who hate you, 28 bless those
who curse you, pray for those who
abuse you. 29 If anyone strikes you
on the cheek, offer the other also;
and from anyone who takes away
your coat do not withhold even
your shirt. 30 Give to everyone who
begs from you; and if anyone takes
away your goods, do not ask for
them again. 31 Do to others as you
would have them do to you.

32 "If you love those who love
you, what credit is that to you? For
even sinners love those who love
them. 33 If you do good to those
who do good to you, what credit is
that to you? For even sinners do the
same. 34 If you lend to those from
whom you hope to receive, what
credit is that to you? Even sinners
lend to sinners, to receive as much
again. 35 But love your enemies, do
good, and lend, expecting nothing in return.[e] Your reward will
be great, and you will be children
of the Most High; for he is kind
to the ungrateful and the wicked.
36 Be merciful, just as your Father
is merciful.

Judging Others

37 "Do not judge, and you will
not be judged; do not condemn,
and you will not be condemned.
Forgive, and you will be forgiven;
38 give, and it will be given to you. A
good measure, pressed down, shak-
en together, running over, will be
put into your lap; for the measure

---

d Gk *cast out your name as evil* *e* Other ancient authorities read *despairing of no one*

you give will be the measure you
get back."
39 He also told them a parable:
"Can a blind person guide a blind
person? Will not both fall into a
pit? 40 A disciple is not above the
teacher, but everyone who is fully
qualified will be like the teacher.
41 Why do you see the speck in your
neighbor's[f] eye, but do not notice
the log in your own eye? 42 Or how
can you say to your neighbor,[g]
'Friend,[h] let me take out the speck
in your eye,' when you yourself do
not see the log in your own eye?
You hypocrite, first take the log out
of your own eye, and then you will
see clearly to take the speck out of
your neighbor's[i] eye.

A Tree and Its Fruit

43 "No good tree bears bad fruit,
nor again does a bad tree bear good
fruit; 44 for each tree is known by
its own fruit. Figs are not gathered
from thorns, nor are grapes picked
from a bramble bush. 45 The good
person out of the good treasure of
the heart produces good, and the
evil person out of evil treasure produces
evil; for it is out of the abundance
of the heart that the mouth
speaks.

The Two Foundations

46 "Why do you call me 'Lord,
Lord,' and do not do what I tell
you? 47 I will show you what someone
is like who comes to me, hears
my words, and acts on them. 48 That
one is like a man building a house,
who dug deeply and laid the foundation
on rock; when a flood arose,
the river burst against that house
but could not shake it, because it
had been well built.[j] 49 But the one
who hears and does not act is like
a man who built a house on the
ground without a foundation. When
the river burst against it, immediately
it fell, and great was the ruin
of that house."

Jesus Heals a Centurion's Servant

7 After Jesus[a] had finished all his
sayings in the hearing of the
people, he entered Capernaum. 2 A
centurion there had a slave whom
he valued highly, and who was ill
and close to death. 3 When he heard
about Jesus, he sent some Jewish
elders to him, asking him to come
and heal his slave. 4 When they
came to Jesus, they appealed to him
earnestly, saying, "He is worthy of
having you do this for him, 5 for he
loves our people, and it is he who
built our synagogue for us." 6 And
Jesus went with them, but when
he was not far from the house, the
centurion sent friends to say to him,
"Lord, do not trouble yourself, for
I am not worthy to have you come
under my roof; 7 therefore I did not
presume to come to you. But only
speak the word, and let my servant
be healed. 8 For I also am a man set
under authority, with soldiers under
me; and I say to one, 'Go,' and he
goes, and to another, 'Come,' and
he comes, and to my slave, 'Do
this,' and the slave does it." 9 When
Jesus heard this he was amazed at
him, and turning to the crowd that
followed him, he said, "I tell you,

f Gk *brother's* *g* Gk *brother* *h* Gk *brother* *i* Gk *brother's* *j* Other ancient authorities read *founded upon the rock* *a* Gk *he*

not even in Israel have I found such
faith." 10 When those who had been
sent returned to the house, they
found the slave in good health.

Jesus Raises the Widow's Son at Nain

11 Soon afterwards[b] he went to
a town called Nain, and his disciples and a large crowd went with
him. 12 As he approached the gate
of the town, a man who had died
was being carried out. He was his
mother's only son, and she was a
widow; and with her was a large
crowd from the town. 13 When the
Lord saw her, he had compassion
for her and said to her, "Do not
weep." 14 Then he came forward
and touched the bier, and the bear-
ers stood still. And he said, "Young
man, I say to you, rise!" 15 The dead
man sat up and began to speak,
and Jesus[c] gave him to his mother.
16 Fear seized all of them; and they
glorified God, saying, "A great
prophet has risen among us!" and
"God has looked favorably on his
people!" 17 This word about him
spread throughout Judea and all the
surrounding country.

Messengers from John the Baptist

18 The disciples of John reported all these things to him. So John
summoned two of his disciples
19 and sent them to the Lord to ask,
"Are you the one who is to come, or
are we to wait for another?" 20 When
the men had come to him, they said,
"John the Baptist has sent us to you
to ask, 'Are you the one who is to
come, or are we to wait for another?' " 21 Jesus[d] had just then cured
many people of diseases, plagues,
and evil spirits, and had given sight
to many who were blind. 22 And he
answered them, "Go and tell John
what you have seen and heard: the
blind receive their sight, the lame
walk, the lepers[e] are cleansed, the
deaf hear, the dead are raised, the
poor have good news brought to
them. 23 And blessed is anyone who
takes no offense at me."

24 When John's messengers had
gone, Jesus[f] began to speak to the
crowds about John:[g] "What did you
go out into the wilderness to look
at? A reed shaken by the wind?
25 What then did you go out to see?
Someone[h] dressed in soft robes?
Look, those who put on fine clothing and live in luxury are in royal
palaces. 26 What then did you go out
to see? A prophet? Yes, I tell you,
and more than a prophet. 27 This is
the one about whom it is written,

'See, I am sending my
messenger ahead of you,
who will prepare your way
before you.'

28 I tell you, among those born of
women no one is greater than John;
yet the least in the kingdom of God
is greater than he." 29 (And all the
people who heard this, including
the tax collectors, acknowledged
the justice of God,[i] because they
had been baptized with John's baptism. 30 But by refusing to be baptized by him, the Pharisees and the
lawyers rejected God's purpose for

---

b Other ancient authorities read *Next day*
c Gk *he* *d* Gk *He* *e* The terms *leper* and *leprosy* can refer to several diseases *f* Gk *he*
g Gk *him* *h* Or *Why then did you go out? To see someone* *i* Or *praised God*

themselves.)
31 "To what then will I compare
the people of this generation, and
what are they like? 32 They are like
children sitting in the marketplace
and calling to one another,

'We played the flute for you, and
you did not dance;
we wailed, and you did not
weep.'

33 For John the Baptist has come
eating no bread and drinking no
wine, and you say, 'He has a demon'; 34 the Son of Man has come
eating and drinking, and you say,
'Look, a glutton and a drunkard,
a friend of tax collectors and sinners!' 35 Nevertheless, wisdom is
vindicated by all her children."

A Sinful Woman Forgiven

36 One of the Pharisees asked
Jesus[j] to eat with him, and he went
into the Pharisee's house and took
his place at the table. 37 And a woman in the city, who was a sinner,
having learned that he was eating in
the Pharisee's house, brought an alabaster jar of ointment. 38 She stood
behind him at his feet, weeping,
and began to bathe his feet with
her tears and to dry them with her
hair. Then she continued kissing his
feet and anointing them with the
ointment. 39 Now when the Pharisee who had invited him saw it, he
said to himself, "If this man were
a prophet, he would have known
who and what kind of woman this
is who is touching him—that she
is a sinner." 40 Jesus spoke up and
said to him, "Simon, I have something to say to you." "Teacher,"
he replied, "speak." 41 "A certain
creditor had two debtors; one owed
five hundred denarii,[k] and the other
fifty. 42 When they could not pay, he
canceled the debts for both of them.
Now which of them will love him
more?" 43 Simon answered, "I suppose the one for whom he canceled
the greater debt." And Jesus[l] said
to him, "You have judged rightly."
44 Then turning toward the woman, he said to Simon, "Do you see
this woman? I entered your house;
you gave me no water for my feet,
but she has bathed my feet with
her tears and dried them with her
hair. 45 You gave me no kiss, but
from the time I came in she has not
stopped kissing my feet. 46 You did
not anoint my head with oil, but she
has anointed my feet with ointment.
47 Therefore, I tell you, her sins,
which were many, have been forgiven; hence she has shown great
love. But the one to whom little is
forgiven, loves little." 48 Then he
said to her, "Your sins are forgiv-
en." 49 But those who were at the
table with him began to say among
themselves, "Who is this who even
forgives sins?" 50 And he said to the
woman, "Your faith has saved you;
go in peace."

Some Women Accompany Jesus

8 Soon afterwards he went on
through cities and villages, proclaiming and bringing the good
news of the kingdom of God. The
twelve were with him, 2 as well as
some women who had been cured
of evil spirits and infirmities: Mary,
called Magdalene, from whom

j Gk *him* *k* The denarius was the usual day's wage for a laborer *l* Gk *he*

seven demons had gone out, 3 and
Joanna, the wife of Herod's steward Chuza, and Susanna, and many
others, who provided for them[a] out
of their resources.

The Parable of the Sower

4 When a great crowd gathered
and people from town after town
came to him, he said in a parable:
5 "A sower went out to sow his seed;
and as he sowed, some fell on the
path and was trampled on, and the
birds of the air ate it up. 6 Some
fell on the rock; and as it grew up,
it withered for lack of moisture.
7 Some fell among thorns, and the
thorns grew with it and choked it.
8 Some fell into good soil, and when
it grew, it produced a hundredfold."
As he said this, he called out, "Let
anyone with ears to hear listen!"

The Purpose of the Parables

9 Then his disciples asked him
what this parable meant. 10 He said,
"To you it has been given to know
the secrets[b] of the kingdom of God;
but to others I speak[c] in parables,
so that

'looking they may not perceive,
and listening they may not
understand.'

The Parable of the Sower Explained

11 "Now the parable is this: The
seed is the word of God. 12 The
ones on the path are those who
have heard; then the devil comes
and takes away the word from
their hearts, so that they may not
believe and be saved. 13 The ones
on the rock are those who, when
they hear the word, receive it with
joy. But these have no root; they
believe only for a while and in a
time of testing fall away. 14 As for
what fell among the thorns, these
are the ones who hear; but as they
go on their way, they are choked by
the cares and riches and pleasures
of life, and their fruit does not ma-
ture. 15 But as for that in the good
soil, these are the ones who, when
they hear the word, hold it fast in
an honest and good heart, and bear
fruit with patient endurance.

A Lamp under a Jar

16 "No one after lighting a lamp
hides it under a jar, or puts it under
a bed, but puts it on a lampstand,
so that those who enter may see the
light. 17 For nothing is hidden that
will not be disclosed, nor is anything secret that will not become
known and come to light. 18 Then
pay attention to how you listen; for
to those who have, more will be
given; and from those who do not
have, even what they seem to have
will be taken away."

The True Kindred of Jesus

19 Then his mother and his
brothers came to him, but they
could not reach him because of the
crowd. 20 And he was told, "Your
mother and your brothers are standing outside, wanting to see you."
21 But he said to them, "My mother
and my brothers are those who hear
the word of God and do it."

Jesus Calms a Storm

22 One day he got into a boat

---

a Other ancient authorities read *him*
b Or *mysteries* *c* Gk lacks *I speak*

with his disciples, and he said to them, "Let us go across to the other side of the lake." So they put out, 23 and while they were sailing he fell asleep. A windstorm swept down on the lake, and the boat was filling with water, and they were in danger. 24 They went to him and woke him up, shouting, "Master, Master, we are perishing!" And he woke up and rebuked the wind and the raging waves; they ceased, and there was a calm. 25 He said to them, "Where is your faith?" They were afraid and amazed, and said to one another, "Who then is this, that he commands even the winds and the water, and they obey him?"

Jesus Heals the Gerasene Demoniac

26 Then they arrived at the country of the Gerasenes,[d] which is opposite Galilee. 27 As he stepped out on land, a man of the city who had demons met him. For a long time he had worn[e] no clothes, and he did not live in a house but in the tombs. 28 When he saw Jesus, he fell down before him and shouted at the top of his voice, "What have you to do with me, Jesus, Son of the Most High God? I beg you, do not torment me"— 29 for Jesus[f] had commanded the unclean spirit to come out of the man. (For many times it had seized him; he was kept under guard and bound with chains and shackles, but he would break the bonds and be driven by the demon into the wilds.) 30 Jesus then asked him, "What is your name?" He said, "Legion"; for many demons had entered him. 31 They begged him not to order them to go back into the abyss.

32 Now there on the hillside a large herd of swine was feeding; and the demons[g] begged Jesus[h] to let them enter these. So he gave them permission. 33 Then the demons came out of the man and entered the swine, and the herd rushed down the steep bank into the lake and was drowned.

34 When the swineherds saw what had happened, they ran off and told it in the city and in the country. 35 Then people came out to see what had happened, and when they came to Jesus, they found the man from whom the demons had gone sitting at the feet of Jesus, clothed and in his right mind. And they were afraid. 36 Those who had seen it told them how the one who had been possessed by demons had been healed. 37 Then all the people of the surrounding country of the Gerasenes[i] asked Jesus[j] to leave them; for they were seized with great fear. So he got into the boat and returned. 38 The man from whom the demons had gone begged that he might be with him; but Jesus[k] sent him away, saying, 39 "Return to your home, and declare how much God has done for you." So he went away, proclaiming throughout the city how much Jesus had done for him.

---

d Other ancient authorities read *Gadarenes*; others, *Gergesenes* *e* Other ancient authorities read *a man of the city who had had demons for a long time met him. He wore* *f* Gk *he* *g* Gk *they* *h* Gk *him* *i* Other ancient authorities read *Gadarenes*; others, *Gergesenes* *j* Gk *him* *k* Gk *he*

A Girl Restored to Life and a Woman Healed

40 Now when Jesus returned, the crowd welcomed him, for they were all waiting for him. 41 Just then there came a man named Jairus, a leader of the synagogue. He fell at Jesus' feet and begged him to come to his house, 42 for he had an only daughter, about twelve years old, who was dying.

As he went, the crowds pressed in on him. 43 Now there was a woman who had been suffering from hemorrhages for twelve years; and though she had spent all she had on physicians,[l] no one could cure her. 44 She came up behind him and touched the fringe of his clothes, and immediately her hemorrhage stopped. 45 Then Jesus asked, "Who touched me?" When all denied it, Peter[m] said, "Master, the crowds surround you and press in on you." 46 But Jesus said, "Someone touched me; for I noticed that power had gone out from me." 47 When the woman saw that she could not remain hidden, she came trembling; and falling down before him, she declared in the presence of all the people why she had touched him, and how she had been immediately healed. 48 He said to her, "Daughter, your faith has made you well; go in peace."

49 While he was still speaking, someone came from the leader's house to say, "Your daughter is dead; do not trouble the teacher any longer." 50 When Jesus heard this, he replied, "Do not fear. Only believe, and she will be saved." 51 When he came to the house, he did not allow anyone to enter with him, except Peter, John, and James, and the child's father and mother. 52 They were all weeping and wailing for her; but he said, "Do not weep; for she is not dead but sleeping." 53 And they laughed at him, knowing that she was dead. 54 But he took her by the hand and called out, "Child, get up!" 55 Her spirit returned, and she got up at once. Then he directed them to give her something to eat. 56 Her parents were astounded; but he ordered them to tell no one what had happened.

The Mission of the Twelve

9 Then Jesus[a] called the twelve together and gave them power and authority over all demons and to cure diseases, 2 and he sent them out to proclaim the kingdom of God and to heal. 3 He said to them, "Take nothing for your journey, no staff, nor bag, nor bread, nor money—not even an extra tunic. 4 Whatever house you enter, stay there, and leave from there. 5 Wherever they do not welcome you, as you are leaving that town shake the dust off your feet as a testimony against them." 6 They departed and went through the villages, bringing the good news and curing diseases everywhere.

Herod's Perplexity

7 Now Herod the ruler[b] heard about all that had taken place, and he was perplexed, because it was

---

l Other ancient authorities lack *and though she had spent all she had on physicians* *m* Other ancient authorities add *and those who were with him* *a* Gk *he* *b* Gk *tetrarch*

said by some that John had been
raised from the dead, 8 by some that
Elijah had appeared, and by others
that one of the ancient prophets
had arisen. 9 Herod said, "John I
beheaded; but who is this about
whom I hear such things?" And he
tried to see him.

Feeding the Five Thousand

10 On their return the apostles
told Jesus[c] all they had done. He
took them with him and withdrew
privately to a city called Bethsaida.
11 When the crowds found out about
it, they followed him; and he welcomed them, and spoke to them
about the kingdom of God, and
healed those who needed to be
cured.

12 The day was drawing to a
close, and the twelve came to him
and said, "Send the crowd away, so
that they may go into the surrounding villages and countryside, to
lodge and get provisions; for we are
here in a deserted place." 13 But he
said to them, "You give them something to eat." They said, "We have
no more than five loaves and two
fish—unless we are to go and buy
food for all these people." 14 For
there were about five thousand
men. And he said to his disciples,
"Make them sit down in groups
of about fifty each." 15 They did so
and made them all sit down. 16 And
taking the five loaves and the two
fish, he looked up to heaven, and
blessed and broke them, and gave
them to the disciples to set before
the crowd. 17 And all ate and were
filled. What was left over was gathered up, twelve baskets of broken
pieces.

Peter's Declaration about Jesus

18 Once when Jesus[d] was praying alone, with only the disciples
near him, he asked them, "Who do
the crowds say that I am?" 19 They
answered, "John the Baptist; but
others, Elijah; and still others, that
one of the ancient prophets has aris-
en." 20 He said to them, "But who do
you say that I am?" Peter answered,
"The Messiah[e] of God."

Jesus Foretells His Death and Resurrection

21 He sternly ordered and commanded them not to tell anyone,
22 saying, "The Son of Man must
undergo great suffering, and be rejected by the elders, chief priests,
and scribes, and be killed, and on
the third day be raised."

23 Then he said to them all, "If
any want to become my followers,
let them deny themselves and take
up their cross daily and follow me.
24 For those who want to save their
life will lose it, and those who lose
their life for my sake will save it.
25 What does it profit them if they
gain the whole world, but lose or
forfeit themselves? 26 Those who
are ashamed of me and of my
words, of them the Son of Man will
be ashamed when he comes in his
glory and the glory of the Father
and of the holy angels. 27 But truly
I tell you, there are some standing
here who will not taste death before
they see the kingdom of God."

---

c Gk *him* *d* Gk *he* *e* Or *The Christ*

The Transfiguration

28 Now about eight days after
these sayings Jesus[f] took with him
Peter and John and James, and went
up on the mountain to pray. [29] And
while he was praying, the appearance of his face changed, and his
clothes became dazzling white.
[30] Suddenly they saw two men,
Moses and Elijah, talking to him.
[31] They appeared in glory and were
speaking of his departure, which
he was about to accomplish at Jerusalem. [32] Now Peter and his companions were weighed down with
sleep; but since they had stayed
awake,[g] they saw his glory and
the two men who stood with him.
[33] Just as they were leaving him, Peter said to Jesus, "Master, it is good
for us to be here; let us make three
dwellings,[h] one for you, one for
Moses, and one for Elijah"—not
knowing what he said. [34] While he
was saying this, a cloud came and
overshadowed them; and they were
terrified as they entered the cloud.
[35] Then from the cloud came a voice
that said, "This is my Son, my Chosen;[i] listen to him!" [36] When the
voice had spoken, Jesus was found
alone. And they kept silent and in
those days told no one any of the
things they had seen.

Jesus Heals a Boy with a Demon

37 On the next day, when they
had come down from the mountain,
a great crowd met him. [38] Just then
a man from the crowd shouted,
"Teacher, I beg you to look at my
son; he is my only child. [39] Suddenly a spirit seizes him, and all at once
he[j] shrieks. It convulses him until
he foams at the mouth; it mauls
him and will scarcely leave him.
[40] I begged your disciples to cast
it out, but they could not." [41] Jesus
answered, "You faithless and perverse generation, how much longer
must I be with you and bear with
you? Bring your son here." [42] While
he was coming, the demon dashed
him to the ground in convulsions.
But Jesus rebuked the unclean spirit, healed the boy, and gave him
back to his father. [43] And all were
astounded at the greatness of God.

Jesus Again Foretells His Death

While everyone was amazed at all
that he was doing, he said to his disciples, [44] "Let these words sink into
your ears: The Son of Man is going
to be betrayed into human hands."
[45] But they did not understand this
saying; its meaning was concealed
from them, so that they could not
perceive it. And they were afraid to
ask him about this saying.

True Greatness

46 An argument arose among
them as to which one of them was
the greatest. [47] But Jesus, aware of
their inner thoughts, took a little
child and put it by his side, [48] and
said to them, "Whoever welcomes
this child in my name welcomes
me, and whoever welcomes me
welcomes the one who sent me;
for the least among all of you is the
greatest."

---

f Gk *he* *g* Or *but when they were fully awake*
h Or *tents* *i* Other ancient authorities read *my Beloved* *j* Or *it*

Another Exorcist

49 John answered, "Master, we
saw someone casting out demons
in your name, and we tried to stop
him, because he does not follow
with us." 50 But Jesus said to him,
"Do not stop him; for whoever is
not against you is for you."

A Samaritan Village Refuses to Receive Jesus

51 When the days drew near for
him to be taken up, he set his face
to go to Jerusalem. 52 And he sent
messengers ahead of him. On their
way they entered a village of the
Samaritans to make ready for him;
53 but they did not receive him, because his face was set toward Jerusalem. 54 When his disciples James
and John saw it, they said, "Lord,
do you want us to command fire to
come down from heaven and consume them?"[k] 55 But he turned and
rebuked them. 56 Then[l] they went on
to another village.

Would-Be Followers of Jesus

57 As they were going along
the road, someone said to him, "I
will follow you wherever you go."
58 And Jesus said to him, "Foxes
have holes, and birds of the air
have nests; but the Son of Man
has nowhere to lay his head." 59 To
another he said, "Follow me." But
he said, "Lord, first let me go and
bury my father." 60 But Jesus[m] said
to him, "Let the dead bury their
own dead; but as for you, go and
proclaim the kingdom of God."
61 Another said, "I will follow you,
Lord; but let me first say farewell
to those at my home." 62 Jesus said
to him, "No one who puts a hand to
the plow and looks back is fit for
the kingdom of God."

The Mission of the Seventy

10 After this the Lord appointed
seventy[a] others and sent them
on ahead of him in pairs to every
town and place where he himself
intended to go. 2 He said to them,
"The harvest is plentiful, but the
laborers are few; therefore ask the
Lord of the harvest to send out laborers into his harvest. 3 Go on your
way. See, I am sending you out like
lambs into the midst of wolves.
4 Carry no purse, no bag, no sandals; and greet no one on the road.
5 Whatever house you enter, first
say, 'Peace to this house!' 6 And
if anyone is there who shares in
peace, your peace will rest on that
person; but if not, it will return to
you. 7 Remain in the same house,
eating and drinking whatever they
provide, for the laborer deserves to
be paid. Do not move about from
house to house. 8 Whenever you
enter a town and its people welcome you, eat what is set before
you; 9 cure the sick who are there,
and say to them, 'The kingdom of
God has come near to you.'[b] 10 But
whenever you enter a town and
they do not welcome you, go out
into its streets and say, 11 'Even the
dust of your town that clings to our
feet, we wipe off in protest against

---

k Other ancient authorities add *as Elijah did*
l Other ancient authorities read *rebuked them, and said, "You do not know what spirit you are of, 56 for the Son of Man has not come to destroy the lives of human beings but to save them." Then*
m Gk *he*
a Other ancient authorities read *seventy-two*
b Or *is at hand for you*

you. Yet know this: the kingdom of
God has come near.'[c] 12 I tell you,
on that day it will be more tolerable
for Sodom than for that town.

Woes to Unrepentant Cities

13 "Woe to you, Chorazin! Woe
to you, Bethsaida! For if the deeds
of power done in you had been
done in Tyre and Sidon, they would
have repented long ago, sitting in
sackcloth and ashes. 14 But at the
judgment it will be more tolerable
for Tyre and Sidon than for you.
15 And you, Capernaum,
will you be exalted to heaven?
No, you will be brought down
to Hades.

16 "Whoever listens to you listens to me, and whoever rejects you
rejects me, and whoever rejects me
rejects the one who sent me."

The Return of the Seventy

17 The seventy[d] returned with
joy, saying, "Lord, in your name
even the demons submit to us!"
18 He said to them, "I watched Satan fall from heaven like a flash of
lightning. 19 See, I have given you
authority to tread on snakes and
scorpions, and over all the power
of the enemy; and nothing will hurt
you. 20 Nevertheless, do not rejoice
at this, that the spirits submit to
you, but rejoice that your names are
written in heaven."

Jesus Rejoices

21 At that same hour Jesus[e] rejoiced in the Holy Spirit[f] and said,
"I thank[g] you, Father, Lord of heav-
en and earth, because you have hidden these things from the wise and
the intelligent and have revealed
them to infants; yes, Father, for
such was your gracious will.[h] 22 All
things have been handed over to me
by my Father; and no one knows
who the Son is except the Father,
or who the Father is except the
Son and anyone to whom the Son
chooses to reveal him."

23 Then turning to the disciples, Jesus[i] said to them privately,
"Blessed are the eyes that see what
you see! 24 For I tell you that many
prophets and kings desired to see
what you see, but did not see it, and
to hear what you hear, but did not
hear it."

The Parable of the Good Samaritan

25 Just then a lawyer stood up
to test Jesus.[j] "Teacher," he said,
"what must I do to inherit eternal
life?" 26 He said to him, "What is
written in the law? What do you
read there?" 27 He answered, "You
shall love the Lord your God with
all your heart, and with all your
soul, and with all your strength, and
with all your mind; and your neighbor as yourself." 28 And he said to
him, "You have given the right
answer; do this, and you will live."

29 But wanting to justify himself, he asked Jesus, "And who is
my neighbor?" 30 Jesus replied, "A
man was going down from Jerusalem to Jericho, and fell into the
hands of robbers, who stripped
him, beat him, and went away,

c Or *is at hand* *d* Other ancient authorities read *seventy-two* *e* Gk *he* *f* Other authorities read *in the spirit* *g* Or *praise* *h* Or *for so it was well-pleasing in your sight* *i* Gk *he* *j* Gk *him*

leaving him half dead. 31 Now by
chance a priest was going down
that road; and when he saw him,
he passed by on the other side.
32 So likewise a Levite, when he
came to the place and saw him,
passed by on the other side. 33 But
a Samaritan while traveling came
near him; and when he saw him,
he was moved with pity. 34 He went
to him and bandaged his wounds,
having poured oil and wine on
them. Then he put him on his own
animal, brought him to an inn, and
took care of him. 35 The next day he
took out two denarii,[k] gave them to
the innkeeper, and said, 'Take care
of him; and when I come back, I
will repay you whatever more you
spend.' 36 Which of these three, do
you think, was a neighbor to the
man who fell into the hands of the
robbers?" 37 He said, "The one who
showed him mercy." Jesus said to
him, "Go and do likewise."

Jesus Visits Martha and Mary

38 Now as they went on their
way, he entered a certain village,
where a woman named Martha
welcomed him into her home. 39 She
had a sister named Mary, who sat at
the Lord's feet and listened to what
he was saying. 40 But Martha was
distracted by her many tasks; so she
came to him and asked, "Lord, do
you not care that my sister has left
me to do all the work by myself?
Tell her then to help me." 41 But the
Lord answered her, "Martha, Martha, you are worried and distracted
by many things; 42 there is need of
only one thing.[l] Mary has chosen
the better part, which will not be
taken away from her."

The Lord's Prayer

11 He was praying in a certain
place, and after he had finished, one of his disciples said to
him, "Lord, teach us to pray, as
John taught his disciples." 2 He said
to them, "When you pray, say:

Father,[a] hallowed be your name.
Your kingdom come.[b]
3 Give us each day our daily
bread.[c]
4 And forgive us our sins,
for we ourselves forgive
everyone indebted to us.
And do not bring us to the
time of trial."[d]

Perseverance in Prayer

5 And he said to them, "Suppose
one of you has a friend, and you
go to him at midnight and say to
him, 'Friend, lend me three loaves
of bread; 6 for a friend of mine has
arrived, and I have nothing to set
before him.' 7 And he answers from
within, 'Do not bother me; the door
has already been locked, and my
children are with me in bed; I cannot get up and give you anything.'
8 I tell you, even though he will not
get up and give him anything because he is his friend, at least because of his persistence he will get
up and give him whatever he needs.

---

k The denarius was the usual day's wage for a laborer *l* Other ancient authorities read *few things are necessary, or only one* *a* Other ancient authorities read *Our Father in heaven* *b* A few ancient authorities read *Your Holy Spirit come upon us and cleanse us.* Other ancient authorities add *Your will be done, on earth as in heaven* *c* Or *our bread for tomorrow* *d* Or *us into temptation.* Other ancient authorities add *but rescue us from the evil one* (or *from evil*)

9 "So I say to you, Ask, and it
will be given you; search, and you
will find; knock, and the door will
be opened for you. [10]For everyone
who asks receives, and everyone
who searches finds, and for everyone who knocks, the door will be
opened. [11]Is there anyone among
you who, if your child asks for[e] a
fish, will give a snake instead of a
fish? [12]Or if the child asks for an
egg, will give a scorpion? [13]If you
then, who are evil, know how to
give good gifts to your children,
how much more will the heavenly
Father give the Holy Spirit[f] to those
who ask him!"

Jesus and Beelzebul

14 Now he was casting out a
demon that was mute; when the
demon had gone out, the one who
had been mute spoke, and the
crowds were amazed. [15]But some
of them said, "He casts out demons
by Beelzebul, the ruler of the demons." [16]Others, to test him, kept
demanding from him a sign from
heaven. [17]But he knew what they
were thinking and said to them,
"Every kingdom divided against
itself becomes a desert, and house
falls on house. [18]If Satan also is divided against himself, how will his
kingdom stand? —for you say that
I cast out the demons by Beelzebul.
[19]Now if I cast out the demons by
Beelzebul, by whom do your exorcists[g] cast them out? Therefore they
will be your judges. [20]But if it is by
the finger of God that I cast out the
demons, then the kingdom of God
has come to you. [21]When a strong
man, fully armed, guards his castle,
his property is safe. [22]But when one
stronger than he attacks him and
overpowers him, he takes away his
armor in which he trusted and divides his plunder. [23]Whoever is not
with me is against me, and whoever
does not gather with me scatters.

The Return of the Unclean Spirit

24 "When the unclean spirit has
gone out of a person, it wanders
through waterless regions looking
for a resting place, but not finding
any, it says, 'I will return to my
house from which I came.' [25]When
it comes, it finds it swept and put
in order. [26]Then it goes and brings
seven other spirits more evil than
itself, and they enter and live there;
and the last state of that person is
worse than the first."

True Blessedness

27 While he was saying this,
a woman in the crowd raised her
voice and said to him, "Blessed is
the womb that bore you and the
breasts that nursed you!" [28]But he
said, "Blessed rather are those who
hear the word of God and obey it!"

The Sign of Jonah

29 When the crowds were increasing, he began to say, "This
generation is an evil generation; it
asks for a sign, but no sign will be
given to it except the sign of Jonah.
[30]For just as Jonah became a sign to
the people of Nineveh, so the Son
of Man will be to this generation.

---

e Other ancient authorities add *bread, will give a stone; or if your child asks for* f Other ancient authorities read *the Father give the Holy Spirit from heaven* g Gk *sons*

31 The queen of the South will rise
at the judgment with the people of
this generation and condemn them,
because she came from the ends of
the earth to listen to the wisdom of
Solomon, and see, something greater than Solomon is here! 32 The people of Nineveh will rise up at the
judgment with this generation and
condemn it, because they repented
at the proclamation of Jonah, and
see, something greater than Jonah
is here!

The Light of the Body

33 "No one after lighting a lamp
puts it in a cellar,[h] but on the lampstand so that those who enter may
see the light. 34 Your eye is the lamp
of your body. If your eye is healthy,
your whole body is full of light;
but if it is not healthy, your body
is full of darkness. 35 Therefore consider whether the light in you is not
darkness. 36 If then your whole body
is full of light, with no part of it in
darkness, it will be as full of light
as when a lamp gives you light with
its rays."

Jesus Denounces Pharisees and Lawyers

37 While he was speaking, a
Pharisee invited him to dine with
him; so he went in and took his
place at the table. 38 The Pharisee
was amazed to see that he did not
first wash before dinner. 39 Then the
Lord said to him, "Now you Pharisees clean the outside of the cup
and of the dish, but inside you are
full of greed and wickedness. 40 You
fools! Did not the one who made
the outside make the inside also?
41 So give for alms those things that
are within; and see, everything will
be clean for you.

42 "But woe to you Pharisees!
For you tithe mint and rue and
herbs of all kinds, and neglect justice and the love of God; it is these
you ought to have practiced, without neglecting the others. 43 Woe to
you Pharisees! For you love to have
the seat of honor in the synagogues
and to be greeted with respect in
the marketplaces. 44 Woe to you!
For you are like unmarked graves,
and people walk over them without
realizing it."

45 One of the lawyers answered
him, "Teacher, when you say these
things, you insult us too." 46 And he
said, "Woe also to you lawyers! For
you load people with burdens hard
to bear, and you yourselves do not
lift a finger to ease them. 47 Woe to
you! For you build the tombs of
the prophets whom your ancestors
killed. 48 So you are witnesses and
approve of the deeds of your ancestors; for they killed them, and you
build their tombs. 49 Therefore also
the Wisdom of God said, 'I will
send them prophets and apostles,
some of whom they will kill and
persecute,' 50 so that this generation
may be charged with the blood of
all the prophets shed since the
foundation of the world, 51 from the
blood of Abel to the blood of Zechariah, who perished between the
altar and the sanctuary. Yes, I tell
you, it will be charged against this
generation. 52 Woe to you lawyers!
For you have taken away the key of

h Other ancient authorities add *or under the bushel basket*

knowledge; you did not enter yourselves, and you hindered those who were entering."

53 When he went outside, the scribes and the Pharisees began to be very hostile toward him and to cross-examine him about many things, 54 lying in wait for him, to catch him in something he might say.

A Warning against Hypocrisy

12 Meanwhile, when the crowd gathered by the thousands, so that they trampled on one another, he began to speak first to his disciples, "Beware of the yeast of the Pharisees, that is, their hypocrisy. 2 Nothing is covered up that will not be uncovered, and nothing secret that will not become known. 3 Therefore whatever you have said in the dark will be heard in the light, and what you have whispered behind closed doors will be proclaimed from the housetops.

Exhortation to Fearless Confession

4 "I tell you, my friends, do not fear those who kill the body, and after that can do nothing more. 5 But I will warn you whom to fear: fear him who, after he has killed, has authority[a] to cast into hell.[b] Yes, I tell you, fear him! 6 Are not five sparrows sold for two pennies? Yet not one of them is forgotten in God's sight. 7 But even the hairs of your head are all counted. Do not be afraid; you are of more value than many sparrows.

8 "And I tell you, everyone who acknowledges me before others, the Son of Man also will acknowledge before the angels of God; 9 but whoever denies me before others will be denied before the angels of God. 10 And everyone who speaks a word against the Son of Man will be forgiven; but whoever blasphemes against the Holy Spirit will not be forgiven. 11 When they bring you before the synagogues, the rulers, and the authorities, do not worry about how[c] you are to defend yourselves or what you are to say; 12 for the Holy Spirit will teach you at that very hour what you ought to say."

The Parable of the Rich Fool

13 Someone in the crowd said to him, "Teacher, tell my brother to divide the family inheritance with me." 14 But he said to him, "Friend, who set me to be a judge or arbitrator over you?" 15 And he said to them, "Take care! Be on your guard against all kinds of greed; for one's life does not consist in the abundance of possessions." 16 Then he told them a parable: "The land of a rich man produced abundantly. 17 And he thought to himself, 'What should I do, for I have no place to store my crops?' 18 Then he said, 'I will do this: I will pull down my barns and build larger ones, and there I will store all my grain and my goods. 19 And I will say to my soul, Soul, you have ample goods laid up for many years; relax, eat, drink, be merry.' 20 But God said to him, 'You fool! This very night your life is being demanded of you. And the things you have prepared,

---

a Or *power* b Gk *Gehenna* c Other ancient authorities add *or what*

whose will they be?' [21]So it is with those who store up treasures for themselves but are not rich toward God."

Do Not Worry

22 He said to his disciples, "Therefore I tell you, do not worry about your life, what you will eat, or about your body, what you will wear. [23]For life is more than food, and the body more than clothing. [24]Consider the ravens: they neither sow nor reap, they have neither storehouse nor barn, and yet God feeds them. Of how much more value are you than the birds! [25]And can any of you by worrying add a single hour to your span of life?[d] [26]If then you are not able to do so small a thing as that, why do you worry about the rest? [27]Consider the lilies, how they grow: they neither toil nor spin;[e] yet I tell you, even Solomon in all his glory was not clothed like one of these. [28]But if God so clothes the grass of the field, which is alive today and tomorrow is thrown into the oven, how much more will he clothe you—you of little faith! [29]And do not keep striving for what you are to eat and what you are to drink, and do not keep worrying. [30]For it is the nations of the world that strive after all these things, and your Father knows that you need them. [31]Instead, strive for his[f] kingdom, and these things will be given to you as well.

32 "Do not be afraid, little flock, for it is your Father's good pleasure to give you the kingdom. [33]Sell your possessions, and give alms. Make purses for yourselves that do not wear out, an unfailing treasure in heaven, where no thief comes near and no moth destroys. [34]For where your treasure is, there your heart will be also.

Watchful Slaves

35 "Be dressed for action and have your lamps lit; [36]be like those who are waiting for their master to return from the wedding banquet, so that they may open the door for him as soon as he comes and knocks. [37]Blessed are those slaves whom the master finds alert when he comes; truly I tell you, he will fasten his belt and have them sit down to eat, and he will come and serve them. [38]If he comes during the middle of the night, or near dawn, and finds them so, blessed are those slaves.

39 "But know this: if the owner of the house had known at what hour the thief was coming, he[g] would not have let his house be broken into. [40]You also must be ready, for the Son of Man is coming at an unexpected hour."

The Faithful or the Unfaithful Slave

41 Peter said, "Lord, are you telling this parable for us or for everyone?" [42]And the Lord said, "Who then is the faithful and prudent manager whom his master will put in charge of his slaves, to give them their allowance of food at the proper time? [43]Blessed is that

d Or *add a cubit to your stature* e Other ancient authorities read *Consider the lilies; they neither spin nor weave* f Other ancient authorities read *God's* g Other ancient authorities add *would have watched and*

slave whom his master will find at
work when he arrives. 44 Truly I tell
you, he will put that one in charge
of all his possessions. 45 But if that
slave says to himself, 'My master
is delayed in coming,' and if he begins to beat the other slaves, men
and women, and to eat and drink
and get drunk, 46 the master of that
slave will come on a day when he
does not expect him and at an hour
that he does not know, and will cut
him in pieces,[h] and put him with
the unfaithful. 47 That slave who
knew what his master wanted, but
did not prepare himself or do what
was wanted, will receive a severe
beating. 48 But the one who did
not know and did what deserved a
beating will receive a light beating.
From everyone to whom much has
been given, much will be required;
and from the one to whom much
has been entrusted, even more will
be demanded.

Jesus the Cause of Division

49 "I came to bring fire to the
earth, and how I wish it were already kindled! 50 I have a baptism
with which to be baptized, and
what stress I am under until it is
completed! 51 Do you think that I
have come to bring peace to the
earth? No, I tell you, but rather division! 52 From now on five in one
household will be divided, three
against two and two against three;
53 they will be divided:

father against son
  and son against father,
mother against daughter
  and daughter against mother,
mother-in-law against her
  daughter-in-law
and daughter-in-law against
  mother-in-law."

Interpreting the Time

54 He also said to the crowds,
"When you see a cloud rising in
the west, you immediately say, 'It
is going to rain'; and so it happens.
55 And when you see the south wind
blowing, you say, 'There will be
scorching heat'; and it happens.
56 You hypocrites! You know how
to interpret the appearance of earth
and sky, but why do you not know
how to interpret the present time?

Settling with Your Opponent

57 "And why do you not judge
for yourselves what is right?
58 Thus, when you go with your
accuser before a magistrate, on
the way make an effort to settle
the case,[i] or you may be dragged
before the judge, and the judge
hand you over to the officer, and
the officer throw you in prison. 59 I
tell you, you will never get out until
you have paid the very last penny."

Repent or Perish

13 At that very time there were
some present who told him
about the Galileans whose blood
Pilate had mingled with their sacrifices. 2 He asked them, "Do you
think that because these Galileans
suffered in this way they were
worse sinners than all other Galileans? 3 No, I tell you; but unless you
repent, you will all perish as they

h Or *cut him off* i Gk *settle with him*

did. 4Or those eighteen who were
killed when the tower of Siloam
fell on them—do you think that
they were worse offenders than all
the others living in Jerusalem? 5No,
I tell you; but unless you repent,
you will all perish just as they did."

The Parable of the Barren Fig Tree

6 Then he told this parable: "A
man had a fig tree planted in his
vineyard; and he came looking for
fruit on it and found none. 7So he
said to the gardener, 'See here! For
three years I have come looking for
fruit on this fig tree, and still I find
none. Cut it down! Why should it
be wasting the soil?' 8He replied,
'Sir, let it alone for one more year,
until I dig around it and put manure
on it. 9If it bears fruit next year,
well and good; but if not, you can
cut it down.' "

Jesus Heals a Crippled Woman

10 Now he was teaching in one
of the synagogues on the sabbath.
11And just then there appeared a
woman with a spirit that had crippled her for eighteen years. She
was bent over and was quite unable
to stand up straight. 12When Jesus
saw her, he called her over and said,
"Woman, you are set free from your
ailment." 13When he laid his hands
on her, immediately she stood up
straight and began praising God.
14But the leader of the synagogue,
indignant because Jesus had cured
on the sabbath, kept saying to the
crowd, "There are six days on
which work ought to be done; come
on those days and be cured, and not
on the sabbath day." 15But the Lord
answered him and said, "You hypocrites! Does not each of you on the
sabbath untie his ox or his donkey
from the manger, and lead it away
to give it water? 16And ought not
this woman, a daughter of Abraham whom Satan bound for eighteen long years, be set free from
this bondage on the sabbath day?"
17When he said this, all his oppo-
nents were put to shame; and the
entire crowd was rejoicing at all the
wonderful things that he was doing.

The Parable of the Mustard Seed

18 He said therefore, "What is
the kingdom of God like? And to
what should I compare it? 19It is
like a mustard seed that someone
took and sowed in the garden; it
grew and became a tree, and the
birds of the air made nests in its
branches."

The Parable of the Yeast

20 And again he said, "To what
should I compare the kingdom of
God? 21It is like yeast that a woman took and mixed in with[a] three
measures of flour until all of it was
leavened."

The Narrow Door

22 Jesus[b] went through one town
and village after another, teaching
as he made his way to Jerusalem.
23Someone asked him, "Lord, will
only a few be saved?" He said to
them, 24"Strive to enter through the
narrow door; for many, I tell you,
will try to enter and will not be
able. 25When once the owner of the

---

a Gk *hid in* *b* Gk *He*

house has got up and shut the door, and you begin to stand outside and to knock at the door, saying, 'Lord, open to us,' then in reply he will say to you, 'I do not know where you come from.' 26 Then you will begin to say, 'We ate and drank with you, and you taught in our streets.' 27 But he will say, 'I do not know where you come from; go away from me, all you evildoers!' 28 There will be weeping and gnashing of teeth when you see Abraham and Isaac and Jacob and all the prophets in the kingdom of God, and you yourselves thrown out. 29 Then people will come from east and west, from north and south, and will eat in the kingdom of God. 30 Indeed, some are last who will be first, and some are first who will be last."

The Lament over Jerusalem

31 At that very hour some Pharisees came and said to him, "Get away from here, for Herod wants to kill you." 32 He said to them, "Go and tell that fox for me,[c] 'Listen, I am casting out demons and performing cures today and tomorrow, and on the third day I finish my work. 33 Yet today, tomorrow, and the next day I must be on my way, because it is impossible for a prophet to be killed outside of Jerusalem.' 34 Jerusalem, Jerusalem, the city that kills the prophets and stones those who are sent to it! How often have I desired to gather your children together as a hen gathers her brood under her wings, and you were not willing! 35 See, your house is left to you. And I tell you, you will not see me until the time comes when[d] you say, 'Blessed is the one who comes in the name of the Lord.' "

Jesus Heals the Man with Dropsy

14 On one occasion when Jesus[a] was going to the house of a leader of the Pharisees to eat a meal on the sabbath, they were watching him closely. 2 Just then, in front of him, there was a man who had dropsy. 3 And Jesus asked the lawyers and Pharisees, "Is it lawful to cure people on the sabbath, or not?" 4 But they were silent. So Jesus[b] took him and healed him, and sent him away. 5 Then he said to them, "If one of you has a child[c] or an ox that has fallen into a well, will you not immediately pull it out on a sabbath day?" 6 And they could not reply to this.

Humility and Hospitality

7 When he noticed how the guests chose the places of honor, he told them a parable. 8 "When you are invited by someone to a wedding banquet, do not sit down at the place of honor, in case someone more distinguished than you has been invited by your host; 9 and the host who invited both of you may come and say to you, 'Give this person your place,' and then in disgrace you would start to take the lowest place. 10 But when you are invited, go and sit down at the lowest place, so that when your host comes, he may say to you, 'Friend, move up higher'; then you will be

---

c Gk lacks *for me* *d* Other ancient authorities lack *the time comes when* *a* Gk *he* *b* Gk *he* *c* Other ancient authorities read *a donkey*

honored in the presence of all who
sit at the table with you. 11 For all
who exalt themselves will be humbled, and those who humble themselves will be exalted."

12 He said also to the one who
had invited him, "When you give a
luncheon or a dinner, do not invite
your friends or your brothers or
your relatives or rich neighbors, in
case they may invite you in return,
and you would be repaid. 13 But
when you give a banquet, invite the
poor, the crippled, the lame, and the
blind. 14 And you will be blessed,
because they cannot repay you, for
you will be repaid at the resurrection of the righteous."

The Parable of the Great Dinner

15 One of the dinner guests, on
hearing this, said to him, "Blessed
is anyone who will eat bread in the
kingdom of God!" 16 Then Jesus[d]
said to him, "Someone gave a great
dinner and invited many. 17 At the
time for the dinner he sent his slave
to say to those who had been invited, 'Come; for everything is ready
now.' 18 But they all alike began
to make excuses. The first said to
him, 'I have bought a piece of land,
and I must go out and see it; please
accept my regrets.' 19 Another said,
'I have bought five yoke of oxen,
and I am going to try them out;
please accept my regrets.' 20 Another said, 'I have just been married,
and therefore I cannot come.' 21 So
the slave returned and reported this
to his master. Then the owner of
the house became angry and said
to his slave, 'Go out at once into
the streets and lanes of the town
and bring in the poor, the crippled,
the blind, and the lame.' 22 And the
slave said, 'Sir, what you ordered
has been done, and there is still
room.' 23 Then the master said to the
slave, 'Go out into the roads and
lanes, and compel people to come
in, so that my house may be filled.
24 For I tell you,[e] none of those who
were invited will taste my dinner.' "

The Cost of Discipleship

25 Now large crowds were traveling with him; and he turned and
said to them, 26 "Whoever comes
to me and does not hate father and
mother, wife and children, brothers
and sisters, yes, and even life itself,
cannot be my disciple. 27 Whoever
does not carry the cross and follow
me cannot be my disciple. 28 For
which of you, intending to build a
tower, does not first sit down and
estimate the cost, to see whether he has enough to complete it?
29 Otherwise, when he has laid a
foundation and is not able to finish,
all who see it will begin to ridicule
him, 30 saying, 'This fellow began
to build and was not able to finish.'
31 Or what king, going out to wage
war against another king, will not
sit down first and consider whether he is able with ten thousand to
oppose the one who comes against
him with twenty thousand? 32 If he
cannot, then, while the other is still
far away, he sends a delegation and
asks for the terms of peace. 33 So
therefore, none of you can become
my disciple if you do not give up all
your possessions.

---

d Gk *he* *e* The Greek word for *you* here is plural

About Salt

34 "Salt is good; but if salt has lost its taste, how can its saltiness be restored?[f] [35]It is fit neither for the soil nor for the manure pile; they throw it away. Let anyone with ears to hear listen!"

The Parable of the Lost Sheep

15 Now all the tax collectors and sinners were coming near to listen to him. [2]And the Pharisees and the scribes were grumbling and saying, "This fellow welcomes sinners and eats with them."

3 So he told them this parable: [4]"Which one of you, having a hundred sheep and losing one of them, does not leave the ninety-nine in the wilderness and go after the one that is lost until he finds it? [5]When he has found it, he lays it on his shoulders and rejoices. [6]And when he comes home, he calls together his friends and neighbors, saying to them, 'Rejoice with me, for I have found my sheep that was lost.' [7]Just so, I tell you, there will be more joy in heaven over one sinner who repents than over ninety-nine righteous persons who need no repentance.

The Parable of the Lost Coin

8 "Or what woman having ten silver coins,[a] if she loses one of them, does not light a lamp, sweep the house, and search carefully until she finds it? [9]When she has found it, she calls together her friends and neighbors, saying, 'Rejoice with me, for I have found the coin that I had lost.' [10]Just so, I tell you, there is joy in the presence of the angels of God over one sinner who repents."

The Parable of the Prodigal and His Brother

11 Then Jesus[b] said, "There was a man who had two sons. [12]The younger of them said to his father, 'Father, give me the share of the property that will belong to me.' So he divided his property between them. [13]A few days later the younger son gathered all he had and traveled to a distant country, and there he squandered his property in dissolute living. [14]When he had spent everything, a severe famine took place throughout that country, and he began to be in need. [15]So he went and hired himself out to one of the citizens of that country, who sent him to his fields to feed the pigs. [16]He would gladly have filled himself with[c] the pods that the pigs were eating; and no one gave him anything. [17]But when he came to himself he said, 'How many of my father's hired hands have bread enough and to spare, but here I am dying of hunger! [18]I will get up and go to my father, and I will say to him, "Father, I have sinned against heaven and before you; [19]I am no longer worthy to be called your son; treat me like one of your hired hands." ' [20]So he set off and went to his father. But while he was still far off, his father saw him and was filled with compassion; he ran and put his arms

---

f Or *how can it be used for seasoning?*
a Gk *drachmas*, each worth about a day's wage for a laborer *b* Gk *he* *c* Other ancient authorities read *filled his stomach with*

around him and kissed him. 21 Then the son said to him, 'Father, I have sinned against heaven and before you; I am no longer worthy to be called your son.'[d] 22 But the father said to his slaves, 'Quickly, bring out a robe—the best one—and put it on him; put a ring on his finger and sandals on his feet. 23 And get the fatted calf and kill it, and let us eat and celebrate; 24 for this son of mine was dead and is alive again; he was lost and is found!' And they began to celebrate.

25 "Now his elder son was in the field; and when he came and approached the house, he heard music and dancing. 26 He called one of the slaves and asked what was going on. 27 He replied, 'Your brother has come, and your father has killed the fatted calf, because he has got him back safe and sound.' 28 Then he became angry and refused to go in. His father came out and began to plead with him. 29 But he answered his father, 'Listen! For all these years I have been working like a slave for you, and I have never disobeyed your command; yet you have never given me even a young goat so that I might celebrate with my friends. 30 But when this son of yours came back, who has devoured your property with prostitutes, you killed the fatted calf for him!' 31 Then the father[e] said to him, 'Son, you are always with me, and all that is mine is yours. 32 But we had to celebrate and rejoice, because this brother of yours was dead and has come to life; he was lost and has been found.' "

The Parable of the Dishonest Manager

16 Then Jesus[a] said to the disciples, "There was a rich man who had a manager, and charges were brought to him that this man was squandering his property. 2 So he summoned him and said to him, 'What is this that I hear about you? Give me an accounting of your management, because you cannot be my manager any longer.' 3 Then the manager said to himself, 'What will I do, now that my master is taking the position away from me? I am not strong enough to dig, and I am ashamed to beg. 4 I have decided what to do so that, when I am dismissed as manager, people may welcome me into their homes.' 5 So, summoning his master's debtors one by one, he asked the first, 'How much do you owe my master?' 6 He answered, 'A hundred jugs of olive oil.' He said to him, 'Take your bill, sit down quickly, and make it fifty.' 7 Then he asked another, 'And how much do you owe?' He replied, 'A hundred containers of wheat.' He said to him, 'Take your bill and make it eighty.' 8 And his master commended the dishonest manager because he had acted shrewdly; for the children of this age are more shrewd in dealing with their own generation than are the children of light. 9 And I tell you, make friends for yourselves by means of dishonest wealth[b] so that when it is gone, they may welcome you into the eternal homes.[c]

---

d Other ancient authorities add *Treat me like one of your hired servants* *e* Gk *he* *a* Gk *he* *b* Gk *mammon* *c* Gk *tents*

10 "Whoever is faithful in a very little is faithful also in much; and whoever is dishonest in a very little is dishonest also in much. [11]If then you have not been faithful with the dishonest wealth,[d] who will entrust to you the true riches? [12]And if you have not been faithful with what belongs to another, who will give you what is your own? [13]No slave can serve two masters; for a slave will either hate the one and love the other, or be devoted to the one and despise the other. You cannot serve God and wealth."[e]

The Law and the Kingdom of God

14 The Pharisees, who were lovers of money, heard all this, and they ridiculed him. [15]So he said to them, "You are those who justify yourselves in the sight of others; but God knows your hearts; for what is prized by human beings is an abomination in the sight of God.

16 "The law and the prophets were in effect until John came; since then the good news of the kingdom of God is proclaimed, and everyone tries to enter it by force.[f] [17]But it is easier for heaven and earth to pass away, than for one stroke of a letter in the law to be dropped.

18 "Anyone who divorces his wife and marries another commits adultery, and whoever marries a woman divorced from her husband commits adultery.

The Rich Man and Lazarus

19 "There was a rich man who was dressed in purple and fine linen and who feasted sumptuously every day. [20]And at his gate lay a poor man named Lazarus, covered with sores, [21]who longed to satisfy his hunger with what fell from the rich man's table; even the dogs would come and lick his sores. [22]The poor man died and was carried away by the angels to be with Abraham.[g] The rich man also died and was buried. [23]In Hades, where he was being tormented, he looked up and saw Abraham far away with Lazarus by his side.[h] [24]He called out, 'Father Abraham, have mercy on me, and send Lazarus to dip the tip of his finger in water and cool my tongue; for I am in agony in these flames.' [25]But Abraham said, 'Child, remember that during your lifetime you received your good things, and Lazarus in like manner evil things; but now he is comforted here, and you are in agony. [26]Besides all this, between you and us a great chasm has been fixed, so that those who might want to pass from here to you cannot do so, and no one can cross from there to us.' [27]He said, 'Then, father, I beg you to send him to my father's house— [28]for I have five brothers—that he may warn them, so that they will not also come into this place of torment.' [29]Abraham replied, 'They have Moses and the prophets; they should listen to them.' [30]He said, 'No, father Abraham; but if someone goes to them from the dead, they will repent.' [31]He said to him, 'If they do not listen to Moses and the prophets, neither will they be

d Gk *mammon* *e* Gk *mammon*
f Or *everyone is strongly urged to enter it*
g Gk *to Abraham's bosom* *h* Gk *in his bosom*

convinced even if someone rises from the dead.' "

Some Sayings of Jesus

17 Jesus[a] said to his disciples, "Occasions for stumbling are bound to come, but woe to anyone by whom they come! 2 It would be better for you if a millstone were hung around your neck and you were thrown into the sea than for you to cause one of these little ones to stumble. 3 Be on your guard! If another disciple[b] sins, you must rebuke the offender, and if there is repentance, you must forgive. 4 And if the same person sins against you seven times a day, and turns back to you seven times and says, 'I repent,' you must forgive."

5 The apostles said to the Lord, "Increase our faith!" 6 The Lord replied, "If you had faith the size of a[c] mustard seed, you could say to this mulberry tree, 'Be uprooted and planted in the sea,' and it would obey you.

7 "Who among you would say to your slave who has just come in from plowing or tending sheep in the field, 'Come here at once and take your place at the table'? 8 Would you not rather say to him, 'Prepare supper for me, put on your apron and serve me while I eat and drink; later you may eat and drink'? 9 Do you thank the slave for doing what was commanded? 10 So you also, when you have done all that you were ordered to do, say, 'We are worthless slaves; we have done only what we ought to have done!' "

Jesus Cleanses Ten Lepers

11 On the way to Jerusalem Jesus[d] was going through the region between Samaria and Galilee. 12 As he entered a village, ten lepers[e] approached him. Keeping their distance, 13 they called out, saying, "Jesus, Master, have mercy on us!" 14 When he saw them, he said to them, "Go and show yourselves to the priests." And as they went, they were made clean. 15 Then one of them, when he saw that he was healed, turned back, praising God with a loud voice. 16 He prostrated himself at Jesus'[f] feet and thanked him. And he was a Samaritan. 17 Then Jesus asked, "Were not ten made clean? But the other nine, where are they? 18 Was none of them found to return and give praise to God except this foreigner?" 19 Then he said to him, "Get up and go on your way; your faith has made you well."

The Coming of the Kingdom

20 Once Jesus[g] was asked by the Pharisees when the kingdom of God was coming, and he answered, "The kingdom of God is not coming with things that can be observed; 21 nor will they say, 'Look, here it is!' or 'There it is!' For, in fact, the kingdom of God is among[h] you."

22 Then he said to the disciples, "The days are coming when you will long to see one of the days of the Son of Man, and you will not

---

a Gk *He* *b* Gk *your brother* *c* Gk *faith as a grain of* *d* Gk *he* *e* The terms *leper* and *leprosy* can refer to several diseases *f* Gk *his* *g* Gk *he* *h* Or *within*

see it. 23 They will say to you, 'Look
there!' or 'Look here!' Do not go,
do not set off in pursuit. 24 For as the
lightning flashes and lights up the
sky from one side to the other, so
will the Son of Man be in his day.[i]
25 But first he must endure much
suffering and be rejected by this
generation. 26 Just as it was in the
days of Noah, so too it will be in
the days of the Son of Man. 27 They
were eating and drinking, and marrying and being given in marriage,
until the day Noah entered the ark,
and the flood came and destroyed
all of them. 28 Likewise, just as it
was in the days of Lot: they were
eating and drinking, buying and
selling, planting and building, 29 but
on the day that Lot left Sodom, it
rained fire and sulfur from heaven
and destroyed all of them 30—it will
be like that on the day that the Son
of Man is revealed. 31 On that day,
anyone on the housetop who has
belongings in the house must not
come down to take them away; and
likewise anyone in the field must
not turn back. 32 Remember Lot's
wife. 33 Those who try to make
their life secure will lose it, but
those who lose their life will keep
it. 34 I tell you, on that night there
will be two in one bed; one will be
taken and the other left. 35 There
will be two women grinding meal
together; one will be taken and the
other left."[j] 37 Then they asked him,
"Where, Lord?" He said to them,
"Where the corpse is, there the vultures will gather."

The Parable of the Widow and the Unjust Judge

18 Then Jesus[a] told them a parable about their need to pray
always and not to lose heart. 2 He
said, "In a certain city there was a
judge who neither feared God nor
had respect for people. 3 In that
city there was a widow who kept
coming to him and saying, 'Grant
me justice against my opponent.'
4 For a while he refused; but later
he said to himself, 'Though I have
no fear of God and no respect for
anyone, 5 yet because this widow
keeps bothering me, I will grant her
justice, so that she may not wear
me out by continually coming.'"[b]
6 And the Lord said, "Listen to what
the unjust judge says. 7 And will not
God grant justice to his chosen ones
who cry to him day and night? Will
he delay long in helping them? 8 I
tell you, he will quickly grant justice to them. And yet, when the Son
of Man comes, will he find faith on
earth?"

The Parable of the Pharisee and the Tax Collector

9 He also told this parable to
some who trusted in themselves
that they were righteous and regarded others with contempt:
10 "Two men went up to the temple
to pray, one a Pharisee and the other a tax collector. 11 The Pharisee,
standing by himself, was praying thus, 'God, I thank you that I

---

i Other ancient authorities lack *in his day*
j Other ancient authorities add verse 36, *"Two will be in the field; one will be taken and the other left."* *a* Gk *he* *b* Or *so that she may not finally come and slap me in the face*

am not like other people: thieves,
rogues, adulterers, or even like this
tax collector. 12 I fast twice a week;
I give a tenth of all my income.'
13 But the tax collector, standing
far off, would not even look up to
heaven, but was beating his breast
and saying, 'God, be merciful to
me, a sinner!' 14 I tell you, this man
went down to his home justified
rather than the other; for all who
exalt themselves will be humbled,
but all who humble themselves will
be exalted."

Jesus Blesses Little Children

15 People were bringing even
infants to him that he might touch
them; and when the disciples saw
it, they sternly ordered them not to
do it. 16 But Jesus called for them
and said, "Let the little children
come to me, and do not stop them;
for it is to such as these that the
kingdom of God belongs. 17 Truly I
tell you, whoever does not receive
the kingdom of God as a little child
will never enter it."

The Rich Ruler

18 A certain ruler asked him,
"Good Teacher, what must I do to
inherit eternal life?" 19 Jesus said to
him, "Why do you call me good?
No one is good but God alone.
20 You know the commandments:
'You shall not commit adultery;
You shall not murder; You shall not
steal; You shall not bear false witness; Honor your father and mother.' " 21 He replied, "I have kept all
these since my youth." 22 When
Jesus heard this, he said to him,
"There is still one thing lacking.
Sell all that you own and distribute
the money[c] to the poor, and you
will have treasure in heaven; then
come, follow me." 23 But when he
heard this, he became sad; for he
was very rich. 24 Jesus looked at him
and said, "How hard it is for those
who have wealth to enter the kingdom of God! 25 Indeed, it is easier
for a camel to go through the eye of
a needle than for someone who is
rich to enter the kingdom of God."

26 Those who heard it said,
"Then who can be saved?" 27 He
replied, "What is impossible for
mortals is possible for God."

28 Then Peter said, "Look, we
have left our homes and followed
you." 29 And he said to them, "Truly I tell you, there is no one who
has left house or wife or brothers
or parents or children, for the sake
of the kingdom of God, 30 who will
not get back very much more in this
age, and in the age to come eternal
life."

A Third Time Jesus Foretells His Death and Resurrection

31 Then he took the twelve aside
and said to them, "See, we are going up to Jerusalem, and everything
that is written about the Son of Man
by the prophets will be accomplished. 32 For he will be handed
over to the Gentiles; and he will be
mocked and insulted and spat upon.
33 After they have flogged him, they
will kill him, and on the third day
he will rise again." 34 But they understood nothing about all these
things; in fact, what he said was

---

c Gk lacks *the money*

hidden from them, and they did not
grasp what was said.

Jesus Heals a Blind Beggar Near Jericho

35 As he approached Jericho, a
blind man was sitting by the roadside begging. 36When he heard a
crowd going by, he asked what was
happening. 37They told him, "Jesus
of Nazareth[d] is passing by." 38Then
he shouted, "Jesus, Son of David,
have mercy on me!" 39Those who
were in front sternly ordered him to
be quiet; but he shouted even more
loudly, "Son of David, have mercy
on me!" 40Jesus stood still and ordered the man to be brought to him;
and when he came near, he asked
him, 41"What do you want me to
do for you?" He said, "Lord, let
me see again." 42Jesus said to him,
"Receive your sight; your faith has
saved you." 43Immediately he regained his sight and followed him,
glorifying God; and all the people,
when they saw it, praised God.

Jesus and Zacchaeus

19 He entered Jericho and was
passing through it. 2A man
was there named Zacchaeus; he
was a chief tax collector and was
rich. 3He was trying to see who
Jesus was, but on account of the
crowd he could not, because he was
short in stature. 4So he ran ahead
and climbed a sycamore tree to see
him, because he was going to pass
that way. 5When Jesus came to the
place, he looked up and said to him,
"Zacchaeus, hurry and come down;
for I must stay at your house today." 6So he hurried down and was
happy to welcome him. 7All who
saw it began to grumble and said,
"He has gone to be the guest of one
who is a sinner." 8Zacchaeus stood
there and said to the Lord, "Look,
half of my possessions, Lord, I
will give to the poor; and if I have
defrauded anyone of anything, I
will pay back four times as much."
9Then Jesus said to him, "Today
salvation has come to this house,
because he too is a son of Abraham.
10For the Son of Man came to seek
out and to save the lost."

The Parable of the Ten Pounds

11 As they were listening to this,
he went on to tell a parable, because
he was near Jerusalem, and because
they supposed that the kingdom of
God was to appear immediately.
12So he said, "A nobleman went to
a distant country to get royal power
for himself and then return. 13He
summoned ten of his slaves, and
gave them ten pounds,[a] and said to
them, 'Do business with these until I come back.' 14But the citizens
of his country hated him and sent
a delegation after him, saying, 'We
do not want this man to rule over
us.' 15When he returned, having
received royal power, he ordered
these slaves, to whom he had giv-
en the money, to be summoned so
that he might find out what they
had gained by trading. 16The first
came forward and said, 'Lord, your
pound has made ten more pounds.'
17He said to him, 'Well done, good
slave! Because you have been trust-

d Gk *the Nazorean* *a* The mina, rendered here by *pound,* was about three months' wages for a laborer

worthy in a very small thing, take charge of ten cities.' [18]Then the second came, saying, 'Lord, your pound has made five pounds.' [19]He said to him, 'And you, rule over five cities.' [20]Then the other came, saying, 'Lord, here is your pound. I wrapped it up in a piece of cloth, [21]for I was afraid of you, because you are a harsh man; you take what you did not deposit, and reap what you did not sow.' [22]He said to him, 'I will judge you by your own words, you wicked slave! You knew, did you, that I was a harsh man, taking what I did not deposit and reaping what I did not sow? [23]Why then did you not put my money into the bank? Then when I returned, I could have collected it with interest.' [24]He said to the bystanders, 'Take the pound from him and give it to the one who has ten pounds.' [25](And they said to him, 'Lord, he has ten pounds!') [26]'I tell you, to all those who have, more will be given; but from those who have nothing, even what they have will be taken away. [27]But as for these enemies of mine who did not want me to be king over them—bring them here and slaughter them in my presence.' "

Jesus' Triumphal Entry into Jerusalem

28 After he had said this, he went on ahead, going up to Jerusalem.

29 When he had come near Bethphage and Bethany, at the place called the Mount of Olives, he sent two of the disciples, [30]saying, "Go into the village ahead of you, and as you enter it you will find tied there a colt that has never been ridden. Untie it and bring it here. [31]If anyone asks you, 'Why are you untying it?' just say this, 'The Lord needs it.' " [32]So those who were sent departed and found it as he had told them. [33]As they were untying the colt, its owners asked them, "Why are you untying the colt?" [34]They said, "The Lord needs it." [35]Then they brought it to Jesus; and after throwing their cloaks on the colt, they set Jesus on it. [36]As he rode along, people kept spreading their cloaks on the road. [37]As he was now approaching the path down from the Mount of Olives, the whole multitude of the disciples began to praise God joyfully with a loud voice for all the deeds of power that they had seen, [38]saying,

"Blessed is the king
who comes in the name of the
Lord!
Peace in heaven,
and glory in the highest
heaven!"

[39]Some of the Pharisees in the crowd said to him, "Teacher, order your disciples to stop." [40]He answered, "I tell you, if these were silent, the stones would shout out."

Jesus Weeps over Jerusalem

41 As he came near and saw the city, he wept over it, [42]saying, "If you, even you, had only recognized on this day the things that make for peace! But now they are hidden from your eyes. [43]Indeed, the days will come upon you, when your enemies will set up ramparts around you and surround you, and hem you in on every side. [44]They

will crush you to the ground, you
and your children within you, and
they will not leave within you one
stone upon another; because you
did not recognize the time of your
visitation from God."[b]

Jesus Cleanses the Temple

45 Then he entered the temple
and began to drive out those who
were selling things there; [46]and he
said, "It is written,

'My house shall be a house of
prayer';
but you have made it a den of
robbers."

47 Every day he was teaching
in the temple. The chief priests,
the scribes, and the leaders of the
people kept looking for a way to
kill him; [48]but they did not find
anything they could do, for all the
people were spellbound by what
they heard.

The Authority of Jesus Questioned

20 One day, as he was teaching
the people in the temple and
telling the good news, the chief
priests and the scribes came with
the elders [2]and said to him, "Tell
us, by what authority are you doing these things? Who is it who
gave you this authority?" [3]He answered them, "I will also ask you a
question, and you tell me: [4]Did the
baptism of John come from heaven,
or was it of human origin?" [5]They
discussed it with one another, saying, "If we say, 'From heaven,' he
will say, 'Why did you not believe
him?' [6]But if we say, 'Of human
origin,' all the people will stone us;
for they are convinced that John
was a prophet." [7]So they answered
that they did not know where it
came from. [8]Then Jesus said to
them, "Neither will I tell you by
what authority I am doing these
things."

The Parable of the Wicked Tenants

9 He began to tell the people this
parable: "A man planted a vineyard, and leased it to tenants, and
went to another country for a long
time. [10]When the season came, he
sent a slave to the tenants in order
that they might give him his share
of the produce of the vineyard; but
the tenants beat him and sent him
away empty-handed. [11]Next he sent
another slave; that one also they
beat and insulted and sent away
empty-handed. [12]And he sent still
a third; this one also they wounded
and threw out. [13]Then the owner of
the vineyard said, 'What shall I do?
I will send my beloved son; perhaps
they will respect him.' [14]But when
the tenants saw him, they discussed
it among themselves and said, 'This
is the heir; let us kill him so that the
inheritance may be ours.' [15]So they
threw him out of the vineyard and
killed him. What then will the owner of the vineyard do to them? [16]He
will come and destroy those tenants
and give the vineyard to others."
When they heard this, they said,
"Heaven forbid!" [17]But he looked
at them and said, "What then does
this text mean:

'The stone that the builders
rejected
has become the cornerstone'?[a]

b Gk lacks *from God* *a* Or *keystone*

18 Everyone who falls on that stone
will be broken to pieces; and it will
crush anyone on whom it falls."
19 When the scribes and chief priests
realized that he had told this parable against them, they wanted to lay
hands on him at that very hour, but
they feared the people.

The Question about Paying Taxes

20 So they watched him and sent
spies who pretended to be honest,
in order to trap him by what he said,
so as to hand him over to the jurisdiction and authority of the governor. 21 So they asked him, "Teacher,
we know that you are right in what
you say and teach, and you show
deference to no one, but teach the
way of God in accordance with
truth. 22 Is it lawful for us to pay taxes to the emperor, or not?" 23 But he
perceived their craftiness and said
to them, 24 "Show me a denarius.
Whose head and whose title does it
bear?" They said, "The emperor's."
25 He said to them, "Then give to the
emperor the things that are the emperor's, and to God the things that
are God's." 26 And they were not
able in the presence of the people
to trap him by what he said; and
being amazed by his answer, they
became silent.

The Question about the Resurrection

27 Some Sadducees, those who
say there is no resurrection, came
to him 28 and asked him a question,
"Teacher, Moses wrote for us that if
a man's brother dies, leaving a wife
but no children, the man[b] shall marry the widow and raise up children
for his brother. 29 Now there were
seven brothers; the first married,
and died childless; 30 then the second 31 and the third married her, and
so in the same way all seven died
childless. 32 Finally the woman also
died. 33 In the resurrection, therefore, whose wife will the woman
be? For the seven had married her."

34 Jesus said to them, "Those
who belong to this age marry and
are given in marriage; 35 but those
who are considered worthy of a
place in that age and in the resurrection from the dead neither marry
nor are given in marriage. 36 Indeed
they cannot die anymore, because
they are like angels and are children
of God, being children of the resurrection. 37 And the fact that the dead
are raised Moses himself showed,
in the story about the bush, where
he speaks of the Lord as the God of
Abraham, the God of Isaac, and the
God of Jacob. 38 Now he is God not
of the dead, but of the living; for to
him all of them are alive." 39 Then
some of the scribes answered,
"Teacher, you have spoken well."
40 For they no longer dared to ask
him another question.

The Question about David's Son

41 Then he said to them, "How
can they say that the Messiah[c] is
David's son? 42 For David himself
says in the book of Psalms,

'The Lord said to my Lord,
"Sit at my right hand,
43 until I make your enemies
your footstool." '

44 David thus calls him Lord; so

b Gk *his brother* *c* Or *the Christ*

how can he be his son?”

Jesus Denounces the Scribes

45 In the hearing of all the people
he said to the[d] disciples, 46“Beware
of the scribes, who like to walk
around in long robes, and love to
be greeted with respect in the marketplaces, and to have the best seats
in the synagogues and places of
honor at banquets. 47They devour
widows’ houses and for the sake of
appearance say long prayers. They
will receive the greater condemnation.”

The Widow’s Offering

21 He looked up and saw rich
people putting their gifts into
the treasury; 2he also saw a poor
widow put in two small copper
coins. 3He said, “Truly I tell you,
this poor widow has put in more
than all of them; 4for all of them
have contributed out of their abundance, but she out of her poverty
has put in all she had to live on.”

The Destruction of the Temple Foretold

5 When some were speaking
about the temple, how it was
adorned with beautiful stones and
gifts dedicated to God, he said,
6“As for these things that you see,
the days will come when not one
stone will be left upon another; all
will be thrown down.”

Signs and Persecutions

7 They asked him, “Teacher,
when will this be, and what will
be the sign that this is about to take
place?” 8And he said, “Beware that
you are not led astray; for many
will come in my name and say, ‘I
am he!’[a] and, ‘The time is near!’[b]
Do not go after them.
9 “When you hear of wars and
insurrections, do not be terrified;
for these things must take place
first, but the end will not follow immediately.” 10Then he said to them,
“Nation will rise against nation,
and kingdom against kingdom;
11there will be great earthquakes,
and in various places famines and
plagues; and there will be dread-
ful portents and great signs from
heaven.
12 “But before all this occurs,
they will arrest you and persecute
you; they will hand you over to
synagogues and prisons, and you
will be brought before kings and
governors because of my name.
13This will give you an opportunity
to testify. 14So make up your minds
not to prepare your defense in ad-
vance; 15for I will give you words[c]
and a wisdom that none of your op-
ponents will be able to withstand or
contradict. 16You will be betrayed
even by parents and brothers, by
relatives and friends; and they will
put some of you to death. 17You
will be hated by all because of my
name. 18But not a hair of your head
will perish. 19By your endurance
you will gain your souls.

The Destruction of Jerusalem Foretold

20 “When you see Jerusalem
surrounded by armies, then know
that its desolation has come near.[d]

d Other ancient authorities read *his* *a* Gk *I am*
b Or *at hand* *c* Gk *a mouth* *d* Or *is at hand*

21 Then those in Judea must flee to the mountains, and those inside the city must leave it, and those out in the country must not enter it; 22 for these are days of vengeance, as a fulfillment of all that is written. 23 Woe to those who are pregnant and to those who are nursing infants in those days! For there will be great distress on the earth and wrath against this people; 24 they will fall by the edge of the sword and be taken away as captives among all nations; and Jerusalem will be trampled on by the Gentiles, until the times of the Gentiles are fulfilled.

The Coming of the Son of Man

25 "There will be signs in the sun, the moon, and the stars, and on the earth distress among nations confused by the roaring of the sea and the waves. 26 People will faint from fear and foreboding of what is coming upon the world, for the powers of the heavens will be shaken. 27 Then they will see 'the Son of Man coming in a cloud' with power and great glory. 28 Now when these things begin to take place, stand up and raise your heads, because your redemption is drawing near."

The Lesson of the Fig Tree

29 Then he told them a parable: "Look at the fig tree and all the trees; 30 as soon as they sprout leaves you can see for yourselves and know that summer is already near. 31 So also, when you see these things taking place, you know that the kingdom of God is near. 32 Truly I tell you, this generation will not pass away until all things have taken place. 33 Heaven and earth will pass away, but my words will not pass away.

Exhortation to Watch

34 "Be on guard so that your hearts are not weighed down with dissipation and drunkenness and the worries of this life, and that day does not catch you unexpectedly, 35 like a trap. For it will come upon all who live on the face of the whole earth. 36 Be alert at all times, praying that you may have the strength to escape all these things that will take place, and to stand before the Son of Man."

37 Every day he was teaching in the temple, and at night he would go out and spend the night on the Mount of Olives, as it was called. 38 And all the people would get up early in the morning to listen to him in the temple.

The Plot to Kill Jesus

22 Now the festival of Unleavened Bread, which is called the Passover, was near. 2 The chief priests and the scribes were looking for a way to put Jesus[a] to death, for they were afraid of the people.

3 Then Satan entered into Judas called Iscariot, who was one of the twelve; 4 he went away and conferred with the chief priests and officers of the temple police about how he might betray him to them. 5 They were greatly pleased and agreed to give him money. 6 So he consented and began to look for an

a Gk *him*

opportunity to betray him to them when no crowd was present.

The Preparation of the Passover

7 Then came the day of Unleavened Bread, on which the Passover lamb had to be sacrificed. 8 So Jesus[b] sent Peter and John, saying, "Go and prepare the Passover meal for us that we may eat it." 9 They asked him, "Where do you want us to make preparations for it?" 10 "Listen," he said to them, "when you have entered the city, a man carrying a jar of water will meet you; follow him into the house he enters 11 and say to the owner of the house, 'The teacher asks you, "Where is the guest room, where I may eat the Passover with my disciples?" ' 12 He will show you a large room upstairs, already furnished. Make preparations for us there." 13 So they went and found everything as he had told them; and they prepared the Passover meal.

The Institution of the Lord's Supper

14 When the hour came, he took his place at the table, and the apostles with him. 15 He said to them, "I have eagerly desired to eat this Passover with you before I suffer; 16 for I tell you, I will not eat it[c] until it is fulfilled in the kingdom of God." 17 Then he took a cup, and after giving thanks he said, "Take this and divide it among yourselves; 18 for I tell you that from now on I will not drink of the fruit of the vine until the kingdom of God comes." 19 Then he took a loaf of bread, and when he had given thanks, he broke it and gave it to them, saying, "This is my body, which is given for you. Do this in remembrance of me." 20 And he did the same with the cup after supper, saying, "This cup that is poured out for you is the new covenant in my blood.[d] 21 But see, the one who betrays me is with me, and his hand is on the table. 22 For the Son of Man is going as it has been determined, but woe to that one by whom he is betrayed!" 23 Then they began to ask one another which one of them it could be who would do this.

The Dispute about Greatness

24 A dispute also arose among them as to which one of them was to be regarded as the greatest. 25 But he said to them, "The kings of the Gentiles lord it over them; and those in authority over them are called benefactors. 26 But not so with you; rather the greatest among you must become like the youngest, and the leader like one who serves. 27 For who is greater, the one who is at the table or the one who serves? Is it not the one at the table? But I am among you as one who serves.

28 "You are those who have stood by me in my trials; 29 and I confer on you, just as my Father has conferred on me, a kingdom, 30 so that you may eat and drink at my table in my kingdom, and you will sit on thrones judging the twelve tribes of Israel.

b Gk *he* *c* Other ancient authorities read *never eat it again* *d* Other ancient authorities lack, in whole or in part, verses 19b-20 (*which is given . . . in my blood*)

Jesus Predicts Peter's Denial

31 "Simon, Simon, listen! Satan
has demanded[e] to sift all of you
like wheat, 32 but I have prayed for
you that your own faith may not
fail; and you, when once you have
turned back, strengthen your brothers." 33 And he said to him, "Lord, I
am ready to go with you to prison
and to death!" 34 Jesus[f] said, "I tell
you, Peter, the cock will not crow
this day, until you have denied
three times that you know me."

Purse, Bag, and Sword

35 He said to them, "When I
sent you out without a purse, bag,
or sandals, did you lack anything?"
They said, "No, not a thing." 36 He
said to them, "But now, the one
who has a purse must take it, and
likewise a bag. And the one who
has no sword must sell his cloak
and buy one. 37 For I tell you, this
scripture must be fulfilled in me,
'And he was counted among the
lawless'; and indeed what is written
about me is being fulfilled." 38 They
said, "Lord, look, here are two
swords." He replied, "It is enough."

Jesus Prays on the Mount of Olives

39 He came out and went, as
was his custom, to the Mount of
Olives; and the disciples followed
him. 40 When he reached the place,
he said to them, "Pray that you may
not come into the time of trial."[g]
41 Then he withdrew from them
about a stone's throw, knelt down,
and prayed, 42 "Father, if you are
willing, remove this cup from me;
yet, not my will but yours be done."
[[43 Then an angel from heaven
appeared to him and gave him
strength. 44 In his anguish he prayed
more earnestly, and his sweat became like great drops of blood falling down on the ground.]][h] 45 When
he got up from prayer, he came to
the disciples and found them sleeping because of grief, 46 and he said
to them, "Why are you sleeping?
Get up and pray that you may not
come into the time of trial."[i]

The Betrayal and Arrest of Jesus

47 While he was still speaking,
suddenly a crowd came, and the
one called Judas, one of the twelve,
was leading them. He approached
Jesus to kiss him; 48 but Jesus said
to him, "Judas, is it with a kiss
that you are betraying the Son of
Man?" 49 When those who were
around him saw what was coming, they asked, "Lord, should we
strike with the sword?" 50 Then
one of them struck the slave of the
high priest and cut off his right ear.
51 But Jesus said, "No more of this!"
And he touched his ear and healed
him. 52 Then Jesus said to the chief
priests, the officers of the temple
police, and the elders who had
come for him, "Have you come out
with swords and clubs as if I were a
bandit? 53 When I was with you day
after day in the temple, you did not
lay hands on me. But this is your
hour, and the power of darkness!"

Peter Denies Jesus

54 Then they seized him and led

e Or *has obtained permission* f Gk *He*
g Or *into temptation* h Other ancient authorities lack verses 43 and 44 i Or *into temptation*

him away, bringing him into the
high priest's house. But Peter was
following at a distance. 55 When
they had kindled a fire in the middle of the courtyard and sat down
together, Peter sat among them.
56 Then a servant-girl, seeing him
in the firelight, stared at him and
said, "This man also was with
him." 57 But he denied it, saying,
"Woman, I do not know him." 58 A
little later someone else, on seeing
him, said, "You also are one of
them." But Peter said, "Man, I am
not!" 59 Then about an hour later
still another kept insisting, "Surely this man also was with him; for
he is a Galilean." 60 But Peter said,
"Man, I do not know what you are
talking about!" At that moment,
while he was still speaking, the
cock crowed. 61 The Lord turned
and looked at Peter. Then Peter
remembered the word of the Lord,
how he had said to him, "Before the
cock crows today, you will deny me
three times." 62 And he went out and
wept bitterly.

The Mocking and Beating of Jesus

63 Now the men who were holding Jesus began to mock him and
beat him; 64 they also blindfolded
him and kept asking him, "Prophesy! Who is it that struck you?"
65 They kept heaping many other
insults on him.

Jesus before the Council

66 When day came, the assembly
of the elders of the people, both
chief priests and scribes, gathered
together, and they brought him
to their council. 67 They said, "If
you are the Messiah,[j] tell us." He
replied, "If I tell you, you will not
believe; 68 and if I question you, you
will not answer. 69 But from now on
the Son of Man will be seated at the
right hand of the power of God."
70 All of them asked, "Are you,
then, the Son of God?" He said to
them, "You say that I am." 71 Then
they said, "What further testimony
do we need? We have heard it ourselves from his own lips!"

Jesus before Pilate

23 Then the assembly rose as a
body and brought Jesus[a] before Pilate. 2 They began to accuse
him, saying, "We found this man
perverting our nation, forbidding
us to pay taxes to the emperor,
and saying that he himself is the
Messiah, a king."[b] 3 Then Pilate
asked him, "Are you the king of the
Jews?" He answered, "You say so."
4 Then Pilate said to the chief priests
and the crowds, "I find no basis for
an accusation against this man."
5 But they were insistent and said,
"He stirs up the people by teaching
throughout all Judea, from Galilee
where he began even to this place."

Jesus before Herod

6 When Pilate heard this, he
asked whether the man was a Galilean. 7 And when he learned that
he was under Herod's jurisdiction,
he sent him off to Herod, who was
himself in Jerusalem at that time.
8 When Herod saw Jesus, he was
very glad, for he had been wanting
to see him for a long time, because

---

j Or *the Christ* *a* Gk *him* *b* Or *is an anointed king* he had heard about him and was hoping to see him perform some sign. 9 He questioned him at some length, but Jesus[c] gave him no answer. 10 The chief priests and the scribes stood by, vehemently accusing him. 11 Even Herod with his soldiers treated him with contempt and mocked him; then he put an elegant robe on him, and sent him back to Pilate. 12 That same day Herod and Pilate became friends with each other; before this they had been enemies.

Jesus Sentenced to Death

13 Pilate then called together the chief priests, the leaders, and the people, 14 and said to them, "You brought me this man as one who was perverting the people; and here I have examined him in your presence and have not found this man guilty of any of your charges against him. 15 Neither has Herod, for he sent him back to us. Indeed, he has done nothing to deserve death. 16 I will therefore have him flogged and release him."[d]

18 Then they all shouted out together, "Away with this fellow! Release Barabbas for us!" 19 (This was a man who had been put in prison for an insurrection that had taken place in the city, and for murder.) 20 Pilate, wanting to release Jesus, addressed them again; 21 but they kept shouting, "Crucify, crucify him!" 22 A third time he said to them, "Why, what evil has he done? I have found in him no ground for the sentence of death; I will therefore have him flogged and then release him." 23 But they kept urgently demanding with loud shouts that he should be crucified; and their voices prevailed. 24 So Pilate gave his verdict that their demand should be granted. 25 He released the man they asked for, the one who had been put in prison for insurrection and murder, and he handed Jesus over as they wished.

The Crucifixion of Jesus

26 As they led him away, they seized a man, Simon of Cyrene, who was coming from the country, and they laid the cross on him, and made him carry it behind Jesus. 27 A great number of the people followed him, and among them were women who were beating their breasts and wailing for him. 28 But Jesus turned to them and said, "Daughters of Jerusalem, do not weep for me, but weep for yourselves and for your children. 29 For the days are surely coming when they will say, 'Blessed are the barren, and the wombs that never bore, and the breasts that never nursed.' 30 Then they will begin to say to the mountains, 'Fall on us'; and to the hills, 'Cover us.' 31 For if they do this when the wood is green, what will happen when it is dry?"

32 Two others also, who were criminals, were led away to be put to death with him. 33 When they came to the place that is called The Skull, they crucified Jesus[e] there with the criminals, one on his right and one on his left. [[34 Then

---

c Gk *he* *d* Here, or after verse 19, other ancient authorities add verse 17, *Now he was obliged to release someone for them at the festival* *e* Gk *him*

Jesus said, "Father, forgive them; for they do not know what they are doing."]][f] And they cast lots to divide his clothing. 35 And the people stood by, watching; but the leaders scoffed at him, saying, "He saved others; let him save himself if he is the Messiah[g] of God, his chosen one!" 36 The soldiers also mocked him, coming up and offering him sour wine, 37 and saying, "If you are the King of the Jews, save yourself!" 38 There was also an inscription over him,[h] "This is the King of the Jews."

39 One of the criminals who were hanged there kept deriding[i] him and saying, "Are you not the Messiah?[j] Save yourself and us!" 40 But the other rebuked him, saying, "Do you not fear God, since you are under the same sentence of condemnation? 41 And we indeed have been condemned justly, for we are getting what we deserve for our deeds, but this man has done nothing wrong." 42 Then he said, "Jesus, remember me when you come into[k] your kingdom." 43 He replied, "Truly I tell you, today you will be with me in Paradise."

The Death of Jesus

44 It was now about noon, and darkness came over the whole land[l] until three in the afternoon, 45 while the sun's light failed;[m] and the curtain of the temple was torn in two. 46 Then Jesus, crying with a loud voice, said, "Father, into your hands I commend my spirit." Having said this, he breathed his last. 47 When the centurion saw what had taken place, he praised God and said, "Certainly this man was innocent."[n] 48 And when all the crowds who had gathered there for this spectacle saw what had taken place, they returned home, beating their breasts. 49 But all his acquaintances, including the women who had followed him from Galilee, stood at a distance, watching these things.

The Burial of Jesus

50 Now there was a good and righteous man named Joseph, who, though a member of the council, 51 had not agreed to their plan and action. He came from the Jewish town of Arimathea, and he was waiting expectantly for the kingdom of God. 52 This man went to Pilate and asked for the body of Jesus. 53 Then he took it down, wrapped it in a linen cloth, and laid it in a rock-hewn tomb where no one had ever been laid. 54 It was the day of Preparation, and the sabbath was beginning.[o] 55 The women who had come with him from Galilee followed, and they saw the tomb and how his body was laid. 56 Then they returned, and prepared spices and ointments.

On the sabbath they rested according to the commandment.

The Resurrection of Jesus

24 But on the first day of the week, at early dawn, they

f Other ancient authorities lack the sentence *Then Jesus . . . what they are doing* *g* Or *the Christ* *h* Other ancient authorities add *written in Greek and Latin and Hebrew* (that is, *Aramaic*) *i* Or *blaspheming* *j* Or *the Christ* *k* Other ancient authorities read *in* *l* Or *earth* *m* Or *the sun was eclipsed.* Other ancient authorities read *the sun was darkened* *n* Or *righteous* *o* Gk *was dawning*

came to the tomb, taking the spices that they had prepared. 2 They
found the stone rolled away from
the tomb, 3 but when they went
in, they did not find the body.[a]
4 While they were perplexed about
this, suddenly two men in dazzling
clothes stood beside them. 5 The
women[b] were terrified and bowed
their faces to the ground, but the
men[c] said to them, "Why do you
look for the living among the dead?
He is not here, but has risen.[d] 6 Remember how he told you, while he
was still in Galilee, 7 that the Son of
Man must be handed over to sinners, and be crucified, and on the
third day rise again." 8 Then they
remembered his words, 9 and re-
turning from the tomb, they told all
this to the eleven and to all the rest.
10 Now it was Mary Magdalene, Joanna, Mary the mother of James,
and the other women with them
who told this to the apostles. 11 But
these words seemed to them an idle
tale, and they did not believe them.
12 But Peter got up and ran to the
tomb; stooping and looking in, he
saw the linen cloths by themselves;
then he went home, amazed at what
had happened.[e]

The Walk to Emmaus

13 Now on that same day two of
them were going to a village called
Emmaus, about seven miles[f] from
Jerusalem, 14 and talking with each
other about all these things that
had happened. 15 While they were
talking and discussing, Jesus himself came near and went with them,
16 but their eyes were kept from
recognizing him. 17 And he said to
them, "What are you discussing
with each other while you walk
along?" They stood still, looking
sad.[g] 18 Then one of them, whose
name was Cleopas, answered him,
"Are you the only stranger in Jerusalem who does not know the
things that have taken place there
in these days?" 19 He asked them,
"What things?" They replied, "The
things about Jesus of Nazareth,[h]
who was a prophet mighty in deed
and word before God and all the
people, 20 and how our chief priests
and leaders handed him over to be
condemned to death and crucified
him. 21 But we had hoped that he
was the one to redeem Israel.[i] Yes,
and besides all this, it is now the
third day since these things took
place. 22 Moreover, some women
of our group astounded us. They
were at the tomb early this morning, 23 and when they did not find
his body there, they came back and
told us that they had indeed seen a
vision of angels who said that he
was alive. 24 Some of those who
were with us went to the tomb and
found it just as the women had said;
but they did not see him." 25 Then
he said to them, "Oh, how foolish
you are, and how slow of heart to
believe all that the prophets have
declared! 26 Was it not necessary
that the Messiah[j] should suffer

a Other ancient authorities add *of the Lord Jesus* *b* Gk *They* *c* Gk *but they* *d* Other ancient authorities lack *He is not here, but has risen* *e* Other ancient authorities lack verse 12 *f* Gk *sixty stadia;* other ancient authorities read *a hundred sixty stadia* *g* Other ancient authorities read *walk along, looking sad?"* *h* Other ancient authorities read *Jesus the Nazorean* *i* Or *to set Israel free* *j* Or *the Christ*

these things and then enter into his glory?" [27]Then beginning with Moses and all the prophets, he interpreted to them the things about himself in all the scriptures.

28 As they came near the village to which they were going, he walked ahead as if he were going on. [29]But they urged him strongly, saying, "Stay with us, because it is almost evening and the day is now nearly over." So he went in to stay with them. [30]When he was at the table with them, he took bread, blessed and broke it, and gave it to them. [31]Then their eyes were opened, and they recognized him; and he vanished from their sight. [32]They said to each other, "Were not our hearts burning within us[k] while he was talking to us on the road, while he was opening the scriptures to us?" [33]That same hour they got up and returned to Jerusalem; and they found the eleven and their companions gathered together. [34]They were saying, "The Lord has risen indeed, and he has appeared to Simon!" [35]Then they told what had happened on the road, and how he had been made known to them in the breaking of the bread.

Jesus Appears to His Disciples

36 While they were talking about this, Jesus himself stood among them and said to them, "Peace be with you."[l] [37]They were startled and terrified, and thought that they were seeing a ghost. [38]He said to them, "Why are you frightened, and why do doubts arise in your hearts? [39]Look at my hands and my feet; see that it is I myself. Touch me and see; for a ghost does not have flesh and bones as you see that I have." [40]And when he had said this, he showed them his hands and his feet.[m] [41]While in their joy they were disbelieving and still wondering, he said to them, "Have you anything here to eat?" [42]They gave him a piece of broiled fish, [43]and he took it and ate in their presence.

44 Then he said to them, "These are my words that I spoke to you while I was still with you—that everything written about me in the law of Moses, the prophets, and the psalms must be fulfilled." [45]Then he opened their minds to understand the scriptures, [46]and he said to them, "Thus it is written, that the Messiah[n] is to suffer and to rise from the dead on the third day, [47]and that repentance and forgiveness of sins is to be proclaimed in his name to all nations, beginning from Jerusalem. [48]You are witnesses[o] of these things. [49]And see, I am sending upon you what my Father promised; so stay here in the city until you have been clothed with power from on high."

The Ascension of Jesus

50 Then he led them out as far as Bethany, and, lifting up his hands, he blessed them. [51]While he was blessing them, he withdrew from them and was carried up into heav-

---

k Other ancient authorities lack *within us*
l Other ancient authorities lack *and said to them, "Peace be with you."* *m* Other ancient authorities lack verse 40 *n* Or *the Christ*
o Or *nations. Beginning from Jerusalem [48]you are witnesses*

en.[p] 52 And they worshiped him, and[q] returned to Jerusalem with great joy; 53 and they were continually in the temple blessing God.[r]

p Other ancient authorities lack *and was carried up into heaven* q Other ancient authorities lack *worshiped him, and* r Other ancient authorities add *Amen*

The Gospel According to JOHN

The Word Became Flesh

1 In the beginning was the Word,
and the Word was with God,
and the Word was God. 2 He was in
the beginning with God. 3 All things
came into being through him, and
without him not one thing came
into being. What has come into being 4 in him was life,[a] and the life
was the light of all people. 5 The
light shines in the darkness, and the
darkness did not overcome it.

6 There was a man sent from
God, whose name was John. 7 He
came as a witness to testify to
the light, so that all might believe
through him. 8 He himself was not
the light, but he came to testify to
the light. 9 The true light, which enlightens everyone, was coming into
the world.[b]

10 He was in the world, and the
world came into being through him;
yet the world did not know him.
11 He came to what was his own,[c]
and his own people did not accept
him. 12 But to all who received him,
who believed in his name, he gave
power to become children of God,
13 who were born, not of blood or of
the will of the flesh or of the will of
man, but of God.

14 And the Word became flesh
and lived among us, and we have
seen his glory, the glory as of a father's only son,[d] full of grace and
truth. 15 (John testified to him and
cried out, "This was he of whom
I said, 'He who comes after me
ranks ahead of me because he was
before me.' ") 16 From his fullness
we have all received, grace upon
grace. 17 The law indeed was giv-
en through Moses; grace and truth
came through Jesus Christ. 18 No
one has ever seen God. It is God
the only Son,[e] who is close to the
Father's heart,[f] who has made him
known.

The Testimony of John the Baptist

19 This is the testimony given by
John when the Jews sent priests and
Levites from Jerusalem to ask him,
"Who are you?" 20 He confessed
and did not deny it, but confessed,
"I am not the Messiah."[g] 21 And
they asked him, "What then? Are
you Elijah?" He said, "I am not."
"Are you the prophet?" He answered, "No." 22 Then they said to
him, "Who are you? Let us have
an answer for those who sent us.
What do you say about yourself?"
23 He said,

"I am the voice of one crying out
in the wilderness,
'Make straight the way of the
Lord,' "

---

a Or [3]*through him. And without him not one thing came into being that has come into being.* [4]*In him was life* b Or *He was the true light that enlightens everyone coming into the world* c Or *to his own home* d Or *the Father's only Son* e Other ancient authorities read *It is an only Son, God,* or *It is the only Son* f Gk *bosom* g Or *the Christ*

as the prophet Isaiah said.
24 Now they had been sent from
the Pharisees. 25 They asked him,
"Why then are you baptizing if
you are neither the Messiah,[h] nor
Elijah, nor the prophet?" 26 John answered them, "I baptize with water.
Among you stands one whom you
do not know, 27 the one who is coming after me; I am not worthy to untie the thong of his sandal." 28 This
took place in Bethany across the
Jordan where John was baptizing.

The Lamb of God

29 The next day he saw Jesus
coming toward him and declared,
"Here is the Lamb of God who
takes away the sin of the world!
30 This is he of whom I said, 'After
me comes a man who ranks ahead
of me because he was before me.'
31 I myself did not know him; but I
came baptizing with water for this
reason, that he might be revealed to
Israel." 32 And John testified, "I saw
the Spirit descending from heaven
like a dove, and it remained on him.
33 I myself did not know him, but
the one who sent me to baptize with
water said to me, 'He on whom you
see the Spirit descend and remain is
the one who baptizes with the Holy
Spirit.' 34 And I myself have seen
and have testified that this is the
Son of God."[i]

The First Disciples of Jesus

35 The next day John again was
standing with two of his disciples,
36 and as he watched Jesus walk by,
he exclaimed, "Look, here is the
Lamb of God!" 37 The two disciples
heard him say this, and they followed Jesus. 38 When Jesus turned
and saw them following, he said to
them, "What are you looking for?"
They said to him, "Rabbi" (which
translated means Teacher), "where
are you staying?" 39 He said to
them, "Come and see." They came
and saw where he was staying, and
they remained with him that day. It
was about four o'clock in the afternoon. 40 One of the two who heard
John speak and followed him was
Andrew, Simon Peter's brother.
41 He first found his brother Simon
and said to him, "We have found
the Messiah" (which is translated
Anointed[j]). 42 He brought Simon[k] to
Jesus, who looked at him and said,
"You are Simon son of John. You
are to be called Cephas" (which is
translated Peter[l]).

Jesus Calls Philip and Nathanael

43 The next day Jesus decided to
go to Galilee. He found Philip and
said to him, "Follow me." 44 Now
Philip was from Bethsaida, the
city of Andrew and Peter. 45 Philip
found Nathanael and said to him,
"We have found him about whom
Moses in the law and also the
prophets wrote, Jesus son of Joseph from Nazareth." 46 Nathanael
said to him, "Can anything good
come out of Nazareth?" Philip said
to him, "Come and see." 47 When
Jesus saw Nathanael coming toward him, he said of him, "Here is
truly an Israelite in whom there is
no deceit!" 48 Nathanael asked him,

---

h Or *the Christ* *i* Other ancient authorities read *is God's chosen one* *j* Or *Christ* *k* Gk *him* *l* From the word for *rock* in Aramaic (*kepha*) and Greek (*petra*), respectively

"Where did you get to know me?" Jesus answered, "I saw you under the fig tree before Philip called you." 49 Nathanael replied, "Rabbi, you are the Son of God! You are the King of Israel!" 50 Jesus answered, "Do you believe because I told you that I saw you under the fig tree? You will see greater things than these." 51 And he said to him, "Very truly, I tell you,[m] you will see heaven opened and the angels of God ascending and descending upon the Son of Man."

The Wedding at Cana

2 On the third day there was a wedding in Cana of Galilee, and the mother of Jesus was there. 2 Jesus and his disciples had also been invited to the wedding. 3 When the wine gave out, the mother of Jesus said to him, "They have no wine." 4 And Jesus said to her, "Woman, what concern is that to you and to me? My hour has not yet come." 5 His mother said to the servants, "Do whatever he tells you." 6 Now standing there were six stone water jars for the Jewish rites of purification, each holding twenty or thirty gallons. 7 Jesus said to them, "Fill the jars with water." And they filled them up to the brim. 8 He said to them, "Now draw some out, and take it to the chief steward." So they took it. 9 When the steward tasted the water that had become wine, and did not know where it came from (though the servants who had drawn the water knew), the steward called the bridegroom 10 and said to him, "Everyone serves the good wine first, and then the inferior wine after the guests have become drunk. But you have kept the good wine until now." 11 Jesus did this, the first of his signs, in Cana of Galilee, and revealed his glory; and his disciples believed in him.

12 After this he went down to Capernaum with his mother, his brothers, and his disciples; and they remained there a few days.

Jesus Cleanses the Temple

13 The Passover of the Jews was near, and Jesus went up to Jerusalem. 14 In the temple he found people selling cattle, sheep, and doves, and the money changers seated at their tables. 15 Making a whip of cords, he drove all of them out of the temple, both the sheep and the cattle. He also poured out the coins of the money changers and overturned their tables. 16 He told those who were selling the doves, "Take these things out of here! Stop making my Father's house a marketplace!" 17 His disciples remembered that it was written, "Zeal for your house will consume me." 18 The Jews then said to him, "What sign can you show us for doing this?" 19 Jesus answered them, "Destroy this temple, and in three days I will raise it up." 20 The Jews then said, "This temple has been under construction for forty-six years, and will you raise it up in three days?" 21 But he was speaking of the temple of his body. 22 After he was raised from the dead, his disciples remembered that he had said this; and they believed the scripture and the word

m Both instances of the Greek word for *you* in this verse are plural

that Jesus had spoken.

23 When he was in Jerusalem during the Passover festival, many believed in his name because they saw the signs that he was doing. 24But Jesus on his part would not entrust himself to them, because he knew all people 25and needed no one to testify about anyone; for he himself knew what was in everyone.

Nicodemus Visits Jesus

3 Now there was a Pharisee named Nicodemus, a leader of the Jews. 2He came to Jesus[a] by night and said to him, "Rabbi, we know that you are a teacher who has come from God; for no one can do these signs that you do apart from the presence of God." 3Jesus answered him, "Very truly, I tell you, no one can see the kingdom of God without being born from above."[b] 4Nicodemus said to him, "How can anyone be born after having grown old? Can one enter a second time into the mother's womb and be born?" 5Jesus answered, "Very truly, I tell you, no one can enter the kingdom of God without being born of water and Spirit. 6What is born of the flesh is flesh, and what is born of the Spirit is spirit.[c] 7Do not be astonished that I said to you, 'You[d] must be born from above.'[e] 8The wind[f] blows where it chooses, and you hear the sound of it, but you do not know where it comes from or where it goes. So it is with everyone who is born of the Spirit." 9Nicodemus said to him, "How can these things be?" 10Jesus answered him, "Are you a teacher of Israel, and yet you do not understand these things?

11 "Very truly, I tell you, we speak of what we know and testify to what we have seen; yet you[g] do not receive our testimony. 12If I have told you about earthly things and you do not believe, how can you believe if I tell you about heavenly things? 13No one has ascended into heaven except the one who descended from heaven, the Son of Man.[h] 14And just as Moses lifted up the serpent in the wilderness, so must the Son of Man be lifted up, 15that whoever believes in him may have eternal life.[i]

16 "For God so loved the world that he gave his only Son, so that everyone who believes in him may not perish but may have eternal life.

17 "Indeed, God did not send the Son into the world to condemn the world, but in order that the world might be saved through him. 18Those who believe in him are not condemned; but those who do not believe are condemned already, because they have not believed in the name of the only Son of God. 19And this is the judgment, that the light has come into the world, and people loved darkness rather than light because their deeds were evil. 20For all who do evil hate the light and do not come to the light, so that their deeds may not be exposed.

a Gk *him* *b* Or *born anew* *c* The same Greek word means both *wind* and *spirit*
d The Greek word for *you* here is plural
e Or *anew* *f* The same Greek word means both *wind* and *spirit* *g* The Greek word for *you* here and in verse 12 is plural *h* Other ancient authorities add *who is in heaven* *i* Some interpreters hold that the quotation concludes with verse 15

21 But those who do what is true
come to the light, so that it may be
clearly seen that their deeds have
been done in God."[j]

Jesus and John the Baptist

22 After this Jesus and his disciples went into the Judean countryside, and he spent some time there
with them and baptized. 23 John also
was baptizing at Aenon near Salim
because water was abundant there;
and people kept coming and were
being baptized 24—John, of course,
had not yet been thrown into prison.

25 Now a discussion about purification arose between John's
disciples and a Jew.[k] 26 They came
to John and said to him, "Rabbi,
the one who was with you across
the Jordan, to whom you testified,
here he is baptizing, and all are going to him." 27 John answered, "No
one can receive anything except
what has been given from heaven.
28 You yourselves are my witnesses
that I said, 'I am not the Messiah,[l]
but I have been sent ahead of him.'
29 He who has the bride is the bridegroom. The friend of the bridegroom, who stands and hears him,
rejoices greatly at the bridegroom's
voice. For this reason my joy has
been fulfilled. 30 He must increase,
but I must decrease."[m]

The One Who Comes from Heaven

31 The one who comes from
above is above all; the one who is
of the earth belongs to the earth
and speaks about earthly things.
The one who comes from heaven
is above all. 32 He testifies to what
he has seen and heard, yet no one
accepts his testimony. 33 Whoever has accepted his testimony has
certified[n] this, that God is true.
34 He whom God has sent speaks
the words of God, for he gives the
Spirit without measure. 35 The Father loves the Son and has placed
all things in his hands. 36 Whoever
believes in the Son has eternal life;
whoever disobeys the Son will not
see life, but must endure God's
wrath.

Jesus and the Woman of Samaria

4 Now when Jesus[a] learned that
the Pharisees had heard, "Jesus
is making and baptizing more disciples than John" 2—although it was
not Jesus himself but his disciples
who baptized— 3 he left Judea and
started back to Galilee. 4 But he had
to go through Samaria. 5 So he came
to a Samaritan city called Sychar,
near the plot of ground that Jacob
had given to his son Joseph. 6 Jacob's well was there, and Jesus,
tired out by his journey, was sitting
by the well. It was about noon.

7 A Samaritan woman came to
draw water, and Jesus said to her,
"Give me a drink." 8 (His disciples
had gone to the city to buy food.)
9 The Samaritan woman said to
him, "How is it that you, a Jew,
ask a drink of me, a woman of Samaria?" (Jews do not share things
in common with Samaritans.)[b]

---

j Some interpreters hold that the quotation concludes with verse 15 *k* Other ancient authorities read *the Jews* *l* Or *the Christ*
m Some interpreters hold that the quotation continues through verse 36 *n* Gk *set a seal to* *a* Other ancient authorities read *the Lord*
b Other ancient authorities lack this sentence

10 Jesus answered her, "If you knew
the gift of God, and who it is that
is saying to you, 'Give me a drink,'
you would have asked him, and
he would have given you living
water." 11 The woman said to him,
"Sir, you have no bucket, and the
well is deep. Where do you get that
living water? 12 Are you greater
than our ancestor Jacob, who gave
us the well, and with his sons and
his flocks drank from it?" 13 Jesus
said to her, "Everyone who drinks
of this water will be thirsty again,
14 but those who drink of the water
that I will give them will never be
thirsty. The water that I will give
will become in them a spring of
water gushing up to eternal life."
15 The woman said to him, "Sir, give
me this water, so that I may never
be thirsty or have to keep coming
here to draw water."

16 Jesus said to her, "Go, call
your husband, and come back."
17 The woman answered him, "I
have no husband." Jesus said to her,
"You are right in saying, 'I have no
husband'; 18 for you have had five
husbands, and the one you have
now is not your husband. What you
have said is true!" 19 The woman
said to him, "Sir, I see that you are a
prophet. 20 Our ancestors worshiped
on this mountain, but you[c] say
that the place where people must
worship is in Jerusalem." 21 Jesus
said to her, "Woman, believe me,
the hour is coming when you will
worship the Father neither on this
mountain nor in Jerusalem. 22 You
worship what you do not know;
we worship what we know, for salvation is from the Jews. 23 But the
hour is coming, and is now here,
when the true worshipers will worship the Father in spirit and truth,
for the Father seeks such as these
to worship him. 24 God is spirit,
and those who worship him must
worship in spirit and truth." 25 The
woman said to him, "I know that
Messiah is coming" (who is called
Christ). "When he comes, he will
proclaim all things to us." 26 Jesus
said to her, "I am he,[d] the one who
is speaking to you."

27 Just then his disciples came.
They were astonished that he was
speaking with a woman, but no
one said, "What do you want?" or,
"Why are you speaking with her?"
28 Then the woman left her water jar
and went back to the city. She said
to the people, 29 "Come and see a
man who told me everything I have
ever done! He cannot be the Messiah,[e] can he?" 30 They left the city
and were on their way to him.

31 Meanwhile the disciples were
urging him, "Rabbi, eat something." 32 But he said to them, "I
have food to eat that you do not
know about." 33 So the disciples
said to one another, "Surely no one
has brought him something to eat?"
34 Jesus said to them, "My food is
to do the will of him who sent me
and to complete his work. 35 Do you
not say, 'Four months more, then
comes the harvest'? But I tell you,
look around you, and see how the
fields are ripe for harvesting. 36 The
reaper is already receiving[f] wages

---

c The Greek word for *you* here and in verses 21 and 22 is plural *d* Gk *I am* *e* Or *the Christ* *f* Or [35]. . . *the fields are already ripe for harvesting.* [36]*The reaper is receiving* and is gathering fruit for eternal life, so that sower and reaper may rejoice together. 37 For here the saying holds true, 'One sows and another reaps.' 38 I sent you to reap that for which you did not labor. Others have labored, and you have entered into their labor."

39 Many Samaritans from that city believed in him because of the woman's testimony, "He told me everything I have ever done." 40 So when the Samaritans came to him, they asked him to stay with them; and he stayed there two days. 41 And many more believed because of his word. 42 They said to the woman, "It is no longer because of what you said that we believe, for we have heard for ourselves, and we know that this is truly the Savior of the world."

Jesus Returns to Galilee

43 When the two days were over, he went from that place to Galilee 44 (for Jesus himself had testified that a prophet has no honor in the prophet's own country). 45 When he came to Galilee, the Galileans welcomed him, since they had seen all that he had done in Jerusalem at the festival; for they too had gone to the festival.

Jesus Heals an Official's Son

46 Then he came again to Cana in Galilee where he had changed the water into wine. Now there was a royal official whose son lay ill in Capernaum. 47 When he heard that Jesus had come from Judea to Galilee, he went and begged him to come down and heal his son, for he was at the point of death. 48 Then Jesus said to him, "Unless you[g] see signs and wonders you will not believe." 49 The official said to him, "Sir, come down before my little boy dies." 50 Jesus said to him, "Go; your son will live." The man believed the word that Jesus spoke to him and started on his way. 51 As he was going down, his slaves met him and told him that his child was alive. 52 So he asked them the hour when he began to recover, and they said to him, "Yesterday at one in the afternoon the fever left him." 53 The father realized that this was the hour when Jesus had said to him, "Your son will live." So he himself believed, along with his whole household. 54 Now this was the second sign that Jesus did after coming from Judea to Galilee.

Jesus Heals on the Sabbath

5 After this there was a festival of the Jews, and Jesus went up to Jerusalem.

2 Now in Jerusalem by the Sheep Gate there is a pool, called in Hebrew[a] Beth-zatha,[b] which has five porticoes. 3 In these lay many invalids—blind, lame, and paralyzed.[c] 5 One man was there who had been ill for thirty-eight years. 6 When Jesus saw him lying there and knew that he had been there a

---

g Both instances of the Greek word for *you* in this verse are plural *a* That is, *Aramaic* *b* Other ancient authorities read *Bethesda*, others *Bethsaida* *c* Other ancient authorities add, wholly or in part, *waiting for the stirring of the water; 4for an angel of the Lord went down at certain seasons into the pool, and stirred up the water; whoever stepped in first after the stirring of the water was made well from whatever disease that person had.*

long time, he said to him, "Do you
want to be made well?" [7]The sick
man answered him, "Sir, I have no
one to put me into the pool when
the water is stirred up; and while I
am making my way, someone else
steps down ahead of me." [8]Jesus
said to him, "Stand up, take your
mat and walk." [9]At once the man
was made well, and he took up his
mat and began to walk.
Now that day was a sabbath. [10]So
the Jews said to the man who had
been cured, "It is the sabbath; it
is not lawful for you to carry your
mat." [11]But he answered them,
"The man who made me well
said to me, 'Take up your mat and
walk.'" [12]They asked him, "Who is
the man who said to you, 'Take it
up and walk'?" [13]Now the man who
had been healed did not know who
it was, for Jesus had disappeared
in[d] the crowd that was there. [14]Lat-
er Jesus found him in the temple
and said to him, "See, you have
been made well! Do not sin any
more, so that nothing worse happens to you." [15]The man went away
and told the Jews that it was Jesus
who had made him well. [16]There-
fore the Jews started persecuting
Jesus, because he was doing such
things on the sabbath. [17]But Jesus
answered them, "My Father is still
working, and I also am working."
[18]For this reason the Jews were
seeking all the more to kill him, because he was not only breaking the
sabbath, but was also calling God
his own Father, thereby making
himself equal to God.

The Authority of the Son

19 Jesus said to them, "Very truly, I tell you, the Son can do nothing on his own, but only what he
sees the Father doing; for whatever
the Father[e] does, the Son does likewise. [20]The Father loves the Son
and shows him all that he himself is
doing; and he will show him greater
works than these, so that you will
be astonished. [21]Indeed, just as the
Father raises the dead and gives
them life, so also the Son gives
life to whomever he wishes. [22]The
Father judges no one but has given
all judgment to the Son, [23]so that
all may honor the Son just as they
honor the Father. Anyone who does
not honor the Son does not honor
the Father who sent him. [24]Very
truly, I tell you, anyone who hears
my word and believes him who
sent me has eternal life, and does
not come under judgment, but has
passed from death to life.
25 "Very truly, I tell you, the hour
is coming, and is now here, when
the dead will hear the voice of the
Son of God, and those who hear
will live. [26]For just as the Father has
life in himself, so he has granted
the Son also to have life in himself;
[27]and he has given him authority to
execute judgment, because he is the
Son of Man. [28]Do not be astonished
at this; for the hour is coming when
all who are in their graves will hear
his voice [29]and will come out—
those who have done good, to the
resurrection of life, and those who
have done evil, to the resurrection
of condemnation.

---

d Or *had left because of* e Gk *that one*

Witnesses to Jesus

30 "I can do nothing on my own.
As I hear, I judge; and my judgment
is just, because I seek to do not my
own will but the will of him who
sent me.

31 "If I testify about myself, my
testimony is not true. 32 There is
another who testifies on my behalf,
and I know that his testimony to me
is true. 33 You sent messengers to
John, and he testified to the truth.
34 Not that I accept such human
testimony, but I say these things
so that you may be saved. 35 He
was a burning and shining lamp,
and you were willing to rejoice for
a while in his light. 36 But I have a
testimony greater than John's. The
works that the Father has given me
to complete, the very works that I
am doing, testify on my behalf that
the Father has sent me. 37 And the
Father who sent me has himself testified on my behalf. You have never
heard his voice or seen his form,
38 and you do not have his word
abiding in you, because you do not
believe him whom he has sent.

39 "You search the scriptures
because you think that in them
you have eternal life; and it is they
that testify on my behalf. 40 Yet you
refuse to come to me to have life.
41 I do not accept glory from human
beings. 42 But I know that you do
not have the love of God in[f] you.
43 I have come in my Father's name,
and you do not accept me; if another comes in his own name, you will
accept him. 44 How can you believe
when you accept glory from one
another and do not seek the glory
that comes from the one who alone
is God? 45 Do not think that I will
accuse you before the Father; your
accuser is Moses, on whom you
have set your hope. 46 If you believed Moses, you would believe
me, for he wrote about me. 47 But if
you do not believe what he wrote,
how will you believe what I say?"

Feeding the Five Thousand

6 After this Jesus went to the other
side of the Sea of Galilee, also
called the Sea of Tiberias.[a] 2 A
large crowd kept following him,
because they saw the signs that he
was doing for the sick. 3 Jesus went
up the mountain and sat down there
with his disciples. 4 Now the Passover, the festival of the Jews, was
near. 5 When he looked up and saw
a large crowd coming toward him,
Jesus said to Philip, "Where are
we to buy bread for these people
to eat?" 6 He said this to test him,
for he himself knew what he was
going to do. 7 Philip answered him,
"Six months' wages[b] would not buy
enough bread for each of them to
get a little." 8 One of his disciples,
Andrew, Simon Peter's brother,
said to him, 9 "There is a boy here
who has five barley loaves and two
fish. But what are they among so
many people?" 10 Jesus said, "Make
the people sit down." Now there
was a great deal of grass in the
place; so they[c] sat down, about five
thousand in all. 11 Then Jesus took
the loaves, and when he had given
thanks, he distributed them to those
who were seated; so also the fish, as

---

f Or *among* *a* Gk *of Galilee of Tiberias*
b Gk *Two hundred denarii*; the denarius was the usual day's wage for a laborer *c* Gk *the men*

much as they wanted. 12 When they
were satisfied, he told his disciples,
"Gather up the fragments left over,
so that nothing may be lost." 13 So
they gathered them up, and from
the fragments of the five barley
loaves, left by those who had eaten,
they filled twelve baskets. 14 When
the people saw the sign that he had
done, they began to say, "This is
indeed the prophet who is to come
into the world."
15 When Jesus realized that
they were about to come and take
him by force to make him king, he
withdrew again to the mountain by
himself.

Jesus Walks on the Water

16 When evening came, his disciples went down to the sea, 17 got
into a boat, and started across the
sea to Capernaum. It was now dark,
and Jesus had not yet come to them.
18 The sea became rough because a
strong wind was blowing. 19 When
they had rowed about three or four
miles,[d] they saw Jesus walking on
the sea and coming near the boat,
and they were terrified. 20 But he
said to them, "It is I;[e] do not be
afraid." 21 Then they wanted to take
him into the boat, and immediately
the boat reached the land toward
which they were going.

The Bread from Heaven

22 The next day the crowd that
had stayed on the other side of the
sea saw that there had been only
one boat there. They also saw that
Jesus had not got into the boat with
his disciples, but that his disciples
had gone away alone. 23 Then some
boats from Tiberias came near the
place where they had eaten the
bread after the Lord had given
thanks.[f] 24 So when the crowd saw
that neither Jesus nor his disciples
were there, they themselves got
into the boats and went to Capernaum looking for Jesus.
25 When they found him on the
other side of the sea, they said to
him, "Rabbi, when did you come
here?" 26 Jesus answered them,
"Very truly, I tell you, you are looking for me, not because you saw
signs, but because you ate your fill
of the loaves. 27 Do not work for the
food that perishes, but for the food
that endures for eternal life, which
the Son of Man will give you. For
it is on him that God the Father
has set his seal." 28 Then they said
to him, "What must we do to perform the works of God?" 29 Jesus
answered them, "This is the work
of God, that you believe in him
whom he has sent." 30 So they said
to him, "What sign are you going
to give us then, so that we may see
it and believe you? What work are
you performing? 31 Our ancestors
ate the manna in the wilderness; as
it is written, 'He gave them bread
from heaven to eat.'" 32 Then Jesus
said to them, "Very truly, I tell you,
it was not Moses who gave you
the bread from heaven, but it is
my Father who gives you the true
bread from heaven. 33 For the bread
of God is that which[g] comes down
from heaven and gives life to the
world." 34 They said to him, "Sir,

---

d Gk *about twenty-five or thirty stadia* e Gk *I am* f Other ancient authorities lack *after the Lord had given thanks* g Or *he who*

give us this bread always."
35 Jesus said to them, "I am the
bread of life. Whoever comes to me
will never be hungry, and whoever
believes in me will never be thirsty.
[36]But I said to you that you have
seen me and yet do not believe.
[37]Everything that the Father gives
me will come to me, and anyone
who comes to me I will never drive
away; [38]for I have come down from
heaven, not to do my own will, but
the will of him who sent me. [39]And
this is the will of him who sent me,
that I should lose nothing of all
that he has given me, but raise it
up on the last day. [40]This is indeed
the will of my Father, that all who
see the Son and believe in him may
have eternal life; and I will raise
them up on the last day."
41 Then the Jews began to complain about him because he said,
"I am the bread that came down
from heaven." [42]They were saying, "Is not this Jesus, the son of
Joseph, whose father and mother
we know? How can he now say, 'I
have come down from heaven'?"
[43]Jesus answered them, "Do not
complain among yourselves. [44]No
one can come to me unless drawn
by the Father who sent me; and I
will raise that person up on the last
day. [45]It is written in the prophets,
'And they shall all be taught by
God.' Everyone who has heard and
learned from the Father comes to
me. [46]Not that anyone has seen the
Father except the one who is from
God; he has seen the Father. [47]Very
truly, I tell you, whoever believes
has eternal life. [48]I am the bread of
life. [49]Your ancestors ate the manna
in the wilderness, and they died.
[50]This is the bread that comes down
from heaven, so that one may eat
of it and not die. [51]I am the living
bread that came down from heaven.
Whoever eats of this bread will live
forever; and the bread that I will
give for the life of the world is my
flesh."
52 The Jews then disputed
among themselves, saying, "How
can this man give us his flesh to
eat?" [53]So Jesus said to them, "Very
truly, I tell you, unless you eat the
flesh of the Son of Man and drink
his blood, you have no life in you.
[54]Those who eat my flesh and drink
my blood have eternal life, and I
will raise them up on the last day;
[55]for my flesh is true food and my
blood is true drink. [56]Those who eat
my flesh and drink my blood abide
in me, and I in them. [57]Just as the
living Father sent me, and I live
because of the Father, so whoever
eats me will live because of me.
[58]This is the bread that came down
from heaven, not like that which
your ancestors ate, and they died.
But the one who eats this bread will
live forever." [59]He said these things
while he was teaching in the synagogue at Capernaum.

The Words of Eternal Life

60 When many of his disciples
heard it, they said, "This teaching
is difficult; who can accept it?"
[61]But Jesus, being aware that his
disciples were complaining about
it, said to them, "Does this offend
you? [62]Then what if you were to see
the Son of Man ascending to where
he was before? [63]It is the spirit that

gives life; the flesh is useless. The
words that I have spoken to you
are spirit and life. 64 But among you
there are some who do not believe."
For Jesus knew from the first who
were the ones that did not believe,
and who was the one that would
betray him. 65 And he said, "For this
reason I have told you that no one
can come to me unless it is granted
by the Father."

66 Because of this many of his
disciples turned back and no longer
went about with him. 67 So Jesus
asked the twelve, "Do you also
wish to go away?" 68 Simon Peter
answered him, "Lord, to whom can
we go? You have the words of eternal life. 69 We have come to believe
and know that you are the Holy
One of God."[h] 70 Jesus answered
them, "Did I not choose you, the
twelve? Yet one of you is a devil."
71 He was speaking of Judas son of
Simon Iscariot,[i] for he, though one
of the twelve, was going to betray
him.

The Unbelief of Jesus' Brothers

7 After this Jesus went about in
Galilee. He did not wish[a] to go
about in Judea because the Jews
were looking for an opportunity to
kill him. 2 Now the Jewish festival
of Booths[b] was near. 3 So his brothers said to him, "Leave here and go
to Judea so that your disciples also
may see the works you are doing;
4 for no one who wants[c] to be widely known acts in secret. If you do
these things, show yourself to the
world." 5 (For not even his brothers believed in him.) 6 Jesus said to
them, "My time has not yet come,
but your time is always here. 7 The
world cannot hate you, but it hates
me because I testify against it that
its works are evil. 8 Go to the festival yourselves. I am not[d] going to
this festival, for my time has not yet
fully come." 9 After saying this, he
remained in Galilee.

Jesus at the Festival of Booths

10 But after his brothers had
gone to the festival, then he also
went, not publicly but as it were[e]
in secret. 11 The Jews were looking
for him at the festival and saying,
"Where is he?" 12 And there was
considerable complaining about
him among the crowds. While
some were saying, "He is a good
man," others were saying, "No, he
is deceiving the crowd." 13 Yet no
one would speak openly about him
for fear of the Jews.

14 About the middle of the festival Jesus went up into the temple
and began to teach. 15 The Jews
were astonished at it, saying, "How
does this man have such learning,[f]
when he has never been taught?"
16 Then Jesus answered them, "My
teaching is not mine but his who
sent me. 17 Anyone who resolves
to do the will of God will know
whether the teaching is from God
or whether I am speaking on my
own. 18 Those who speak on their
own seek their own glory; but the

---

h Other ancient authorities read *the Christ, the Son of the living God* *i* Other ancient authorities read *Judas Iscariot son of Simon;* others, *Judas son of Simon from Karyot* (Kerioth) *a* Other ancient authorities read *was not at liberty* *b* Or *Tabernacles* *c* Other ancient authorities read *wants it* *d* Other ancient authorities add *yet* *e* Other ancient authorities lack *as it were* *f* Or *this man know his letters*

one who seeks the glory of him who sent him is true, and there is nothing false in him.

19 "Did not Moses give you the law? Yet none of you keeps the law. Why are you looking for an opportunity to kill me?" 20 The crowd answered, "You have a demon! Who is trying to kill you?" 21 Jesus answered them, "I performed one work, and all of you are astonished. 22 Moses gave you circumcision (it is, of course, not from Moses, but from the patriarchs), and you circumcise a man on the sabbath. 23 If a man receives circumcision on the sabbath in order that the law of Moses may not be broken, are you angry with me because I healed a man's whole body on the sabbath? 24 Do not judge by appearances, but judge with right judgment."

Is This the Christ?

25 Now some of the people of Jerusalem were saying, "Is not this the man whom they are trying to kill? 26 And here he is, speaking openly, but they say nothing to him! Can it be that the authorities really know that this is the Messiah?[g] 27 Yet we know where this man is from; but when the Messiah[h] comes, no one will know where he is from." 28 Then Jesus cried out as he was teaching in the temple, "You know me, and you know where I am from. I have not come on my own. But the one who sent me is true, and you do not know him. 29 I know him, because I am from him, and he sent me." 30 Then they tried to arrest him, but no one laid hands on him, because his hour had not yet come. 31 Yet many in the crowd believed in him and were saying, "When the Messiah[i] comes, will he do more signs than this man has done?"[j]

Officers Are Sent to Arrest Jesus

32 The Pharisees heard the crowd muttering such things about him, and the chief priests and Pharisees sent temple police to arrest him. 33 Jesus then said, "I will be with you a little while longer, and then I am going to him who sent me. 34 You will search for me, but you will not find me; and where I am, you cannot come." 35 The Jews said to one another, "Where does this man intend to go that we will not find him? Does he intend to go to the Dispersion among the Greeks and teach the Greeks? 36 What does he mean by saying, 'You will search for me and you will not find me' and 'Where I am, you cannot come'?"

Rivers of Living Water

37 On the last day of the festival, the great day, while Jesus was standing there, he cried out, "Let anyone who is thirsty come to me, 38 and let the one who believes in me drink. As[k] the scripture has said, 'Out of the believer's heart[l] shall flow rivers of living water.'" 39 Now he said this about the Spirit, which believers in him were to receive; for as yet there was no

g Or *the Christ* h Or *the Christ* i Or *the Christ* j Other ancient authorities read *is doing* k Or *come to me and drink.* [38] *The one who believes in me, as* l Gk *out of his belly*

Spirit,[m] because Jesus was not yet
glorified.

Division among the People

40 When they heard these words,
some in the crowd said, "This is
really the prophet." 41 Others said,
"This is the Messiah."[n] But some
asked, "Surely the Messiah[o] does
not come from Galilee, does he?
42 Has not the scripture said that the
Messiah[p] is descended from David
and comes from Bethlehem, the
village where David lived?" 43 So
there was a division in the crowd
because of him. 44 Some of them
wanted to arrest him, but no one
laid hands on him.

The Unbelief of Those in Authority

45 Then the temple police went
back to the chief priests and Pharisees, who asked them, "Why did
you not arrest him?" 46 The police
answered, "Never has anyone
spoken like this!" 47 Then the Pharisees replied, "Surely you have
not been deceived too, have you?
48 Has any one of the authorities or
of the Pharisees believed in him?
49 But this crowd, which does not
know the law—they are accursed."
50 Nicodemus, who had gone to Jesus[q] before, and who was one of
them, asked, 51 "Our law does not
judge people without first giving
them a hearing to find out what they
are doing, does it?" 52 They replied,
"Surely you are not also from Galilee, are you? Search and you will
see that no prophet is to arise from
Galilee."

The Woman Caught in Adultery

[[53 Then each of them went home,
8 1 while Jesus went to the Mount
of Olives. 2 Early in the morning he came again to the temple.
All the people came to him and he
sat down and began to teach them.
3 The scribes and the Pharisees
brought a woman who had been
caught in adultery; and making her
stand before all of them, 4 they said
to him, "Teacher, this woman was
caught in the very act of commit-
ting adultery. 5 Now in the law Moses commanded us to stone such
women. Now what do you say?"
6 They said this to test him, so that
they might have some charge to
bring against him. Jesus bent down
and wrote with his finger on the
ground. 7 When they kept on questioning him, he straightened up and
said to them, "Let anyone among
you who is without sin be the first
to throw a stone at her." 8 And once
again he bent down and wrote on
the ground.[a] 9 When they heard it,
they went away, one by one, beginning with the elders; and Jesus was
left alone with the woman standing
before him. 10 Jesus straightened up
and said to her, "Woman, where
are they? Has no one condemned
you?" 11 She said, "No one, sir."[b]
And Jesus said, "Neither do I condemn you. Go your way, and from
now on do not sin again."]][c]

---

m Other ancient authorities read *for as yet the Spirit* (others, *Holy Spirit*) *had not been given*
n Or *the Christ* *o* Or *the Christ* *p* Or *the Christ* *q* Gk *him* *a* Other ancient authorities add *the sins of each of them* *b* Or *Lord*
c The most ancient authorities lack 7.53--8.11; other authorities add the passage here or after 7.36 or after 21.25 or after Luke 21.38, with variations of text; some mark the passage as doubtful.

Jesus the Light of the World

12 Again Jesus spoke to them, saying, "I am the light of the world. Whoever follows me will never walk in darkness but will have the light of life." 13 Then the Pharisees said to him, "You are testifying on your own behalf; your testimony is not valid." 14 Jesus answered, "Even if I testify on my own behalf, my testimony is valid because I know where I have come from and where I am going, but you do not know where I come from or where I am going. 15 You judge by human standards;[d] I judge no one. 16 Yet even if I do judge, my judgment is valid; for it is not I alone who judge, but I and the Father[e] who sent me. 17 In your law it is written that the testimony of two witnesses is valid. 18 I testify on my own behalf, and the Father who sent me testifies on my behalf." 19 Then they said to him, "Where is your Father?" Jesus answered, "You know neither me nor my Father. If you knew me, you would know my Father also." 20 He spoke these words while he was teaching in the treasury of the temple, but no one arrested him, because his hour had not yet come.

Jesus Foretells His Death

21 Again he said to them, "I am going away, and you will search for me, but you will die in your sin. Where I am going, you cannot come." 22 Then the Jews said, "Is he going to kill himself? Is that what he means by saying, 'Where I am going, you cannot come'?" 23 He said to them, "You are from below, I am from above; you are of this world, I am not of this world. 24 I told you that you would die in your sins, for you will die in your sins unless you believe that I am he."[f] 25 They said to him, "Who are you?" Jesus said to them, "Why do I speak to you at all?[g] 26 I have much to say about you and much to condemn; but the one who sent me is true, and I declare to the world what I have heard from him." 27 They did not understand that he was speaking to them about the Father. 28 So Jesus said, "When you have lifted up the Son of Man, then you will realize that I am he,[h] and that I do nothing on my own, but I speak these things as the Father instructed me. 29 And the one who sent me is with me; he has not left me alone, for I always do what is pleasing to him." 30 As he was saying these things, many believed in him.

True Disciples

31 Then Jesus said to the Jews who had believed in him, "If you continue in my word, you are truly my disciples; 32 and you will know the truth, and the truth will make you free." 33 They answered him, "We are descendants of Abraham and have never been slaves to anyone. What do you mean by saying, 'You will be made free'?"

34 Jesus answered them, "Very truly, I tell you, everyone who commits sin is a slave to sin. 35 The slave does not have a permanent place in the household; the son has a place there forever. 36 So if the Son makes

---

d Gk *according to the flesh* e Other ancient authorities read *he* f Gk *I am* g Or *What I have told you from the beginning* h Gk *I am*

you free, you will be free indeed.
37I know that you are descendants
of Abraham; yet you look for an
opportunity to kill me, because
there is no place in you for my
word. 38I declare what I have seen
in the Father's presence; as for you,
you should do what you have heard
from the Father."[i]

Jesus and Abraham

39 They answered him, "Abraham is our father." Jesus said to
them, "If you were Abraham's
children, you would be doing[j] what
Abraham did, 40but now you are
trying to kill me, a man who has
told you the truth that I heard from
God. This is not what Abraham did.
41You are indeed doing what your
father does." They said to him, "We
are not illegitimate children; we
have one father, God himself." 42Jesus said to them, "If God were your
Father, you would love me, for I
came from God and now I am here.
I did not come on my own, but he
sent me. 43Why do you not understand what I say? It is because you
cannot accept my word. 44You are
from your father the devil, and you
choose to do your father's desires.
He was a murderer from the beginning and does not stand in the truth,
because there is no truth in him.
When he lies, he speaks according
to his own nature, for he is a liar
and the father of lies. 45But because
I tell the truth, you do not believe
me. 46Which of you convicts me of
sin? If I tell the truth, why do you
not believe me? 47Whoever is from
God hears the words of God. The
reason you do not hear them is that
you are not from God."

48 The Jews answered him, "Are
we not right in saying that you are
a Samaritan and have a demon?"
49Jesus answered, "I do not have a
demon; but I honor my Father, and
you dishonor me. 50Yet I do not seek
my own glory; there is one who
seeks it and he is the judge. 51Very
truly, I tell you, whoever keeps my
word will never see death." 52The
Jews said to him, "Now we know
that you have a demon. Abraham
died, and so did the prophets; yet
you say, 'Whoever keeps my word
will never taste death.' 53Are you
greater than our father Abraham,
who died? The prophets also died.
Who do you claim to be?" 54Jesus
answered, "If I glorify myself, my
glory is nothing. It is my Father
who glorifies me, he of whom you
say, 'He is our God,' 55though you
do not know him. But I know him;
if I would say that I do not know
him, I would be a liar like you. But
I do know him and I keep his word.
56Your ancestor Abraham rejoiced
that he would see my day; he saw it
and was glad." 57Then the Jews said
to him, "You are not yet fifty years
old, and have you seen Abraham?"[k]
58Jesus said to them, "Very truly,
I tell you, before Abraham was, I
am." 59So they picked up stones to
throw at him, but Jesus hid himself
and went out of the temple.

---

i Other ancient authorities read *you do what you have heard from your father* *j* Other ancient authorities read *If you are Abraham's children, then do* *k* Other ancient authorities read *has Abraham seen you?*

A Man Born Blind Receives Sight

9 As he walked along, he saw a man blind from birth. 2 His disciples asked him, "Rabbi, who sinned, this man or his parents, that he was born blind?" 3 Jesus answered, "Neither this man nor his parents sinned; he was born blind so that God's works might be revealed in him. 4 We[a] must work the works of him who sent me[b] while it is day; night is coming when no one can work. 5 As long as I am in the world, I am the light of the world." 6 When he had said this, he spat on the ground and made mud with the saliva and spread the mud on the man's eyes, 7 saying to him, "Go, wash in the pool of Siloam" (which means Sent). Then he went and washed and came back able to see. 8 The neighbors and those who had seen him before as a beggar began to ask, "Is this not the man who used to sit and beg?" 9 Some were saying, "It is he." Others were saying, "No, but it is someone like him." He kept saying, "I am the man." 10 But they kept asking him, "Then how were your eyes opened?" 11 He answered, "The man called Jesus made mud, spread it on my eyes, and said to me, 'Go to Siloam and wash.' Then I went and washed and received my sight." 12 They said to him, "Where is he?" He said, "I do not know."

The Pharisees Investigate the Healing

13 They brought to the Pharisees the man who had formerly been blind. 14 Now it was a sabbath day when Jesus made the mud and opened his eyes. 15 Then the Pharisees also began to ask him how he had received his sight. He said to them, "He put mud on my eyes. Then I washed, and now I see." 16 Some of the Pharisees said, "This man is not from God, for he does not observe the sabbath." But others said, "How can a man who is a sinner perform such signs?" And they were divided. 17 So they said again to the blind man, "What do you say about him? It was your eyes he opened." He said, "He is a prophet."

18 The Jews did not believe that he had been blind and had received his sight until they called the parents of the man who had received his sight 19 and asked them, "Is this your son, who you say was born blind? How then does he now see?" 20 His parents answered, "We know that this is our son, and that he was born blind; 21 but we do not know how it is that now he sees, nor do we know who opened his eyes. Ask him; he is of age. He will speak for himself." 22 His parents said this because they were afraid of the Jews; for the Jews had already agreed that anyone who confessed Jesus[c] to be the Messiah[d] would be put out of the synagogue. 23 Therefore his parents said, "He is of age; ask him."

24 So for the second time they called the man who had been blind, and they said to him, "Give glory to God! We know that this man is a sinner." 25 He answered, "I do not know whether he is a sinner.

---

a Other ancient authorities read *I* *b* Other ancient authorities read *us* *c* Gk *him* *d* Or *the Christ*

One thing I do know, that though I was blind, now I see." 26 They said to him, "What did he do to you? How did he open your eyes?" 27 He answered them, "I have told you already, and you would not listen. Why do you want to hear it again? Do you also want to become his disciples?" 28 Then they reviled him, saying, "You are his disciple, but we are disciples of Moses. 29 We know that God has spoken to Moses, but as for this man, we do not know where he comes from." 30 The man answered, "Here is an astonishing thing! You do not know where he comes from, and yet he opened my eyes. 31 We know that God does not listen to sinners, but he does listen to one who worships him and obeys his will. 32 Never since the world began has it been heard that anyone opened the eyes of a person born blind. 33 If this man were not from God, he could do nothing." 34 They answered him, "You were born entirely in sins, and are you trying to teach us?" And they drove him out.

Spiritual Blindness

35 Jesus heard that they had driven him out, and when he found him, he said, "Do you believe in the Son of Man?"[e] 36 He answered, "And who is he, sir?[f] Tell me, so that I may believe in him." 37 Jesus said to him, "You have seen him, and the one speaking with you is he." 38 He said, "Lord,[g] I believe." And he worshiped him. 39 Jesus said, "I came into this world for judgment so that those who do not see may see, and those who do see may become blind." 40 Some of the Pharisees near him heard this and said to him, "Surely we are not blind, are we?" 41 Jesus said to them, "If you were blind, you would not have sin. But now that you say, 'We see,' your sin remains.

Jesus the Good Shepherd

10 "Very truly, I tell you, anyone who does not enter the sheepfold by the gate but climbs in by another way is a thief and a bandit. 2 The one who enters by the gate is the shepherd of the sheep. 3 The gatekeeper opens the gate for him, and the sheep hear his voice. He calls his own sheep by name and leads them out. 4 When he has brought out all his own, he goes ahead of them, and the sheep follow him because they know his voice. 5 They will not follow a stranger, but they will run from him because they do not know the voice of strangers." 6 Jesus used this figure of speech with them, but they did not understand what he was saying to them.

7 So again Jesus said to them, "Very truly, I tell you, I am the gate for the sheep. 8 All who came before me are thieves and bandits; but the sheep did not listen to them. 9 I am the gate. Whoever enters by me will be saved, and will come in and go out and find pasture. 10 The thief comes only to steal and kill and destroy. I came that they may have life, and have it abundantly.

11 "I am the good shepherd. The

e Other ancient authorities read *the Son of God*
f *Sir* and *Lord* translate the same Greek word
g *Sir* and *Lord* translate the same Greek word

good shepherd lays down his life for the sheep. [12]The hired hand, who is not the shepherd and does not own the sheep, sees the wolf coming and leaves the sheep and runs away—and the wolf snatches them and scatters them. [13]The hired hand runs away because a hired hand does not care for the sheep. [14]I am the good shepherd. I know my own and my own know me, [15]just as the Father knows me and I know the Father. And I lay down my life for the sheep. [16]I have other sheep that do not belong to this fold. I must bring them also, and they will listen to my voice. So there will be one flock, one shepherd. [17]For this reason the Father loves me, because I lay down my life in order to take it up again. [18]No one takes[a] it from me, but I lay it down of my own accord. I have power to lay it down, and I have power to take it up again. I have received this command from my Father."

19 Again the Jews were divided because of these words. [20]Many of them were saying, "He has a demon and is out of his mind. Why listen to him?" [21]Others were saying, "These are not the words of one who has a demon. Can a demon open the eyes of the blind?"

Jesus Is Rejected by the Jews

22 At that time the festival of the Dedication took place in Jerusalem. It was winter, [23]and Jesus was walking in the temple, in the portico of Solomon. [24]So the Jews gathered around him and said to him, "How long will you keep us in suspense? If you are the Messiah,[b] tell us plainly." [25]Jesus answered, "I have told you, and you do not believe. The works that I do in my Father's name testify to me; [26]but you do not believe, because you do not belong to my sheep. [27]My sheep hear my voice. I know them, and they follow me. [28]I give them eternal life, and they will never perish. No one will snatch them out of my hand. [29]What my Father has given me is greater than all else, and no one can snatch it out of the Father's hand.[c] [30]The Father and I are one."

31 The Jews took up stones again to stone him. [32]Jesus replied, "I have shown you many good works from the Father. For which of these are you going to stone me?" [33]The Jews answered, "It is not for a good work that we are going to stone you, but for blasphemy, because you, though only a human being, are making yourself God." [34]Jesus answered, "Is it not written in your law,[d] 'I said, you are gods'? [35]If those to whom the word of God came were called 'gods'—and the scripture cannot be annulled— [36]can you say that the one whom the Father has sanctified and sent into the world is blaspheming because I said, 'I am God's Son'? [37]If I am not doing the works of my Father, then do not believe me. [38]But if I do them, even though you do not believe me, believe the works, so that you may know and under-

a Other ancient authorities read *has taken*
b Or *the Christ* *c* Other ancient authorities read *My Father who has given them to me is greater than all, and no one can snatch them out of the Father's hand* *d* Other ancient authorities read *in the law*

stand[e] that the Father is in me and I
am in the Father." 39 Then they tried
to arrest him again, but he escaped
from their hands.

40 He went away again across the
Jordan to the place where John had
been baptizing earlier, and he remained there. 41 Many came to him,
and they were saying, "John performed no sign, but everything that
John said about this man was true."
42 And many believed in him there.

The Death of Lazarus

11 Now a certain man was ill,
Lazarus of Bethany, the village of Mary and her sister Martha.
2 Mary was the one who anointed
the Lord with perfume and wiped
his feet with her hair; her brother Lazarus was ill. 3 So the sisters
sent a message to Jesus,[a] "Lord, he
whom you love is ill." 4 But when
Jesus heard it, he said, "This illness
does not lead to death; rather it is
for God's glory, so that the Son of
God may be glorified through it."
5 Accordingly, though Jesus loved
Martha and her sister and Lazarus,
6 after having heard that Lazarus[b]
was ill, he stayed two days longer
in the place where he was.

7 Then after this he said to the disciples, "Let us go to Judea again."
8 The disciples said to him, "Rabbi,
the Jews were just now trying to
stone you, and are you going there
again?" 9 Jesus answered, "Are
there not twelve hours of daylight?
Those who walk during the day do
not stumble, because they see the
light of this world. 10 But those who
walk at night stumble, because the
light is not in them." 11 After saying this, he told them, "Our friend
Lazarus has fallen asleep, but I am
going there to awaken him." 12 The
disciples said to him, "Lord, if he
has fallen asleep, he will be all
right." 13 Jesus, however, had been
speaking about his death, but they
thought that he was referring mere-
ly to sleep. 14 Then Jesus told them
plainly, "Lazarus is dead. 15 For
your sake I am glad I was not there,
so that you may believe. But let us
go to him." 16 Thomas, who was
called the Twin,[c] said to his fellow
disciples, "Let us also go, that we
may die with him."

Jesus the Resurrection and the Life

17 When Jesus arrived, he found
that Lazarus[d] had already been in
the tomb four days. 18 Now Bethany was near Jerusalem, some two
miles[e] away, 19 and many of the
Jews had come to Martha and Mary
to console them about their brother. 20 When Martha heard that Jesus
was coming, she went and met him,
while Mary stayed at home. 21 Martha said to Jesus, "Lord, if you had
been here, my brother would not
have died. 22 But even now I know
that God will give you whatever
you ask of him." 23 Jesus said to
her, "Your brother will rise again."
24 Martha said to him, "I know that
he will rise again in the resurrection on the last day." 25 Jesus said
to her, "I am the resurrection and
the life.[f] Those who believe in me,
even though they die, will live,

---

e Other ancient authorities lack *and understand*; others read *and believe* *a* Gk *him* *b* Gk *he* *c* Gk *Didymus* *d* Gk *he* *e* Gk *fifteen stadia* *f* Other ancient authorities lack *and the life*

26 and everyone who lives and believes in me will never die. Do you
believe this?" 27 She said to him,
"Yes, Lord, I believe that you are
the Messiah,[g] the Son of God, the
one coming into the world."

Jesus Weeps

28 When she had said this, she
went back and called her sister
Mary, and told her privately, "The
Teacher is here and is calling for
you." 29 And when she heard it, she
got up quickly and went to him.
30 Now Jesus had not yet come
to the village, but was still at the
place where Martha had met him.
31 The Jews who were with her
in the house, consoling her, saw
Mary get up quickly and go out.
They followed her because they
thought that she was going to the
tomb to weep there. 32 When Mary
came where Jesus was and saw
him, she knelt at his feet and said
to him, "Lord, if you had been here,
my brother would not have died."
33 When Jesus saw her weeping, and
the Jews who came with her also
weeping, he was greatly disturbed
in spirit and deeply moved. 34 He
said, "Where have you laid him?"
They said to him, "Lord, come and
see." 35 Jesus began to weep. 36 So
the Jews said, "See how he loved
him!" 37 But some of them said,
"Could not he who opened the eyes
of the blind man have kept this man
from dying?"

Jesus Raises Lazarus to Life

38 Then Jesus, again greatly
disturbed, came to the tomb. It
was a cave, and a stone was lying
against it. 39 Jesus said, "Take away
the stone." Martha, the sister of
the dead man, said to him, "Lord,
already there is a stench because
he has been dead four days." 40 Jesus said to her, "Did I not tell you
that if you believed, you would see
the glory of God?" 41 So they took
away the stone. And Jesus looked
upward and said, "Father, I thank
you for having heard me. 42 I knew
that you always hear me, but I have
said this for the sake of the crowd
standing here, so that they may believe that you sent me." 43 When he
had said this, he cried with a loud
voice, "Lazarus, come out!" 44 The
dead man came out, his hands and
feet bound with strips of cloth, and
his face wrapped in a cloth. Jesus
said to them, "Unbind him, and let
him go."

The Plot to Kill Jesus

45 Many of the Jews therefore,
who had come with Mary and had
seen what Jesus did, believed in
him. 46 But some of them went to
the Pharisees and told them what
he had done. 47 So the chief priests
and the Pharisees called a meeting
of the council, and said, "What are
we to do? This man is performing
many signs. 48 If we let him go on
like this, everyone will believe in
him, and the Romans will come
and destroy both our holy place[h]
and our nation." 49 But one of them,
Caiaphas, who was high priest that
year, said to them, "You know
nothing at all! 50 You do not understand that it is better for you to have

g Or *the Christ* *h* Or *our temple*; Greek *our place*

one man die for the people than to
have the whole nation destroyed."
51 He did not say this on his own,
but being high priest that year he
prophesied that Jesus was about to
die for the nation, 52 and not for the
nation only, but to gather into one
the dispersed children of God. 53 So
from that day on they planned to
put him to death.

54 Jesus therefore no longer
walked about openly among the
Jews, but went from there to a town
called Ephraim in the region near
the wilderness; and he remained
there with the disciples.

55 Now the Passover of the Jews
was near, and many went up from
the country to Jerusalem before
the Passover to purify themselves.
56 They were looking for Jesus and
were asking one another as they
stood in the temple, "What do you
think? Surely he will not come to
the festival, will he?" 57 Now the
chief priests and the Pharisees had
given orders that anyone who knew
where Jesus[i] was should let them
know, so that they might arrest him.

Mary Anoints Jesus

12 Six days before the Passover
Jesus came to Bethany, the
home of Lazarus, whom he had
raised from the dead. 2 There they
gave a dinner for him. Martha
served, and Lazarus was one of
those at the table with him. 3 Mary
took a pound of costly perfume
made of pure nard, anointed Jesus'
feet, and wiped them[a] with her hair.
The house was filled with the fra-
grance of the perfume. 4 But Judas
Iscariot, one of his disciples (the
one who was about to betray him),
said, 5 "Why was this perfume not
sold for three hundred denarii[b] and
the money given to the poor?" 6 (He
said this not because he cared about
the poor, but because he was a thief;
he kept the common purse and used
to steal what was put into it.) 7 Jesus
said, "Leave her alone. She bought
it[c] so that she might keep it for the
day of my burial. 8 You always have
the poor with you, but you do not
always have me."

The Plot to Kill Lazarus

9 When the great crowd of the
Jews learned that he was there, they
came not only because of Jesus but
also to see Lazarus, whom he had
raised from the dead. 10 So the chief
priests planned to put Lazarus to
death as well, 11 since it was on account of him that many of the Jews
were deserting and were believing
in Jesus.

Jesus' Triumphal Entry into Jerusalem

12 The next day the great crowd
that had come to the festival heard
that Jesus was coming to Jerusalem. 13 So they took branches of
palm trees and went out to meet
him, shouting,

"Hosanna!
Blessed is the one who comes in
the name of the Lord—
the King of Israel!"

14 Jesus found a young donkey and
sat on it; as it is written:

---

i Gk *he* *a* Gk *his feet* *b* Three hundred denarii would be nearly a year's wages for a laborer *c* Gk lacks *She bought it*

15 "Do not be afraid, daughter of
Zion.
Look, your king is coming,
sitting on a donkey's colt!"

16 His disciples did not understand these things at first; but when Jesus was glorified, then they remembered that these things had been written of him and had been done to him. 17 So the crowd that had been with him when he called Lazarus out of the tomb and raised him from the dead continued to testify.[d] 18 It was also because they heard that he had performed this sign that the crowd went to meet him. 19 The Pharisees then said to one another, "You see, you can do nothing. Look, the world has gone after him!"

Some Greeks Wish to See Jesus

20 Now among those who went up to worship at the festival were some Greeks. 21 They came to Philip, who was from Bethsaida in Galilee, and said to him, "Sir, we wish to see Jesus." 22 Philip went and told Andrew; then Andrew and Philip went and told Jesus. 23 Jesus answered them, "The hour has come for the Son of Man to be glorified. 24 Very truly, I tell you, unless a grain of wheat falls into the earth and dies, it remains just a single grain; but if it dies, it bears much fruit. 25 Those who love their life lose it, and those who hate their life in this world will keep it for eternal life. 26 Whoever serves me must follow me, and where I am, there will my servant be also. Whoever serves me, the Father will honor.

Jesus Speaks about His Death

27 "Now my soul is troubled. And what should I say—'Father, save me from this hour'? No, it is for this reason that I have come to this hour. 28 Father, glorify your name." Then a voice came from heaven, "I have glorified it, and I will glorify it again." 29 The crowd standing there heard it and said that it was thunder. Others said, "An angel has spoken to him." 30 Jesus answered, "This voice has come for your sake, not for mine. 31 Now is the judgment of this world; now the ruler of this world will be driven out. 32 And I, when I am lifted up from the earth, will draw all people[e] to myself." 33 He said this to indicate the kind of death he was to die. 34 The crowd answered him, "We have heard from the law that the Messiah[f] remains forever. How can you say that the Son of Man must be lifted up? Who is this Son of Man?" 35 Jesus said to them, "The light is with you for a little longer. Walk while you have the light, so that the darkness may not overtake you. If you walk in the darkness, you do not know where you are going. 36 While you have the light, believe in the light, so that you may become children of light."

The Unbelief of the People

After Jesus had said this, he departed and hid from them. 37 Although he had performed so many signs in their presence, they did not

---

d Other ancient authorities read *with him began to testify that he had called . . . from the dead* *e* Other ancient authorities read *all things* *f* Or *the Christ*

believe in him. [38]This was to fulfill
the word spoken by the prophet
Isaiah:

"Lord, who has believed our
message,
and to whom has the arm of
the Lord been revealed?"

[39]And so they could not believe,
because Isaiah also said,
[40]"He has blinded their eyes
and hardened their heart,
so that they might not look with
their eyes,
and understand with their
heart and turn—
and I would heal them."

[41]Isaiah said this because[g] he saw
his glory and spoke about him.
[42]Nevertheless many, even of the
authorities, believed in him. But
because of the Pharisees they did
not confess it, for fear that they
would be put out of the synagogue;
[43]for they loved human glory more
than the glory that comes from
God.

Summary of Jesus' Teaching

44 Then Jesus cried aloud:
"Whoever believes in me believes
not in me but in him who sent me.
[45]And whoever sees me sees him
who sent me. [46]I have come as
light into the world, so that everyone who believes in me should not
remain in the darkness. [47]I do not
judge anyone who hears my words
and does not keep them, for I came
not to judge the world, but to save
the world. [48]The one who rejects
me and does not receive my word
has a judge; on the last day the
word that I have spoken will serve
as judge, [49]for I have not spoken on
my own, but the Father who sent
me has himself given me a commandment about what to say and
what to speak. [50]And I know that
his commandment is eternal life.
What I speak, therefore, I speak just
as the Father has told me."

Jesus Washes the Disciples' Feet

13 Now before the festival of
the Passover, Jesus knew that
his hour had come to depart from
this world and go to the Father.
Having loved his own who were
in the world, he loved them to the
end. [2]The devil had already put it
into the heart of Judas son of Simon
Iscariot to betray him. And during
supper [3]Jesus, knowing that the
Father had given all things into his
hands, and that he had come from
God and was going to God, [4]got up
from the table,[a] took off his outer
robe, and tied a towel around himself. [5]Then he poured water into a
basin and began to wash the disciples' feet and to wipe them with the
towel that was tied around him. [6]He
came to Simon Peter, who said to
him, "Lord, are you going to wash
my feet?" [7]Jesus answered, "You
do not know now what I am doing, but later you will understand."
[8]Peter said to him, "You will never wash my feet." Jesus answered,
"Unless I wash you, you have no
share with me." [9]Simon Peter said
to him, "Lord, not my feet only
but also my hands and my head!"
[10]Jesus said to him, "One who has
bathed does not need to wash, ex-

---

g Other ancient witnesses read *when*
a Gk *from supper*

cept for the feet,[b] but is entirely
clean. And you[c] are clean, though
not all of you." 11 For he knew who
was to betray him; for this reason
he said, "Not all of you are clean."
12 After he had washed their
feet, had put on his robe, and had
returned to the table, he said to
them, "Do you know what I have
done to you? 13 You call me Teacher
and Lord—and you are right, for
that is what I am. 14 So if I, your
Lord and Teacher, have washed
your feet, you also ought to wash
one another's feet. 15 For I have
set you an example, that you also
should do as I have done to you.
16 Very truly, I tell you, servants[d] are
not greater than their master, nor
are messengers greater than the one
who sent them. 17 If you know these
things, you are blessed if you do
them. 18 I am not speaking of all of
you; I know whom I have chosen.
But it is to fulfill the scripture, 'The
one who ate my bread[e] has lifted
his heel against me.' 19 I tell you this
now, before it occurs, so that when
it does occur, you may believe that
I am he.[f] 20 Very truly, I tell you,
whoever receives one whom I send
receives me; and whoever receives
me receives him who sent me."

Jesus Foretells His Betrayal

21 After saying this Jesus was
troubled in spirit, and declared,
"Very truly, I tell you, one of you
will betray me." 22 The disciples
looked at one another, uncertain of
whom he was speaking. 23 One of
his disciples—the one whom Jesus
loved—was reclining next to him;
24 Simon Peter therefore motioned
to him to ask Jesus of whom he
was speaking. 25 So while reclining
next to Jesus, he asked him, "Lord,
who is it?" 26 Jesus answered, "It is
the one to whom I give this piece
of bread when I have dipped it in
the dish."[g] So when he had dipped
the piece of bread, he gave it to Judas son of Simon Iscariot.[h] 27 After
he received the piece of bread,[i]
Satan entered into him. Jesus said
to him, "Do quickly what you are
going to do." 28 Now no one at the
table knew why he said this to him.
29 Some thought that, because Judas
had the common purse, Jesus was
telling him, "Buy what we need
for the festival"; or, that he should
give something to the poor. 30 So,
after receiving the piece of bread,
he immediately went out. And it
was night.

The New Commandment

31 When he had gone out, Jesus
said, "Now the Son of Man has
been glorified, and God has been
glorified in him. 32 If God has been
glorified in him,[j] God will also glorify him in himself and will glorify
him at once. 33 Little children, I am
with you only a little longer. You
will look for me; and as I said to the
Jews so now I say to you, 'Where
I am going, you cannot come.' 34 I
give you a new commandment, that
you love one another. Just as I have

---

b Other ancient authorities lack *except for the feet* *c* The Greek word for *you* here is plural *d* Gk *slaves* *e* Other ancient authorities read *ate bread with me* *f* Gk *I am* *g* Gk *dipped it* *h* Other ancient authorities read *Judas Iscariot son of Simon*; others, *Judas son of Simon from Karyot* (Kerioth) *i* Gk *After the piece of bread* *j* Other ancient authorities lack *If God has been glorified in him*

loved you, you also should love one another. 35 By this everyone will know that you are my disciples, if you have love for one another.”

Jesus Foretells Peter’s Denial

36 Simon Peter said to him, “Lord, where are you going?” Jesus answered, “Where I am going, you cannot follow me now; but you will follow afterward.” 37 Peter said to him, “Lord, why can I not follow you now? I will lay down my life for you.” 38 Jesus answered, “Will you lay down your life for me? Very truly, I tell you, before the cock crows, you will have denied me three times.

Jesus the Way to the Father

14 “Do not let your hearts be troubled. Believe[a] in God, believe also in me. 2 In my Father’s house there are many dwelling places. If it were not so, would I have told you that I go to prepare a place for you?[b] 3 And if I go and prepare a place for you, I will come again and will take you to myself, so that where I am, there you may be also. 4 And you know the way to the place where I am going.”[c] 5 Thomas said to him, “Lord, we do not know where you are going. How can we know the way?” 6 Jesus said to him, “I am the way, and the truth, and the life. No one comes to the Father except through me. 7 If you know me, you will know[d] my Father also. From now on you do know him and have seen him.”

8 Philip said to him, “Lord, show us the Father, and we will be satisfied.” 9 Jesus said to him, “Have I been with you all this time, Philip, and you still do not know me? Whoever has seen me has seen the Father. How can you say, ‘Show us the Father’? 10 Do you not believe that I am in the Father and the Father is in me? The words that I say to you I do not speak on my own; but the Father who dwells in me does his works. 11 Believe me that I am in the Father and the Father is in me; but if you do not, then believe me because of the works themselves. 12 Very truly, I tell you, the one who believes in me will also do the works that I do and, in fact, will do greater works than these, because I am going to the Father. 13 I will do whatever you ask in my name, so that the Father may be glorified in the Son. 14 If in my name you ask me[e] for anything, I will do it.

The Promise of the Holy Spirit

15 “If you love me, you will keep[f] my commandments. 16 And I will ask the Father, and he will give you another Advocate,[g] to be with you forever. 17 This is the Spirit of truth, whom the world cannot receive, because it neither sees him nor knows him. You know him, because he abides with you, and he will be in[h] you.

18 “I will not leave you orphaned; I am coming to you. 19 In

---

a Or *You believe* *b* Or *If it were not so, I would have told you; for I go to prepare a place for you* *c* Other ancient authorities read *Where I am going you know, and the way you know* *d* Other ancient authorities read *If you had known me, you would have known* *e* Other ancient authorities lack *me* *f* Other ancient authorities read *me, keep* *g* Or *Helper* *h* Or *among*

a little while the world will no longer see me, but you will see me; because I live, you also will live. [20]On that day you will know that I am in my Father, and you in me, and I in you. [21]They who have my commandments and keep them are those who love me; and those who love me will be loved by my Father, and I will love them and reveal myself to them." [22]Judas (not Iscariot) said to him, "Lord, how is it that you will reveal yourself to us, and not to the world?" [23]Jesus answered him, "Those who love me will keep my word, and my Father will love them, and we will come to them and make our home with them. [24]Whoever does not love me does not keep my words; and the word that you hear is not mine, but is from the Father who sent me.

25 "I have said these things to you while I am still with you. [26]But the Advocate,[i] the Holy Spirit, whom the Father will send in my name, will teach you everything, and remind you of all that I have said to you. [27]Peace I leave with you; my peace I give to you. I do not give to you as the world gives. Do not let your hearts be troubled, and do not let them be afraid. [28]You heard me say to you, 'I am going away, and I am coming to you.' If you loved me, you would rejoice that I am going to the Father, because the Father is greater than I. [29]And now I have told you this before it occurs, so that when it does occur, you may believe. [30]I will no longer talk much with you, for the ruler of this world is coming. He has no power over me; [31]but I do as the Father has commanded me, so that the world may know that I love the Father. Rise, let us be on our way.

Jesus the True Vine

15 "I am the true vine, and my Father is the vinegrower. [2]He removes every branch in me that bears no fruit. Every branch that bears fruit he prunes[a] to make it bear more fruit. [3]You have already been cleansed[b] by the word that I have spoken to you. [4]Abide in me as I abide in you. Just as the branch cannot bear fruit by itself unless it abides in the vine, neither can you unless you abide in me. [5]I am the vine, you are the branches. Those who abide in me and I in them bear much fruit, because apart from me you can do nothing. [6]Whoever does not abide in me is thrown away like a branch and withers; such branches are gathered, thrown into the fire, and burned. [7]If you abide in me, and my words abide in you, ask for whatever you wish, and it will be done for you. [8]My Father is glorified by this, that you bear much fruit and become[c] my disciples. [9]As the Father has loved me, so I have loved you; abide in my love. [10]If you keep my commandments, you will abide in my love, just as I have kept my Father's commandments and abide in his love. [11]I have said these things to you so that my joy may be in you, and that your joy may be complete.

12 "This is my command-

i Or *Helper* *a* The same Greek root refers to pruning and cleansing *b* The same Greek root refers to pruning and cleansing *c* Or *be*

ment, that you love one another as I have loved you. 13 No one has greater love than this, to lay down one's life for one's friends. 14 You are my friends if you do what I command you. 15 I do not call you servants[d] any longer, because the servant[e] does not know what the master is doing; but I have called you friends, because I have made known to you everything that I have heard from my Father. 16 You did not choose me but I chose you. And I appointed you to go and bear fruit, fruit that will last, so that the Father will give you whatever you ask him in my name. 17 I am giving you these commands so that you may love one another.

The World's Hatred

18 "If the world hates you, be aware that it hated me before it hated you. 19 If you belonged to the world,[f] the world would love you as its own. Because you do not belong to the world, but I have chosen you out of the world—therefore the world hates you. 20 Remember the word that I said to you, 'Servants[g] are not greater than their master.' If they persecuted me, they will persecute you; if they kept my word, they will keep yours also. 21 But they will do all these things to you on account of my name, because they do not know him who sent me. 22 If I had not come and spoken to them, they would not have sin; but now they have no excuse for their sin. 23 Whoever hates me hates my Father also. 24 If I had not done among them the works that no one else did, they would not have sin. But now they have seen and hated both me and my Father. 25 It was to fulfill the word that is written in their law, 'They hated me without a cause.'

26 "When the Advocate[h] comes, whom I will send to you from the Father, the Spirit of truth who comes from the Father, he will testify on my behalf. 27 You also are to testify because you have been with me from the beginning.

16 "I have said these things to you to keep you from stumbling. 2 They will put you out of the synagogues. Indeed, an hour is coming when those who kill you will think that by doing so they are offering worship to God. 3 And they will do this because they have not known the Father or me. 4 But I have said these things to you so that when their hour comes you may remember that I told you about them.

The Work of the Spirit

"I did not say these things to you from the beginning, because I was with you. 5 But now I am going to him who sent me; yet none of you asks me, 'Where are you going?' 6 But because I have said these things to you, sorrow has filled your hearts. 7 Nevertheless I tell you the truth: it is to your advantage that I go away, for if I do not go away, the Advocate[a] will not come to you; but if I go, I will send him to you. 8 And when he comes, he will prove the world wrong about[b] sin

---

d Gk *slaves* *e* Gk *slave* *f* Gk *were of the world* *g* Gk *Slaves* *h* Or *Helper*
a Or *Helper* *b* Or *convict the world of*

and righteousness and judgment:
9 about sin, because they do not believe in me; 10 about righteousness,
because I am going to the Father
and you will see me no longer;
11 about judgment, because the ruler
of this world has been condemned.
12 "I still have many things to
say to you, but you cannot bear
them now. 13 When the Spirit of
truth comes, he will guide you into
all the truth; for he will not speak
on his own, but will speak whatever he hears, and he will declare
to you the things that are to come.
14 He will glorify me, because he
will take what is mine and declare
it to you. 15 All that the Father has is
mine. For this reason I said that he
will take what is mine and declare
it to you.

Sorrow Will Turn into Joy

16 "A little while, and you will
no longer see me, and again a little
while, and you will see me." 17 Then
some of his disciples said to one another, "What does he mean by saying to us, 'A little while, and you
will no longer see me, and again a
little while, and you will see me';
and 'Because I am going to the Father'?" 18 They said, "What does he
mean by this 'a little while'? We do
not know what he is talking about."
19 Jesus knew that they wanted to
ask him, so he said to them, "Are
you discussing among yourselves
what I meant when I said, 'A little
while, and you will no longer see
me, and again a little while, and
you will see me'? 20 Very truly, I
tell you, you will weep and mourn,
but the world will rejoice; you will
have pain, but your pain will turn
into joy. 21 When a woman is in
labor, she has pain, because her
hour has come. But when her child
is born, she no longer remembers
the anguish because of the joy of
having brought a human being into
the world. 22 So you have pain now;
but I will see you again, and your
hearts will rejoice, and no one will
take your joy from you. 23 On that
day you will ask nothing of me.[c]
Very truly, I tell you, if you ask
anything of the Father in my name,
he will give it to you.[d] 24 Until now
you have not asked for anything in
my name. Ask and you will receive,
so that your joy may be complete.

Peace for the Disciples

25 "I have said these things to
you in figures of speech. The hour
is coming when I will no longer
speak to you in figures, but will tell
you plainly of the Father. 26 On that
day you will ask in my name. I do
not say to you that I will ask the
Father on your behalf; 27 for the Father himself loves you, because you
have loved me and have believed
that I came from God.[e] 28 I came
from the Father and have come into
the world; again, I am leaving the
world and am going to the Father."
29 His disciples said, "Yes, now
you are speaking plainly, not in any
figure of speech! 30 Now we know
that you know all things, and do not
need to have anyone question you;
by this we believe that you came

---

c Or *will ask me no question* d Other ancient authorities read *Father, he will give it to you in my name* e Other ancient authorities read *the Father* from God." 31 Jesus answered them, "Do you now believe? 32 The hour is coming, indeed it has come, when you will be scattered, each one to his home, and you will leave me alone. Yet I am not alone because the Father is with me. 33 I have said this to you, so that in me you may have peace. In the world you face persecution. But take courage; I have conquered the world!"

Jesus Prays for His Disciples

17 After Jesus had spoken these words, he looked up to heaven and said, "Father, the hour has come; glorify your Son so that the Son may glorify you, 2 since you have given him authority over all people,[a] to give eternal life to all whom you have given him. 3 And this is eternal life, that they may know you, the only true God, and Jesus Christ whom you have sent. 4 I glorified you on earth by finishing the work that you gave me to do. 5 So now, Father, glorify me in your own presence with the glory that I had in your presence before the world existed.

6 "I have made your name known to those whom you gave me from the world. They were yours, and you gave them to me, and they have kept your word. 7 Now they know that everything you have given me is from you; 8 for the words that you gave to me I have given to them, and they have received them and know in truth that I came from you; and they have believed that you sent me. 9 I am asking on their behalf; I am not asking on behalf of the world, but on behalf of those whom you gave me, because they are yours. 10 All mine are yours, and yours are mine; and I have been glorified in them. 11 And now I am no longer in the world, but they are in the world, and I am coming to you. Holy Father, protect them in your name that you have given me, so that they may be one, as we are one. 12 While I was with them, I protected them in your name that[b] you have given me. I guarded them, and not one of them was lost except the one destined to be lost,[c] so that the scripture might be fulfilled. 13 But now I am coming to you, and I speak these things in the world so that they may have my joy made complete in themselves.[d] 14 I have given them your word, and the world has hated them because they do not belong to the world, just as I do not belong to the world. 15 I am not asking you to take them out of the world, but I ask you to protect them from the evil one.[e] 16 They do not belong to the world, just as I do not belong to the world. 17 Sanctify them in the truth; your word is truth. 18 As you have sent me into the world, so I have sent them into the world. 19 And for their sakes I sanctify myself, so that they also may be sanctified in truth.

20 "I ask not only on behalf of these, but also on behalf of those who will believe in me through their word, 21 that they may all be one. As you, Father, are in me and I am in you, may they also be in

---

a Gk *flesh* *b* Other ancient authorities read *protected in your name those whom* *c* Gk *except the son of destruction* *d* Or *among themselves* *e* Or *from evil*

us,[f] so that the world may believe that you have sent me. 22 The glory that you have given me I have given them, so that they may be one, as we are one, 23 I in them and you in me, that they may become completely one, so that the world may know that you have sent me and have loved them even as you have loved me. 24 Father, I desire that those also, whom you have given me, may be with me where I am, to see my glory, which you have given me because you loved me before the foundation of the world.

25 "Righteous Father, the world does not know you, but I know you; and these know that you have sent me. 26 I made your name known to them, and I will make it known, so that the love with which you have loved me may be in them, and I in them."

The Betrayal and Arrest of Jesus

18 After Jesus had spoken these words, he went out with his disciples across the Kidron valley to a place where there was a garden, which he and his disciples entered. 2 Now Judas, who betrayed him, also knew the place, because Jesus often met there with his disciples. 3 So Judas brought a detachment of soldiers together with police from the chief priests and the Pharisees, and they came there with lanterns and torches and weapons. 4 Then Jesus, knowing all that was to happen to him, came forward and asked them, "Whom are you looking for?" 5 They answered, "Jesus of Nazareth."[a] Jesus replied, "I am he."[b] Judas, who betrayed him, was standing with them. 6 When Jesus[c] said to them, "I am he,"[d] they stepped back and fell to the ground. 7 Again he asked them, "Whom are you looking for?" And they said, "Jesus of Nazareth."[e] 8 Jesus answered, "I told you that I am he.[f] So if you are looking for me, let these men go." 9 This was to fulfill the word that he had spoken, "I did not lose a single one of those whom you gave me." 10 Then Simon Peter, who had a sword, drew it, struck the high priest's slave, and cut off his right ear. The slave's name was Malchus. 11 Jesus said to Peter, "Put your sword back into its sheath. Am I not to drink the cup that the Father has given me?"

Jesus before the High Priest

12 So the soldiers, their officer, and the Jewish police arrested Jesus and bound him. 13 First they took him to Annas, who was the father-in-law of Caiaphas, the high priest that year. 14 Caiaphas was the one who had advised the Jews that it was better to have one person die for the people.

Peter Denies Jesus

15 Simon Peter and another disciple followed Jesus. Since that disciple was known to the high priest, he went with Jesus into the courtyard of the high priest, 16 but Peter was standing outside at the gate. So the other disciple, who was known to the high priest, went out, spoke

---

f Other ancient authorities read *be one in us*
a Gk *the Nazorean* *b* Gk *I am* *c* Gk *he*
d Gk *I am* *e* Gk *the Nazorean* *f* Gk *I am*

to the woman who guarded the
gate, and brought Peter in. 17 The
woman said to Peter, "You are not
also one of this man's disciples, are
you?" He said, "I am not." 18 Now
the slaves and the police had made
a charcoal fire because it was cold,
and they were standing around it
and warming themselves. Peter
also was standing with them and
warming himself.

The High Priest Questions Jesus

19 Then the high priest questioned Jesus about his disciples
and about his teaching. 20 Jesus
answered, "I have spoken openly
to the world; I have always taught
in synagogues and in the temple,
where all the Jews come together. I have said nothing in secret.
21 Why do you ask me? Ask those
who heard what I said to them; they
know what I said." 22 When he had
said this, one of the police standing
nearby struck Jesus on the face,
saying, "Is that how you answer the
high priest?" 23 Jesus answered, "If I
have spoken wrongly, testify to the
wrong. But if I have spoken rightly,
why do you strike me?" 24 Then Annas sent him bound to Caiaphas the
high priest.

Peter Denies Jesus Again

25 Now Simon Peter was standing and warming himself. They
asked him, "You are not also one of
his disciples, are you?" He denied
it and said, "I am not." 26 One of the
slaves of the high priest, a relative
of the man whose ear Peter had cut
off, asked, "Did I not see you in the
garden with him?" 27 Again Peter
denied it, and at that moment the
cock crowed.

Jesus before Pilate

28 Then they took Jesus from
Caiaphas to Pilate's headquarters.[g]
It was early in the morning. They
themselves did not enter the headquarters,[h] so as to avoid ritual de-
filement and to be able to eat the
Passover. 29 So Pilate went out to
them and said, "What accusation
do you bring against this man?"
30 They answered, "If this man were
not a criminal, we would not have
handed him over to you." 31 Pilate
said to them, "Take him yourselves
and judge him according to your
law." The Jews replied, "We are not
permitted to put anyone to death."
32 (This was to fulfill what Jesus had
said when he indicated the kind of
death he was to die.)

33 Then Pilate entered the headquarters[i] again, summoned Jesus,
and asked him, "Are you the King
of the Jews?" 34 Jesus answered,
"Do you ask this on your own, or
did others tell you about me?" 35 Pilate replied, "I am not a Jew, am
I? Your own nation and the chief
priests have handed you over to
me. What have you done?" 36 Jesus answered, "My kingdom is not
from this world. If my kingdom
were from this world, my followers
would be fighting to keep me from
being handed over to the Jews. But
as it is, my kingdom is not from
here." 37 Pilate asked him, "So you
are a king?" Jesus answered, "You
say that I am a king. For this I was

---

g Gk *the praetorium* *h* Gk *the praetorium*
i Gk *the praetorium*

born, and for this I came into the
world, to testify to the truth. Everyone who belongs to the truth listens
to my voice." 38 Pilate asked him,
"What is truth?"

Jesus Sentenced to Death

After he had said this, he went out
to the Jews again and told them, "I
find no case against him. 39 But you
have a custom that I release someone for you at the Passover. Do you
want me to release for you the King
of the Jews?" 40 They shouted in reply, "Not this man, but Barabbas!"
Now Barabbas was a bandit.

19 Then Pilate took Jesus and
had him flogged. 2 And the
soldiers wove a crown of thorns
and put it on his head, and they
dressed him in a purple robe. 3 They
kept coming up to him, saying,
"Hail, King of the Jews!" and strik-
ing him on the face. 4 Pilate went
out again and said to them, "Look,
I am bringing him out to you to let
you know that I find no case against
him." 5 So Jesus came out, wearing
the crown of thorns and the purple
robe. Pilate said to them, "Here is
the man!" 6 When the chief priests
and the police saw him, they shouted, "Crucify him! Crucify him!"
Pilate said to them, "Take him
yourselves and crucify him; I find
no case against him." 7 The Jews
answered him, "We have a law, and
according to that law he ought to
die because he has claimed to be
the Son of God."
8 Now when Pilate heard this,
he was more afraid than ever. 9 He
entered his headquarters[a] again
and asked Jesus, "Where are you
from?" But Jesus gave him no answer. 10 Pilate therefore said to him,
"Do you refuse to speak to me? Do
you not know that I have power
to release you, and power to crucify you?" 11 Jesus answered him,
"You would have no power over
me unless it had been given you
from above; therefore the one who
handed me over to you is guilty of
a greater sin." 12 From then on Pilate
tried to release him, but the Jews
cried out, "If you release this man,
you are no friend of the emperor.
Everyone who claims to be a king
sets himself against the emperor."
13 When Pilate heard these
words, he brought Jesus outside
and sat[b] on the judge's bench at a
place called The Stone Pavement,
or in Hebrew[c] Gabbatha. 14 Now it
was the day of Preparation for the
Passover; and it was about noon.
He said to the Jews, "Here is your
King!" 15 They cried out, "Away
with him! Away with him! Crucify him!" Pilate asked them, "Shall
I crucify your King?" The chief
priests answered, "We have no king
but the emperor." 16 Then he handed
him over to them to be crucified.

The Crucifixion of Jesus

So they took Jesus; 17 and carrying
the cross by himself, he went out
to what is called The Place of the
Skull, which in Hebrew[d] is called
Golgotha. 18 There they crucified
him, and with him two others, one
on either side, with Jesus between
them. 19 Pilate also had an inscrip-

a Gk *the praetorium* *b* Or *seated him* *c* That is, *Aramaic* *d* That is, *Aramaic*

tion written and put on the cross.
It read, "Jesus of Nazareth,[e] the
King of the Jews." [20]Many of the
Jews read this inscription, because
the place where Jesus was crucified
was near the city; and it was written
in Hebrew,[f] in Latin, and in Greek.
[21]Then the chief priests of the Jews
said to Pilate, "Do not write, 'The
King of the Jews,' but, 'This man
said, I am King of the Jews.'"
[22]Pilate answered, "What I have
written I have written." [23]When the
soldiers had crucified Jesus, they
took his clothes and divided them
into four parts, one for each soldier.
They also took his tunic; now the
tunic was seamless, woven in one
piece from the top. [24]So they said
to one another, "Let us not tear it,
but cast lots for it to see who will
get it." This was to fulfill what the
scripture says,

"They divided my clothes among
themselves,
and for my clothing they cast
lots."

[25]And that is what the soldiers did.
Meanwhile, standing near the
cross of Jesus were his mother,
and his mother's sister, Mary the
wife of Clopas, and Mary Magdalene. [26]When Jesus saw his mother
and the disciple whom he loved
standing beside her, he said to his
mother, "Woman, here is your
son." [27]Then he said to the disciple,
"Here is your mother." And from
that hour the disciple took her into
his own home.

28 After this, when Jesus knew
that all was now finished, he said
(in order to fulfill the scripture),
"I am thirsty." [29]A jar full of sour
wine was standing there. So they
put a sponge full of the wine on a
branch of hyssop and held it to his
mouth. [30]When Jesus had received
the wine, he said, "It is finished."
Then he bowed his head and gave
up his spirit.

Jesus' Side Is Pierced

31 Since it was the day of Preparation, the Jews did not want the
bodies left on the cross during the
sabbath, especially because that
sabbath was a day of great solemni-
ty. So they asked Pilate to have the
legs of the crucified men broken
and the bodies removed. [32]Then the
soldiers came and broke the legs
of the first and of the other who
had been crucified with him. [33]But
when they came to Jesus and saw
that he was already dead, they did
not break his legs. [34]Instead, one of
the soldiers pierced his side with a
spear, and at once blood and water
came out. [35](He who saw this has
testified so that you also may believe. His testimony is true, and
he knows[g] that he tells the truth.)
[36]These things occurred so that the
scripture might be fulfilled, "None
of his bones shall be broken."
[37]And again another passage of
scripture says, "They will look on
the one whom they have pierced."

The Burial of Jesus

38 After these things, Joseph of
Arimathea, who was a disciple of
Jesus, though a secret one because
of his fear of the Jews, asked Pilate
to let him take away the body of

e Gk *the Nazorean* *f* That is, *Aramaic*
g Or *there is one who knows*

Jesus. Pilate gave him permission; so he came and removed his body. 39 Nicodemus, who had at first come to Jesus by night, also came, bringing a mixture of myrrh and aloes, weighing about a hundred pounds. 40 They took the body of Jesus and wrapped it with the spices in linen cloths, according to the burial custom of the Jews. 41 Now there was a garden in the place where he was crucified, and in the garden there was a new tomb in which no one had ever been laid. 42 And so, because it was the Jewish day of Preparation, and the tomb was nearby, they laid Jesus there.

The Resurrection of Jesus

20 Early on the first day of the week, while it was still dark, Mary Magdalene came to the tomb and saw that the stone had been removed from the tomb. 2 So she ran and went to Simon Peter and the other disciple, the one whom Jesus loved, and said to them, "They have taken the Lord out of the tomb, and we do not know where they have laid him." 3 Then Peter and the other disciple set out and went toward the tomb. 4 The two were running together, but the other disciple outran Peter and reached the tomb first. 5 He bent down to look in and saw the linen wrappings lying there, but he did not go in. 6 Then Simon Peter came, following him, and went into the tomb. He saw the linen wrappings lying there, 7 and the cloth that had been on Jesus' head, not lying with the linen wrappings but rolled up in a place by itself. 8 Then the other disciple, who reached the tomb first, also went in, and he saw and believed; 9 for as yet they did not understand the scripture, that he must rise from the dead. 10 Then the disciples returned to their homes.

Jesus Appears to Mary Magdalene

11 But Mary stood weeping outside the tomb. As she wept, she bent over to look[a] into the tomb; 12 and she saw two angels in white, sitting where the body of Jesus had been lying, one at the head and the other at the feet. 13 They said to her, "Woman, why are you weeping?" She said to them, "They have taken away my Lord, and I do not know where they have laid him." 14 When she had said this, she turned around and saw Jesus standing there, but she did not know that it was Jesus. 15 Jesus said to her, "Woman, why are you weeping? Whom are you looking for?" Supposing him to be the gardener, she said to him, "Sir, if you have carried him away, tell me where you have laid him, and I will take him away." 16 Jesus said to her, "Mary!" She turned and said to him in Hebrew,[b] "Rabbouni!" (which means Teacher). 17 Jesus said to her, "Do not hold on to me, because I have not yet ascended to the Father. But go to my brothers and say to them, 'I am ascending to my Father and your Father, to my God and your God.' " 18 Mary Magdalene went and announced to the disciples, "I have seen the Lord"; and she told them that he had said these things to her.

---

a Gk lacks *to look* · *b* That is, *Aramaic*

Jesus Appears to the Disciples

19 When it was evening on that
day, the first day of the week, and
the doors of the house where the
disciples had met were locked for
fear of the Jews, Jesus came and
stood among them and said, "Peace
be with you." 20 After he said this,
he showed them his hands and his
side. Then the disciples rejoiced
when they saw the Lord. 21 Jesus
said to them again, "Peace be with
you. As the Father has sent me, so I
send you." 22 When he had said this,
he breathed on them and said to
them, "Receive the Holy Spirit. 23 If
you forgive the sins of any, they are
forgiven them; if you retain the sins
of any, they are retained."

Jesus and Thomas

24 But Thomas (who was called
the Twin[c]), one of the twelve, was
not with them when Jesus came.
25 So the other disciples told him,
"We have seen the Lord." But he
said to them, "Unless I see the mark
of the nails in his hands, and put my
finger in the mark of the nails and
my hand in his side, I will not believe."

26 A week later his disciples
were again in the house, and Thomas was with them. Although the
doors were shut, Jesus came and
stood among them and said, "Peace
be with you." 27 Then he said to
Thomas, "Put your finger here and
see my hands. Reach out your hand
and put it in my side. Do not doubt
but believe." 28 Thomas answered
him, "My Lord and my God!" 29 Jesus said to him, "Have you believed
because you have seen me? Blessed
are those who have not seen and yet
have come to believe."

The Purpose of This Book

30 Now Jesus did many other
signs in the presence of his disciples, which are not written in this
book. 31 But these are written so that
you may come to believe[d] that Jesus is the Messiah,[e] the Son of God,
and that through believing you may
have life in his name.

Jesus Appears to Seven Disciples

21 After these things Jesus
showed himself again to the
disciples by the Sea of Tiberias;
and he showed himself in this way.
2 Gathered there together were
Simon Peter, Thomas called the
Twin,[a] Nathanael of Cana in Galilee, the sons of Zebedee, and two
others of his disciples. 3 Simon Peter said to them, "I am going fish-
ing." They said to him, "We will go
with you." They went out and got
into the boat, but that night they
caught nothing.

4 Just after daybreak, Jesus stood
on the beach; but the disciples did
not know that it was Jesus. 5 Jesus
said to them, "Children, you have
no fish, have you?" They answered
him, "No." 6 He said to them, "Cast
the net to the right side of the boat,
and you will find some." So they
cast it, and now they were not able
to haul it in because there were so
many fish. 7 That disciple whom
Jesus loved said to Peter, "It is the
Lord!" When Simon Peter heard

c Gk *Didymus* *d* Other ancient authorities read *may continue to believe* *e* Or *the Christ*
a Gk *Didymus*

that it was the Lord, he put on some
clothes, for he was naked, and
jumped into the sea. 8 But the other
disciples came in the boat, dragging
the net full of fish, for they were not
far from the land, only about a hundred yards[b] off.
9 When they had gone ashore,
they saw a charcoal fire there, with
fish on it, and bread. 10 Jesus said
to them, "Bring some of the fish
that you have just caught." 11 So Simon Peter went aboard and hauled
the net ashore, full of large fish, a
hundred fifty-three of them; and
though there were so many, the net
was not torn. 12 Jesus said to them,
"Come and have breakfast." Now
none of the disciples dared to ask
him, "Who are you?" because they
knew it was the Lord. 13 Jesus came
and took the bread and gave it to
them, and did the same with the
fish. 14 This was now the third time
that Jesus appeared to the disciples
after he was raised from the dead.

Jesus and Peter

15 When they had finished
breakfast, Jesus said to Simon Peter, "Simon son of John, do you
love me more than these?" He said
to him, "Yes, Lord; you know that I
love you." Jesus said to him, "Feed
my lambs." 16 A second time he
said to him, "Simon son of John,
do you love me?" He said to him,
"Yes, Lord; you know that I love
you." Jesus said to him, "Tend my
sheep." 17 He said to him the third
time, "Simon son of John, do you
love me?" Peter felt hurt because
he said to him the third time, "Do
you love me?" And he said to him,
"Lord, you know everything; you
know that I love you." Jesus said to
him, "Feed my sheep. 18 Very truly,
I tell you, when you were younger,
you used to fasten your own belt
and to go wherever you wished.
But when you grow old, you will
stretch out your hands, and someone else will fasten a belt around
you and take you where you do not
wish to go." 19 (He said this to indicate the kind of death by which
he would glorify God.) After this he
said to him, "Follow me."

Jesus and the Beloved Disciple

20 Peter turned and saw the disciple whom Jesus loved following
them; he was the one who had reclined next to Jesus at the supper
and had said, "Lord, who is it that is
going to betray you?" 21 When Peter
saw him, he said to Jesus, "Lord,
what about him?" 22 Jesus said to
him, "If it is my will that he remain
until I come, what is that to you?
Follow me!" 23 So the rumor spread
in the community[c] that this disciple
would not die. Yet Jesus did not say
to him that he would not die, but,
"If it is my will that he remain until
I come, what is that to you?"[d]
24 This is the disciple who is
testifying to these things and has
written them, and we know that his
testimony is true. 25 But there are
also many other things that Jesus
did; if every one of them were written down, I suppose that the world
itself could not contain the books
that would be written.

---

b Gk *two hundred cubits* *c* Gk *among the brothers* *d* Other ancient authorities lack *what is that to you*

THE PSALMS

BOOK I
(Psalms 1–41)

Psalm 1

The Two Ways

1 Happy are those
who do not follow the advice of the wicked,
or take the path that sinners tread,
or sit in the seat of scoffers;
2 but their delight is in the law of the LORD,
and on his law they meditate day and night.
3 They are like trees
planted by streams of water,
which yield their fruit in its season,
and their leaves do not wither.
In all that they do, they prosper.

4 The wicked are not so,
but are like chaff that the wind drives away.
5 Therefore the wicked will not stand in the judgment,
nor sinners in the congregation of the righteous;
6 for the LORD watches over the way of the righteous,
but the way of the wicked will perish.

Psalm 2

God's Promise to His Anointed

1 Why do the nations conspire,
and the peoples plot in vain?
2 The kings of the earth set themselves,
and the rulers take counsel together,
against the LORD and his anointed, saying,
3 "Let us burst their bonds asunder,
and cast their cords from us."

4 He who sits in the heavens laughs;
the LORD has them in derision.
5 Then he will speak to them in his wrath,
and terrify them in his fury, saying,
6 "I have set my king on Zion, my holy hill."

7 I will tell of the decree of the LORD:
He said to me, "You are my son;
today I have begotten you.
8 Ask of me, and I will make the nations your heritage,
and the ends of the earth your possession.
9 You shall break them with a rod of iron,
and dash them in pieces like a potter's vessel."

10 Now therefore, O kings, be wise;
be warned, O rulers of the earth.
11 Serve the LORD with fear,
with trembling 12 kiss his feet,[a]
or he will be angry, and you will perish in the way;
for his wrath is quickly kindled.

Happy are all who take refuge in him.

Psalm 3

Trust in God under Adversity

A Psalm of David, when he fled from his son Absalom.

1 O LORD, how many are my foes!
Many are rising against me;
2 many are saying to me,
"There is no help for you[b] in God." *Selah*

3 But you, O LORD, are a shield around me,
my glory, and the one who lifts up my head.
4 I cry aloud to the LORD,
and he answers me from his holy hill. *Selah*

5 I lie down and sleep;
I wake again, for the LORD sustains me.
6 I am not afraid of ten thousands of people
who have set themselves against me all around.

7 Rise up, O LORD!
Deliver me, O my God!
For you strike all my enemies on the cheek;
you break the teeth of the wicked.

8 Deliverance belongs to the LORD;
may your blessing be on your people! *Selah*

Psalm 4

Confident Plea for Deliverance from Enemies

To the leader: with stringed instruments. A Psalm of David.

1 Answer me when I call, O God of my right!
You gave me room when I was in distress.
Be gracious to me, and hear my prayer.

2 How long, you people, shall my honor suffer shame?
How long will you love vain words, and seek after lies?
Selah

---

a Cn: Meaning of Heb of verses 11b and 12a is uncertain *b* Syr: Heb *him*

[3] But know that the LORD has
set apart the faithful for
himself;
the LORD hears when I call to
him.

[4] When you are disturbed,[c] do
not sin;
ponder it on your beds, and be
silent. *Selah*
[5] Offer right sacrifices,
and put your trust in the
LORD.

[6] There are many who say,
"O that we might see
some good!
Let the light of your face shine
on us, O LORD!"
[7] You have put gladness in my
heart
more than when their grain
and wine abound.

[8] I will both lie down and sleep
in peace;
for you alone, O LORD, make
me lie down in safety.

Psalm 5

Trust in God for Deliverance from Enemies

To the leader: for the flutes. A
Psalm of David.

[1] Give ear to my words, O LORD;
give heed to my sighing.
[2] Listen to the sound of my cry,
my King and my God,
for to you I pray.
[3] O LORD, in the morning you
hear my voice;
in the morning I plead my
case to you, and watch.

[4] For you are not a God who
delights in wickedness;
evil will not sojourn with
you.
[5] The boastful will not stand
before your eyes;
you hate all evildoers.
[6] You destroy those who speak
lies;
the LORD abhors the
bloodthirsty and deceitful.

[7] But I, through the abundance of
your steadfast love,
will enter your house,
I will bow down toward your
holy temple
in awe of you.
[8] Lead me, O LORD, in your
righteousness
because of my enemies;
make your way straight
before me.

[9] For there is no truth in their
mouths;
their hearts are destruction;
their throats are open graves;
they flatter with their
tongues.
[10] Make them bear their guilt,
O God;

c Or *are angry*

let them fall by their own counsels;
because of their many transgressions cast them out,
for they have rebelled against you.

[11] But let all who take refuge in you rejoice;
let them ever sing for joy.
Spread your protection over them,
so that those who love your name may exult in you.
[12] For you bless the righteous, O LORD;
you cover them with favor as with a shield.

Psalm 6

Prayer for Recovery from Grave Illness

To the leader: with stringed instruments; according to The Sheminith. A Psalm of David.

[1] O LORD, do not rebuke me in your anger,
or discipline me in your wrath.
[2] Be gracious to me, O LORD, for I am languishing;
O LORD, heal me, for my bones are shaking with terror.
[3] My soul also is struck with terror,
while you, O LORD—how long?
[4] Turn, O LORD, save my life;
deliver me for the sake of your steadfast love.
[5] For in death there is no remembrance of you;
in Sheol who can give you praise?

[6] I am weary with my moaning;
every night I flood my bed with tears;
I drench my couch with my weeping.
[7] My eyes waste away because of grief;
they grow weak because of all my foes.

[8] Depart from me, all you workers of evil,
for the LORD has heard the sound of my weeping.
[9] The LORD has heard my supplication;
the LORD accepts my prayer.
[10] All my enemies shall be ashamed and struck with terror;
they shall turn back, and in a moment be put to shame.

Psalm 7

Plea for Help against Persecutors

A Shiggaion of David, which he sang to the LORD concerning Cush, a Benjaminite.

[1] O LORD my God, in you I take refuge;

save me from all my
pursuers, and deliver me,
2 or like a lion they will tear me
apart;
they will drag me away, with
no one to rescue.

3 O LORD my God, if I have done
this,
if there is wrong in my hands,
4 if I have repaid my ally with
harm
or plundered my foe without
cause,
5 then let the enemy pursue and
overtake me,
trample my life to the ground,
and lay my soul in the dust.
Selah

6 Rise up, O LORD, in your anger;
lift yourself up against the fury
of my enemies;
awake, O my God;[d] you have
appointed a judgment.
7 Let the assembly of the peoples
be gathered around you,
and over it take your seat[e] on
high.
8 The LORD judges the peoples;
judge me, O LORD, according
to my righteousness
and according to the integrity
that is in me.

9 O let the evil of the wicked
come to an end,
but establish the righteous,
you who test the minds and
hearts,
O righteous God.

10 God is my shield,
who saves the upright in
heart.
11 God is a righteous judge,
and a God who has
indignation every day.

12 If one does not repent, God[f]
will whet his sword;
he has bent and strung his bow;
13 he has prepared his deadly
weapons,
making his arrows fiery shafts.
14 See how they conceive evil,
and are pregnant with
mischief,
and bring forth lies.
15 They make a pit, digging it out,
and fall into the hole that
they have made.
16 Their mischief returns upon
their own heads,
and on their own heads their
violence descends.

17 I will give to the LORD the
thanks due to his
righteousness,
and sing praise to the name
of the LORD, the Most
High.

---

d Or *awake for me* *e* Cn: Heb *return*
f Heb *he*

Psalm 8

Divine Majesty and Human Dignity

To the leader: according to The Gittith. A Psalm of David.

1 O LORD, our Sovereign,
how majestic is your name in all the earth!

You have set your glory above the heavens.
2 Out of the mouths of babes and infants
you have founded a bulwark because of your foes,
to silence the enemy and the avenger.

3 When I look at your heavens, the work of your fingers,
the moon and the stars that you have established;
4 what are human beings that you are mindful of them,
mortals[g] that you care for them?

5 Yet you have made them a little lower than God,[h]
and crowned them with glory and honor.
6 You have given them dominion over the works of your hands;
you have put all things under their feet,
7 all sheep and oxen,
and also the beasts of the field,
8 the birds of the air, and the fish of the sea,
whatever passes along the paths of the seas.

9 O LORD, our Sovereign,
how majestic is your name in all the earth!

Psalm 9

God's Power and Justice

To the leader: according to Muth-labben. A Psalm of David.

1 I will give thanks to the LORD with my whole heart;
I will tell of all your wonderful deeds.
2 I will be glad and exult in you;
I will sing praise to your name, O Most High.

3 When my enemies turned back,
they stumbled and perished before you.
4 For you have maintained my just cause;
you have sat on the throne giving righteous judgment.

5 You have rebuked the nations,
you have destroyed the wicked;

g Heb *ben adam*, lit. *son of man* h Or *than the divine beings* or *angels*: Heb *elohim*

you have blotted out their
name forever and ever.
6 The enemies have vanished in
everlasting ruins;
their cities you have rooted
out;
the very memory of them has
perished.

7 But the LORD sits enthroned
forever,
he has established his throne
for judgment.
8 He judges the world with
righteousness;
he judges the peoples with
equity.

9 The LORD is a stronghold for
the oppressed,
a stronghold in times of
trouble.
10 And those who know your
name put their trust in
you,
for you, O LORD, have not
forsaken those who seek
you.

11 Sing praises to the LORD, who
dwells in Zion.
Declare his deeds among the
peoples.
12 For he who avenges blood is
mindful of them;
he does not forget the cry of the
afflicted.

13 Be gracious to me, O LORD.
See what I suffer from those
who hate me;
you are the one who lifts me up
from the gates of death,
14 so that I may recount all your
praises,
and, in the gates of daughter
Zion,
rejoice in your deliverance.

15 The nations have sunk in the pit
that they made;
in the net that they hid has
their own foot been
caught.
16 The LORD has made himself
known, he has executed
judgment;
the wicked are snared in the
work of their own hands.
Higgaion. Selah

17 The wicked shall depart to
Sheol,
all the nations that forget
God.

18 For the needy shall not always
be forgotten,
nor the hope of the poor perish
forever.

19 Rise up, O LORD! Do not let
mortals prevail;
let the nations be judged
before you.
20 Put them in fear, O LORD;
let the nations know that they
are only human. *Selah*

Psalm 10

Prayer for Deliverance from Enemies

[1] Why, O LORD, do you stand far off?
Why do you hide yourself in times of trouble?
[2] In arrogance the wicked persecute the poor—
let them be caught in the schemes they have devised.

[3] For the wicked boast of the desires of their heart,
those greedy for gain curse and renounce the LORD.
[4] In the pride of their countenance the wicked say, "God will not seek it out";
all their thoughts are, "There is no God."

[5] Their ways prosper at all times;
your judgments are on high, out of their sight;
as for their foes, they scoff at them.
[6] They think in their heart, "We shall not be moved;
throughout all generations we shall not meet adversity."

[7] Their mouths are filled with cursing and deceit and oppression;
under their tongues are mischief and iniquity.
[8] They sit in ambush in the villages;
in hiding places they murder the innocent.

Their eyes stealthily watch for the helpless;
[9] they lurk in secret like a lion in its covert;
they lurk that they may seize the poor;
they seize the poor and drag them off in their net.

[10] They stoop, they crouch,
and the helpless fall by their might.
[11] They think in their heart, "God has forgotten,
he has hidden his face, he will never see it."

[12] Rise up, O LORD; O God, lift up your hand;
do not forget the oppressed.
[13] Why do the wicked renounce God,
and say in their hearts,
"You will not call us to account"?

[14] But you do see! Indeed you note trouble and grief,
that you may take it into your hands;
the helpless commit themselves to you;
you have been the helper of the orphan.

15 Break the arm of the wicked
and evildoers;
seek out their wickedness
until you find none.
16 The LORD is king forever and
ever;
the nations shall perish from his
land.

17 O LORD, you will hear the
desire of the meek;
you will strengthen their
heart, you will incline
your ear
18 to do justice for the orphan and
the oppressed,
so that those from earth may
strike terror no more.[i]

Psalm 11

Song of Trust in God

To the leader. Of David.

1 In the LORD I take refuge; how
can you say to me,
"Flee like a bird to the
mountains;[j]
2 for look, the wicked bend the
bow,
they have fitted their arrow to
the string,
to shoot in the dark at the
upright in heart.
3 If the foundations are
destroyed,
what can the righteous do?"

4 The LORD is in his holy temple;
the LORD's throne is in
heaven.
His eyes behold, his gaze
examines humankind.
5 The LORD tests the righteous
and the wicked,
and his soul hates the lover of
violence.
6 On the wicked he will rain
coals of fire and sulfur;
a scorching wind shall be the
portion of their cup.
7 For the LORD is righteous;
he loves righteous deeds;
the upright shall behold his
face.

Psalm 12

Plea for Help in Evil Times

To the leader: according to The
Sheminith. A Psalm of David.

1 Help, O LORD, for there is no
longer anyone who is
godly;
the faithful have disappeared
from humankind.
2 They utter lies to each other;
with flattering lips and a double
heart they speak.

3 May the LORD cut off all
flattering lips,
the tongue that makes great
boasts,
4 those who say, "With our
tongues we will prevail;

i Meaning of Heb uncertain *j* Gk Syr Jerome Tg: Heb *flee to your mountain, O bird*

our lips are our own—who is
our master?"

5 "Because the poor are
despoiled, because the
needy groan,
I will now rise up," says the
LORD;
"I will place them in the
safety for which they
long."
6 The promises of the LORD are
promises that are pure,
silver refined in a furnace on
the ground,
purified seven times.

7 You, O LORD, will protect us;
you will guard us from this
generation forever.
8 On every side the wicked
prowl,
as vileness is exalted among
humankind.

Psalm 13

Prayer for Deliverance from Enemies

To the leader. A Psalm of David.

1 How long, O LORD? Will you
forget me forever?
How long will you hide your
face from me?
2 How long must I bear pain[k] in
my soul,
and have sorrow in my heart all
day long?
How long shall my enemy be
exalted over me?

3 Consider and answer me,
O LORD my God!
Give light to my eyes, or I
will sleep the sleep of
death,
4 and my enemy will say, "I have
prevailed";
my foes will rejoice because I
am shaken.

5 But I trusted in your steadfast
love;
my heart shall rejoice in your
salvation.
6 I will sing to the LORD,
because he has dealt
bountifully with me.

Psalm 14

Denunciation of Godlessness

To the leader. Of David.

1 Fools say in their hearts, "There
is no God."
They are corrupt, they do
abominable deeds;
there is no one who does
good.

2 The LORD looks down from
heaven on humankind
to see if there are any who
are wise,

k Syr: Heb *hold counsels*

who seek after God.

[3] They have all gone astray, they
are all alike perverse;
there is no one who does
good,
no, not one.

[4] Have they no knowledge, all
the evildoers
who eat up my people as they
eat bread,
and do not call upon the LORD?

[5] There they shall be in great
terror,
for God is with the company
of the righteous.
[6] You would confound the plans
of the poor,
but the LORD is their refuge.

[7] O that deliverance for Israel
would come from Zion!
When the LORD restores the
fortunes of his people,
Jacob will rejoice; Israel will
be glad.

Psalm 15

Who Shall Abide in God's Sanctuary?

A Psalm of David.

[1] O LORD, who may abide in your
tent?
Who may dwell on your holy
hill?

[2] Those who walk blamelessly,
and do what is right,
and speak the truth from their
heart;
[3] who do not slander with their
tongue,
and do no evil to their friends,
nor take up a reproach against
their neighbors;
[4] in whose eyes the wicked are
despised,
but who honor those who fear
the LORD;
who stand by their oath even to
their hurt;
[5] who do not lend money at
interest,
and do not take a bribe
against the innocent.

Those who do these things shall
never be moved.

Psalm 16

Song of Trust and Security in God

A Miktam of David.

[1] Protect me, O God, for in you I
take refuge.
[2] I say to the LORD, "You are my
Lord;
I have no good apart from
you."[l]

l Jerome Tg: Meaning of Heb uncertain

3 As for the holy ones in the land,
they are the noble,
in whom is all my delight.

4 Those who choose another god
multiply their sorrows;[m]
their drink offerings of blood
I will not pour out
or take their names upon my
lips.

5 The LORD is my chosen portion
and my cup;
you hold my lot.
6 The boundary lines have fallen
for me in pleasant places;
I have a goodly heritage.

7 I bless the LORD who gives me
counsel;
in the night also my heart
instructs me.
8 I keep the LORD always before
me;
because he is at my right
hand, I shall not be
moved.

9 Therefore my heart is glad, and
my soul rejoices;
my body also rests secure.
10 For you do not give me up to
Sheol,
or let your faithful one see
the Pit.

11 You show me the path of life.
In your presence there is
fullness of joy;
in your right hand are
pleasures forevermore.

Psalm 17

Prayer for Deliverance from Persecutors

A Prayer of David.

1 Hear a just cause, O LORD;
attend to my cry;
give ear to my prayer from lips
free of deceit.
2 From you let my vindication
come;
let your eyes see the right.

3 If you try my heart, if you visit
me by night,
if you test me, you will find
no wickedness in me;
my mouth does not
transgress.
4 As for what others do, by the
word of your lips
I have avoided the ways of the
violent.
5 My steps have held fast to your
paths;
my feet have not slipped.

6 I call upon you, for you will
answer me, O God;
incline your ear to me, hear
my words.
7 Wondrously show your
steadfast love,

m Cn: Meaning of Heb uncertain

O savior of those who seek
refuge
from their adversaries at your
right hand.

8 Guard me as the apple of the
eye;
hide me in the shadow of
your wings,
9 from the wicked who despoil
me,
my deadly enemies who
surround me.
10 They close their hearts to pity;
with their mouths they speak
arrogantly.
11 They track me down;[n] now they
surround me;
they set their eyes to cast me to
the ground.
12 They are like a lion eager to
tear,
like a young lion lurking in
ambush.

13 Rise up, O LORD, confront
them, overthrow them!
By your sword deliver my
life from the wicked,
14 from mortals—by your hand,
O LORD—
from mortals whose portion
in life is in this world.
May their bellies be filled with
what you have stored up
for them;
may their children have more
than enough;
may they leave something
over to their little ones.
15 As for me, I shall behold your
face in righteousness;
when I awake I shall be
satisfied, beholding your
likeness.

Psalm 18

Royal Thanksgiving for Victory

To the leader. A Psalm of David the servant of the LORD, who addressed the words of this song to the LORD on the day when the LORD delivered him from the hand of all his enemies, and from the hand of Saul. He said:

1 I love you, O LORD, my
strength.
2 The LORD is my rock, my
fortress, and my deliverer,
my God, my rock in whom I
take refuge,
my shield, and the horn
of my salvation, my
stronghold.
3 I call upon the LORD, who is
worthy to be praised,
so I shall be saved from my
enemies.

4 The cords of death
encompassed me;
the torrents of perdition
assailed me;
5 the cords of Sheol entangled
me;
the snares of death
confronted me.

n One Ms Compare Syr: MT *Our steps*

[6] In my distress I called upon the LORD;
to my God I cried for help.
From his temple he heard my voice,
and my cry to him reached his ears.

[7] Then the earth reeled and rocked;
the foundations also of the mountains trembled
and quaked, because he was angry.
[8] Smoke went up from his nostrils,
and devouring fire from his mouth;
glowing coals flamed forth from him.
[9] He bowed the heavens, and came down;
thick darkness was under his feet.
[10] He rode on a cherub, and flew;
he came swiftly upon the wings of the wind.
[11] He made darkness his covering around him,
his canopy thick clouds dark with water.
[12] Out of the brightness before him
there broke through his clouds
hailstones and coals of fire.
[13] The LORD also thundered in the heavens,
and the Most High uttered his voice.[o]
[14] And he sent out his arrows, and scattered them;
he flashed forth lightnings, and routed them.
[15] Then the channels of the sea were seen,
and the foundations of the world were laid bare
at your rebuke, O LORD,
at the blast of the breath of your nostrils.

[16] He reached down from on high, he took me;
he drew me out of mighty waters.
[17] He delivered me from my strong enemy,
and from those who hated me;
for they were too mighty for me.
[18] They confronted me in the day of my calamity;
but the LORD was my support.
[19] He brought me out into a broad place;
he delivered me, because he delighted in me.

[20] The LORD rewarded me according to my righteousness;
according to the cleanness of my hands he recompensed me.
[21] For I have kept the ways of the LORD,
and have not wickedly departed from my God.
[22] For all his ordinances were before me,

o Gk See 2 Sam 22.14: Heb adds *hailstones and coals of fire*

and his statutes I did not put
away from me.
23 I was blameless before him,
and I kept myself from guilt.
24 Therefore the LORD has
recompensed me
according to my
righteousness,
according to the cleanness of
my hands in his sight.

25 With the loyal you show
yourself loyal;
with the blameless you show
yourself blameless;
26 with the pure you show yourself
pure;
and with the crooked you
show yourself perverse.
27 For you deliver a humble
people,
but the haughty eyes you
bring down.
28 It is you who light my lamp;
the LORD, my God, lights up
my darkness.
29 By you I can crush a troop,
and by my God I can leap
over a wall.
30 This God—his way is perfect;
the promise of the LORD
proves true;
he is a shield for all who take
refuge in him.

31 For who is God except the
LORD?
And who is a rock besides
our God?—
32 the God who girded me with
strength,
and made my way safe.
33 He made my feet like the feet
of a deer,
and set me secure on the
heights.
34 He trains my hands for war,
so that my arms can bend a
bow of bronze.
35 You have given me the shield of
your salvation,
and your right hand has
supported me;
your help[p] has made me
great.
36 You gave me a wide place for
my steps under me,
and my feet did not slip.
37 I pursued my enemies and
overtook them;
and did not turn back until they
were consumed.
38 I struck them down, so that they
were not able to rise;
they fell under my feet.
39 For you girded me with strength
for the battle;
you made my assailants sink
under me.
40 You made my enemies turn
their backs to me,
and those who hated me I
destroyed.
41 They cried for help, but there
was no one to save them;
they cried to the LORD, but he
did not answer them.
42 I beat them fine, like dust
before the wind;
I cast them out like the mire
of the streets.

p Or *gentleness*

43 You delivered me from strife
with the peoples;[q]
you made me head of the
nations;
people whom I had not known
served me.
44 As soon as they heard of me
they obeyed me;
foreigners came cringing to me.
45 Foreigners lost heart,
and came trembling out of
their strongholds.

46 The LORD lives! Blessed be my
rock,
and exalted be the God of my
salvation,
47 the God who gave me
vengeance
and subdued peoples under me;
48 who delivered me from my
enemies;
indeed, you exalted me above
my adversaries;
you delivered me from the
violent.

49 For this I will extol you,
O LORD, among the
nations,
and sing praises to your name.
50 Great triumphs he gives to his
king,
and shows steadfast love to
his anointed,
to David and his descendants
forever.

Psalm 19

God's Glory in Creation and the Law

To the leader. A Psalm of David.

1 The heavens are telling the
glory of God;
and the firmament[r] proclaims
his handiwork.
2 Day to day pours forth speech,
and night to night declares
knowledge.
3 There is no speech, nor are
there words;
their voice is not heard;
4 yet their voice[s] goes out
through all the earth,
and their words to the end of
the world.

In the heavens[t] he has set a tent
for the sun,
5 which comes out like a
bridegroom from his
wedding canopy,
and like a strong man runs its
course with joy.
6 Its rising is from the end of the
heavens,
and its circuit to the end of
them;
and nothing is hid from its
heat.

7 The law of the LORD is perfect,
reviving the soul;

---

q Gk Tg: Heb *people* *r* Or *dome*
s Gk Jerome Compare Syr: Heb *line* *t* Heb *In them*

the decrees of the LORD are
sure,
making wise the simple;
8 the precepts of the LORD are
right,
rejoicing the heart;
the commandment of the LORD
is clear,
enlightening the eyes;
9 the fear of the LORD is pure,
enduring forever;
the ordinances of the LORD are
true
and righteous altogether.
10 More to be desired are they
than gold,
even much fine gold;
sweeter also than honey,
and drippings of the
honeycomb.

11 Moreover by them is your
servant warned;
in keeping them there is great
reward.
12 But who can detect their errors?
Clear me from hidden faults.
13 Keep back your servant also
from the insolent;[u]
do not let them have dominion
over me.
Then I shall be blameless,
and innocent of great
transgression.

14 Let the words of my mouth and
the meditation of my heart
be acceptable to you,
O LORD, my rock and my
redeemer.

Psalm 20

Prayer for Victory

To the leader. A Psalm of David.

1 The LORD answer you in the
day of trouble!
The name of the God of Jacob
protect you!
2 May he send you help from the
sanctuary,
and give you support from
Zion.
3 May he remember all your
offerings,
and regard with favor your
burnt sacrifices. *Selah*

4 May he grant you your heart's
desire,
and fulfill all your plans.
5 May we shout for joy over your
victory,
and in the name of our God set
up our banners.
May the LORD fulfill all your
petitions.

6 Now I know that the LORD will
help his anointed;
he will answer him from his
holy heaven
with mighty victories by his
right hand.
7 Some take pride in chariots, and
some in horses,
but our pride is in the name of
the LORD our God.
8 They will collapse and fall,

u Or *from proud thoughts*

but we shall rise and stand
upright.

9 Give victory to the king,
O LORD;
answer us when we call.[v]

Psalm 21

Thanksgiving for Victory

To the leader. A Psalm of David.

1 In your strength the king
rejoices, O LORD,
and in your help how greatly he
exults!
2 You have given him his heart's
desire,
and have not withheld the
request of his lips.
Selah
3 For you meet him with rich
blessings;
you set a crown of fine gold on
his head.
4 He asked you for life; you gave
it to him—
length of days forever and ever.
5 His glory is great through your
help;
splendor and majesty you
bestow on him.
6 You bestow on him blessings
forever;
you make him glad with the joy
of your presence.
7 For the king trusts in the LORD,
and through the steadfast
love of the Most High he
shall not be moved.

8 Your hand will find out all your
enemies;
your right hand will find out
those who hate you.
9 You will make them like a fiery
furnace
when you appear.
The LORD will swallow them up
in his wrath,
and fire will consume them.
10 You will destroy their offspring
from the earth,
and their children from among
humankind.
11 If they plan evil against you,
if they devise mischief, they
will not succeed.
12 For you will put them to flight;
you will aim at their faces
with your bows.

13 Be exalted, O LORD, in your
strength!
We will sing and praise your
power.

Psalm 22

Plea for Deliverance from Suffering and Hostility

To the leader: according to The
Deer of the Dawn. A Psalm of
David.

1 My God, my God, why have
you forsaken me?
Why are you so far from
helping me, from the
words of my groaning?

---

v Gk: Heb *give victory, O LORD*; let the King answer us when we call

[2] O my God, I cry by day, but
you do not answer;
and by night, but find no rest.

[3] Yet you are holy,
enthroned on the praises of
Israel.
[4] In you our ancestors trusted;
they trusted, and you
delivered them.
[5] To you they cried, and were
saved;
in you they trusted, and were
not put to shame.

[6] But I am a worm, and not
human;
scorned by others, and despised
by the people.
[7] All who see me mock at me;
they make mouths at me, they
shake their heads;
[8] "Commit your cause to the
Lord; let him deliver—
let him rescue the one in
whom he delights!"

[9] Yet it was you who took me
from the womb;
you kept me safe on my
mother's breast.
[10] On you I was cast from my
birth,
and since my mother bore me
you have been my God.
[11] Do not be far from me,
for trouble is near
and there is no one to help.

[12] Many bulls encircle me,
strong bulls of Bashan
surround me;
[13] they open wide their mouths at
me,
like a ravening and roaring
lion.

[14] I am poured out like water,
and all my bones are out of
joint;
my heart is like wax;
it is melted within my breast;
[15] my mouth[w] is dried up like a
potsherd,
and my tongue sticks to my
jaws;
you lay me in the dust of
death.

[16] For dogs are all around me;
a company of evildoers
encircles me.
My hands and feet have
shriveled;[x]
[17] I can count all my bones.
They stare and gloat over me;
[18] they divide my clothes among
themselves,
and for my clothing they cast
lots.

[19] But you, O Lord, do not be far
away!
O my help, come quickly to
my aid!
[20] Deliver my soul from the
sword,
my life[y] from the power of
the dog!

w Cn: Heb *strength* *x* Meaning of Heb uncertain *y* Heb *my only one*

21 Save me from the mouth of
the lion!

From the horns of the wild oxen
you have rescued[z] me.
22 I will tell of your name to my
brothers and sisters;[a]
in the midst of the
congregation I will praise
you:
23 You who fear the LORD, praise
him!
All you offspring of Jacob,
glorify him;
stand in awe of him, all you
offspring of Israel!
24 For he did not despise or abhor
the affliction of the afflicted;
he did not hide his face from
me,[b]
but heard when I[c] cried to
him.

25 From you comes my praise in
the great congregation;
my vows I will pay before
those who fear him.
26 The poor[d] shall eat and be
satisfied;
those who seek him shall
praise the LORD.
May your hearts live forever!

27 All the ends of the earth shall
remember
and turn to the LORD;
and all the families of the
nations
shall worship before him.[e]
28 For dominion belongs to the
LORD,
and he rules over the nations.

29 To him,[f] indeed, shall all who
sleep in[g] the earth bow
down;
before him shall bow all who
go down to the dust,
and I shall live for him.[h]
30 Posterity will serve him;
future generations will be
told about the Lord,
31 and[i] proclaim his deliverance to
a people yet unborn,
saying that he has done it.

Psalm 23

The Divine Shepherd

A Psalm of David.

1 The LORD is my shepherd, I
shall not want.
2 He makes me lie down in
green pastures;
he leads me beside still waters;[j]
3 he restores my soul.[k]
He leads me in right paths[l]
for his name's sake.

4 Even though I walk through the
darkest valley,[m]
I fear no evil;

z Heb *answered* a Or *kindred* b Heb *him* c Heb *he* d Or *afflicted* e Gk Syr Jerome: Heb *you* f Cn: Heb *They have eaten and* g Cn: Heb *all the fat ones* h Compare Gk Syr Vg: Heb *and he who cannot keep himself alive* i Compare Gk: Heb *it will be told about the Lord to the generation, [31]they will come and* j Heb *waters of rest* k Or *life* l Or *paths of righteousness* m Or *the valley of the shadow of death*

for you are with me;
your rod and your staff—
they comfort me.

5 You prepare a table before me
in the presence of my enemies;
you anoint my head with oil;
my cup overflows.
6 Surely[n] goodness and mercy[o]
shall follow me
all the days of my life,
and I shall dwell in the house of
the LORD
my whole life long.[p]

Psalm 24

Entrance into the Temple

Of David. A Psalm.

1 The earth is the LORD's and all
that is in it,
the world, and those who live
in it;
2 for he has founded it on the
seas,
and established it on the rivers.

3 Who shall ascend the hill of the
LORD?
And who shall stand in his
holy place?
4 Those who have clean hands
and pure hearts,
who do not lift up their souls to
what is false,
and do not swear deceitfully.
5 They will receive blessing from
the LORD,
and vindication from the God
of their salvation.
6 Such is the company of those
who seek him,
who seek the face of the God of
Jacob.[q] *Selah*

7 Lift up your heads, O gates!
and be lifted up, O ancient
doors!
that the King of glory may
come in.
8 Who is the King of glory?
The LORD, strong and mighty,
the LORD, mighty in battle.
9 Lift up your heads, O gates!
and be lifted up, O ancient
doors!
that the King of glory may
come in.
10 Who is this King of glory?
The LORD of hosts,
he is the King of glory.
Selah

Psalm 25

Prayer for Guidance and for Deliverance

Of David.

1 To you, O LORD, I lift up my
soul.
2 O my God, in you I trust;
do not let me be put to
shame;
do not let my enemies exult
over me.

n Or *Only* *o* Or *kindness* *p* Heb *for length of days* *q* Gk Syr: Heb *your face, O Jacob*

[3] Do not let those who wait for
you be put to shame;
let them be ashamed who are
wantonly treacherous.

[4] Make me to know your ways,
O LORD;
teach me your paths.
[5] Lead me in your truth, and
teach me,
for you are the God of my
salvation;
for you I wait all day long.

[6] Be mindful of your mercy,
O LORD, and of your
steadfast love,
for they have been from of
old.
[7] Do not remember the sins
of my youth or my
transgressions;
according to your steadfast
love remember me,
for your goodness' sake,
O LORD!

[8] Good and upright is the LORD;
therefore he instructs sinners in
the way.
[9] He leads the humble in what is
right,
and teaches the humble his
way.
[10] All the paths of the LORD
are steadfast love and
faithfulness,
for those who keep his covenant
and his decrees.

[11] For your name's sake, O LORD,
pardon my guilt, for it is
great.
[12] Who are they that fear the
LORD?
He will teach them the way that
they should choose.

[13] They will abide in prosperity,
and their children shall
possess the land.
[14] The friendship of the LORD is
for those who fear him,
and he makes his covenant
known to them.
[15] My eyes are ever toward the
LORD,
for he will pluck my feet out of
the net.

[16] Turn to me and be gracious to
me,
for I am lonely and afflicted.
[17] Relieve the troubles of my
heart,
and bring me[r] out of my
distress.
[18] Consider my affliction and my
trouble,
and forgive all my sins.

[19] Consider how many are my
foes,
and with what violent hatred
they hate me.
[20] O guard my life, and deliver
me;

r Or *The troubles of my heart are enlarged; bring me*

do not let me be put to
shame, for I take refuge in
you.
21 May integrity and uprightness
preserve me,
for I wait for you.

22 Redeem Israel, O God,
out of all its troubles.

Psalm 26

Plea for Justice and Declaration of Righteousness

Of David.

1 Vindicate me, O LORD,
for I have walked in my
integrity,
and I have trusted in the LORD
without wavering.
2 Prove me, O LORD, and try me;
test my heart and mind.
3 For your steadfast love is before
my eyes,
and I walk in faithfulness to
you.[s]

4 I do not sit with the worthless,
nor do I consort with
hypocrites;
5 I hate the company of evildoers,
and will not sit with the
wicked.

6 I wash my hands in innocence,
and go around your altar,
O LORD,
7 singing aloud a song of
thanksgiving,
and telling all your wondrous
deeds.

8 O LORD, I love the house in
which you dwell,
and the place where your glory
abides.
9 Do not sweep me away with
sinners,
nor my life with the
bloodthirsty,
10 those in whose hands are evil
devices,
and whose right hands are full
of bribes.

11 But as for me, I walk in my
integrity;
redeem me, and be gracious
to me.
12 My foot stands on level ground;
in the great congregation I
will bless the LORD.

Psalm 27

Triumphant Song of Confidence

Of David.

1 The LORD is my light and my
salvation;
whom shall I fear?
The LORD is the stronghold[t] of
my life;
of whom shall I be afraid?

---

s Or *in your faithfulness* t Or *refuge*

[2] When evildoers assail me
to devour my flesh—
my adversaries and foes—
they shall stumble and fall.

[3] Though an army encamp
against me,
my heart shall not fear;
though war rise up against me,
yet I will be confident.

[4] One thing I asked of the LORD,
that will I seek after:
to live in the house of the LORD
all the days of my life,
to behold the beauty of the
LORD,
and to inquire in his temple.

[5] For he will hide me in his
shelter
in the day of trouble;
he will conceal me under the
cover of his tent;
he will set me high on a rock.

[6] Now my head is lifted up
above my enemies all around
me,
and I will offer in his tent
sacrifices with shouts of joy;
I will sing and make melody to
the LORD.

[7] Hear, O LORD, when I cry
aloud,
be gracious to me and answer
me!

[8] "Come," my heart says, "seek
his face!"
Your face, LORD, do I seek.
[9] Do not hide your face from me.

Do not turn your servant away
in anger,
you who have been my help.
Do not cast me off, do not
forsake me,
O God of my salvation!
[10] If my father and mother forsake
me,
the LORD will take me up.

[11] Teach me your way, O LORD,
and lead me on a level path
because of my enemies.
[12] Do not give me up to the will of
my adversaries,
for false witnesses have risen
against me,
and they are breathing out
violence.

[13] I believe that I shall see the
goodness of the LORD
in the land of the living.
[14] Wait for the LORD;
be strong, and let your heart
take courage;
wait for the LORD!

Psalm 28

Prayer for Help and Thanksgiving for It

Of David.

1 To you, O LORD, I call;
my rock, do not refuse to hear me,
for if you are silent to me,
I shall be like those who go down to the Pit.
2 Hear the voice of my supplication,
as I cry to you for help,
as I lift up my hands
toward your most holy sanctuary.[u]

3 Do not drag me away with the wicked,
with those who are workers of evil,
who speak peace with their neighbors,
while mischief is in their hearts.
4 Repay them according to their work,
and according to the evil of their deeds;
repay them according to the work of their hands;
render them their due reward.
5 Because they do not regard the works of the LORD,
or the work of his hands,
he will break them down and build them up no more.

6 Blessed be the LORD,
for he has heard the sound of my pleadings.
7 The LORD is my strength and my shield;
in him my heart trusts;
so I am helped, and my heart exults,
and with my song I give thanks to him.

8 The LORD is the strength of his people;
he is the saving refuge of his anointed.
9 O save your people, and bless your heritage;
be their shepherd, and carry them forever.

Psalm 29

The Voice of God in a Great Storm

A Psalm of David.

1 Ascribe to the LORD,
O heavenly beings,[v]
ascribe to the LORD glory and strength.
2 Ascribe to the LORD the glory of his name;
worship the LORD in holy splendor.

3 The voice of the LORD is over the waters;
the God of glory thunders,

---

u Heb *your innermost sanctuary* *v* Heb *sons of gods*

the LORD, over mighty
waters.
4 The voice of the LORD is
powerful;
the voice of the LORD is full
of majesty.

5 The voice of the LORD breaks
the cedars;
the LORD breaks the cedars of
Lebanon.
6 He makes Lebanon skip like a
calf,
and Sirion like a young wild
ox.

7 The voice of the LORD flashes
forth flames of fire.
8 The voice of the LORD shakes
the wilderness;
the LORD shakes the
wilderness of Kadesh.

9 The voice of the LORD causes
the oaks to whirl,[w]
and strips the forest bare;
and in his temple all say,
"Glory!"

10 The LORD sits enthroned over
the flood;
the LORD sits enthroned as
king forever.
11 May the LORD give strength to
his people!
May the LORD bless his people
with peace!

Psalm 30

Thanksgiving for Recovery from Grave Illness

A Psalm. A Song at the dedication of the temple. Of David.

1 I will extol you, O LORD, for
you have drawn me up,
and did not let my foes rejoice
over me.
2 O LORD my God, I cried to you
for help,
and you have healed me.
3 O LORD, you brought up my
soul from Sheol,
restored me to life from
among those gone down
to the Pit.[x]

4 Sing praises to the LORD, O you
his faithful ones,
and give thanks to his holy
name.
5 For his anger is but for a
moment;
his favor is for a lifetime.
Weeping may linger for the
night,
but joy comes with the
morning.

6 As for me, I said in my
prosperity,
"I shall never be moved."
7 By your favor, O LORD,
you had established me as a
strong mountain;

w Or *causes the deer to calve* x Or *that I should not go down to the Pit*

you hid your face;
I was dismayed.

8 To you, O LORD, I cried,
and to the LORD I made supplication:
9 "What profit is there in my death,
if I go down to the Pit?
Will the dust praise you?
Will it tell of your faithfulness?
10 Hear, O LORD, and be gracious to me!
O LORD, be my helper!"

11 You have turned my mourning into dancing;
you have taken off my sackcloth
and clothed me with joy,
12 so that my soul[y] may praise you
and not be silent.
O LORD my God, I will give thanks to you forever.

Psalm 31

Prayer and Praise for Deliverance from Enemies

To the leader. A Psalm of David.

1 In you, O LORD, I seek refuge;
do not let me ever be put to shame;
in your righteousness deliver me.
2 Incline your ear to me;
rescue me speedily.
Be a rock of refuge for me,
a strong fortress to save me.
3 You are indeed my rock and my fortress;
for your name's sake lead me and guide me,
4 take me out of the net that is hidden for me,
for you are my refuge.
5 Into your hand I commit my spirit;
you have redeemed me,
O LORD, faithful God.

6 You hate[z] those who pay regard to worthless idols,
but I trust in the LORD.
7 I will exult and rejoice in your steadfast love,
because you have seen my affliction;
you have taken heed of my adversities,
8 and have not delivered me into the hand of the enemy;
you have set my feet in a broad place.

9 Be gracious to me, O LORD, for I am in distress;
my eye wastes away from grief,
my soul and body also.
10 For my life is spent with sorrow,
and my years with sighing;
my strength fails because of my misery,[a]
and my bones waste away.

11 I am the scorn of all my adversaries,

---

y Heb *that glory* *z* One Heb Ms Gk Syr Jerome: MT *I hate* *a* Gk Syr: Heb *my iniquity*

a horror[b] to my neighbors,
an object of dread to my acquaintances;
those who see me in the street flee from me.
12 I have passed out of mind like one who is dead;
I have become like a broken vessel.
13 For I hear the whispering of many—
terror all around!—
as they scheme together against me,
as they plot to take my life.

14 But I trust in you, O LORD;
I say, "You are my God."
15 My times are in your hand;
deliver me from the hand of my enemies and persecutors.
16 Let your face shine upon your servant;
save me in your steadfast love.
17 Do not let me be put to shame, O LORD,
for I call on you;
let the wicked be put to shame;
let them go dumbfounded to Sheol.
18 Let the lying lips be stilled
that speak insolently against the righteous
with pride and contempt.

19 O how abundant is your goodness
that you have laid up for those who fear you,
and accomplished for those who take refuge in you,
in the sight of everyone!
20 In the shelter of your presence you hide them
from human plots;
you hold them safe under your shelter
from contentious tongues.

21 Blessed be the LORD,
for he has wondrously shown his steadfast love to me
when I was beset as a city under siege.
22 I had said in my alarm,
"I am driven far[c] from your sight."
But you heard my supplications
when I cried out to you for help.

23 Love the LORD, all you his saints.
The LORD preserves the faithful,
but abundantly repays the one who acts haughtily.
24 Be strong, and let your heart take courage,
all you who wait for the LORD.

Psalm 32

The Joy of Forgiveness

Of David. A Maskil.

1 Happy are those whose transgression is forgiven,
whose sin is covered.

b Cn: Heb *exceedingly* *c* Another reading is *cut off*

2 Happy are those to whom the
LORD imputes no iniquity,
and in whose spirit there is
no deceit.

3 While I kept silence, my body
wasted away
through my groaning all day
long.
4 For day and night your hand
was heavy upon me;
my strength was dried up[d] as
by the heat of summer.
Selah

5 Then I acknowledged my sin to
you,
and I did not hide my
iniquity;
I said, "I will confess my
transgressions to the
LORD,"
and you forgave the guilt of
my sin. *Selah*

6 Therefore let all who are
faithful
offer prayer to you;
at a time of distress,[e] the rush of
mighty waters
shall not reach them.
7 You are a hiding place for me;
you preserve me from
trouble;
you surround me with glad
cries of deliverance.
Selah

8 I will instruct you and teach
you the way you should
go;
I will counsel you with my
eye upon you.
9 Do not be like a horse
or a mule, without
understanding,
whose temper must be curbed
with bit and bridle,
else it will not stay near you.

10 Many are the torments of the
wicked,
but steadfast love surrounds
those who trust in the
LORD.
11 Be glad in the LORD and rejoice,
O righteous,
and shout for joy, all you
upright in heart.

Psalm 33

The Greatness and Goodness of God

1 Rejoice in the LORD, O you
righteous.
Praise befits the upright.
2 Praise the LORD with the lyre;
make melody to him with the
harp of ten strings.
3 Sing to him a new song;
play skillfully on the strings,
with loud shouts.

4 For the word of the LORD is
upright,

d Meaning of Heb uncertain *e* Cn: Heb *at a time of finding only*

and all his work is done in
faithfulness.
5 He loves righteousness and
justice;
the earth is full of the
steadfast love of the LORD.

6 By the word of the LORD the
heavens were made,
and all their host by the
breath of his mouth.
7 He gathered the waters of the
sea as in a bottle;
he put the deeps in
storehouses.

8 Let all the earth fear the LORD;
let all the inhabitants of the
world stand in awe of
him.
9 For he spoke, and it came to be;
he commanded, and it stood
firm.

10 The LORD brings the counsel of
the nations to nothing;
he frustrates the plans of the
peoples.
11 The counsel of the LORD stands
forever,
the thoughts of his heart to all
generations.
12 Happy is the nation whose God
is the LORD,
the people whom he has
chosen as his heritage.

13 The LORD looks down from
heaven;
he sees all humankind.
14 From where he sits enthroned
he watches
all the inhabitants of the
earth—
15 he who fashions the hearts of
them all,
and observes all their deeds.
16 A king is not saved by his great
army;
a warrior is not delivered by
his great strength.
17 The war horse is a vain hope
for victory,
and by its great might it
cannot save.

18 Truly the eye of the LORD is on
those who fear him,
on those who hope in his
steadfast love,
19 to deliver their soul from death,
and to keep them alive in
famine.

20 Our soul waits for the LORD;
he is our help and shield.
21 Our heart is glad in him,
because we trust in his holy
name.
22 Let your steadfast love,
O LORD, be upon us,
even as we hope in you.

Psalm 34

Praise for Deliverance from Trouble

Of David, when he feigned madness before Abimelech, so that he drove him out, and he went away.

[1] I will bless the LORD at all times;
his praise shall continually be in my mouth.
[2] My soul makes its boast in the LORD;
let the humble hear and be glad.
[3] O magnify the LORD with me,
and let us exalt his name together.

[4] I sought the LORD, and he answered me,
and delivered me from all my fears.
[5] Look to him, and be radiant;
so your[f] faces shall never be ashamed.
[6] This poor soul cried, and was heard by the LORD,
and was saved from every trouble.
[7] The angel of the LORD encamps around those who fear him,
and delivers them.
[8] O taste and see that the LORD is good;
happy are those who take refuge in him.
[9] O fear the LORD, you his holy ones,
for those who fear him have no want.
[10] The young lions suffer want and hunger,
but those who seek the LORD lack no good thing.

[11] Come, O children, listen to me;
I will teach you the fear of the LORD.
[12] Which of you desires life,
and covets many days to enjoy good?
[13] Keep your tongue from evil,
and your lips from speaking deceit.
[14] Depart from evil, and do good;
seek peace, and pursue it.

[15] The eyes of the LORD are on the righteous,
and his ears are open to their cry.
[16] The face of the LORD is against evildoers,
to cut off the remembrance of them from the earth.
[17] When the righteous cry for help, the LORD hears,
and rescues them from all their troubles.
[18] The LORD is near to the brokenhearted,
and saves the crushed in spirit.

[19] Many are the afflictions of the righteous,

---

f Gk Syr Jerome: Heb *their*

but the LORD rescues them
from them all.
20 He keeps all their bones;
not one of them will be
broken.
21 Evil brings death to the wicked,
and those who hate the
righteous will be
condemned.
22 The LORD redeems the life of
his servants;
none of those who take
refuge in him will be
condemned.

Psalm 35

Prayer for Deliverance from Enemies

Of David.

1 Contend, O LORD, with those
who contend with me;
fight against those who fight
against me!
2 Take hold of shield and buckler,
and rise up to help me!
3 Draw the spear and javelin
against my pursuers;
say to my soul,
"I am your salvation."

4 Let them be put to shame and
dishonor
who seek after my life.
Let them be turned back and
confounded
who devise evil against me.
5 Let them be like chaff before
the wind,
with the angel of the LORD
driving them on.
6 Let their way be dark and
slippery,
with the angel of the LORD
pursuing them.

7 For without cause they hid their
net[g] for me;
without cause they dug a pit[h]
for my life.
8 Let ruin come on them
unawares.
And let the net that they hid
ensnare them;
let them fall in it—to their
ruin.

9 Then my soul shall rejoice in
the LORD,
exulting in his deliverance.
10 All my bones shall say,
"O LORD, who is like you?
You deliver the weak
from those too strong for
them,
the weak and needy from
those who despoil them."

11 Malicious witnesses rise up;
they ask me about things I do
not know.
12 They repay me evil for good;
my soul is forlorn.
13 But as for me, when they were
sick,
I wore sackcloth;
I afflicted myself with
fasting.

---

g Heb *a pit, their net* h The word *pit* is transposed from the preceding line

I prayed with head bowed[i] on
my bosom,
14 as though I grieved for a
friend or a brother;
I went about as one who
laments for a mother,
bowed down and in mourning.

15 But at my stumbling they
gathered in glee,
they gathered together against
me;
ruffians whom I did not know
tore at me without ceasing;
16 they impiously mocked more
and more,[j]
gnashing at me with their teeth.

17 How long, O LORD, will you
look on?
Rescue me from their
ravages,
my life from the lions!
18 Then I will thank you in the
great congregation;
in the mighty throng I will
praise you.

19 Do not let my treacherous
enemies rejoice over me,
or those who hate me without
cause wink the eye.
20 For they do not speak peace,
but they conceive deceitful
words
against those who are quiet in
the land.
21 They open wide their mouths
against me;
they say, "Aha, Aha,
our eyes have seen it."
22 You have seen, O LORD; do not
be silent!
O Lord, do not be far from me!
23 Wake up! Bestir yourself for
my defense,
for my cause, my God and my
Lord!
24 Vindicate me, O LORD, my God,
according to your
righteousness,
and do not let them rejoice
over me.
25 Do not let them say to
themselves,
"Aha, we have our heart's
desire."
Do not let them say, "We have
swallowed you[k] up."

26 Let all those who rejoice at my
calamity
be put to shame and
confusion;
let those who exalt themselves
against me
be clothed with shame and
dishonor.

27 Let those who desire my
vindication
shout for joy and be glad,
and say evermore,
"Great is the LORD,
who delights in the welfare of
his servant."
28 Then my tongue shall tell of
your righteousness
and of your praise all day long.

---

i Or *My prayer turned back* *j* Cn Compare Gk: Heb *like the profanest of mockers of a cake* *k* Heb *him*

Psalm 36

Human Wickedness and Divine Goodness

To the leader. Of David, the servant of the LORD.

1 Transgression speaks to the wicked
deep in their hearts;
there is no fear of God
before their eyes.
2 For they flatter themselves in their own eyes
that their iniquity cannot be found out and hated.
3 The words of their mouths are mischief and deceit;
they have ceased to act wisely and do good.
4 They plot mischief while on their beds;
they are set on a way that is not good;
they do not reject evil.

5 Your steadfast love, O LORD, extends to the heavens,
your faithfulness to the clouds.
6 Your righteousness is like the mighty mountains,
your judgments are like the great deep;
you save humans and animals alike, O LORD.

7 How precious is your steadfast love, O God!
All people may take refuge in the shadow of your wings.
8 They feast on the abundance of your house,
and you give them drink from the river of your delights.
9 For with you is the fountain of life;
in your light we see light.

10 O continue your steadfast love to those who know you,
and your salvation to the upright of heart!
11 Do not let the foot of the arrogant tread on me,
or the hand of the wicked drive me away.
12 There the evildoers lie prostrate;
they are thrust down, unable to rise.

Psalm 37

Exhortation to Patience and Trust

Of David.

1 Do not fret because of the wicked;
do not be envious of wrongdoers,
2 for they will soon fade like the grass,
and wither like the green herb.

3 Trust in the LORD, and do good;
so you will live in the land, and enjoy security.
4 Take delight in the LORD,
and he will give you the desires of your heart.

5 Commit your way to the LORD;
trust in him, and he will act.
6 He will make your vindication shine like the light,
and the justice of your cause like the noonday.

7 Be still before the LORD, and wait patiently for him;
do not fret over those who prosper in their way,
over those who carry out evil devices.

8 Refrain from anger, and forsake wrath.
Do not fret—it leads only to evil.
9 For the wicked shall be cut off,
but those who wait for the LORD shall inherit the land.

10 Yet a little while, and the wicked will be no more;
though you look diligently for their place, they will not be there.
11 But the meek shall inherit the land,
and delight themselves in abundant prosperity.

12 The wicked plot against the righteous,
and gnash their teeth at them;
13 but the LORD laughs at the wicked,
for he sees that their day is coming.

14 The wicked draw the sword and bend their bows
to bring down the poor and needy,
to kill those who walk uprightly;
15 their sword shall enter their own heart,
and their bows shall be broken.

16 Better is a little that the righteous person has
than the abundance of many wicked.
17 For the arms of the wicked shall be broken,
but the LORD upholds the righteous.

18 The LORD knows the days of the blameless,
and their heritage will abide forever;
19 they are not put to shame in evil times,
in the days of famine they have abundance.

20 But the wicked perish,
and the enemies of the LORD are like the glory of the pastures;
they vanish—like smoke they vanish away.

21 The wicked borrow, and do not pay back,
but the righteous are generous and keep giving;

22 for those blessed by the LORD
shall inherit the land,
but those cursed by him shall be
cut off.

23 Our steps[l] are made firm by the
LORD,
when he delights in our[m]
way;
24 though we stumble,[n] we[o] shall
not fall headlong,
for the LORD holds us[p] by the
hand.

25 I have been young, and now am
old,
yet I have not seen the
righteous forsaken
or their children begging
bread.
26 They are ever giving liberally
and lending,
and their children become a
blessing.

27 Depart from evil, and do good;
so you shall abide forever.
28 For the LORD loves justice;
he will not forsake his faithful
ones.

The righteous shall be kept safe
forever,
but the children of the wicked
shall be cut off.
29 The righteous shall inherit the
land,
and live in it forever.

30 The mouths of the righteous
utter wisdom,
and their tongues speak
justice.
31 The law of their God is in their
hearts;
their steps do not slip.

32 The wicked watch for the
righteous,
and seek to kill them.
33 The LORD will not abandon
them to their power,
or let them be condemned
when they are brought to
trial.

34 Wait for the LORD, and keep to
his way,
and he will exalt you to
inherit the land;
you will look on the
destruction of the wicked.

35 I have seen the wicked
oppressing,
and towering like a cedar of
Lebanon.[q]
36 Again I[r] passed by, and they
were no more;
though I sought them, they
could not be found.

37 Mark the blameless, and behold
the upright,

---

l Heb *A man's steps* *m* Heb *his* *n* Heb *he stumbles* *o* Heb *he* *p* Heb *him*
q Gk: Meaning of Heb uncertain *r* Gk Syr Jerome: Heb *he*

for there is posterity for the
peaceable.
38 But transgressors shall be
altogether destroyed;
the posterity of the wicked shall
be cut off.

39 The salvation of the righteous is
from the LORD;
he is their refuge in the time
of trouble.
40 The LORD helps them and
rescues them;
he rescues them from the
wicked, and saves them,
because they take refuge in
him.

Psalm 38

A Penitent Sufferer's Plea for Healing

A Psalm of David, for the memorial offering.

1 O LORD, do not rebuke me in
your anger,
or discipline me in your
wrath.
2 For your arrows have sunk into
me,
and your hand has come
down on me.

3 There is no soundness in my
flesh
because of your indignation;
there is no health in my bones
because of my sin.
4 For my iniquities have gone
over my head;
they weigh like a burden too
heavy for me.

5 My wounds grow foul and
fester
because of my foolishness;
6 I am utterly bowed down and
prostrate;
all day long I go around
mourning.
7 For my loins are filled with
burning,
and there is no soundness in
my flesh.
8 I am utterly spent and crushed;
I groan because of the tumult of
my heart.

9 O Lord, all my longing is
known to you;
my sighing is not hidden from
you.
10 My heart throbs, my strength
fails me;
as for the light of my eyes—
it also has gone from me.
11 My friends and companions
stand aloof from my
affliction,
and my neighbors stand far
off.

12 Those who seek my life lay
their snares;
those who seek to hurt me
speak of ruin,
and meditate treachery all day
long.

13 But I am like the deaf, I do not
hear;
like the mute, who cannot
speak.
14 Truly, I am like one who does
not hear,
and in whose mouth is no
retort.

15 But it is for you, O LORD, that I
wait;
it is you, O Lord my God,
who will answer.
16 For I pray, "Only do not let
them rejoice over me,
those who boast against me
when my foot slips."

17 For I am ready to fall,
and my pain is ever with me.
18 I confess my iniquity;
I am sorry for my sin.
19 Those who are my foes without
cause[s] are mighty,
and many are those who hate
me wrongfully.
20 Those who render me evil for
good
are my adversaries because I
follow after good.

21 Do not forsake me, O LORD;
O my God, do not be far from
me;
22 make haste to help me,
O Lord, my salvation.

Psalm 39

Prayer for Wisdom and Forgiveness

To the leader: to Jeduthun. A Psalm of David.

1 I said, "I will guard my ways
that I may not sin with my
tongue;
I will keep a muzzle on my
mouth
as long as the wicked are in my
presence."
2 I was silent and still;
I held my peace to no avail;
my distress grew worse,
3 my heart became hot within me.
While I mused, the fire burned;
then I spoke with my tongue:

4 "LORD, let me know my end,
and what is the measure of my
days;
let me know how fleeting my
life is.
5 You have made my days a few
handbreadths,
and my lifetime is as nothing in
your sight.
Surely everyone stands as a
mere breath. *Selah*
6 Surely everyone goes about like
a shadow.
Surely for nothing they are in
turmoil;
they heap up, and do not
know who will gather.

---

s Q Ms: MT *my living foes*

7 "And now, O Lord, what do I
wait for?
My hope is in you.
8 Deliver me from all my
transgressions.
Do not make me the scorn of
the fool.
9 I am silent; I do not open my
mouth,
for it is you who have done it.
10 Remove your stroke from me;
I am worn down by the
blows[t] of your hand.

11 "You chastise mortals
in punishment for sin,
consuming like a moth what is
dear to them;
surely everyone is a mere
breath. *Selah*

12 "Hear my prayer, O LORD,
and give ear to my cry;
do not hold your peace at my
tears.
For I am your passing guest,
an alien, like all my forebears.
13 Turn your gaze away from me,
that I may smile again,
before I depart and am no
more."

Psalm 40

Thanksgiving for Deliverance and Prayer for Help

To the leader. Of David. A Psalm.

1 I waited patiently for the LORD;
he inclined to me and heard my
cry.
2 He drew me up from the
desolate pit,[u]
out of the miry bog,
and set my feet upon a rock,
making my steps secure.
3 He put a new song in my
mouth,
a song of praise to our God.
Many will see and fear,
and put their trust in the
LORD.

4 Happy are those who make
the LORD their trust,
who do not turn to the proud,
to those who go astray after
false gods.
5 You have multiplied, O LORD
my God,
your wondrous deeds and your
thoughts toward us;
none can compare with you.
Were I to proclaim and tell of
them,
they would be more than can
be counted.

6 Sacrifice and offering you do
not desire,
but you have given me an open
ear.[v]
Burnt offering and sin offering
you have not required.
7 Then I said, "Here I am;
in the scroll of the book it is
written of me.[w]

---

t Heb *hostility* *u* Cn: Heb *pit of tumult*
v Heb *ears you have dug for me* *w* Meaning of Heb uncertain

8 I delight to do your will, O my God;
your law is within my heart."

9 I have told the glad news of deliverance
in the great congregation;
see, I have not restrained my lips,
as you know, O LORD.
10 I have not hidden your saving help within my heart,
I have spoken of your faithfulness and your salvation;
I have not concealed your steadfast love and your faithfulness
from the great congregation.

11 Do not, O LORD, withhold
your mercy from me;
let your steadfast love and your faithfulness
keep me safe forever.
12 For evils have encompassed me
without number;
my iniquities have overtaken me,
until I cannot see;
they are more than the hairs of my head,
and my heart fails me.

13 Be pleased, O LORD, to deliver me;
O LORD, make haste to help me.
14 Let all those be put to shame and confusion
who seek to snatch away my life;
let those be turned back and brought to dishonor
who desire my hurt.
15 Let those be appalled because of their shame
who say to me, "Aha, Aha!"

16 But may all who seek you
rejoice and be glad in you;
may those who love your salvation
say continually, "Great is the LORD!"
17 As for me, I am poor and needy,
but the Lord takes thought for me.
You are my help and my deliverer;
do not delay, O my God.

Psalm 41

Assurance of God's Help and a Plea for Healing

To the leader. A Psalm of David.

1 Happy are those who consider the poor;[x]
the LORD delivers them in the day of trouble.
2 The LORD protects them and keeps them alive;
they are called happy in the land.
You do not give them up to the will of their enemies.
3 The LORD sustains them on their sickbed;

x Or *weak*

in their illness you heal all
their infirmities.[y]

4 As for me, I said, "O LORD, be
gracious to me;
heal me, for I have sinned
against you."
5 My enemies wonder in malice
when I will die, and my name
perish.
6 And when they come to see me,
they utter empty words,
while their hearts gather
mischief;
when they go out, they tell it
abroad.
7 All who hate me whisper
together about me;
they imagine the worst for
me.

8 They think that a deadly thing
has fastened on me,
that I will not rise again from
where I lie.
9 Even my bosom friend in whom
I trusted,
who ate of my bread, has lifted
the heel against me.
10 But you, O LORD, be gracious to
me,
and raise me up, that I may
repay them.

11 By this I know that you are
pleased with me;
because my enemy has not
triumphed over me.
12 But you have upheld me
because of my integrity,
and set me in your presence
forever.

13 Blessed be the LORD, the God of
Israel,
from everlasting to
everlasting.
Amen and Amen.

BOOK II
(Psalms 42–72)

Psalm 42

Longing for God and His Help in Distress

To the leader. A Maskil of the
Korahites.

1 As a deer longs for flowing
streams,
so my soul longs for you,
O God.
2 My soul thirsts for God,
for the living God.
When shall I come and behold
the face of God?
3 My tears have been my food
day and night,
while people say to me
continually,
"Where is your God?"

4 These things I remember,
as I pour out my soul:
how I went with the throng,[z]

y Heb *you change all his bed* z Meaning of Heb uncertain

and led them in procession to
the house of God,
with glad shouts and songs of
thanksgiving,
a multitude keeping festival.
5 Why are you cast down, O my
soul,
and why are you disquieted
within me?
Hope in God; for I shall again
praise him,
my help 6 and my God.

My soul is cast down within
me;
therefore I remember you
from the land of Jordan and of
Hermon,
from Mount Mizar.
7 Deep calls to deep
at the thunder of your
cataracts;
all your waves and your billows
have gone over me.
8 By day the LORD commands his
steadfast love,
and at night his song is with
me,
a prayer to the God of my
life.

9 I say to God, my rock,
"Why have you forgotten
me?
Why must I walk about
mournfully
because the enemy oppresses
me?"
10 As with a deadly wound in my
body,
my adversaries taunt me,
while they say to me
continually,
"Where is your God?"

11 Why are you cast down, O my
soul,
and why are you disquieted
within me?
Hope in God; for I shall again
praise him,
my help and my God.

Psalm 43

Prayer to God in Time of Trouble

1 Vindicate me, O God, and
defend my cause
against an ungodly people;
from those who are deceitful
and unjust
deliver me!
2 For you are the God in whom I
take refuge;
why have you cast me off?
Why must I walk about
mournfully
because of the oppression of
the enemy?

3 O send out your light and your
truth;
let them lead me;
let them bring me to your holy
hill
and to your dwelling.
4 Then I will go to the altar of
God,
to God my exceeding joy;
and I will praise you with the
harp,

O God, my God.

[5] Why are you cast down, O my soul,
and why are you disquieted within me?
Hope in God; for I shall again praise him,
my help and my God.

Psalm 44

National Lament and Prayer for Help

To the leader. Of the Korahites. A Maskil.

[1] We have heard with our ears, O God,
our ancestors have told us,
what deeds you performed in their days,
in the days of old:
[2] you with your own hand drove out the nations,
but them you planted;
you afflicted the peoples,
but them you set free;
[3] for not by their own sword did they win the land,
nor did their own arm give them victory;
but your right hand, and your arm,
and the light of your countenance,
for you delighted in them.

[4] You are my King and my God;
you command[a] victories for Jacob.
[5] Through you we push down our foes;
through your name we tread down our assailants.
[6] For not in my bow do I trust,
nor can my sword save me.
[7] But you have saved us from our foes,
and have put to confusion those who hate us.
[8] In God we have boasted continually,
and we will give thanks to your name forever.
Selah

[9] Yet you have rejected us and abased us,
and have not gone out with our armies.
[10] You made us turn back from the foe,
and our enemies have gotten spoil.
[11] You have made us like sheep for slaughter,
and have scattered us among the nations.
[12] You have sold your people for a trifle,
demanding no high price for them.

[13] You have made us the taunt of our neighbors,
the derision and scorn of those around us.

---

a Gk Syr: Heb *You are my King, O God; command*

14 You have made us a byword
among the nations,
a laughingstock[b] among the
peoples.
15 All day long my disgrace is
before me,
and shame has covered my
face
16 at the words of the taunters and
revilers,
at the sight of the enemy and
the avenger.

17 All this has come upon us,
yet we have not forgotten
you,
or been false to your
covenant.
18 Our heart has not turned back,
nor have our steps departed
from your way,
19 yet you have broken us in the
haunt of jackals,
and covered us with deep
darkness.

20 If we had forgotten the name of
our God,
or spread out our hands to a
strange god,
21 would not God discover this?
For he knows the secrets of
the heart.
22 Because of you we are being
killed all day long,
and accounted as sheep for
the slaughter.

23 Rouse yourself! Why do you
sleep, O Lord?
Awake, do not cast us off
forever!
24 Why do you hide your face?
Why do you forget our
affliction and oppression?
25 For we sink down to the dust;
our bodies cling to the
ground.
26 Rise up, come to our help.
Redeem us for the sake of
your steadfast love.

Psalm 45

Ode for a Royal Wedding

To the leader: according to Lilies.
Of the Korahites. A Maskil. A
love song.

1 My heart overflows with a
goodly theme;
I address my verses to the
king;
my tongue is like the pen of a
ready scribe.

2 You are the most handsome of
men;
grace is poured upon your
lips;
therefore God has blessed
you forever.
3 Gird your sword on your thigh,
O mighty one,
in your glory and majesty.

4 In your majesty ride on
victoriously

b Heb *a shaking of the head*

for the cause of truth and to
defend[c] the right;
let your right hand teach you
dread deeds.
5 Your arrows are sharp
in the heart of the king's
enemies;
the peoples fall under you.

6 Your throne, O God,[d] endures
forever and ever.
Your royal scepter is a scepter
of equity;
7 you love righteousness and hate
wickedness.
Therefore God, your God, has
anointed you
with the oil of gladness beyond
your companions;
8 your robes are all fragrant with
myrrh and aloes and
cassia.
From ivory palaces stringed
instruments make you
glad;
9 daughters of kings are among
your ladies of honor;
at your right hand stands the
queen in gold of Ophir.

10 Hear, O daughter, consider and
incline your ear;
forget your people and your
father's house,
11 and the king will desire your
beauty.
Since he is your lord, bow to
him;
12 the people[e] of Tyre will seek
your favor with gifts,
the richest of the people
13 with all kinds of wealth.
The princess is decked in her
chamber with gold-woven
robes;[f]
14 in many-colored robes she is
led to the king;
behind her the virgins, her
companions, follow.
15 With joy and gladness they are
led along
as they enter the palace of the
king.

16 In the place of ancestors you,
O king,[g] shall have sons;
you will make them princes
in all the earth.
17 I will cause your name to
be celebrated in all
generations;
therefore the peoples will
praise you forever and
ever.

Psalm 46

God's Defense of His City and People

To the leader. Of the Korahites.
According to Alamoth. A Song.

1 God is our refuge and strength,
a very present[h] help in
trouble.
2 Therefore we will not fear,
though the earth should
change,

c Cn: Heb *and the meekness of* d Or *Your throne is a throne of God, it* e Heb *daughter* f Or *people.* 13*All glorious is the princess within, gold embroidery is her clothing* g Heb lacks *O king* h Or *well proved*

though the mountains shake
in the heart of the sea;
3 though its waters roar and foam,
though the mountains tremble
with its tumult. *Selah*

4 There is a river whose streams
make glad the city of God,
the holy habitation of the Most High.
5 God is in the midst of the city;[i]
it shall not be moved;
God will help it when the morning dawns.
6 The nations are in an uproar,
the kingdoms totter;
he utters his voice, the earth melts.
7 The LORD of hosts is with us;
the God of Jacob is our refuge.[j]
Selah

8 Come, behold the works of the LORD;
see what desolations he has
brought on the earth.
9 He makes wars cease to the end
of the earth;
he breaks the bow, and
shatters the spear;
he burns the shields with fire.
10 "Be still, and know that I am God!
I am exalted among the nations,
I am exalted in the earth."
11 The LORD of hosts is with us;
the God of Jacob is our refuge.[k]
Selah

Psalm 47

God's Rule over the Nations

To the leader. Of the Korahites.
A Psalm.

1 Clap your hands, all you peoples;
shout to God with loud songs of joy.
2 For the LORD, the Most High, is awesome,
a great king over all the earth.
3 He subdued peoples under us,
and nations under our feet.
4 He chose our heritage for us,
the pride of Jacob whom he loves. *Selah*

5 God has gone up with a shout,
the LORD with the sound of a trumpet.
6 Sing praises to God, sing praises;
sing praises to our King, sing praises.
7 For God is the king of all the earth;
sing praises with a psalm.[l]

8 God is king over the nations;
God sits on his holy throne.
9 The princes of the peoples gather
as the people of the God of Abraham.
For the shields of the earth
belong to God;
he is highly exalted.

i Heb *of it* *j* Or *fortress* *k* Or *fortress*
l Heb *Maskil*

Psalm 48

The Glory and Strength of Zion

A Song. A Psalm of the Korahites.

1 Great is the LORD and greatly to be praised
in the city of our God.
His holy mountain, 2 beautiful in elevation,
is the joy of all the earth,
Mount Zion, in the far north,
the city of the great King.
3 Within its citadels God
has shown himself a sure defense.

4 Then the kings assembled,
they came on together.
5 As soon as they saw it, they were astounded;
they were in panic, they took to flight;
6 trembling took hold of them there,
pains as of a woman in labor,
7 as when an east wind shatters
the ships of Tarshish.
8 As we have heard, so have we seen
in the city of the LORD of hosts,
in the city of our God,
which God establishes forever. *Selah*

9 We ponder your steadfast love, O God,
in the midst of your temple.
10 Your name, O God, like your praise,
reaches to the ends of the earth.
Your right hand is filled with victory.
11 Let Mount Zion be glad,
let the towns[m] of Judah rejoice
because of your judgments.

12 Walk about Zion, go all around it,
count its towers,
13 consider well its ramparts;
go through its citadels,
that you may tell the next generation
14 that this is God,
our God forever and ever.
He will be our guide forever.

Psalm 49

The Folly of Trust in Riches

To the leader. Of the Korahites. A Psalm.

1 Hear this, all you peoples;
give ear, all inhabitants of the world,
2 both low and high,
rich and poor together.
3 My mouth shall speak wisdom;
the meditation of my heart shall be understanding.
4 I will incline my ear to a proverb;
I will solve my riddle to the music of the harp.

m Heb *daughters*

[5] Why should I fear in times of
trouble,
when the iniquity of my
persecutors surrounds me,
[6] those who trust in their wealth
and boast of the abundance of
their riches?
[7] Truly, no ransom avails for
one's life,[n]
there is no price one can give
to God for it.
[8] For the ransom of life is costly,
and can never suffice,
[9] that one should live on forever
and never see the grave.[o]

[10] When we look at the wise, they
die;
fool and dolt perish together
and leave their wealth to others.
[11] Their graves[p] are their homes
forever,
their dwelling places to all
generations,
though they named lands
their own.
[12] Mortals cannot abide in their
pomp;
they are like the animals that
perish.

[13] Such is the fate of the
foolhardy,
the end of those[q] who are
pleased with their lot.
Selah
[14] Like sheep they are appointed
for Sheol;
Death shall be their shepherd;
straight to the grave they
descend,[r]
and their form shall waste
away;
Sheol shall be their home.[s]
[15] But God will ransom my soul
from the power of Sheol,
for he will receive me.
Selah

[16] Do not be afraid when some
become rich,
when the wealth of their
houses increases.
[17] For when they die they will
carry nothing away;
their wealth will not go down
after them.
[18] Though in their lifetime they
count themselves happy
—for you are praised when you
do well for yourself—
[19] they[t] will go to the company of
their ancestors,
who will never again see the
light.
[20] Mortals cannot abide in their
pomp;
they are like the animals that
perish.

Psalm 50

The Acceptable Sacrifice

A Psalm of Asaph.

[1] The mighty one, God the LORD,

n Another reading is *no one can ransom a brother* *o* Heb *the pit* *p* Gk Syr Compare Tg: Heb *their inward* (thought) *q* Tg: Heb *after them* *r* Cn: Heb *the upright shall have dominion over them in the morning* *s* Meaning of Heb uncertain *t* Cn: Heb *you*

speaks and summons the earth
from the rising of the sun to its setting.
2 Out of Zion, the perfection of beauty,
God shines forth.

3 Our God comes and does not keep silence,
before him is a devouring fire,
and a mighty tempest all around him.
4 He calls to the heavens above
and to the earth, that he may judge his people:
5 "Gather to me my faithful ones,
who made a covenant with me by sacrifice!"
6 The heavens declare his righteousness,
for God himself is judge. *Selah*

7 "Hear, O my people, and I will speak,
O Israel, I will testify against you.
I am God, your God.
8 Not for your sacrifices do I rebuke you;
your burnt offerings are continually before me.
9 I will not accept a bull from your house,
or goats from your folds.
10 For every wild animal of the forest is mine,
the cattle on a thousand hills.
11 I know all the birds of the air,[u]
and all that moves in the field is mine.
12 "If I were hungry, I would not tell you,
for the world and all that is in it is mine.
13 Do I eat the flesh of bulls,
or drink the blood of goats?
14 Offer to God a sacrifice of thanksgiving,[v]
and pay your vows to the Most High.
15 Call on me in the day of trouble;
I will deliver you, and you shall glorify me."

16 But to the wicked God says:
"What right have you to recite my statutes,
or take my covenant on your lips?
17 For you hate discipline,
and you cast my words behind you.
18 You make friends with a thief when you see one,
and you keep company with adulterers.

19 "You give your mouth free rein for evil,
and your tongue frames deceit.
20 You sit and speak against your kin;
you slander your own mother's child.
21 These things you have done and I have been silent;
you thought that I was one just like yourself.

u Gk Syr Tg: Heb *mountains* *v* Or *make thanksgiving your sacrifice to God*

But now I rebuke you, and lay
the charge before you.

22 "Mark this, then, you who
forget God,
or I will tear you apart, and
there will be no one to
deliver.
23 Those who bring thanksgiving
as their sacrifice honor
me;
to those who go the right way[w]
I will show the salvation of
God."

Psalm 51

Prayer for Cleansing and Pardon

To the leader. A Psalm of David, when the prophet Nathan came to him, after he had gone in to Bathsheba.

1 Have mercy on me, O God,
according to your steadfast
love;
according to your abundant
mercy
blot out my transgressions.
2 Wash me thoroughly from my
iniquity,
and cleanse me from my sin.

3 For I know my transgressions,
and my sin is ever before me.
4 Against you, you alone, have I
sinned,
and done what is evil in your
sight,
so that you are justified in your
sentence
and blameless when you pass
judgment.
5 Indeed, I was born guilty,
a sinner when my mother
conceived me.

6 You desire truth in the inward
being;[x]
therefore teach me wisdom in
my secret heart.
7 Purge me with hyssop, and I
shall be clean;
wash me, and I shall be whiter
than snow.
8 Let me hear joy and gladness;
let the bones that you have
crushed rejoice.
9 Hide your face from my sins,
and blot out all my iniquities.

10 Create in me a clean heart,
O God,
and put a new and right[y] spirit
within me.
11 Do not cast me away from your
presence,
and do not take your holy spirit
from me.
12 Restore to me the joy of your
salvation,
and sustain in me a willing[z]
spirit.

13 Then I will teach transgressors
your ways,
and sinners will return to you.

---

w Heb *who set a way* *x* Meaning of Heb uncertain *y* Or *steadfast* *z* Or *generous*

14 Deliver me from bloodshed,
O God,
O God of my salvation,
and my tongue will sing
aloud of your deliverance.

15 O Lord, open my lips,
and my mouth will declare your
praise.
16 For you have no delight in
sacrifice;
if I were to give a burnt
offering, you would not
be pleased.
17 The sacrifice acceptable to
God[a] is a broken spirit;
a broken and contrite heart,
O God, you will not
despise.

18 Do good to Zion in your good
pleasure;
rebuild the walls of Jerusalem,
19 then you will delight in right
sacrifices,
in burnt offerings and whole
burnt offerings;
then bulls will be offered on
your altar.

Psalm 52

Judgment on the Deceitful

To the leader. A Maskil of David, when Doeg the Edomite came to Saul and said to him, "David has come to the house of Ahimelech."

1 Why do you boast, O mighty
one,
of mischief done against the
godly?[b]
All day long 2 you are plotting
destruction.
Your tongue is like a sharp
razor,
you worker of treachery.
3 You love evil more than good,
and lying more than speaking
the truth. *Selah*
4 You love all words that devour,
O deceitful tongue.

5 But God will break you down
forever;
he will snatch and tear you
from your tent;
he will uproot you from the
land of the living.
Selah
6 The righteous will see, and fear,
and will laugh at the evildoer,[c]
saying,
7 "See the one who would not
take
refuge in God,
but trusted in abundant riches,

---

a Or *My sacrifice, O God,* b Cn Compare Syr: Heb *the kindness of God* c Heb *him*

and sought refuge in
wealth!"[d]

8 But I am like a green olive tree
in the house of God.
I trust in the steadfast love of
God
forever and ever.
9 I will thank you forever,
because of what you have done.
In the presence of the faithful
I will proclaim[e] your name,
for it is good.

Psalm 53

Denunciation of Godlessness

To the leader: according to Mahalath. A Maskil of David.

1 Fools say in their hearts, "There
is no God."
They are corrupt, they
commit abominable acts;
there is no one who does
good.

2 God looks down from heaven
on humankind
to see if there are any who
are wise,
who seek after God.

3 They have all fallen away, they
are all alike perverse;
there is no one who does
good,
no, not one.

4 Have they no knowledge, those
evildoers,
who eat up my people as they
eat bread,
and do not call upon God?

5 There they shall be in great
terror,
in terror such as has not been.
For God will scatter the bones
of the ungodly;[f]
they will be put to shame,[g]
for God has rejected
them.

6 O that deliverance for Israel
would come from Zion!
When God restores the
fortunes of his people,
Jacob will rejoice; Israel will
be glad.

Psalm 54

Prayer for Vindication

To the leader: with stringed instruments. A Maskil of David, when the Ziphites went and told Saul, "David is in hiding among us."

1 Save me, O God, by your name,
and vindicate me by your
might.
2 Hear my prayer, O God;

---

d Syr Tg: Heb *in his destruction* *e* Cn: Heb *wait for* *f* Cn Compare Gk Syr: Heb *him who encamps against you* *g* Gk: Heb *you have put (them) to shame*

give ear to the words of my
mouth.

3 For the insolent have risen
against me,
the ruthless seek my life;
they do not set God before
them. *Selah*

4 But surely, God is my helper;
the Lord is the upholder of[h] my
life.
5 He will repay my enemies for
their evil.
In your faithfulness, put an
end to them.

6 With a freewill offering I will
sacrifice to you;
I will give thanks to your name,
O LORD, for it is good.
7 For he has delivered me from
every trouble,
and my eye has looked in
triumph on my enemies.

Psalm 55

Complaint about a Friend's Treachery

To the leader: with stringed
instruments. A Maskil of David.

1 Give ear to my prayer, O God;
do not hide yourself from my
supplication.
2 Attend to me, and answer me;
I am troubled in my
complaint.
I am distraught 3 by the noise of
the enemy,
because of the clamor of the
wicked.
For they bring[i] trouble upon
me,
and in anger they cherish
enmity against me.

4 My heart is in anguish within
me,
the terrors of death have
fallen upon me.
5 Fear and trembling come upon
me,
and horror overwhelms me.
6 And I say, "O that I had wings
like a dove!
I would fly away and be at
rest;
7 truly, I would flee far away;
I would lodge in the
wilderness; *Selah*
8 I would hurry to find a shelter
for myself
from the raging wind and
tempest."

9 Confuse, O Lord, confound
their speech;
for I see violence and strife in
the city.
10 Day and night they go around it
on its walls,
and iniquity and trouble are
within it;
11 ruin is in its midst;
oppression and fraud

h Gk Syr Jerome: Heb *is of those who uphold* or *is with those who uphold* *i* Cn Compare Gk: Heb *they cause to totter*

do not depart from its
marketplace.

12 It is not enemies who taunt
me—
I could bear that;
it is not adversaries who deal
insolently with me—
I could hide from them.
13 But it is you, my equal,
my companion, my familiar
friend,
14 with whom I kept pleasant
company;
we walked in the house of
God with the throng.
15 Let death come upon them;
let them go down alive to
Sheol;
for evil is in their homes and
in their hearts.

16 But I call upon God,
and the LORD will save me.
17 Evening and morning and at
noon
I utter my complaint and moan,
and he will hear my voice.
18 He will redeem me unharmed
from the battle that I wage,
for many are arrayed against
me.
19 God, who is enthroned from of
old, *Selah*
will hear, and will humble
them—
because they do not change,
and do not fear God.

20 My companion laid hands on a
friend
and violated a covenant with
me[j]
21 with speech smoother than
butter,
but with a heart set on war;
with words that were softer
than oil,
but in fact were drawn
swords.

22 Cast your burden[k] on the LORD,
and he will sustain you;
he will never permit
the righteous to be moved.

23 But you, O God, will cast them
down
into the lowest pit;
the bloodthirsty and treacherous
shall not live out half their
days.
But I will trust in you.

Psalm 56

Trust in God under Persecution

To the leader: according to The
Dove on Far-off Terebinths.
Of David. A Miktam, when the
Philistines seized him in Gath.

1 Be gracious to me, O God, for
people trample on me;
all day long foes oppress me;
2 my enemies trample on me all
day long,
for many fight against me.

---

j Heb lacks *with me* *k* Or *Cast what he has given you*

O Most High, [3]when I am
afraid,
I put my trust in you.
4 In God, whose word I praise,
in God I trust; I am not
afraid;
what can flesh do to me?

5 All day long they seek to injure
my cause;
all their thoughts are against
me for evil.
6 They stir up strife, they lurk,
they watch my steps.
As they hoped to have my life,
7 so repay[l] them for their
crime;
in wrath cast down the
peoples, O God!

8 You have kept count of my
tossings;
put my tears in your bottle.
Are they not in your record?
9 Then my enemies will retreat
in the day when I call.
This I know, that[m] God is for
me.
10 In God, whose word I praise,
in the LORD, whose word I
praise,
11 in God I trust; I am not afraid.
What can a mere mortal do to
me?

12 My vows to you I must
perform, O God;
I will render thank offerings
to you.
13 For you have delivered my soul
from death,
and my feet from falling,
so that I may walk before God
in the light of life.

Psalm 57

Praise and Assurance under Persecution

To the leader: Do Not Destroy.
Of David. A Miktam, when he
fled from Saul, in the cave.

1 Be merciful to me, O God, be
merciful to me,
for in you my soul takes
refuge;
in the shadow of your wings I
will take refuge,
until the destroying storms pass
by.
2 I cry to God Most High,
to God who fulfills his
purpose for me.
3 He will send from heaven and
save me,
he will put to shame those
who trample on me.
Selah
God will send forth his
steadfast love and his
faithfulness.

4 I lie down among lions
that greedily devour[n] human
prey;
their teeth are spears and
arrows,
their tongues sharp swords.

---

l Cn: Heb *rescue* *m* Or *because* *n* Cn: Heb *are aflame for*

5 Be exalted, O God, above the
heavens.
Let your glory be over all the
earth.

6 They set a net for my steps;
my soul was bowed down.
They dug a pit in my path,
but they have fallen into it
themselves. *Selah*
7 My heart is steadfast, O God,
my heart is steadfast.
I will sing and make melody.
8 Awake, my soul!
Awake, O harp and lyre!
I will awake the dawn.
9 I will give thanks to you,
O Lord, among the
peoples;
I will sing praises to you
among the nations.
10 For your steadfast love is as
high as the heavens;
your faithfulness extends to
the clouds.

11 Be exalted, O God, above the
heavens.
Let your glory be over all the
earth.

Psalm 58

Prayer for Vengeance

To the leader: Do Not Destroy.
Of David. A Miktam.

1 Do you indeed decree what is
right, you gods?[o]
Do you judge people fairly?
2 No, in your hearts you devise
wrongs;
your hands deal out violence on
earth.

3 The wicked go astray from the
womb;
they err from their birth,
speaking lies.
4 They have venom like the
venom of a serpent,
like the deaf adder that stops
its ear,
5 so that it does not hear the voice
of charmers
or of the cunning enchanter.

6 O God, break the teeth in their
mouths;
tear out the fangs of the
young lions, O Lord!
7 Let them vanish like water that
runs away;
like grass let them be trodden
down[p] and wither.
8 Let them be like the snail that
dissolves into slime;
like the untimely birth that
never sees the sun.
9 Sooner than your pots can feel
the heat of thorns,
whether green or ablaze, may
he sweep them away!

10 The righteous will rejoice when
they see vengeance done;
they will bathe their feet in
the blood of the wicked.

o Or *mighty lords* *p* Cn: Meaning of Heb uncertain

[11] People will say, "Surely there is
a reward for the righteous;
surely there is a God who
judges on earth."

Psalm 59

Prayer for Deliverance from Enemies

To the leader: Do Not Destroy.
Of David. A Miktam, when Saul
ordered his house to be watched
in order to kill him.

[1] Deliver me from my enemies,
O my God;
protect me from those who
rise up against me.
[2] Deliver me from those who
work evil;
from the bloodthirsty save me.

[3] Even now they lie in wait for
my life;
the mighty stir up strife
against me.
For no transgression or sin of
mine, O LORD,
[4] for no fault of mine, they run
and make ready.

Rouse yourself, come to my
help and see!
[5] You, LORD God of hosts, are
God of Israel.
Awake to punish all the nations;
spare none of those who
treacherously plot evil.
Selah

[6] Each evening they come back,
howling like dogs
and prowling about the city.
[7] There they are, bellowing with
their mouths,
with sharp words[q] on their
lips—
for "Who," they think,[r] "will
hear us?"

[8] But you laugh at them, O LORD;
you hold all the nations in
derision.
[9] O my strength, I will watch for
you;
for you, O God, are my
fortress.
[10] My God in his steadfast love
will meet me;
my God will let me look in
triumph on my enemies.

[11] Do not kill them, or my people
may forget;
make them totter by your
power, and bring them
down,
O Lord, our shield.
[12] For the sin of their mouths, the
words of their lips,
let them be trapped in their
pride.
For the cursing and lies that
they utter,
[13] consume them in wrath;
consume them until they are
no more.
Then it will be known to the
ends of the earth

q Heb *with swords* *r* Heb lacks *they think*

that God rules over Jacob.
Selah

14 Each evening they come back,
howling like dogs
and prowling about the city.
15 They roam about for food,
and growl if they do not get
their fill.

16 But I will sing of your might;
I will sing aloud of your
steadfast love in the
morning.
For you have been a fortress for
me
and a refuge in the day of my
distress.
17 O my strength, I will sing
praises to you,
for you, O God, are my
fortress,
the God who shows me
steadfast love.

Psalm 60

Prayer for National Victory after Defeat

To the leader: according to the Lily of the Covenant. A Miktam of David; for instruction; when he struggled with Aram-naharaim and with Aram-zobah, and when Joab on his return killed twelve thousand Edomites in the Valley of Salt.

1 O God, you have rejected us,
broken our defenses;
you have been angry; now
restore us!
2 You have caused the land to
quake; you have torn it
open;
repair the cracks in it, for it is
tottering.
3 You have made your people
suffer hard things;
you have given us wine to drink
that made us reel.

4 You have set up a banner for
those who fear you,
to rally to it out of bowshot.[s]
Selah
5 Give victory with your right
hand, and answer us,[t]
so that those whom you love
may be rescued.

6 God has promised in his
sanctuary:[u]
"With exultation I will divide
up Shechem,
and portion out the Vale of
Succoth.
7 Gilead is mine, and Manasseh
is mine;
Ephraim is my helmet;
Judah is my scepter.
8 Moab is my washbasin;
on Edom I hurl my shoe;
over Philistia I shout in
triumph."

9 Who will bring me to the
fortified city?
Who will lead me to Edom?

s Gk Syr Jerome: Heb *because of the truth*
t Another reading is *me* *u* Or *by his holiness*

10 Have you not rejected us,
O God?
You do not go out, O God,
with our armies.
11 O grant us help against the foe,
for human help is worthless.
12 With God we shall do valiantly;
it is he who will tread down our
foes.

Psalm 61

Assurance of God's Protection

To the leader: with stringed
instruments. Of David.

1 Hear my cry, O God;
listen to my prayer.
2 From the end of the earth I call
to you,
when my heart is faint.

Lead me to the rock
that is higher than I;
3 for you are my refuge,
a strong tower against the
enemy.

4 Let me abide in your tent
forever,
find refuge under the shelter
of your wings. *Selah*
5 For you, O God, have heard my
vows;
you have given me the heritage
of those who fear your
name.

6 Prolong the life of the king;
may his years endure to all
generations!
7 May he be enthroned forever
before God;
appoint steadfast love and
faithfulness to watch over
him!

8 So I will always sing praises to
your name,
as I pay my vows day after
day.

Psalm 62

Song of Trust in God Alone

To the leader: according to
Jeduthun. A Psalm of David.

1 For God alone my soul waits in
silence;
from him comes my
salvation.
2 He alone is my rock and my
salvation,
my fortress; I shall never be
shaken.

3 How long will you assail a
person,
will you batter your victim,
all of you,
as you would a leaning wall,
a tottering fence?
4 Their only plan is to bring
down a person of
prominence.
They take pleasure in
falsehood;
they bless with their mouths,

but inwardly they curse.
Selah

5 For God alone my soul waits in silence,
for my hope is from him.
6 He alone is my rock and my salvation,
my fortress; I shall not be shaken.
7 On God rests my deliverance and my honor;
my mighty rock, my refuge is in God.

8 Trust in him at all times, O people;
pour out your heart before him;
God is a refuge for us. *Selah*

9 Those of low estate are but a breath,
those of high estate are a delusion;
in the balances they go up;
they are together lighter than a breath.
10 Put no confidence in extortion,
and set no vain hopes on robbery;
if riches increase, do not set your heart on them.

11 Once God has spoken;
twice have I heard this:
that power belongs to God,
12 and steadfast love belongs to you, O Lord.
For you repay to all
according to their work.

Psalm 63

Comfort and Assurance in God's Presence

A Psalm of David, when he was in the Wilderness of Judah.

1 O God, you are my God, I seek you,
my soul thirsts for you;
my flesh faints for you,
as in a dry and weary land
where there is no water.
2 So I have looked upon you in the sanctuary,
beholding your power and glory.
3 Because your steadfast love is better than life,
my lips will praise you.
4 So I will bless you as long as I live;
I will lift up my hands and call on your name.

5 My soul is satisfied as with a rich feast,[v]
and my mouth praises you with joyful lips
6 when I think of you on my bed,
and meditate on you in the watches of the night;
7 for you have been my help,
and in the shadow of your wings I sing for joy.
8 My soul clings to you;
your right hand upholds me.

---

v Heb *with fat and fatness*

9 But those who seek to destroy
my life
shall go down into the depths
of the earth;
10 they shall be given over to the
power of the sword,
they shall be prey for jackals.
11 But the king shall rejoice in
God;
all who swear by him shall
exult,
for the mouths of liars will be
stopped.

Psalm 64

Prayer for Protection from Enemies

To the leader. A Psalm of David.

1 Hear my voice, O God, in my
complaint;
preserve my life from the
dread enemy.
2 Hide me from the secret plots
of the wicked,
from the scheming of evildoers,
3 who whet their tongues like
swords,
who aim bitter words like
arrows,
4 shooting from ambush at the
blameless;
they shoot suddenly and
without fear.
5 They hold fast to their evil
purpose;
they talk of laying snares
secretly,
thinking, "Who can see us?[w]
6 Who can search out our
crimes?[x]
We have thought out a
cunningly conceived
plot."
For the human heart and
mind are deep.

7 But God will shoot his arrow at
them;
they will be wounded
suddenly.
8 Because of their tongue he will
bring them to ruin;[y]
all who see them will shake
with horror.
9 Then everyone will fear;
they will tell what God has
brought about,
and ponder what he has done.

10 Let the righteous rejoice in the
LORD
and take refuge in him.
Let all the upright in heart
glory.

Psalm 65

Thanksgiving for Earth's Bounty

To the leader. A Psalm of David.
A Song.

1 Praise is due to you,
O God, in Zion;
and to you shall vows be
performed,
2 O you who answer prayer!
To you all flesh shall come.

---

w Syr: Heb *them* *x* Cn: Heb *They search out crimes* *y* Cn: Heb *They will bring him to ruin, their tongue being against them*

[3] When deeds of iniquity
overwhelm us,
you forgive our
transgressions.
[4] Happy are those whom you
choose and bring near
to live in your courts.
We shall be satisfied with the
goodness of your house,
your holy temple.

[5] By awesome deeds you answer
us with deliverance,
O God of our salvation;
you are the hope of all the ends
of the earth
and of the farthest seas.
[6] By your[z] strength you
established the mountains;
you are girded with might.
[7] You silence the roaring of the
seas,
the roaring of their waves,
the tumult of the peoples.
[8] Those who live at earth's
farthest bounds are awed
by your signs;
you make the gateways of the
morning and the evening
shout for joy.

[9] You visit the earth and water it,
you greatly enrich it;
the river of God is full of water;
you provide the people with
grain,
for so you have prepared it.
[10] You water its furrows
abundantly,
settling its ridges,
softening it with showers,
and blessing its growth.
[11] You crown the year with your
bounty;
your wagon tracks overflow
with richness.
[12] The pastures of the wilderness
overflow,
the hills gird themselves with
joy,
[13] the meadows clothe themselves
with flocks,
the valleys deck themselves
with grain,
they shout and sing together
for joy.

Psalm 66

Praise for God's Goodness to Israel

To the leader. A Song. A Psalm.

[1] Make a joyful noise to God, all
the earth;
[2] sing the glory of his name;
give to him glorious praise.
[3] Say to God, "How awesome are
your deeds!
Because of your great power,
your enemies cringe
before you.
[4] All the earth worships you;
they sing praises to you,
sing praises to your name."
Selah

[5] Come and see what God has
done:
he is awesome in his deeds
among mortals.

---

z Gk Jerome: Heb *his*

6 He turned the sea into dry land;
they passed through the river on foot.
There we rejoiced in him,
7 who rules by his might forever,
whose eyes keep watch on the nations—
let the rebellious not exalt themselves. *Selah*

8 Bless our God, O peoples,
let the sound of his praise be heard,
9 who has kept us among the living,
and has not let our feet slip.
10 For you, O God, have tested us;
you have tried us as silver is tried.
11 You brought us into the net;
you laid burdens on our backs;
12 you let people ride over our heads;
we went through fire and through water;
yet you have brought us out to a spacious place.[a]

13 I will come into your house with burnt offerings;
I will pay you my vows,
14 those that my lips uttered
and my mouth promised when I was in trouble.
15 I will offer to you burnt offerings of fatlings,
with the smoke of the sacrifice of rams;
I will make an offering of bulls and goats. *Selah*

16 Come and hear, all you who fear God,
and I will tell what he has done for me.
17 I cried aloud to him,
and he was extolled with my tongue.
18 If I had cherished iniquity in my heart,
the Lord would not have listened.
19 But truly God has listened;
he has given heed to the words of my prayer.

20 Blessed be God,
because he has not rejected my prayer
or removed his steadfast love from me.

Psalm 67

The Nations Called to Praise God

To the leader: with stringed instruments. A Psalm. A Song.

1 May God be gracious to us and bless us
and make his face to shine upon us, *Selah*
2 that your way may be known upon earth,
your saving power among all nations.
3 Let the peoples praise you, O God;
let all the peoples praise you.

a Cn Compare Gk Syr Jerome Tg: Heb *to a saturation*

4 Let the nations be glad and sing
for joy,
for you judge the peoples with
equity
and guide the nations upon
earth. *Selah*
5 Let the peoples praise you,
O God;
let all the peoples praise you.

6 The earth has yielded its
increase;
God, our God, has blessed us.
7 May God continue to bless us;
let all the ends of the earth
revere him.

Psalm 68

Praise and Thanksgiving

To the leader. Of David. A Psalm.
A Song.

1 Let God rise up, let his enemies
be scattered;
let those who hate him flee
before him.
2 As smoke is driven away, so
drive them away;
as wax melts before the fire,
let the wicked perish before
God.
3 But let the righteous be joyful;
let them exult before God;
let them be jubilant with joy.

4 Sing to God, sing praises to his
name;
lift up a song to him who rides
upon the clouds[b]—
his name is the LORD—
be exultant before him.

5 Father of orphans and protector
of widows
is God in his holy habitation.
6 God gives the desolate a home
to live in;
he leads out the prisoners to
prosperity,
but the rebellious live in a
parched land.

7 O God, when you went out
before your people,
when you marched through the
wilderness, *Selah*
8 the earth quaked, the heavens
poured down rain
at the presence of God, the God
of Sinai,
at the presence of God, the God
of Israel.
9 Rain in abundance, O God, you
showered abroad;
you restored your heritage
when it languished;
10 your flock found a dwelling in
it;
in your goodness, O God,
you provided for the
needy.

11 The Lord gives the command;
great is the company of those[c]
who bore the tidings:
12 "The kings of the armies, they
flee, they flee!"

---

b Or *cast up a highway for him who rides through the deserts* c Or *company of the women*

The women at home divide the spoil,
[13] though they stay among the sheepfolds—
the wings of a dove covered with silver,
its pinions with green gold.
[14] When the Almighty[d] scattered kings there,
snow fell on Zalmon.

[15] O mighty mountain, mountain of Bashan;
O many-peaked mountain, mountain of Bashan!
[16] Why do you look with envy, O many-peaked mountain,
at the mount that God desired for his abode,
where the LORD will reside forever?

[17] With mighty chariotry, twice ten thousand,
thousands upon thousands,
the Lord came from Sinai into the holy place.[e]
[18] You ascended the high mount,
leading captives in your train
and receiving gifts from people,
even from those who rebel against the LORD God's abiding there.
[19] Blessed be the Lord,
who daily bears us up;
God is our salvation. *Selah*
[20] Our God is a God of salvation,
and to GOD, the Lord, belongs escape from death.

[21] But God will shatter the heads of his enemies,
the hairy crown of those who walk in their guilty ways.
[22] The Lord said,
"I will bring them back from Bashan,
I will bring them back from the depths of the sea,
[23] so that you may bathe[f] your feet in blood,
so that the tongues of your dogs may have their share from the foe."

[24] Your solemn processions are seen,[g] O God,
the processions of my God, my King, into the sanctuary—
[25] the singers in front, the musicians last,
between them girls playing tambourines:
[26] "Bless God in the great congregation,
the LORD, O you who are of Israel's fountain!"
[27] There is Benjamin, the least of them, in the lead,
the princes of Judah in a body,
the princes of Zebulun, the princes of Naphtali.

[28] Summon your might, O God;
show your strength, O God,
as you have done for us before.

---

d Traditional rendering of Heb *Shaddai*
e Cn: Heb *The Lord among them Sinai in the holy* (place) *f* Gk Syr Tg: Heb *shatter*
g Or *have been seen*

29 Because of your temple at Jerusalem
kings bear gifts to you.
30 Rebuke the wild animals that live among the reeds,
the herd of bulls with the calves of the peoples.
Trample[h] under foot those who lust after tribute;
scatter the peoples who delight in war.[i]
31 Let bronze be brought from Egypt;
let Ethiopia[j] hasten to stretch out its hands to God.

32 Sing to God, O kingdoms of the earth;
sing praises to the Lord, *Selah*
33 O rider in the heavens, the ancient heavens;
listen, he sends out his voice, his mighty voice.
34 Ascribe power to God,
whose majesty is over Israel;
and whose power is in the skies.
35 Awesome is God in his[k] sanctuary,
the God of Israel;
he gives power and strength to his people.

Blessed be God!

Psalm 69

Prayer for Deliverance from Persecution

To the leader: according to Lilies. Of David.

1 Save me, O God,
for the waters have come up to my neck.
2 I sink in deep mire,
where there is no foothold;
I have come into deep waters,
and the flood sweeps over me.
3 I am weary with my crying;
my throat is parched.
My eyes grow dim
with waiting for my God.

4 More in number than the hairs of my head
are those who hate me without cause;
many are those who would destroy me,
my enemies who accuse me falsely.
What I did not steal
must I now restore?
5 O God, you know my folly;
the wrongs I have done are not hidden from you.

6 Do not let those who hope in you be put to shame because of me,
O Lord God of hosts;

h Cn: Heb *Trampling* *i* Meaning of Heb of verse 30 is uncertain *j* Or *Nubia*; Heb *Cush*
k Gk: Heb *from your*

do not let those who seek you
be dishonored because of
me,
O God of Israel.
7 It is for your sake that I have
borne reproach,
that shame has covered my
face.
8 I have become a stranger to my
kindred,
an alien to my mother's
children.

9 It is zeal for your house that has
consumed me;
the insults of those who insult
you have fallen on me.
10 When I humbled my soul with
fasting,[l]
they insulted me for doing so.
11 When I made sackcloth my
clothing,
I became a byword to them.
12 I am the subject of gossip for
those who sit in the gate,
and the drunkards make
songs about me.

13 But as for me, my prayer is to
you, O LORD.
At an acceptable time, O God,
in the abundance of your
steadfast love, answer me.
With your faithful help 14rescue
me
from sinking in the mire;
let me be delivered from my
enemies
and from the deep waters.
15 Do not let the flood sweep over
me,
or the deep swallow me up,
or the Pit close its mouth
over me.

16 Answer me, O LORD, for your
steadfast love is good;
according to your abundant
mercy, turn to me.
17 Do not hide your face from
your servant,
for I am in distress—make
haste to answer me.
18 Draw near to me, redeem me,
set me free because of my
enemies.

19 You know the insults I receive,
and my shame and dishonor;
my foes are all known to you.
20 Insults have broken my heart,
so that I am in despair.
I looked for pity, but there was
none;
and for comforters, but I
found none.
21 They gave me poison for food,
and for my thirst they gave
me vinegar to drink.

22 Let their table be a trap for
them,
a snare for their allies.
23 Let their eyes be darkened so
that they cannot see,
and make their loins tremble
continually.
24 Pour out your indignation upon
them,
and let your burning anger
overtake them.

---

l Gk Syr: Heb *I wept, with fasting my soul*, or *I made my soul mourn with fasting*

25 May their camp be a desolation;
let no one live in their tents.
26 For they persecute those whom
you have struck down,
and those whom you have
wounded, they attack still
more.[m]
27 Add guilt to their guilt;
may they have no acquittal
from you.
28 Let them be blotted out of the
book of the living;
let them not be enrolled
among the righteous.
29 But I am lowly and in pain;
let your salvation, O God,
protect me.

30 I will praise the name of God
with a song;
I will magnify him with
thanksgiving.
31 This will please the LORD more
than an ox
or a bull with horns and
hoofs.
32 Let the oppressed see it and be
glad;
you who seek God, let your
hearts revive.
33 For the LORD hears the needy,
and does not despise his own
that are in bonds.

34 Let heaven and earth praise
him,
the seas and everything that
moves in them.
35 For God will save Zion
and rebuild the cities of
Judah;
and his servants shall live[n] there
and possess it;
36 the children of his servants
shall inherit it,
and those who love his name
shall live in it.

Psalm 70

Prayer for Deliverance from Enemies

To the leader. Of David, for the memorial offering.

1 Be pleased, O God, to deliver
me.
O LORD, make haste to help
me!
2 Let those be put to shame and
confusion
who seek my life.
Let those be turned back and
brought to dishonor
who desire to hurt me.
3 Let those who say, "Aha, Aha!"
turn back because of their
shame.

4 Let all who seek you
rejoice and be glad in you.
Let those who love your
salvation
say evermore, "God is great!"
5 But I am poor and needy;
hasten to me, O God!
You are my help and my
deliverer;
O LORD, do not delay!

m Gk Syr: Heb *recount the pain of* *n* Syr: Heb *and they shall live*

Psalm 71

Prayer for Lifelong Protection and Help

1 In you, O LORD, I take refuge;
let me never be put to shame.
2 In your righteousness deliver me and rescue me;
incline your ear to me and save me.
3 Be to me a rock of refuge,
a strong fortress,[o] to save me,
for you are my rock and my fortress.

4 Rescue me, O my God, from the hand of the wicked,
from the grasp of the unjust and cruel.
5 For you, O Lord, are my hope,
my trust, O LORD, from my youth.
6 Upon you I have leaned from my birth;
it was you who took me from my mother's womb.
My praise is continually of you.

7 I have been like a portent to many,
but you are my strong refuge.
8 My mouth is filled with your praise,
and with your glory all day long.
9 Do not cast me off in the time of old age;
do not forsake me when my strength is spent.
10 For my enemies speak concerning me,
and those who watch for my life consult together.
11 They say, "Pursue and seize that person
whom God has forsaken,
for there is no one to deliver."

12 O God, do not be far from me;
O my God, make haste to help me!
13 Let my accusers be put to shame and consumed;
let those who seek to hurt me
be covered with scorn and disgrace.
14 But I will hope continually,
and will praise you yet more and more.
15 My mouth will tell of your righteous acts,
of your deeds of salvation all day long,
though their number is past my knowledge.
16 I will come praising the mighty deeds of the Lord GOD,
I will praise your righteousness, yours alone.

17 O God, from my youth you have taught me,
and I still proclaim your wondrous deeds.
18 So even to old age and gray hairs,
O God, do not forsake me,
until I proclaim your might

o Gk Compare 31.3: Heb *to come continually you have commanded*

to all the generations to
come.[p]
Your power [19] and your
righteousness, O God,
reach the high heavens.

You who have done great
things,
O God, who is like you?
20 You who have made me see
many troubles and
calamities
will revive me again;
from the depths of the earth
you will bring me up again.
21 You will increase my honor,
and comfort me once again.

22 I will also praise you with the
harp
for your faithfulness, O my
God;
I will sing praises to you with
the lyre,
O Holy One of Israel.
23 My lips will shout for joy
when I sing praises to you;
my soul also, which you have
rescued.
24 All day long my tongue will
talk of your righteous
help,
for those who tried to do me
harm
have been put to shame, and
disgraced.

Psalm 72

Prayer for Guidance and Support for the King

Of Solomon.

1 Give the king your justice,
O God,
and your righteousness to a
king's son.
2 May he judge your people with
righteousness,
and your poor with justice.
3 May the mountains yield
prosperity for the people,
and the hills, in
righteousness.
4 May he defend the cause of the
poor of the people,
give deliverance to the needy,
and crush the oppressor.

5 May he live[q] while the sun
endures,
and as long as the
moon, throughout all
generations.
6 May he be like rain that falls on
the mown grass,
like showers that water the
earth.
7 In his days may righteousness
flourish
and peace abound, until the
moon is no more.

8 May he have dominion from
sea to sea,

p Gk Compare Syr: Heb *to a generation, to all that come* *q* Gk: Heb *may they fear you*

and from the River to the ends
of the earth.
9 May his foes[r] bow down before
him,
and his enemies lick the dust.
10 May the kings of Tarshish and
of the isles
render him tribute,
may the kings of Sheba and
Seba
bring gifts.
11 May all kings fall down before
him,
all nations give him service.

12 For he delivers the needy when
they call,
the poor and those who have no
helper.
13 He has pity on the weak and the
needy,
and saves the lives of the
needy.
14 From oppression and violence
he redeems their life;
and precious is their blood in
his sight.

15 Long may he live!
May gold of Sheba be given to
him.
May prayer be made for him
continually,
and blessings invoked for
him all day long.
16 May there be abundance of
grain in the land;
may it wave on the tops of
the mountains;
may its fruit be like Lebanon;
and may people blossom in the
cities
like the grass of the field.
17 May his name endure forever,
his fame continue as long as
the sun.
May all nations be blessed in
him;[s]
may they pronounce him happy.

18 Blessed be the LORD, the God of
Israel,
who alone does wondrous
things.
19 Blessed be his glorious name
forever;
may his glory fill the whole
earth.
Amen and Amen.

20 The prayers of David son of
Jesse are ended.

BOOK III
(Psalms 73–89)

Psalm 73

Plea for Relief from Oppressors

A Psalm of Asaph.

1 Truly God is good to the
upright,[t]
to those who are pure in heart.
2 But as for me, my feet had
almost stumbled;
my steps had nearly slipped.

---

r Cn: Heb *those who live in the wilderness*
s Or *bless themselves by him* t Or *good to Israel*

3 For I was envious of the arrogant;
I saw the prosperity of the wicked.

4 For they have no pain;
their bodies are sound and sleek.
5 They are not in trouble as others are;
they are not plagued like other people.
6 Therefore pride is their necklace;
violence covers them like a garment.
7 Their eyes swell out with fatness;
their hearts overflow with follies.
8 They scoff and speak with malice;
loftily they threaten oppression.
9 They set their mouths against heaven,
and their tongues range over the earth.

10 Therefore the people turn and praise them,[u]
and find no fault in them.[v]
11 And they say, "How can God know?
Is there knowledge in the Most High?"
12 Such are the wicked;
always at ease, they increase in riches.
13 All in vain I have kept my heart clean
and washed my hands in innocence.
14 For all day long I have been plagued,
and am punished every morning.

15 If I had said, "I will talk on in this way,"
I would have been untrue to the circle of your children.
16 But when I thought how to understand this,
it seemed to me a wearisome task,
17 until I went into the sanctuary of God;
then I perceived their end.
18 Truly you set them in slippery places;
you make them fall to ruin.
19 How they are destroyed in a moment,
swept away utterly by terrors!
20 They are[w] like a dream when one awakes;
on awaking you despise their phantoms.

21 When my soul was embittered,
when I was pricked in heart,
22 I was stupid and ignorant;
I was like a brute beast toward you.
23 Nevertheless I am continually with you;
you hold my right hand.
24 You guide me with your counsel,

u Cn: Heb *his people return here* *v* Cn: Heb *abundant waters are drained by them*
w Cn: Heb *Lord*

and afterward you will receive
me with honor.[x]
25 Whom have I in heaven but
you?
And there is nothing on earth
that I desire other than
you.
26 My flesh and my heart may fail,
but God is the strength[y] of
my heart and my portion
forever.

27 Indeed, those who are far from
you will perish;
you put an end to those who
are false to you.
28 But for me it is good to be near
God;
I have made the Lord God
my refuge,
to tell of all your works.

Psalm 74

Plea for Help in Time of National Humiliation

A Maskil of Asaph.

1 O God, why do you cast us off
forever?
Why does your anger smoke
against the sheep of your
pasture?
2 Remember your congregation,
which you acquired long
ago,
which you redeemed to be
the tribe of your heritage.
Remember Mount Zion,
where you came to dwell.
3 Direct your steps to the
perpetual ruins;
the enemy has destroyed
everything in the
sanctuary.

4 Your foes have roared within
your holy place;
they set up their emblems
there.
5 At the upper entrance they
hacked
the wooden trellis with axes.[z]
6 And then, with hatchets and
hammers,
they smashed all its carved
work.
7 They set your sanctuary on fire;
they desecrated the dwelling
place of your name,
bringing it to the ground.
8 They said to themselves, "We
will utterly subdue them";
they burned all the meeting
places of God in the land.

9 We do not see our emblems;
there is no longer any
prophet,
and there is no one among us
who knows how long.
10 How long, O God, is the foe to
scoff?
Is the enemy to revile your
name forever?
11 Why do you hold back your
hand;

x Or *to glory* *y* Heb *rock* *z* Cn Compare Gk Syr: Meaning of Heb uncertain

why do you keep your hand
in[a] your bosom?

12 Yet God my King is from of
old,
working salvation in the
earth.
13 You divided the sea by your
might;
you broke the heads of the
dragons in the waters.
14 You crushed the heads of
Leviathan;
you gave him as food[b] for
the creatures of the
wilderness.
15 You cut openings for springs
and torrents;
you dried up ever-flowing
streams.
16 Yours is the day, yours also the
night;
you established the
luminaries[c] and the sun.
17 You have fixed all the bounds
of the earth;
you made summer and
winter.

18 Remember this, O LORD, how
the enemy scoffs,
and an impious people reviles
your name.
19 Do not deliver the soul of your
dove to the wild animals;
do not forget the life of your
poor forever.

20 Have regard for your[d] covenant,
for the dark places of the land
are full of the haunts of
violence.
21 Do not let the downtrodden be
put to shame;
let the poor and needy praise
your name.
22 Rise up, O God, plead your
cause;
remember how the impious
scoff at you all day long.
23 Do not forget the clamor of
your foes,
the uproar of your adversaries
that goes up continually.

Psalm 75

Thanksgiving for God's Wondrous Deeds

To the leader: Do Not Destroy. A
Psalm of Asaph. A Song.

1 We give thanks to you, O God;
we give thanks; your name is
near.
People tell of your wondrous
deeds.

2 At the set time that I appoint
I will judge with equity.
3 When the earth totters, with all
its inhabitants,
it is I who keep its pillars
steady. *Selah*
4 I say to the boastful, "Do not
boast,"

a Cn: Heb *do you consume your right hand from*
b Heb *food for the people* *c* Or *moon*; Heb
light *d* Gk Syr: Heb *the*

and to the wicked, "Do not lift
up your horn;
5 do not lift up your horn on high,
or speak with insolent neck."

6 For not from the east or from
the west
and not from the wilderness
comes lifting up;
7 but it is God who executes
judgment,
putting down one and lifting up
another.
8 For in the hand of the LORD
there is a cup
with foaming wine, well mixed;
he will pour a draught from it,
and all the wicked of the earth
shall drain it down to the dregs.
9 But I will rejoice[e] forever;
I will sing praises to the God
of Jacob.

10 All the horns of the wicked I
will cut off,
but the horns of the righteous
shall be exalted.

Psalm 76

Israel's God—Judge of All the Earth

To the leader: with stringed instruments. A Psalm of Asaph. A Song.

1 In Judah God is known,
his name is great in Israel.
2 His abode has been established
in Salem,
his dwelling place in Zion.
3 There he broke the flashing
arrows,
the shield, the sword, and the
weapons of war. *Selah*

4 Glorious are you, more majestic
than the everlasting mountains.[f]
5 The stouthearted were stripped
of their spoil;
they sank into sleep;
none of the troops
was able to lift a hand.
6 At your rebuke, O God of
Jacob,
both rider and horse lay
stunned.

7 But you indeed are awesome!
Who can stand before you
when once your anger is
roused?
8 From the heavens you uttered
judgment;
the earth feared and was still
9 when God rose up to establish
judgment,
to save all the oppressed of
the earth. *Selah*

10 Human wrath serves only to
praise you,
when you bind the last bit of
your[g] wrath around you.
11 Make vows to the LORD your
God, and perform them;
let all who are around him bring
gifts
to the one who is awesome,

---

e Gk: Heb *declare* f Gk: Heb *the mountains of prey* g Heb lacks *your*

12 who cuts off the spirit of princes,
who inspires fear in the kings of the earth.

Psalm 77

God's Mighty Deeds Recalled

To the leader: according to Jeduthun. Of Asaph. A Psalm.

1 I cry aloud to God,
aloud to God, that he may hear me.
2 In the day of my trouble I seek the Lord;
in the night my hand is stretched out without wearying;
my soul refuses to be comforted.
3 I think of God, and I moan;
I meditate, and my spirit faints. *Selah*

4 You keep my eyelids from closing;
I am so troubled that I cannot speak.
5 I consider the days of old,
and remember the years of long ago.
6 I commune[h] with my heart in the night;
I meditate and search my spirit:[i]
7 "Will the Lord spurn forever,
and never again be favorable?
8 Has his steadfast love ceased forever?
Are his promises at an end for all time?
9 Has God forgotten to be gracious?
Has he in anger shut up his compassion?" *Selah*
10 And I say, "It is my grief
that the right hand of the Most High has changed."

11 I will call to mind the deeds of the LORD;
I will remember your wonders of old.
12 I will meditate on all your work,
and muse on your mighty deeds.
13 Your way, O God, is holy.
What god is so great as our God?
14 You are the God who works wonders;
you have displayed your might among the peoples.
15 With your strong arm you redeemed your people,
the descendants of Jacob and Joseph. *Selah*

16 When the waters saw you, O God,
when the waters saw you, they were afraid;
the very deep trembled.
17 The clouds poured out water;
the skies thundered;
your arrows flashed on every side.
18 The crash of your thunder was in the whirlwind;
your lightnings lit up the world;

h Gk Syr: Heb *My music* *i* Syr Jerome: Heb *my spirit searches*

the earth trembled and shook.
19 Your way was through the sea,
your path, through the mighty waters;
yet your footprints were unseen.
20 You led your people like a flock
by the hand of Moses and Aaron.

Psalm 78

God's Goodness and Israel's Ingratitude

A Maskil of Asaph.

1 Give ear, O my people, to my teaching;
incline your ears to the words of my mouth.
2 I will open my mouth in a parable;
I will utter dark sayings from of old,
3 things that we have heard and known,
that our ancestors have told us.
4 We will not hide them from their children;
we will tell to the coming generation
the glorious deeds of the LORD, and his might,
and the wonders that he has done.

5 He established a decree in Jacob,
and appointed a law in Israel,
which he commanded our ancestors
to teach to their children;
6 that the next generation might know them,
the children yet unborn,
and rise up and tell them to their children,
7 so that they should set their hope in God,
and not forget the works of God,
but keep his commandments;
8 and that they should not be like their ancestors,
a stubborn and rebellious generation,
a generation whose heart was not steadfast,
whose spirit was not faithful to God.

9 The Ephraimites, armed with[j] the bow,
turned back on the day of battle.
10 They did not keep God's covenant,
but refused to walk according to his law.
11 They forgot what he had done,
and the miracles that he had shown them.
12 In the sight of their ancestors he worked marvels
in the land of Egypt, in the fields of Zoan.
13 He divided the sea and let them pass through it,
and made the waters stand like a heap.
14 In the daytime he led them with a cloud,

j Heb *armed with shooting*

and all night long with a fiery
light.
15 He split rocks open in the
wilderness,
and gave them drink
abundantly as from the
deep.
16 He made streams come out of
the rock,
and caused waters to flow
down like rivers.

17 Yet they sinned still more
against him,
rebelling against the Most
High in the desert.
18 They tested God in their heart
by demanding the food they
craved.
19 They spoke against God,
saying,
"Can God spread a table in
the wilderness?
20 Even though he struck the rock
so that water gushed out
and torrents overflowed,
can he also give bread,
or provide meat for his
people?"

21 Therefore, when the LORD
heard, he was full of rage;
a fire was kindled against
Jacob,
his anger mounted against
Israel,
22 because they had no faith in
God,
and did not trust his saving
power.
23 Yet he commanded the skies
above,
and opened the doors of
heaven;
24 he rained down on them manna
to eat,
and gave them the grain of
heaven.
25 Mortals ate of the bread of
angels;
he sent them food in
abundance.
26 He caused the east wind to
blow in the heavens,
and by his power he led out
the south wind;
27 he rained flesh upon them like
dust,
winged birds like the sand of
the seas;
28 he let them fall within their
camp,
all around their dwellings.
29 And they ate and were well
filled,
for he gave them what they
craved.
30 But before they had satisfied
their craving,
while the food was still in
their mouths,
31 the anger of God rose against
them
and he killed the strongest of
them,
and laid low the flower of
Israel.

32 In spite of all this they still
sinned;
they did not believe in his
wonders.
33 So he made their days vanish
like a breath,
and their years in terror.

[34] When he killed them, they
sought for him;
they repented and sought
God earnestly.
[35] They remembered that God was
their rock,
the Most High God their
redeemer.
[36] But they flattered him with their
mouths;
they lied to him with their
tongues.
[37] Their heart was not steadfast
toward him;
they were not true to his
covenant.
[38] Yet he, being compassionate,
forgave their iniquity,
and did not destroy them;
often he restrained his anger,
and did not stir up all his
wrath.
[39] He remembered that they were
but flesh,
a wind that passes and does
not come again.
[40] How often they rebelled against
him in the wilderness
and grieved him in the desert!
[41] They tested God again and
again,
and provoked the Holy One
of Israel.
[42] They did not keep in mind his
power,
or the day when he redeemed
them from the foe;
[43] when he displayed his signs in
Egypt,
and his miracles in the fields
of Zoan.
[44] He turned their rivers to blood,
so that they could not drink
of their streams.
[45] He sent among them swarms
of flies, which devoured
them,
and frogs, which destroyed
them.
[46] He gave their crops to the
caterpillar,
and the fruit of their labor to
the locust.
[47] He destroyed their vines with
hail,
and their sycamores with
frost.
[48] He gave over their cattle to the
hail,
and their flocks to
thunderbolts.
[49] He let loose on them his fierce
anger,
wrath, indignation, and distress,
a company of destroying
angels.
[50] He made a path for his anger;
he did not spare them from
death,
but gave their lives over to the
plague.
[51] He struck all the firstborn in
Egypt,
the first issue of their strength
in the tents of Ham.
[52] Then he led out his people like
sheep,
and guided them in the
wilderness like a flock.
[53] He led them in safety, so that
they were not afraid;
but the sea overwhelmed
their enemies.
[54] And he brought them to his
holy hill,
to the mountain that his right
hand had won.

55 He drove out nations before
them;
he apportioned them for a
possession
and settled the tribes of Israel
in their tents.

56 Yet they tested the Most High
God,
and rebelled against him.
They did not observe his
decrees,
57 but turned away and were
faithless like their
ancestors;
they twisted like a
treacherous bow.
58 For they provoked him to anger
with their high places;
they moved him to jealousy
with their idols.
59 When God heard, he was full of
wrath,
and he utterly rejected Israel.
60 He abandoned his dwelling at
Shiloh,
the tent where he dwelt
among mortals,
61 and delivered his power to
captivity,
his glory to the hand of the
foe.
62 He gave his people to the
sword,
and vented his wrath on his
heritage.
63 Fire devoured their young men,
and their girls had no
marriage song.
64 Their priests fell by the sword,
and their widows made no
lamentation.
65 Then the Lord awoke as from
sleep,
like a warrior shouting
because of wine.
66 He put his adversaries to rout;
he put them to everlasting
disgrace.

67 He rejected the tent of Joseph,
he did not choose the tribe of
Ephraim;
68 but he chose the tribe of Judah,
Mount Zion, which he loves.
69 He built his sanctuary like the
high heavens,
like the earth, which he has
founded forever.
70 He chose his servant David,
and took him from the
sheepfolds;
71 from tending the nursing ewes
he brought him
to be the shepherd of his people
Jacob,
of Israel, his inheritance.
72 With upright heart he tended
them,
and guided them with skillful
hand.

Psalm 79

Plea for Mercy for Jerusalem

A Psalm of Asaph.

1 O God, the nations have come
into your inheritance;
they have defiled your holy
temple;
they have laid Jerusalem in
ruins.

2 They have given the bodies of your servants
to the birds of the air for food,
the flesh of your faithful to the wild animals of the earth.
3 They have poured out their blood like water
all around Jerusalem,
and there was no one to bury them.
4 We have become a taunt to our neighbors,
mocked and derided by those around us.

5 How long, O LORD? Will you be angry forever?
Will your jealous wrath burn like fire?
6 Pour out your anger on the nations
that do not know you,
and on the kingdoms
that do not call on your name.
7 For they have devoured Jacob
and laid waste his habitation.

8 Do not remember against us the iniquities of our ancestors;
let your compassion come speedily to meet us,
for we are brought very low.
9 Help us, O God of our salvation,
for the glory of your name;
deliver us, and forgive our sins,
for your name's sake.
10 Why should the nations say,
"Where is their God?"
Let the avenging of the outpoured blood of your servants
be known among the nations before our eyes.

11 Let the groans of the prisoners come before you;
according to your great power preserve those doomed to die.
12 Return sevenfold into the bosom of our neighbors
the taunts with which they taunted you, O Lord!
13 Then we your people, the flock of your pasture,
will give thanks to you forever;
from generation to generation we will recount your praise.

Psalm 80

Prayer for Israel's Restoration

To the leader: on Lilies, a Covenant. Of Asaph. A Psalm.

1 Give ear, O Shepherd of Israel,
you who lead Joseph like a flock!
You who are enthroned upon the cherubim, shine forth
2 before Ephraim and Benjamin and Manasseh.
Stir up your might,
and come to save us!

3 Restore us, O God;
let your face shine, that we may be saved.

[4] O LORD God of hosts,
how long will you be angry
with your people's
prayers?
[5] You have fed them with the
bread of tears,
and given them tears to drink
in full measure.
[6] You make us the scorn[k] of our
neighbors;
our enemies laugh among
themselves.

[7] Restore us, O God of hosts;
let your face shine, that we
may be saved.

[8] You brought a vine out of
Egypt;
you drove out the nations and
planted it.
[9] You cleared the ground for it;
it took deep root and filled
the land.
[10] The mountains were covered
with its shade,
the mighty cedars with its
branches;
[11] it sent out its branches to the
sea,
and its shoots to the River.
[12] Why then have you broken
down its walls,
so that all who pass along the
way pluck its fruit?
[13] The boar from the forest
ravages it,
and all that move in the field
feed on it.

[14] Turn again, O God of hosts;
look down from heaven, and
see;
have regard for this vine,
[15] the stock that your right hand
planted.[l]
[16] They have burned it with fire,
they have cut it down;[m]
may they perish at the rebuke
of your countenance.
[17] But let your hand be upon the
one at your right hand,
the one whom you made
strong for yourself.
[18] Then we will never turn back
from you;
give us life, and we will call
on your name.

[19] Restore us, O LORD God of
hosts;
let your face shine, that we
may be saved.

Psalm 81

God's Appeal to Stubborn Israel

To the leader: according to The
Gittith. Of Asaph.

[1] Sing aloud to God our strength;
shout for joy to the God of
Jacob.
[2] Raise a song, sound the
tambourine,
the sweet lyre with the harp.
[3] Blow the trumpet at the new
moon,

---

k Syr: Heb *strife* *l* Heb adds from verse 17 *and upon the one whom you made strong for yourself* *m* Cn: Heb *it is cut down*

at the full moon, on our festal
day.
4 For it is a statute for Israel,
an ordinance of the God of
Jacob.
5 He made it a decree in Joseph,
when he went out over[n] the
land of Egypt.

I hear a voice I had not known:
6 "I relieved your[o] shoulder of
the burden;
your[p] hands were freed from
the basket.
7 In distress you called, and I
rescued you;
I answered you in the secret
place of thunder;
I tested you at the waters of
Meribah. *Selah*
8 Hear, O my people, while I
admonish you;
O Israel, if you would but listen
to me!
9 There shall be no strange god
among you;
you shall not bow down to a
foreign god.
10 I am the LORD your God,
who brought you up out of
the land of Egypt.
Open your mouth wide and I
will fill it.

11 "But my people did not listen to
my voice;
Israel would not submit to me.
12 So I gave them over to their
stubborn hearts,
to follow their own counsels.
13 O that my people would listen
to me,
that Israel would walk in my
ways!
14 Then I would quickly subdue
their enemies,
and turn my hand against their
foes.
15 Those who hate the LORD would
cringe before him,
and their doom would last
forever.
16 I would feed you[q] with the
finest of the wheat,
and with honey from the rock I
would satisfy you."

Psalm 82

A Plea for Justice

A Psalm of Asaph.

1 God has taken his place in the
divine council;
in the midst of the gods he
holds judgment:
2 "How long will you judge
unjustly
and show partiality to the
wicked? *Selah*
3 Give justice to the weak and the
orphan;
maintain the right of the
lowly and the destitute.
4 Rescue the weak and the needy;
deliver them from the hand of
the wicked."

5 They have neither knowledge
nor understanding,

---

n Or *against* *o* Heb *his* *p* Heb *his*
q Cn Compare verse 16b: Heb *he would feed him*

they walk around in darkness;
all the foundations of the earth
are shaken.

6 I say, "You are gods,
children of the Most High, all
of you;
7 nevertheless, you shall die like
mortals,
and fall like any prince."[r]

8 Rise up, O God, judge the
earth;
for all the nations belong to
you!

Psalm 83

Prayer for Judgment on Israel's Foes

A Song. A Psalm of Asaph.

1 O God, do not keep silence;
do not hold your peace or be
still, O God!
2 Even now your enemies are in
tumult;
those who hate you have raised
their heads.
3 They lay crafty plans against
your people;
they consult together against
those you protect.
4 They say, "Come, let us wipe
them out as a nation;
let the name of Israel be
remembered no more."
5 They conspire with one accord;
against you they make a
covenant—
6 the tents of Edom and the
Ishmaelites,
Moab and the Hagrites,
7 Gebal and Ammon and Amalek,
Philistia with the inhabitants
of Tyre;
8 Assyria also has joined them;
they are the strong arm of the
children of Lot. *Selah*

9 Do to them as you did to
Midian,
as to Sisera and Jabin at the
Wadi Kishon,
10 who were destroyed at En-dor,
who became dung for the
ground.
11 Make their nobles like Oreb
and Zeeb,
all their princes like Zebah
and Zalmunna,
12 who said, "Let us take the
pastures of God
for our own possession."

13 O my God, make them like
whirling dust,[s]
like chaff before the wind.
14 As fire consumes the forest,
as the flame sets the
mountains ablaze,
15 so pursue them with your
tempest
and terrify them with your
hurricane.
16 Fill their faces with shame,
so that they may seek your
name, O LORD.
17 Let them be put to shame and
dismayed forever;

---

r Or *fall as one man, O princes* *s* Or *a tumbleweed*

let them perish in disgrace.
18 Let them know that you alone,
whose name is the LORD,
are the Most High over all the earth.

Psalm 84

The Joy of Worship in the Temple

To the leader: according to The Gittith. Of the Korahites. A Psalm.

1 How lovely is your dwelling place,
O LORD of hosts!
2 My soul longs, indeed it faints
for the courts of the LORD;
my heart and my flesh sing for joy
to the living God.

3 Even the sparrow finds a home,
and the swallow a nest for herself,
where she may lay her young,
at your altars, O LORD of hosts,
my King and my God.
4 Happy are those who live in your house,
ever singing your praise.
Selah

5 Happy are those whose strength is in you,
in whose heart are the highways to Zion.[t]
6 As they go through the valley of Baca
they make it a place of springs;
the early rain also covers it with pools.
7 They go from strength to strength;
the God of gods will be seen in Zion.

8 O LORD God of hosts, hear my prayer;
give ear, O God of Jacob!
Selah
9 Behold our shield, O God;
look on the face of your anointed.

10 For a day in your courts is better
than a thousand elsewhere.
I would rather be a doorkeeper
in the house of my God
than live in the tents of wickedness.
11 For the LORD God is a sun and shield;
he bestows favor and honor.
No good thing does the LORD withhold
from those who walk uprightly.
12 O LORD of hosts,
happy is everyone who trusts in you.

t Heb lacks *to Zion*

Psalm 85

Prayer for the Restoration of God's Favor

To the leader. Of the Korahites. A Psalm.

1 LORD, you were favorable to your land;
you restored the fortunes of Jacob.
2 You forgave the iniquity of your people;
you pardoned all their sin. *Selah*
3 You withdrew all your wrath;
you turned from your hot anger.

4 Restore us again, O God of our salvation,
and put away your indignation toward us.
5 Will you be angry with us forever?
Will you prolong your anger to all generations?
6 Will you not revive us again,
so that your people may rejoice in you?
7 Show us your steadfast love, O LORD,
and grant us your salvation.

8 Let me hear what God the LORD will speak,
for he will speak peace to his people,
to his faithful, to those who turn to him in their hearts.[u]
9 Surely his salvation is at hand for those who fear him,
that his glory may dwell in our land.

10 Steadfast love and faithfulness will meet;
righteousness and peace will kiss each other.
11 Faithfulness will spring up from the ground,
and righteousness will look down from the sky.
12 The LORD will give what is good,
and our land will yield its increase.
13 Righteousness will go before him,
and will make a path for his steps.

Psalm 86

Supplication for Help against Enemies

A Prayer of David.

1 Incline your ear, O LORD, and answer me,
for I am poor and needy.
2 Preserve my life, for I am devoted to you;
save your servant who trusts in you.
You are my God; 3 be gracious to me, O Lord,
for to you do I cry all day long.

---

u Gk: Heb *but let them not turn back to folly*

4 Gladden the soul of your
servant,
for to you, O Lord, I lift up my
soul.
5 For you, O Lord, are good and
forgiving,
abounding in steadfast love to
all who call on you.
6 Give ear, O LORD, to my prayer;
listen to my cry of supplication.
7 In the day of my trouble I call
on you,
for you will answer me.

8 There is none like you among
the gods, O Lord,
nor are there any works like
yours.
9 All the nations you have made
shall come
and bow down before you,
O Lord,
and shall glorify your name.
10 For you are great and do
wondrous things;
you alone are God.
11 Teach me your way, O LORD,
that I may walk in your truth;
give me an undivided heart to
revere your name.
12 I give thanks to you, O Lord
my God, with my whole
heart,
and I will glorify your name
forever.
13 For great is your steadfast love
toward me;
you have delivered my soul
from the depths of Sheol.

14 O God, the insolent rise up
against me;
a band of ruffians seeks my life,
and they do not set you before
them.
15 But you, O Lord, are a God
merciful and gracious,
slow to anger and abounding
in steadfast love and
faithfulness.
16 Turn to me and be gracious to
me;
give your strength to your
servant;
save the child of your serving
girl.
17 Show me a sign of your favor,
so that those who hate me
may see it and be put to
shame,
because you, LORD, have
helped me and comforted
me.

Psalm 87

The Joy of Living in Zion

Of the Korahites. A Psalm. A Song.

1 On the holy mount stands the
city he founded;
2 the LORD loves the gates of
Zion
more than all the dwellings of
Jacob.
3 Glorious things are spoken of
you,
O city of God. *Selah*

4 Among those who know me
I mention Rahab and
Babylon;

Philistia too, and Tyre, with
Ethiopia[v]—
"This one was born there,"
they say.

5 And of Zion it shall be said,
"This one and that one were
born in it";
for the Most High himself will
establish it.
6 The LORD records, as he
registers the peoples,
"This one was born there."
Selah

7 Singers and dancers alike say,
"All my springs are in you."

Psalm 88

Prayer for Help in Despondency

A Song. A Psalm of the
Korahites. To the leader:
according to Mahalath Leannoth.
A Maskil of Heman the Ezrahite.

1 O LORD, God of my salvation,
when, at night, I cry out in your
presence,
2 let my prayer come before you;
incline your ear to my cry.

3 For my soul is full of troubles,
and my life draws near to
Sheol.
4 I am counted among those who
go down to the Pit;
I am like those who have no
help,
5 like those forsaken among the
dead,
like the slain that lie in the
grave,
like those whom you remember
no more,
for they are cut off from your
hand.
6 You have put me in the depths
of the Pit,
in the regions dark and deep.
7 Your wrath lies heavy upon me,
and you overwhelm me with
all your waves. *Selah*

8 You have caused my
companions to shun me;
you have made me a thing of
horror to them.
I am shut in so that I cannot
escape;
9 my eye grows dim through
sorrow.
Every day I call on you,
O LORD;
I spread out my hands to you.
10 Do you work wonders for the
dead?
Do the shades rise up to praise
you? *Selah*
11 Is your steadfast love declared
in the grave,
or your faithfulness in
Abaddon?
12 Are your wonders known in the
darkness,
or your saving help in the
land of forgetfulness?

13 But I, O LORD, cry out to you;

v Or *Nubia*; Heb *Cush*

in the morning my prayer
comes before you.
14 O LORD, why do you cast me
off?
Why do you hide your face
from me?
15 Wretched and close to death
from my youth up,
I suffer your terrors; I am
desperate.[w]
16 Your wrath has swept over me;
your dread assaults destroy
me.
17 They surround me like a flood
all day long;
from all sides they close in
on me.
18 You have caused friend and
neighbor to shun me;
my companions are in
darkness.

Psalm 89

God's Covenant with David

A Maskil of Ethan the Ezrahite.

1 I will sing of your steadfast
love, O LORD,[x] forever;
with my mouth I will proclaim
your faithfulness to all
generations.
2 I declare that your steadfast
love is established
forever;
your faithfulness is as firm as
the heavens.

3 You said, "I have made a
covenant with my chosen
one,
I have sworn to my servant
David:
4 'I will establish your
descendants forever,
and build your throne for all
generations.' " *Selah*

5 Let the heavens praise your
wonders, O LORD,
your faithfulness in the
assembly of the holy
ones.
6 For who in the skies can be
compared to the LORD?
Who among the heavenly
beings is like the LORD,
7 a God feared in the council of
the holy ones,
great and awesome[y] above all
that are around him?
8 O LORD God of hosts,
who is as mighty as you,
O LORD?
Your faithfulness surrounds
you.
9 You rule the raging of the sea;
when its waves rise, you still
them.
10 You crushed Rahab like a
carcass;
you scattered your enemies
with your mighty arm.
11 The heavens are yours, the
earth also is yours;
the world and all that is in it—
you have founded them.
12 The north and the south[z]—you
created them;
Tabor and Hermon joyously
praise your name.

w Meaning of Heb uncertain *x* Gk: Heb *the steadfast love of the* LORD *y* Gk Syr: Heb *greatly awesome* *z* Or *Zaphon and Yamin*

13 You have a mighty arm;
strong is your hand, high
your right hand.
14 Righteousness and justice are
the foundation of your
throne;
steadfast love and
faithfulness go before
you.
15 Happy are the people who
know the festal shout,
who walk, O LORD, in the
light of your countenance;
16 they exult in your name all day
long,
and extol[a] your
righteousness.
17 For you are the glory of their
strength;
by your favor our horn is
exalted.
18 For our shield belongs to the
LORD,
our king to the Holy One of
Israel.

19 Then you spoke in a vision to
your faithful one, and
said:
"I have set the crown[b] on one
who is mighty,
I have exalted one chosen from
the people.
20 I have found my servant David;
with my holy oil I have
anointed him;
21 my hand shall always remain
with him;
my arm also shall strengthen
him.
22 The enemy shall not outwit
him,
the wicked shall not humble
him.
23 I will crush his foes before him
and strike down those who
hate him.
24 My faithfulness and steadfast
love shall be with him;
and in my name his horn
shall be exalted.
25 I will set his hand on the sea
and his right hand on the
rivers.
26 He shall cry to me, 'You are my
Father,
my God, and the Rock of my
salvation!'
27 I will make him the firstborn,
the highest of the kings of the
earth.
28 Forever I will keep my steadfast
love for him,
and my covenant with him
will stand firm.
29 I will establish his line forever,
and his throne as long as the
heavens endure.
30 If his children forsake my law
and do not walk according to
my ordinances,
31 if they violate my statutes
and do not keep my
commandments,
32 then I will punish their
transgression with the rod
and their iniquity with
scourges;
33 but I will not remove from him
my steadfast love,
or be false to my faithfulness.
34 I will not violate my covenant,
or alter the word that went
forth from my lips.

a Cn: Heb *are exalted in* *b* Cn: Heb *help*

[35] Once and for all I have sworn
by my holiness;
I will not lie to David.
[36] His line shall continue forever,
and his throne endure before
me like the sun.
[37] It shall be established forever
like the moon,
an enduring witness in the
skies." *Selah*

[38] But now you have spurned and
rejected him;
you are full of wrath against
your anointed.
[39] You have renounced the
covenant with your
servant;
you have defiled his crown in
the dust.
[40] You have broken through all his
walls;
you have laid his strongholds
in ruins.
[41] All who pass by plunder him;
he has become the scorn of
his neighbors.
[42] You have exalted the right hand
of his foes;
you have made all his
enemies rejoice.
[43] Moreover, you have turned
back the edge of his
sword,
and you have not supported
him in battle.
[44] You have removed the scepter
from his hand,[c]
and hurled his throne to the
ground.
[45] You have cut short the days of
his youth;
you have covered him with
shame. *Selah*

[46] How long, O LORD? Will you
hide yourself forever?
How long will your wrath
burn like fire?
[47] Remember how short my time
is—[d]
for what vanity you have
created all mortals!
[48] Who can live and never see
death?
Who can escape the power of
Sheol? *Selah*

[49] Lord, where is your steadfast
love of old,
which by your faithfulness
you swore to David?
[50] Remember, O Lord, how your
servant is taunted;
how I bear in my bosom the
insults of the peoples,[e]
[51] with which your enemies taunt,
O LORD,
with which they taunted
the footsteps of your
anointed.

[52] Blessed be the LORD forever.

---

c Cn: Heb *removed his cleanness* *d* Meaning of Heb uncertain *e* Cn: Heb *bosom all of many peoples*

Amen and Amen.

BOOK IV

(Psalms 90–106)

Psalm 90

God's Eternity and Human Frailty

A Prayer of Moses, the man of God.

1 Lord, you have been our
dwelling place[f]
in all generations.
2 Before the mountains were
brought forth,
or ever you had formed the
earth and the world,
from everlasting to
everlasting you are God.

3 You turn us[g] back to dust,
and say, "Turn back, you
mortals."
4 For a thousand years in your
sight
are like yesterday when it is
past,
or like a watch in the night.

5 You sweep them away; they are
like a dream,
like grass that is renewed in
the morning;
6 in the morning it flourishes and
is renewed;
in the evening it fades and
withers.

7 For we are consumed by your
anger;
by your wrath we are
overwhelmed.
8 You have set our iniquities
before you,
our secret sins in the light of
your countenance.

9 For all our days pass away
under your wrath;
our years come to an end[h]
like a sigh.
10 The days of our life are seventy
years,
or perhaps eighty, if we are
strong;
even then their span[i] is only toil
and trouble;
they are soon gone, and we
fly away.

11 Who considers the power of
your anger?
Your wrath is as great as the
fear that is due you.
12 So teach us to count our days
that we may gain a wise heart.

13 Turn, O LORD! How long?
Have compassion on your
servants!
14 Satisfy us in the morning with
your steadfast love,
so that we may rejoice and be
glad all our days.

---

f Another reading is *our refuge*
g Heb *humankind* h Syr: Heb *we bring our years to an end* i Cn Compare Gk Syr Jerome Tg: Heb *pride*

[15] Make us glad as many days as
you have afflicted us,
and as many years as we
have seen evil.
[16] Let your work be manifest to
your servants,
and your glorious power to
their children.
[17] Let the favor of the Lord our
God be upon us,
and prosper for us the work
of our hands—
O prosper the work of our
hands!

Psalm 91

Assurance of God's Protection

[1] You who live in the shelter of
the Most High,
who abide in the shadow of
the Almighty,[j]
[2] will say to the LORD, "My
refuge and my fortress;
my God, in whom I trust."
[3] For he will deliver you from the
snare of the fowler
and from the deadly
pestilence;
[4] he will cover you with his
pinions,
and under his wings you will
find refuge;
his faithfulness is a shield
and buckler.
[5] You will not fear the terror of
the night,
or the arrow that flies by day,
[6] or the pestilence that stalks in
darkness,
or the destruction that wastes at
noonday.
[7] A thousand may fall at your
side,
ten thousand at your right
hand,
but it will not come near you.
[8] You will only look with your
eyes
and see the punishment of the
wicked.

[9] Because you have made the
LORD your refuge,[k]
the Most High your dwelling
place,
[10] no evil shall befall you,
no scourge come near your tent.

[11] For he will command his angels
concerning you
to guard you in all your ways.
[12] On their hands they will bear
you up,
so that you will not dash your
foot against a stone.
[13] You will tread on the lion and
the adder,
the young lion and the
serpent you will trample
under foot.

[14] Those who love me, I will
deliver;
I will protect those who know
my name.
[15] When they call to me, I will
answer them;
I will be with them in trouble,

---

j Traditional rendering of Heb *Shaddai*
k Cn: Heb *Because you, LORD,* are my refuge; you have made

I will rescue them and honor them.
16 With long life I will satisfy them,
and show them my salvation.

Psalm 92

Thanksgiving for Vindication

A Psalm. A Song for the Sabbath Day.

1 It is good to give thanks to the LORD,
to sing praises to your name, O Most High;
2 to declare your steadfast love in the morning,
and your faithfulness by night,
3 to the music of the lute and the harp,
to the melody of the lyre.
4 For you, O LORD, have made me glad by your work;
at the works of your hands I sing for joy.

5 How great are your works, O LORD!
Your thoughts are very deep!
6 The dullard cannot know,
the stupid cannot understand this:
7 though the wicked sprout like grass
and all evildoers flourish,
they are doomed to destruction forever,
8 but you, O LORD, are on high forever.
9 For your enemies, O LORD,
for your enemies shall perish;
all evildoers shall be scattered.

10 But you have exalted my horn like that of the wild ox;
you have poured over me[l] fresh oil.
11 My eyes have seen the downfall of my enemies;
my ears have heard the doom of my evil assailants.

12 The righteous flourish like the palm tree,
and grow like a cedar in Lebanon.
13 They are planted in the house of the LORD;
they flourish in the courts of our God.
14 In old age they still produce fruit;
they are always green and full of sap,
15 showing that the LORD is upright;
he is my rock, and there is no unrighteousness in him.

Psalm 93

The Majesty of God's Rule

1 The LORD is king, he is robed in majesty;
the LORD is robed, he is girded with strength.

l Syr: Meaning of Heb uncertain

He has established the world; it
shall never be moved;
2 your throne is established
from of old;
you are from everlasting.

3 The floods have lifted up,
O LORD,
the floods have lifted up their
voice;
the floods lift up their
roaring.
4 More majestic than the thunders
of mighty waters,
more majestic than the
waves[m] of the sea,
majestic on high is the LORD!

5 Your decrees are very sure;
holiness befits your house,
O LORD, forevermore.

Psalm 94

God the Avenger of the Righteous

1 O LORD, you God of vengeance,
you God of vengeance, shine
forth!
2 Rise up, O judge of the earth;
give to the proud what they
deserve!
3 O LORD, how long shall the
wicked,
how long shall the wicked
exult?

4 They pour out their arrogant
words;
all the evildoers boast.
5 They crush your people,
O LORD,
and afflict your heritage.
6 They kill the widow and the
stranger,
they murder the orphan,
7 and they say, "The LORD does
not see;
the God of Jacob does not
perceive."

8 Understand, O dullest of the
people;
fools, when will you be wise?
9 He who planted the ear, does he
not hear?
He who formed the eye, does
he not see?
10 He who disciplines the nations,
he who teaches knowledge to
humankind,
does he not chastise?
11 The LORD knows our thoughts,[n]
that they are but an empty
breath.

12 Happy are those whom you
discipline, O LORD,
and whom you teach out of
your law,
13 giving them respite from days
of trouble,
until a pit is dug for the
wicked.
14 For the LORD will not forsake
his people;
he will not abandon his
heritage;
15 for justice will return to the
righteous,

m Cn: Heb *majestic are the waves* *n* Heb *the thoughts of humankind*

and all the upright in heart will
follow it.

16 Who rises up for me against the
wicked?
Who stands up for me against
evildoers?
17 If the LORD had not been my
help,
my soul would soon have lived
in the land of silence.
18 When I thought, "My foot is
slipping,"
your steadfast love, O LORD,
held me up.
19 When the cares of my heart are
many,
your consolations cheer my
soul.
20 Can wicked rulers be allied
with you,
those who contrive mischief by
statute?
21 They band together against the
life of the righteous,
and condemn the innocent to
death.
22 But the LORD has become my
stronghold,
and my God the rock of my
refuge.
23 He will repay them for their
iniquity
and wipe them out for their
wickedness;
the LORD our God will wipe
them out.

Psalm 95

A Call to Worship and Obedience

1 O come, let us sing to the LORD;
let us make a joyful noise to the
rock of our salvation!
2 Let us come into his presence
with thanksgiving;
let us make a joyful noise to
him with songs of praise!
3 For the LORD is a great God,
and a great King above all
gods.
4 In his hand are the depths of the
earth;
the heights of the mountains
are his also.
5 The sea is his, for he made it,
and the dry land, which his
hands have formed.

6 O come, let us worship and
bow down,
let us kneel before the LORD,
our Maker!
7 For he is our God,
and we are the people of his
pasture,
and the sheep of his hand.

O that today you would listen to
his voice!
8 Do not harden your hearts, as at
Meribah,
as on the day at Massah in the
wilderness,
9 when your ancestors tested me,
and put me to the proof, though
they had seen my work.
10 For forty years I loathed that
generation

and said, "They are a people
whose hearts go astray,
and they do not regard my
ways."
11 Therefore in my anger I swore,
"They shall not enter my rest."

Psalm 96

Praise to God Who Comes in Judgment

1 O sing to the LORD a new song;
sing to the LORD, all the earth.
2 Sing to the LORD, bless his
name;
tell of his salvation from day
to day.
3 Declare his glory among the
nations,
his marvelous works among
all the peoples.
4 For great is the LORD, and
greatly to be praised;
he is to be revered above all
gods.
5 For all the gods of the peoples
are idols,
but the LORD made the
heavens.
6 Honor and majesty are before
him;
strength and beauty are in his
sanctuary.

7 Ascribe to the LORD, O families
of the peoples,
ascribe to the LORD glory and
strength.
8 Ascribe to the LORD the glory
due his name;
bring an offering, and come
into his courts.
9 Worship the LORD in holy
splendor;
tremble before him, all the
earth.

10 Say among the nations, "The
LORD is king!
The world is firmly
established; it shall never
be moved.
He will judge the peoples
with equity."
11 Let the heavens be glad, and let
the earth rejoice;
let the sea roar, and all that fills
it;
12 let the field exult, and
everything in it.
Then shall all the trees of the
forest sing for joy
13 before the LORD; for he is
coming,
for he is coming to judge the
earth.
He will judge the world with
righteousness,
and the peoples with his
truth.

Psalm 97

The Glory of God's Reign

1 The LORD is king! Let the earth
rejoice;
let the many coastlands be
glad!
2 Clouds and thick darkness are
all around him;

righteousness and justice
are the foundation of his throne.
3 Fire goes before him,
and consumes his adversaries on every side.
4 His lightnings light up the world;
the earth sees and trembles.
5 The mountains melt like wax before the LORD,
before the Lord of all the earth.

6 The heavens proclaim his righteousness;
and all the peoples behold his glory.
7 All worshipers of images are put to shame,
those who make their boast in worthless idols;
all gods bow down before him.
8 Zion hears and is glad,
and the towns[o] of Judah rejoice,
because of your judgments, O God.
9 For you, O LORD, are most high over all the earth;
you are exalted far above all gods.

10 The LORD loves those who hate[p] evil;
he guards the lives of his faithful;
he rescues them from the hand of the wicked.
11 Light dawns[q] for the righteous,
and joy for the upright in heart.
12 Rejoice in the LORD, O you righteous,
and give thanks to his holy name!

Psalm 98

Praise the Judge of the World

A Psalm.

1 O sing to the LORD a new song,
for he has done marvelous things.
His right hand and his holy arm
have gotten him victory.
2 The LORD has made known his victory;
he has revealed his vindication
in the sight of the nations.
3 He has remembered his steadfast love and faithfulness
to the house of Israel.
All the ends of the earth have seen
the victory of our God.

4 Make a joyful noise to the LORD, all the earth;
break forth into joyous song and sing praises.
5 Sing praises to the LORD with the lyre,
with the lyre and the sound of melody.
6 With trumpets and the sound of the horn
make a joyful noise before the King, the LORD.

o Heb *daughters* p Cn: Heb *You who love the LORD hate* q Gk Syr Jerome: Heb *is sown*

[7] Let the sea roar, and all that fills it;
the world and those who live in it.
[8] Let the floods clap their hands;
let the hills sing together for joy
[9] at the presence of the LORD, for he is coming
to judge the earth.
He will judge the world with righteousness,
and the peoples with equity.

Psalm 99

Praise to God for His Holiness

[1] The LORD is king; let the peoples tremble!
He sits enthroned upon the cherubim; let the earth quake!
[2] The LORD is great in Zion;
he is exalted over all the peoples.
[3] Let them praise your great and awesome name.
Holy is he!
[4] Mighty King,[r] lover of justice,
you have established equity;
you have executed justice
and righteousness in Jacob.
[5] Extol the LORD our God;
worship at his footstool.
Holy is he!

[6] Moses and Aaron were among his priests,
Samuel also was among those who called on his name.
They cried to the LORD, and he answered them.
[7] He spoke to them in the pillar of cloud;
they kept his decrees,
and the statutes that he gave them.

[8] O LORD our God, you answered them;
you were a forgiving God to them,
but an avenger of their wrongdoings.
[9] Extol the LORD our God,
and worship at his holy mountain;
for the LORD our God is holy.

Psalm 100

All Lands Summoned to Praise God

A Psalm of thanksgiving.

[1] Make a joyful noise to the LORD, all the earth.
[2] Worship the LORD with gladness;
come into his presence with singing.

[3] Know that the LORD is God.
It is he that made us, and we are his;[s]
we are his people, and the sheep of his pasture.

r Cn: Heb *And a king's strength* *s* Another reading is *and not we ourselves*

4 Enter his gates with
thanksgiving,
and his courts with praise.
Give thanks to him, bless his
name.

5 For the LORD is good;
his steadfast love endures
forever,
and his faithfulness to all
generations.

Psalm 101

A Sovereign's Pledge of Integrity and Justice

Of David. A Psalm.

1 I will sing of loyalty and of
justice;
to you, O LORD, I will sing.
2 I will study the way that is
blameless.
When shall I attain it?

I will walk with integrity of
heart
within my house;
3 I will not set before my eyes
anything that is base.

I hate the work of those who
fall away;
it shall not cling to me.
4 Perverseness of heart shall be
far from me;
I will know nothing of evil.

5 One who secretly slanders a
neighbor
I will destroy.
A haughty look and an arrogant
heart
I will not tolerate.

6 I will look with favor on the
faithful in the land,
so that they may live with me;
whoever walks in the way that
is blameless
shall minister to me.

7 No one who practices deceit
shall remain in my house;
no one who utters lies
shall continue in my
presence.

8 Morning by morning I will
destroy
all the wicked in the land,
cutting off all evildoers
from the city of the LORD.

Psalm 102

Prayer to the Eternal King for Help

A prayer of one afflicted, when
faint and pleading before the
LORD.

1 Hear my prayer, O LORD;
let my cry come to you.
2 Do not hide your face from me
in the day of my distress.
Incline your ear to me;

answer me speedily in the
day when I call.

[3] For my days pass away like
smoke,
and my bones burn like a
furnace.
[4] My heart is stricken and
withered like grass;
I am too wasted to eat my
bread.
[5] Because of my loud groaning
my bones cling to my skin.
[6] I am like an owl of the
wilderness,
like a little owl of the waste
places.
[7] I lie awake;
I am like a lonely bird on the
housetop.
[8] All day long my enemies taunt
me;
those who deride me use my
name for a curse.
[9] For I eat ashes like bread,
and mingle tears with my
drink,
[10] because of your indignation and
anger;
for you have lifted me up and
thrown me aside.
[11] My days are like an evening
shadow;
I wither away like grass.

[12] But you, O LORD, are enthroned
forever;
your name endures to all
generations.
[13] You will rise up and have
compassion on Zion,
for it is time to favor it;
the appointed time has come.
[14] For your servants hold its
stones dear,
and have pity on its dust.
[15] The nations will fear the name
of the LORD,
and all the kings of the earth
your glory.
[16] For the LORD will build up
Zion;
he will appear in his glory.
[17] He will regard the prayer of the
destitute,
and will not despise their
prayer.

[18] Let this be recorded for a
generation to come,
so that a people yet unborn may
praise the LORD:
[19] that he looked down from his
holy height,
from heaven the LORD looked at
the earth,
[20] to hear the groans of the
prisoners,
to set free those who were
doomed to die;
[21] so that the name of the LORD
may be declared in Zion,
and his praise in Jerusalem,
[22] when peoples gather together,
and kingdoms, to worship the
LORD.

[23] He has broken my strength in
midcourse;
he has shortened my days.
[24] "O my God," I say, "do not take
me away
at the midpoint of my life,
you whose years endure

throughout all generations."

[25] Long ago you laid the
foundation of the earth,
and the heavens are the work
of your hands.
[26] They will perish, but you
endure;
they will all wear out like a
garment.
You change them like clothing,
and they pass away;
[27] but you are the same, and your
years have no end.
[28] The children of your servants
shall live secure;
their offspring shall be
established in your
presence.

Psalm 103

Thanksgiving for God's Goodness

Of David.

[1] Bless the LORD, O my soul,
and all that is within me,
bless his holy name.
[2] Bless the LORD, O my soul,
and do not forget all his
benefits—
[3] who forgives all your iniquity,
who heals all your diseases,
[4] who redeems your life from the
Pit,
who crowns you with
steadfast love and mercy,
[5] who satisfies you with good as
long as you live[t]
so that your youth is renewed
like the eagle's.

[6] The LORD works vindication
and justice for all who are
oppressed.
[7] He made known his ways to
Moses,
his acts to the people of
Israel.
[8] The LORD is merciful and
gracious,
slow to anger and abounding
in steadfast love.
[9] He will not always accuse,
nor will he keep his anger
forever.
[10] He does not deal with us
according to our sins,
nor repay us according to our
iniquities.
[11] For as the heavens are high
above the earth,
so great is his steadfast love
toward those who fear
him;
[12] as far as the east is from the
west,
so far he removes our
transgressions from us.
[13] As a father has compassion for
his children,
so the LORD has compassion
for those who fear him.
[14] For he knows how we were
made;
he remembers that we are
dust.

[15] As for mortals, their days are
like grass;
they flourish like a flower of
the field;

t Meaning of Heb uncertain

16 for the wind passes over it, and
it is gone,
and its place knows it no
more.
17 But the steadfast love of the
LORD is from everlasting
to everlasting
on those who fear him,
and his righteousness to
children's children,
18 to those who keep his covenant
and remember to do his
commandments.

19 The LORD has established his
throne in the heavens,
and his kingdom rules over
all.
20 Bless the LORD, O you his
angels,
you mighty ones who do his
bidding,
obedient to his spoken word.
21 Bless the LORD, all his hosts,
his ministers that do his will.
22 Bless the LORD, all his works,
in all places of his dominion.
Bless the LORD, O my soul.

Psalm 104

God the Creator and Provider

1 Bless the LORD, O my soul.
O LORD my God, you are
very great.
You are clothed with honor and
majesty,
2 wrapped in light as with a
garment.
You stretch out the heavens like
a tent,
3 you set the beams of your[u]
chambers on the waters,
you make the clouds your[v]
chariot,
you ride on the wings of the
wind,
4 you make the winds your[w]
messengers,
fire and flame your[x]
ministers.

5 You set the earth on its
foundations,
so that it shall never be
shaken.
6 You cover it with the deep as
with a garment;
the waters stood above the
mountains.
7 At your rebuke they flee;
at the sound of your thunder
they take to flight.
8 They rose up to the mountains,
ran down to the valleys
to the place that you
appointed for them.
9 You set a boundary that they
may not pass,
so that they might not again
cover the earth.

10 You make springs gush forth in
the valleys;
they flow between the hills,
11 giving drink to every wild
animal;
the wild asses quench their
thirst.
12 By the streams[y] the birds of the
air have their habitation;

u Heb *his* *v* Heb *his* *w* Heb *his* *x* Heb *his*
y Heb *By them*

they sing among the
branches.
13 From your lofty abode you
water the mountains;
the earth is satisfied with the
fruit of your work.

14 You cause the grass to grow for
the cattle,
and plants for people to use,[z]
to bring forth food from the
earth,
15 and wine to gladden the human
heart,
oil to make the face shine,
and bread to strengthen the
human heart.
16 The trees of the LORD are
watered abundantly,
the cedars of Lebanon that he
planted.
17 In them the birds build their
nests;
the stork has its home in the
fir trees.
18 The high mountains are for the
wild goats;
the rocks are a refuge for the
coneys.
19 You have made the moon to
mark the seasons;
the sun knows its time for
setting.
20 You make darkness, and it is
night,
when all the animals of the
forest come creeping out.
21 The young lions roar for their
prey,
seeking their food from God.
22 When the sun rises, they
withdraw
and lie down in their dens.
23 People go out to their work
and to their labor until the
evening.

24 O LORD, how manifold are your
works!
In wisdom you have made
them all;
the earth is full of your
creatures.
25 Yonder is the sea, great and
wide,
creeping things innumerable are
there,
living things both small and
great.
26 There go the ships,
and Leviathan that you formed
to sport in it.

27 These all look to you
to give them their food in due
season;
28 when you give to them, they
gather it up;
when you open your hand,
they are filled with good
things.
29 When you hide your face, they
are dismayed;
when you take away their
breath, they die
and return to their dust.
30 When you send forth your
spirit,[a] they are created;
and you renew the face of the
ground.

---

z Or *to cultivate* a Or *your breath*

[31] May the glory of the LORD
endure forever;
may the LORD rejoice in his
works—
[32] who looks on the earth and it
trembles,
who touches the mountains
and they smoke.
[33] I will sing to the LORD as long
as I live;
I will sing praise to my God
while I have being.
[34] May my meditation be pleasing
to him,
for I rejoice in the LORD.
[35] Let sinners be consumed from
the earth,
and let the wicked be no
more.
Bless the LORD, O my soul.
Praise the LORD!

Psalm 105

God's Faithfulness to Israel

[1] O give thanks to the LORD, call
on his name,
make known his deeds
among the peoples.
[2] Sing to him, sing praises to
him;
tell of all his wonderful works.
[3] Glory in his holy name;
let the hearts of those who
seek the LORD rejoice.
[4] Seek the LORD and his strength;
seek his presence continually.
[5] Remember the wonderful works
he has done,
his miracles, and the
judgments he has uttered,
[6] O offspring of his servant
Abraham,[b]
children of Jacob, his chosen
ones.

[7] He is the LORD our God;
his judgments are in all the
earth.
[8] He is mindful of his covenant
forever,
of the word that he
commanded, for a
thousand generations,
[9] the covenant that he made with
Abraham,
his sworn promise to Isaac,
[10] which he confirmed to Jacob as
a statute,
to Israel as an everlasting
covenant,
[11] saying, "To you I will give the
land of Canaan
as your portion for an
inheritance."

[12] When they were few in number,
of little account, and strangers
in it,
[13] wandering from nation to
nation,
from one kingdom to another
people,
[14] he allowed no one to oppress
them;
he rebuked kings on their
account,
[15] saying, "Do not touch my
anointed ones;
do my prophets no harm."

b Another reading is *Israel* (compare 1 Chr 16.13)

16 When he summoned famine
against the land,
and broke every staff of bread,
17 he had sent a man ahead of
them,
Joseph, who was sold as a
slave.
18 His feet were hurt with fetters,
his neck was put in a collar of
iron;
19 until what he had said came to
pass,
the word of the LORD kept
testing him.
20 The king sent and released him;
the ruler of the peoples set him
free.
21 He made him lord of his house,
and ruler of all his
possessions,
22 to instruct[c] his officials at his
pleasure,
and to teach his elders wisdom.

23 Then Israel came to Egypt;
Jacob lived as an alien in the
land of Ham.
24 And the LORD made his people
very fruitful,
and made them stronger than
their foes,
25 whose hearts he then turned to
hate his people,
to deal craftily with his
servants.

26 He sent his servant Moses,
and Aaron whom he had
chosen.
27 They performed his signs
among them,
and miracles in the land of
Ham.
28 He sent darkness, and made the
land dark;
they rebelled[d] against his
words.
29 He turned their waters into
blood,
and caused their fish to die.
30 Their land swarmed with frogs,
even in the chambers of their
kings.
31 He spoke, and there came
swarms of flies,
and gnats throughout their
country.
32 He gave them hail for rain,
and lightning that flashed
through their land.
33 He struck their vines and fig
trees,
and shattered the trees of their
country.
34 He spoke, and the locusts came,
and young locusts without
number;
35 they devoured all the vegetation
in their land,
and ate up the fruit of their
ground.
36 He struck down all the firstborn
in their land,
the first issue of all their
strength.

37 Then he brought Israel[e] out
with silver and gold,
and there was no one among
their tribes who stumbled.
38 Egypt was glad when they
departed,

c Gk Syr Jerome: Heb *to bind* *d* Cn Compare Gk Syr: Heb *they did not rebel* *e* Heb *them*

for dread of them had fallen
upon it.
39 He spread a cloud for a
covering,
and fire to give light by night.
40 They asked, and he brought
quails,
and gave them food from
heaven in abundance.
41 He opened the rock, and water
gushed out;
it flowed through the desert
like a river.
42 For he remembered his holy
promise,
and Abraham, his servant.

43 So he brought his people out
with joy,
his chosen ones with singing.
44 He gave them the lands of the
nations,
and they took possession of
the wealth of the peoples,
45 that they might keep his statutes
and observe his laws.
Praise the LORD!

Psalm 106

A Confession of Israel's Sins

1 Praise the LORD!
O give thanks to the LORD,
for he is good;
for his steadfast love endures
forever.
2 Who can utter the mighty
doings of the LORD,
or declare all his praise?
3 Happy are those who observe
justice,
who do righteousness at all
times.

4 Remember me, O LORD, when
you show favor to your
people;
help me when you deliver
them;
5 that I may see the prosperity of
your chosen ones,
that I may rejoice in the
gladness of your nation,
that I may glory in your
heritage.

6 Both we and our ancestors have
sinned;
we have committed iniquity,
have done wickedly.
7 Our ancestors, when they were
in Egypt,
did not consider your
wonderful works;
they did not remember the
abundance of your
steadfast love,
but rebelled against the Most
High[f] at the Red Sea.[g]
8 Yet he saved them for his
name's sake,
so that he might make known
his mighty power.
9 He rebuked the Red Sea,[h] and it
became dry;
he led them through the deep as
through a desert.
10 So he saved them from the hand
of the foe,
and delivered them from the
hand of the enemy.

f Cn Compare 78.17, 56: Heb *rebelled at the sea*
g Or *Sea of Reeds* *h* Or *Sea of Reeds*

11 The waters covered their
adversaries;
not one of them was left.
12 Then they believed his words;
they sang his praise.

13 But they soon forgot his works;
they did not wait for his
counsel.
14 But they had a wanton craving
in the wilderness,
and put God to the test in the
desert;
15 he gave them what they asked,
but sent a wasting disease
among them.

16 They were jealous of Moses in
the camp,
and of Aaron, the holy one of
the LORD.
17 The earth opened and
swallowed up Dathan,
and covered the faction of
Abiram.
18 Fire also broke out in their
company;
the flame burned up the
wicked.

19 They made a calf at Horeb
and worshiped a cast image.
20 They exchanged the glory of
God[i]
for the image of an ox that eats
grass.
21 They forgot God, their Savior,
who had done great things in
Egypt,
22 wondrous works in the land of
Ham,
and awesome deeds by the Red
Sea.[j]
23 Therefore he said he would
destroy them—
had not Moses, his chosen
one,
stood in the breach before him,
to turn away his wrath from
destroying them.

24 Then they despised the pleasant
land,
having no faith in his
promise.
25 They grumbled in their tents,
and did not obey the voice of
the LORD.
26 Therefore he raised his hand
and swore to them
that he would make them fall
in the wilderness,
27 and would disperse[k] their
descendants among the
nations,
scattering them over the lands.

28 Then they attached themselves
to the Baal of Peor,
and ate sacrifices offered to the
dead;
29 they provoked the LORD to
anger with their deeds,
and a plague broke out
among them.
30 Then Phinehas stood up and
interceded,
and the plague was stopped.
31 And that has been reckoned to
him as righteousness

i Compare Gk Mss: Heb *exchanged their glory*
j Or *Sea of Reeds* *k* Syr Compare Ezek 20.23: Heb *cause to fall*

from generation to generation
forever.

32 They angered the LORD[l] at the
waters of Meribah,
and it went ill with Moses on
their account;
33 for they made his spirit bitter,
and he spoke words that were
rash.

34 They did not destroy the
peoples,
as the LORD commanded
them,
35 but they mingled with the
nations
and learned to do as they did.
36 They served their idols,
which became a snare to
them.
37 They sacrificed their sons
and their daughters to the
demons;
38 they poured out innocent blood,
the blood of their sons and
daughters,
whom they sacrificed to the
idols of Canaan;
and the land was polluted
with blood.
39 Thus they became unclean by
their acts,
and prostituted themselves in
their doings.

40 Then the anger of the LORD
was kindled against his
people,
and he abhorred his heritage;
41 he gave them into the hand of
the nations,
so that those who hated them
ruled over them.
42 Their enemies oppressed them,
and they were brought into
subjection under their
power.
43 Many times he delivered them,
but they were rebellious in
their purposes,
and were brought low
through their iniquity.
44 Nevertheless he regarded their
distress
when he heard their cry.
45 For their sake he remembered
his covenant,
and showed compassion
according to the
abundance of his steadfast
love.
46 He caused them to be pitied
by all who held them captive.

47 Save us, O LORD our God,
and gather us from among the
nations,
that we may give thanks to your
holy name
and glory in your praise.

48 Blessed be the LORD, the God of
Israel,
from everlasting to
everlasting.
And let all the people say,
"Amen."
Praise the LORD!

---

l Heb *him*

BOOK V
(Psalms 107–150)

Psalm 107

Thanksgiving for Deliverance from Many Troubles

1 O give thanks to the LORD, for he is good;
for his steadfast love endures forever.
2 Let the redeemed of the LORD say so,
those he redeemed from trouble
3 and gathered in from the lands,
from the east and from the west,
from the north and from the south.[m]

4 Some wandered in desert wastes,
finding no way to an inhabited town;
5 hungry and thirsty,
their soul fainted within them.
6 Then they cried to the LORD in their trouble,
and he delivered them from their distress;
7 he led them by a straight way,
until they reached an inhabited town.
8 Let them thank the LORD for his steadfast love,
for his wonderful works to humankind.
9 For he satisfies the thirsty,
and the hungry he fills with good things.

10 Some sat in darkness and in gloom,
prisoners in misery and in irons,
11 for they had rebelled against the words of God,
and spurned the counsel of the Most High.
12 Their hearts were bowed down with hard labor;
they fell down, with no one to help.
13 Then they cried to the LORD in their trouble,
and he saved them from their distress;
14 he brought them out of darkness and gloom,
and broke their bonds asunder.
15 Let them thank the LORD for his steadfast love,
for his wonderful works to humankind.
16 For he shatters the doors of bronze,
and cuts in two the bars of iron.

17 Some were sick[n] through their sinful ways,
and because of their iniquities endured affliction;
18 they loathed any kind of food,
and they drew near to the gates of death.
19 Then they cried to the LORD in their trouble,
and he saved them from their distress;
20 he sent out his word and healed them,

---

m Cn: Heb *sea* *n* Cn: Heb *fools*

and delivered them from
destruction.
21 Let them thank the LORD for his
steadfast love,
for his wonderful works to
humankind.
22 And let them offer thanksgiving
sacrifices,
and tell of his deeds with
songs of joy.

23 Some went down to the sea in
ships,
doing business on the mighty
waters;
24 they saw the deeds of the LORD,
his wondrous works in the
deep.
25 For he commanded and raised
the stormy wind,
which lifted up the waves of the
sea.
26 They mounted up to heaven,
they went down to the
depths;
their courage melted away in
their calamity;
27 they reeled and staggered like
drunkards,
and were at their wits' end.
28 Then they cried to the LORD in
their trouble,
and he brought them out from
their distress;
29 he made the storm be still,
and the waves of the sea were
hushed.
30 Then they were glad because
they had quiet,
and he brought them to their
desired haven.
31 Let them thank the LORD for his
steadfast love,
for his wonderful works to
humankind.
32 Let them extol him in the
congregation of the
people,
and praise him in the
assembly of the elders.

33 He turns rivers into a desert,
springs of water into thirsty
ground,
34 a fruitful land into a salty waste,
because of the wickedness of its
inhabitants.
35 He turns a desert into pools of
water,
a parched land into springs of
water.
36 And there he lets the hungry
live,
and they establish a town to live
in;
37 they sow fields, and plant
vineyards,
and get a fruitful yield.
38 By his blessing they multiply
greatly,
and he does not let their
cattle decrease.

39 When they are diminished and
brought low
through oppression, trouble,
and sorrow,
40 he pours contempt on princes
and makes them wander in
trackless wastes;
41 but he raises up the needy out
of distress,
and makes their families like
flocks.
42 The upright see it and are glad;

and all wickedness stops its
mouth.
43 Let those who are wise give
heed to these things,
and consider the steadfast
love of the LORD.

Psalm 108

Praise and Prayer for Victory

A Song. A Psalm of David.

1 My heart is steadfast, O God,
my heart is steadfast;[o]
I will sing and make melody.
Awake, my soul![p]
2 Awake, O harp and lyre!
I will awake the dawn.
3 I will give thanks to you,
O LORD, among the
peoples,
and I will sing praises to you
among the nations.
4 For your steadfast love is higher
than the heavens,
and your faithfulness reaches
to the clouds.

5 Be exalted, O God, above the
heavens,
and let your glory be over all
the earth.
6 Give victory with your right
hand, and answer me,
so that those whom you love
may be rescued.

7 God has promised in his
sanctuary:[q]
"With exultation I will divide
up Shechem,
and portion out the Vale of
Succoth.
8 Gilead is mine; Manasseh is
mine;
Ephraim is my helmet;
Judah is my scepter.
9 Moab is my washbasin;
on Edom I hurl my shoe;
over Philistia I shout in
triumph."

10 Who will bring me to the
fortified city?
Who will lead me to Edom?
11 Have you not rejected us,
O God?
You do not go out, O God, with
our armies.
12 O grant us help against the foe,
for human help is worthless.
13 With God we shall do valiantly;
it is he who will tread down
our foes.

Psalm 109

Prayer for Vindication and Vengeance

To the leader. Of David. A Psalm.

1 Do not be silent, O God of my
praise.
2 For wicked and deceitful
mouths are opened against
me,

---

o Heb Mss Gk Syr: MT lacks *my heart is steadfast* *p* Compare 57.8: Heb *also my soul* *q* Or *by his holiness*

speaking against me with lying
tongues.
3 They beset me with words of
hate,
and attack me without cause.
4 In return for my love they
accuse me,
even while I make prayer for
them.[r]
5 So they reward me evil for
good,
and hatred for my love.

6 They say,[s] "Appoint a wicked
man against him;
let an accuser stand on his right.
7 When he is tried, let him be
found guilty;
let his prayer be counted as sin.
8 May his days be few;
may another seize his
position.
9 May his children be orphans,
and his wife a widow.
10 May his children wander about
and beg;
may they be driven out of[t] the
ruins they inhabit.
11 May the creditor seize all that
he has;
may strangers plunder the fruits
of his toil.
12 May there be no one to do him
a kindness,
nor anyone to pity his orphaned
children.
13 May his posterity be cut off;
may his name be blotted out in
the second generation.
14 May the iniquity of his father[u]
be remembered before the
LORD,
and do not let the sin of his
mother be blotted out.
15 Let them be before the LORD
continually,
and may his[v] memory be cut off
from the earth.
16 For he did not remember to
show kindness,
but pursued the poor and needy
and the brokenhearted to their
death.
17 He loved to curse; let curses
come on him.
He did not like blessing; may it
be far from him.
18 He clothed himself with cursing
as his coat,
may it soak into his body like
water,
like oil into his bones.
19 May it be like a garment that he
wraps around himself,
like a belt that he wears every
day."

20 May that be the reward of my
accusers from the LORD,
of those who speak evil against
my life.
21 But you, O LORD my Lord,
act on my behalf for your
name's sake;
because your steadfast love is
good, deliver me.
22 For I am poor and needy,
and my heart is pierced
within me.
23 I am gone like a shadow at
evening;
I am shaken off like a locust.

---

r Syr: Heb *I prayer* *s* Heb lacks *They say* *t* Gk: Heb *and seek* *u* Cn: Heb *fathers* *v* Gk: Heb *their*

24 My knees are weak through
fasting;
my body has become gaunt.
25 I am an object of scorn to my
accusers;
when they see me, they shake
their heads.

26 Help me, O LORD my God!
Save me according to your
steadfast love.
27 Let them know that this is your
hand;
you, O LORD, have done it.
28 Let them curse, but you will
bless.
Let my assailants be put to
shame;[w] may your servant
be glad.
29 May my accusers be clothed
with dishonor;
may they be wrapped in their
own shame as in a mantle.
30 With my mouth I will give great
thanks to the LORD;
I will praise him in the midst of
the throng.
31 For he stands at the right hand
of the needy,
to save them from those who
would condemn them to
death.

Psalm 110

Assurance of Victory for God's Priest-King

Of David. A Psalm.

1 The LORD says to my lord,
"Sit at my right hand
until I make your enemies your
footstool."

2 The LORD sends out from Zion
your mighty scepter.
Rule in the midst of your foes.
3 Your people will offer
themselves willingly
on the day you lead your forces
on the holy mountains.[x]
From the womb of the morning,
like dew, your youth[y] will
come to you.
4 The LORD has sworn and will
not change his mind,
"You are a priest forever
according to the order of
Melchizedek."[z]

5 The Lord is at your right hand;
he will shatter kings on the
day of his wrath.
6 He will execute judgment
among the nations,
filling them with corpses;
he will shatter heads
over the wide earth.
7 He will drink from the stream
by the path;
therefore he will lift up his
head.

Psalm 111

Praise for God's Wonderful Works

1 Praise the LORD!

---

w Gk: Heb *They have risen up and have been put to shame* *x* Another reading is *in holy splendor* *y* Cn: Heb *the dew of your youth*
z Or *forever, a rightful king by my edict*

I will give thanks to the LORD
with my whole heart,
in the company of
the upright, in the
congregation.
2 Great are the works of the
LORD,
studied by all who delight in
them.
3 Full of honor and majesty is his
work,
and his righteousness endures
forever.
4 He has gained renown by his
wonderful deeds;
the LORD is gracious and
merciful.
5 He provides food for those who
fear him;
he is ever mindful of his
covenant.
6 He has shown his people the
power of his works,
in giving them the heritage of
the nations.
7 The works of his hands are
faithful and just;
all his precepts are
trustworthy.
8 They are established forever
and ever,
to be performed with
faithfulness and
uprightness.
9 He sent redemption to his
people;
he has commanded his
covenant forever.
Holy and awesome is his name.
10 The fear of the LORD is the
beginning of wisdom;
all those who practice
it[a] have a good
understanding.
His praise endures forever.

Psalm 112

Blessings of the Righteous

1 Praise the LORD!
Happy are those who fear the
LORD,
who greatly delight in his
commandments.
2 Their descendants will be
mighty in the land;
the generation of the upright
will be blessed.
3 Wealth and riches are in their
houses,
and their righteousness
endures forever.
4 They rise in the darkness as a
light for the upright;
they are gracious, merciful,
and righteous.
5 It is well with those who deal
generously and lend,
who conduct their affairs
with justice.
6 For the righteous will never be
moved;
they will be remembered
forever.
7 They are not afraid of evil
tidings;
their hearts are firm, secure in
the LORD.
8 Their hearts are steady, they
will not be afraid;
in the end they will look in
triumph on their foes.

---

a Gk Syr: Heb *them*

9 They have distributed freely,
they have given to the poor;
their righteousness endures forever;
their horn is exalted in honor.
10 The wicked see it and are angry;
they gnash their teeth and melt away;
the desire of the wicked comes to nothing.

Psalm 113

God the Helper of the Needy

1 Praise the LORD!
Praise, O servants of the LORD;
praise the name of the LORD.

2 Blessed be the name of the LORD
from this time on and forevermore.
3 From the rising of the sun to its setting
the name of the LORD is to be praised.
4 The LORD is high above all nations,
and his glory above the heavens.

5 Who is like the LORD our God,
who is seated on high,
6 who looks far down
on the heavens and the earth?
7 He raises the poor from the dust,
and lifts the needy from the ash heap,
8 to make them sit with princes,
with the princes of his people.
9 He gives the barren woman a home,
making her the joyous mother of children.
Praise the LORD!

Psalm 114

God's Wonders at the Exodus

1 When Israel went out from Egypt,
the house of Jacob from a people of strange language,
2 Judah became God's[b] sanctuary,
Israel his dominion.

3 The sea looked and fled;
Jordan turned back.
4 The mountains skipped like rams,
the hills like lambs.

5 Why is it, O sea, that you flee?
O Jordan, that you turn back?
6 O mountains, that you skip like rams?
O hills, like lambs?

7 Tremble, O earth, at the presence of the LORD,
at the presence of the God of Jacob,

---

b Heb *his*

8 who turns the rock into a pool of water,
the flint into a spring of water.

Psalm 115

The Impotence of Idols and the Greatness of God

1 Not to us, O LORD, not to us,
but to your name give glory,
for the sake of your steadfast love and your faithfulness.
2 Why should the nations say,
"Where is their God?"

3 Our God is in the heavens;
he does whatever he pleases.
4 Their idols are silver and gold,
the work of human hands.
5 They have mouths, but do not speak;
eyes, but do not see.
6 They have ears, but do not hear;
noses, but do not smell.
7 They have hands, but do not feel;
feet, but do not walk;
they make no sound in their throats.
8 Those who make them are like them;
so are all who trust in them.

9 O Israel, trust in the LORD!
He is their help and their shield.
10 O house of Aaron, trust in the LORD!
He is their help and their shield.
11 You who fear the LORD, trust in the LORD!
He is their help and their shield.

12 The LORD has been mindful of us; he will bless us;
he will bless the house of Israel;
he will bless the house of Aaron;
13 he will bless those who fear the LORD,
both small and great.

14 May the LORD give you increase,
both you and your children.
15 May you be blessed by the LORD,
who made heaven and earth.

16 The heavens are the LORD's heavens,
but the earth he has given to human beings.
17 The dead do not praise the LORD,
nor do any that go down into silence.
18 But we will bless the LORD
from this time on and forevermore.
Praise the LORD!

Psalm 116

Thanksgiving for Recovery from Illness

[1] I love the LORD, because he has heard
my voice and my supplications.
[2] Because he inclined his ear to me,
therefore I will call on him as long as I live.
[3] The snares of death encompassed me;
the pangs of Sheol laid hold on me;
I suffered distress and anguish.
[4] Then I called on the name of the LORD:
"O LORD, I pray, save my life!"

[5] Gracious is the LORD, and righteous;
our God is merciful.
[6] The LORD protects the simple;
when I was brought low, he saved me.
[7] Return, O my soul, to your rest,
for the LORD has dealt bountifully with you.

[8] For you have delivered my soul from death,
my eyes from tears,
my feet from stumbling.
[9] I walk before the LORD
in the land of the living.
[10] I kept my faith, even when I said,
"I am greatly afflicted";
[11] I said in my consternation,
"Everyone is a liar."

[12] What shall I return to the LORD
for all his bounty to me?
[13] I will lift up the cup of salvation
and call on the name of the LORD,
[14] I will pay my vows to the LORD
in the presence of all his people.
[15] Precious in the sight of the LORD
is the death of his faithful ones.
[16] O LORD, I am your servant;
I am your servant, the child of your serving girl.
You have loosed my bonds.
[17] I will offer to you a thanksgiving sacrifice
and call on the name of the LORD.
[18] I will pay my vows to the LORD
in the presence of all his people,
[19] in the courts of the house of the LORD,
in your midst, O Jerusalem.
Praise the LORD!

Psalm 117

Universal Call to Worship

[1] Praise the LORD, all you nations!
Extol him, all you peoples!
[2] For great is his steadfast love toward us,
and the faithfulness of the LORD endures forever.
Praise the LORD!

Psalm 118

A Song of Victory

1 O give thanks to the LORD, for
he is good;
his steadfast love endures
forever!

2 Let Israel say,
"His steadfast love endures
forever."
3 Let the house of Aaron say,
"His steadfast love endures
forever."
4 Let those who fear the LORD
say,
"His steadfast love endures
forever."

5 Out of my distress I called on
the LORD;
the LORD answered me and
set me in a broad place.
6 With the LORD on my side I do
not fear.
What can mortals do to me?
7 The LORD is on my side to help
me;
I shall look in triumph on
those who hate me.
8 It is better to take refuge in the
LORD
than to put confidence in
mortals.
9 It is better to take refuge in the
LORD
than to put confidence in
princes.

10 All nations surrounded me;
in the name of the LORD I cut
them off!
11 They surrounded me,
surrounded me on every
side;
in the name of the LORD I cut
them off!
12 They surrounded me like bees;
they blazed[c] like a fire of
thorns;
in the name of the LORD I cut
them off!
13 I was pushed hard,[d] so that I
was falling,
but the LORD helped me.
14 The LORD is my strength and
my might;
he has become my salvation.

15 There are glad songs of
victory in the tents of the
righteous:
"The right hand of the LORD
does valiantly;
16 the right hand of the LORD is
exalted;
the right hand of the LORD does
valiantly."
17 I shall not die, but I shall live,
and recount the deeds of the
LORD.
18 The LORD has punished me
severely,
but he did not give me over
to death.

19 Open to me the gates of
righteousness,
that I may enter through them
and give thanks to the LORD.

c Gk: Heb *were extinguished* *d* Gk Syr Jerome: Heb *You pushed me hard*

20 This is the gate of the LORD;
the righteous shall enter
through it.

21 I thank you that you have
answered me
and have become my salvation.
22 The stone that the builders
rejected
has become the chief
cornerstone.
23 This is the LORD's doing;
it is marvelous in our eyes.
24 This is the day that the LORD
has made;
let us rejoice and be glad in
it.[e]
25 Save us, we beseech you,
O LORD!
O LORD, we beseech you,
give us success!

26 Blessed is the one who comes
in the name of the LORD.[f]
We bless you from the house
of the LORD.
27 The LORD is God,
and he has given us light.
Bind the festal procession with
branches,
up to the horns of the altar.[g]

28 You are my God, and I will give
thanks to you;
you are my God, I will extol
you.

29 O give thanks to the LORD, for
he is good,
for his steadfast love endures
forever.

Psalm 119

The Glories of God's Law

1 Happy are those whose way is
blameless,
who walk in the law of the
LORD.
2 Happy are those who keep his
decrees,
who seek him with their
whole heart,
3 who also do no wrong,
but walk in his ways.
4 You have commanded your
precepts
to be kept diligently.
5 O that my ways may be
steadfast
in keeping your statutes!
6 Then I shall not be put to
shame,
having my eyes fixed on all
your commandments.
7 I will praise you with an upright
heart,
when I learn your righteous
ordinances.
8 I will observe your statutes;
do not utterly forsake me.

9 How can young people keep
their way pure?
By guarding it according to
your word.

e Or *in him* *f* Or *Blessed in the name of the LORD is the one who comes* *g* Meaning of Heb uncertain

[10] With my whole heart I seek you;
do not let me stray from your commandments.
[11] I treasure your word in my heart,
so that I may not sin against you.
[12] Blessed are you, O Lord;
teach me your statutes.
[13] With my lips I declare
all the ordinances of your mouth.
[14] I delight in the way of your decrees
as much as in all riches.
[15] I will meditate on your precepts,
and fix my eyes on your ways.
[16] I will delight in your statutes;
I will not forget your word.

[17] Deal bountifully with your servant,
so that I may live and observe your word.
[18] Open my eyes, so that I may behold
wondrous things out of your law.
[19] I live as an alien in the land;
do not hide your commandments from me.
[20] My soul is consumed with longing
for your ordinances at all times.
[21] You rebuke the insolent, accursed ones,
who wander from your commandments;
[22] take away from me their scorn and contempt,
for I have kept your decrees.
[23] Even though princes sit plotting against me,
your servant will meditate on your statutes.
[24] Your decrees are my delight,
they are my counselors.

[25] My soul clings to the dust;
revive me according to your word.
[26] When I told of my ways, you answered me;
teach me your statutes.
[27] Make me understand the way of your precepts,
and I will meditate on your wondrous works.
[28] My soul melts away for sorrow;
strengthen me according to your word.
[29] Put false ways far from me;
and graciously teach me your law.
[30] I have chosen the way of faithfulness;
I set your ordinances before me.
[31] I cling to your decrees, O Lord;
let me not be put to shame.
[32] I run the way of your commandments,
for you enlarge my understanding.

[33] Teach me, O Lord, the way of your statutes,
and I will observe it to the end.
[34] Give me understanding, that I may keep your law
and observe it with my whole heart.

35 Lead me in the path of your
commandments,
for I delight in it.
36 Turn my heart to your decrees,
and not to selfish gain.
37 Turn my eyes from looking at
vanities;
give me life in your ways.
38 Confirm to your servant your
promise,
which is for those who fear
you.
39 Turn away the disgrace that I
dread,
for your ordinances are good.
40 See, I have longed for your
precepts;
in your righteousness give
me life.

41 Let your steadfast love come to
me, O LORD,
your salvation according to
your promise.
42 Then I shall have an answer for
those who taunt me,
for I trust in your word.
43 Do not take the word of truth
utterly out of my mouth,
for my hope is in your
ordinances.
44 I will keep your law
continually,
forever and ever.
45 I shall walk at liberty,
for I have sought your
precepts.
46 I will also speak of your
decrees before kings,
and shall not be put to shame;
47 I find my delight in your
commandments,
because I love them.
48 I revere your commandments,
which I love,
and I will meditate on your
statutes.

49 Remember your word to your
servant,
in which you have made me
hope.
50 This is my comfort in my
distress,
that your promise gives me
life.
51 The arrogant utterly deride me,
but I do not turn away from
your law.
52 When I think of your
ordinances from of old,
I take comfort, O LORD.
53 Hot indignation seizes me
because of the wicked,
those who forsake your law.
54 Your statutes have been my
songs
wherever I make my home.
55 I remember your name in the
night, O LORD,
and keep your law.
56 This blessing has fallen to me,
for I have kept your precepts.

57 The LORD is my portion;
I promise to keep your
words.
58 I implore your favor with all
my heart;
be gracious to me according
to your promise.
59 When I think of your ways,
I turn my feet to your
decrees;
60 I hurry and do not delay

to keep your commandments.
61 Though the cords of the wicked
ensnare me,
I do not forget your law.
62 At midnight I rise to praise you,
because of your righteous
ordinances.
63 I am a companion of all who
fear you,
of those who keep your
precepts.
64 The earth, O LORD, is full of
your steadfast love;
teach me your statutes.

65 You have dealt well with your
servant,
O LORD, according to your
word.
66 Teach me good judgment and
knowledge,
for I believe in your
commandments.
67 Before I was humbled I went
astray,
but now I keep your word.
68 You are good and do good;
teach me your statutes.
69 The arrogant smear me with
lies,
but with my whole heart I
keep your precepts.
70 Their hearts are fat and gross,
but I delight in your law.
71 It is good for me that I was
humbled,
so that I might learn your
statutes.
72 The law of your mouth is better
to me
than thousands of gold and
silver pieces.

73 Your hands have made and
fashioned me;
give me understanding
that I may learn your
commandments.
74 Those who fear you shall see
me and rejoice,
because I have hoped in your
word.
75 I know, O LORD, that your
judgments are right,
and that in faithfulness you
have humbled me.
76 Let your steadfast love become
my comfort
according to your promise to
your servant.
77 Let your mercy come to me,
that I may live;
for your law is my delight.
78 Let the arrogant be put to
shame,
because they have subverted
me with guile;
as for me, I will meditate on
your precepts.
79 Let those who fear you turn to
me,
so that they may know your
decrees.
80 May my heart be blameless in
your statutes,
so that I may not be put to
shame.

81 My soul languishes for your
salvation;
I hope in your word.
82 My eyes fail with watching for
your promise;
I ask, "When will you
comfort me?"

83 For I have become like a
wineskin in the smoke,
yet I have not forgotten your
statutes.
84 How long must your servant
endure?
When will you judge those who
persecute me?
85 The arrogant have dug pitfalls
for me;
they flout your law.
86 All your commandments are
enduring;
I am persecuted without cause;
help me!
87 They have almost made an end
of me on earth;
but I have not forsaken your
precepts.
88 In your steadfast love spare my
life,
so that I may keep the
decrees of your mouth.

89 The LORD exists forever;
your word is firmly fixed in
heaven.
90 Your faithfulness endures to all
generations;
you have established the earth,
and it stands fast.
91 By your appointment they stand
today,
for all things are your servants.
92 If your law had not been my
delight,
I would have perished in my
misery.
93 I will never forget your
precepts,
for by them you have given me
life.
94 I am yours; save me,
for I have sought your precepts.
95 The wicked lie in wait to
destroy me,
but I consider your decrees.
96 I have seen a limit to all
perfection,
but your commandment is
exceedingly broad.

97 Oh, how I love your law!
It is my meditation all day
long.
98 Your commandment makes me
wiser than my enemies,
for it is always with me.
99 I have more understanding
than all my teachers,
for your decrees are my
meditation.
100 I understand more than the
aged,
for I keep your precepts.
101 I hold back my feet from every
evil way,
in order to keep your word.
102 I do not turn away from your
ordinances,
for you have taught me.
103 How sweet are your words to
my taste,
sweeter than honey to my
mouth!
104 Through your precepts I get
understanding;
therefore I hate every false
way.

105 Your word is a lamp to my feet
and a light to my path.
106 I have sworn an oath and
confirmed it,

to observe your righteous
ordinances.
107 I am severely afflicted;
give me life, O LORD,
according to your word.
108 Accept my offerings of praise,
O LORD,
and teach me your
ordinances.
109 I hold my life in my hand
continually,
but I do not forget your law.
110 The wicked have laid a snare
for me,
but I do not stray from your
precepts.
111 Your decrees are my heritage
forever;
they are the joy of my heart.
112 I incline my heart to perform
your statutes
forever, to the end.

113 I hate the double-minded,
but I love your law.
114 You are my hiding place and
my shield;
I hope in your word.
115 Go away from me, you
evildoers,
that I may keep the
commandments of my
God.
116 Uphold me according to your
promise, that I may live,
and let me not be put to
shame in my hope.
117 Hold me up, that I may be safe
and have regard for your
statutes continually.
118 You spurn all who go astray
from your statutes;
for their cunning is in vain.
119 All the wicked of the earth you
count as dross;
therefore I love your decrees.
120 My flesh trembles for fear of
you,
and I am afraid of your
judgments.

121 I have done what is just and
right;
do not leave me to my
oppressors.
122 Guarantee your servant's well-
being;
do not let the godless oppress
me.
123 My eyes fail from watching for
your salvation,
and for the fulfillment of your
righteous promise.
124 Deal with your servant
according to your
steadfast love,
and teach me your statutes.
125 I am your servant; give me
understanding,
so that I may know your
decrees.
126 It is time for the LORD to act,
for your law has been broken.
127 Truly I love your
commandments
more than gold, more than
fine gold.
128 Truly I direct my steps by all
your precepts;[h]
I hate every false way.

129 Your decrees are wonderful;

h Gk Jerome: Meaning of Heb uncertain

therefore my soul keeps
them.
130 The unfolding of your words
gives light;
it imparts understanding to
the simple.
131 With open mouth I pant,
because I long for your
commandments.
132 Turn to me and be gracious to
me,
as is your custom toward
those who love your
name.
133 Keep my steps steady
according to your
promise,
and never let iniquity have
dominion over me.
134 Redeem me from human
oppression,
that I may keep your
precepts.
135 Make your face shine upon
your servant,
and teach me your statutes.
136 My eyes shed streams of tears
because your law is not kept.

137 You are righteous, O LORD,
and your judgments are right.
138 You have appointed your
decrees in righteousness
and in all faithfulness.
139 My zeal consumes me
because my foes forget your
words.
140 Your promise is well tried,
and your servant loves it.
141 I am small and despised,
yet I do not forget your
precepts.
142 Your righteousness is an
everlasting righteousness,
and your law is the truth.
143 Trouble and anguish have
come upon me,
but your commandments are
my delight.
144 Your decrees are righteous
forever;
give me understanding that I
may live.

145 With my whole heart I cry;
answer me, O LORD.
I will keep your statutes.
146 I cry to you; save me,
that I may observe your
decrees.
147 I rise before dawn and cry for
help;
I put my hope in your words.
148 My eyes are awake before
each watch of the night,
that I may meditate on your
promise.
149 In your steadfast love hear my
voice;
O LORD, in your justice
preserve my life.
150 Those who persecute me with
evil purpose draw near;
they are far from your law.
151 Yet you are near, O LORD,
and all your commandments
are true.
152 Long ago I learned from your
decrees
that you have established
them forever.

153 Look on my misery and rescue
me,

for I do not forget your law.
154 Plead my cause and redeem me;
give me life according to your promise.
155 Salvation is far from the wicked,
for they do not seek your statutes.
156 Great is your mercy, O LORD;
give me life according to your justice.
157 Many are my persecutors and my adversaries,
yet I do not swerve from your decrees.
158 I look at the faithless with disgust,
because they do not keep your commands.
159 Consider how I love your precepts;
preserve my life according to your steadfast love.
160 The sum of your word is truth;
and every one of your righteous ordinances endures forever.

161 Princes persecute me without cause,
but my heart stands in awe of your words.
162 I rejoice at your word
like one who finds great spoil.
163 I hate and abhor falsehood,
but I love your law.
164 Seven times a day I praise you
for your righteous ordinances.
165 Great peace have those who love your law;
nothing can make them stumble.
166 I hope for your salvation, O LORD,
and I fulfill your commandments.
167 My soul keeps your decrees;
I love them exceedingly.
168 I keep your precepts and decrees,
for all my ways are before you.

169 Let my cry come before you, O LORD;
give me understanding according to your word.
170 Let my supplication come before you;
deliver me according to your promise.
171 My lips will pour forth praise,
because you teach me your statutes.
172 My tongue will sing of your promise,
for all your commandments are right.
173 Let your hand be ready to help me,
for I have chosen your precepts.
174 I long for your salvation, O LORD,
and your law is my delight.
175 Let me live that I may praise you,
and let your ordinances help me.
176 I have gone astray like a lost sheep; seek out your servant,

for I do not forget your
commandments.

Psalm 120

Prayer for Deliverance from Slanderers

A Song of Ascents.

1 In my distress I cry to the LORD,
that he may answer me:
2 "Deliver me, O LORD,
from lying lips,
from a deceitful tongue."

3 What shall be given to you?
And what more shall be done
to you,
you deceitful tongue?
4 A warrior's sharp arrows,
with glowing coals of the
broom tree!

5 Woe is me, that I am an alien in
Meshech,
that I must live among the tents
of Kedar.
6 Too long have I had my
dwelling
among those who hate peace.
7 I am for peace;
but when I speak,
they are for war.

Psalm 121

Assurance of God's Protection

A Song of Ascents.

1 I lift up my eyes to the hills—
from where will my help come?
2 My help comes from the LORD,
who made heaven and earth.

3 He will not let your foot be
moved;
he who keeps you will not
slumber.
4 He who keeps Israel
will neither slumber nor
sleep.

5 The LORD is your keeper;
the LORD is your shade at your
right hand.
6 The sun shall not strike you by
day,
nor the moon by night.

7 The LORD will keep you from
all evil;
he will keep your life.
8 The LORD will keep
your going out and your
coming in
from this time on and
forevermore.

Psalm 122

Song of Praise and Prayer for Jerusalem

A Song of Ascents. Of David.

1 I was glad when they said to
me,
"Let us go to the house of the
LORD!"
2 Our feet are standing
within your gates,
O Jerusalem.

3 Jerusalem—built as a city
that is bound firmly together.
4 To it the tribes go up,
the tribes of the LORD,
as was decreed for Israel,
to give thanks to the name of
the LORD.
5 For there the thrones for
judgment were set up,
the thrones of the house of
David.

6 Pray for the peace of Jerusalem:
"May they prosper who love
you.
7 Peace be within your walls,
and security within your
towers."
8 For the sake of my relatives and
friends
I will say, "Peace be within
you."
9 For the sake of the house of the
LORD our God,
I will seek your good.

Psalm 123

Supplication for Mercy

A Song of Ascents.

1 To you I lift up my eyes,
O you who are enthroned in
the heavens!
2 As the eyes of servants
look to the hand of their
master,
as the eyes of a maid
to the hand of her mistress,
so our eyes look to the LORD
our God,
until he has mercy upon us.

3 Have mercy upon us, O LORD,
have mercy upon us,
for we have had more than
enough of contempt.
4 Our soul has had more than its
fill
of the scorn of those who are
at ease,
of the contempt of the proud.

Psalm 124

Thanksgiving for Israel's Deliverance

A Song of Ascents. Of David.

1 If it had not been the LORD who
was on our side
—let Israel now say—
2 if it had not been the LORD who
was on our side,
when our enemies attacked
us,

3 then they would have
swallowed us up alive,
when their anger was kindled
against us;
4 then the flood would have
swept us away,
the torrent would have gone
over us;
5 then over us would have gone
the raging waters.

6 Blessed be the LORD,
who has not given us
as prey to their teeth.
7 We have escaped like a bird
from the snare of the fowlers;
the snare is broken,
and we have escaped.

8 Our help is in the name of the
LORD,
who made heaven and earth.

Psalm 125

The Security of God's People

A Song of Ascents.

1 Those who trust in the LORD are
like Mount Zion,
which cannot be moved, but
abides forever.
2 As the mountains surround
Jerusalem,
so the LORD surrounds his
people,
from this time on and
forevermore.
3 For the scepter of wickedness
shall not rest
on the land allotted to the
righteous,
so that the righteous might not
stretch out
their hands to do wrong.
4 Do good, O LORD, to those who
are good,
and to those who are upright
in their hearts.
5 But those who turn aside to
their own crooked ways
the LORD will lead away with
evildoers.
Peace be upon Israel!

Psalm 126

A Harvest of Joy

A Song of Ascents.

1 When the LORD restored the
fortunes of Zion,[i]
we were like those who
dream.
2 Then our mouth was filled with
laughter,
and our tongue with shouts of
joy;
then it was said among the
nations,
"The LORD has done great
things for them."
3 The LORD has done great things
for us,
and we rejoiced.

4 Restore our fortunes, O LORD,
like the watercourses in the
Negeb.

---

i Or *brought back those who returned to Zion*

[5] May those who sow in tears
reap with shouts of joy.
[6] Those who go out weeping,
bearing the seed for sowing,
shall come home with shouts of joy,
carrying their sheaves.

Psalm 127

God's Blessings in the Home

A Song of Ascents. Of Solomon.

[1] Unless the LORD builds the house,
those who build it labor in vain.
Unless the LORD guards the city,
the guard keeps watch in vain.
[2] It is in vain that you rise up early
and go late to rest,
eating the bread of anxious toil;
for he gives sleep to his beloved.[j]

[3] Sons are indeed a heritage from the LORD,
the fruit of the womb a reward.
[4] Like arrows in the hand of a warrior
are the sons of one's youth.
[5] Happy is the man who has
his quiver full of them.
He shall not be put to shame
when he speaks with his enemies in the gate.

Psalm 128

The Happy Home of the Faithful

A Song of Ascents.

[1] Happy is everyone who fears the LORD,
who walks in his ways.
[2] You shall eat the fruit of the labor of your hands;
you shall be happy, and it shall go well with you.

[3] Your wife will be like a fruitful vine
within your house;
your children will be like olive shoots
around your table.
[4] Thus shall the man be blessed
who fears the LORD.

[5] The LORD bless you from Zion.
May you see the prosperity of Jerusalem
all the days of your life.
[6] May you see your children's children.
Peace be upon Israel!

---

j Or *for he provides for his beloved during sleep*

Psalm 129

Prayer for the Downfall of Israel's Enemies

A Song of Ascents.

1 "Often have they attacked me
from my youth"
—let Israel now say—
2 "often have they attacked me
from my youth,
yet they have not prevailed
against me.
3 The plowers plowed on my
back;
they made their furrows long."
4 The LORD is righteous;
he has cut the cords of the
wicked.
5 May all who hate Zion
be put to shame and turned
backward.
6 Let them be like the grass on
the housetops
that withers before it grows up,
7 with which reapers do not fill
their hands
or binders of sheaves their
arms,
8 while those who pass by do not
say,
"The blessing of the LORD be
upon you!
We bless you in the name of
the LORD!"

Psalm 130

Waiting for Divine Redemption

A Song of Ascents.

1 Out of the depths I cry to you,
O LORD.
2 Lord, hear my voice!
Let your ears be attentive
to the voice of my
supplications!

3 If you, O LORD, should mark
iniquities,
Lord, who could stand?
4 But there is forgiveness with
you,
so that you may be revered.

5 I wait for the LORD, my soul
waits,
and in his word I hope;
6 my soul waits for the Lord
more than those who watch
for the morning,
more than those who watch
for the morning.

7 O Israel, hope in the LORD!
For with the LORD there is
steadfast love,
and with him is great power to
redeem.
8 It is he who will redeem Israel
from all its iniquities.

Psalm 131

Song of Quiet Trust

A Song of Ascents. Of David.

1 O LORD, my heart is not lifted up,
my eyes are not raised too high;
I do not occupy myself with things
too great and too marvelous for me.
2 But I have calmed and quieted my soul,
like a weaned child with its mother;
my soul is like the weaned child that is with me.[k]

3 O Israel, hope in the LORD
from this time on and forevermore.

Psalm 132

The Eternal Dwelling of God in Zion

A Song of Ascents.

1 O LORD, remember in David's favor
all the hardships he endured;
2 how he swore to the LORD
and vowed to the Mighty One of Jacob,
3 "I will not enter my house
or get into my bed;
4 I will not give sleep to my eyes
or slumber to my eyelids,
5 until I find a place for the LORD,
a dwelling place for the Mighty One of Jacob."

6 We heard of it in Ephrathah;
we found it in the fields of Jaar.
7 "Let us go to his dwelling place;
let us worship at his footstool."

8 Rise up, O LORD, and go to your resting place,
you and the ark of your might.
9 Let your priests be clothed with righteousness,
and let your faithful shout for joy.
10 For your servant David's sake
do not turn away the face of your anointed one.

11 The LORD swore to David a sure oath
from which he will not turn back:
"One of the sons of your body
I will set on your throne.
12 If your sons keep my covenant
and my decrees that I shall teach them,
their sons also, forevermore,
shall sit on your throne."

13 For the LORD has chosen Zion;
he has desired it for his habitation:
14 "This is my resting place forever;

k Or *my soul within me is like a weaned child*

here I will reside, for I have desired it.
15 I will abundantly bless its provisions;
I will satisfy its poor with bread.
16 Its priests I will clothe with salvation,
and its faithful will shout for joy.
17 There I will cause a horn to sprout up for David;
I have prepared a lamp for my anointed one.
18 His enemies I will clothe with disgrace,
but on him, his crown will gleam."

Psalm 133

The Blessedness of Unity

A Song of Ascents.

1 How very good and pleasant it is
when kindred live together in unity!
2 It is like the precious oil on the head,
running down upon the beard,
on the beard of Aaron,
running down over the collar of his robes.
3 It is like the dew of Hermon,
which falls on the mountains of Zion.
For there the LORD ordained his blessing,
life forevermore.

Psalm 134

Praise in the Night

A Song of Ascents.

1 Come, bless the LORD, all you servants of the LORD,
who stand by night in the house of the LORD!
2 Lift up your hands to the holy place,
and bless the LORD.

3 May the LORD, maker of heaven and earth,
bless you from Zion.

Psalm 135

Praise for God's Goodness and Might

1 Praise the LORD!
Praise the name of the LORD;
give praise, O servants of the LORD,
2 you that stand in the house of the LORD,
in the courts of the house of our God.
3 Praise the LORD, for the LORD is good;
sing to his name, for he is gracious.
4 For the LORD has chosen Jacob for himself,
Israel as his own possession.

5 For I know that the LORD is great;

our Lord is above all gods.
6 Whatever the LORD pleases he does,
in heaven and on earth,
in the seas and all deeps.
7 He it is who makes the clouds rise at the end of the earth;
he makes lightnings for the rain
and brings out the wind from his storehouses.

8 He it was who struck down the firstborn of Egypt,
both human beings and animals;
9 he sent signs and wonders
into your midst, O Egypt,
against Pharaoh and all his servants.
10 He struck down many nations
and killed mighty kings—
11 Sihon, king of the Amorites,
and Og, king of Bashan,
and all the kingdoms of Canaan—
12 and gave their land as a heritage,
a heritage to his people Israel.

13 Your name, O LORD, endures forever,
your renown, O LORD, throughout all ages.
14 For the LORD will vindicate his people,
and have compassion on his servants.

15 The idols of the nations are silver and gold,
the work of human hands.
16 They have mouths, but they do not speak;
they have eyes, but they do not see;
17 they have ears, but they do not hear,
and there is no breath in their mouths.
18 Those who make them
and all who trust them
shall become like them.

19 O house of Israel, bless the LORD!
O house of Aaron, bless the LORD!
20 O house of Levi, bless the LORD!
You that fear the LORD, bless the LORD!
21 Blessed be the LORD from Zion,
he who resides in Jerusalem.
Praise the LORD!

Psalm 136

God's Work in Creation and in History

1 O give thanks to the LORD, for he is good,
for his steadfast love endures forever.
2 O give thanks to the God of gods,
for his steadfast love endures forever.
3 O give thanks to the Lord of lords,

for his steadfast love endures
forever;

[4] who alone does great wonders,
for his steadfast love endures
forever;
[5] who by understanding made the
heavens,
for his steadfast love endures
forever;
[6] who spread out the earth on the
waters,
for his steadfast love endures
forever;
[7] who made the great lights,
for his steadfast love endures
forever;
[8] the sun to rule over the day,
for his steadfast love endures
forever;
[9] the moon and stars to rule over
the night,
for his steadfast love endures
forever;

[10] who struck Egypt through their
firstborn,
for his steadfast love endures
forever;
[11] and brought Israel out from
among them,
for his steadfast love endures
forever;
[12] with a strong hand and an
outstretched arm,
for his steadfast love endures
forever;
[13] who divided the Red Sea[l] in
two,
for his steadfast love endures
forever;
[14] and made Israel pass through
the midst of it,
for his steadfast love endures
forever;
[15] but overthrew Pharaoh and his
army in the Red Sea,[m]
for his steadfast love endures
forever;
[16] who led his people through the
wilderness,
for his steadfast love endures
forever;
[17] who struck down great kings,
for his steadfast love endures
forever;
[18] and killed famous kings,
for his steadfast love endures
forever;
[19] Sihon, king of the Amorites,
for his steadfast love endures
forever;
[20] and Og, king of Bashan,
for his steadfast love endures
forever;
[21] and gave their land as a
heritage,
for his steadfast love endures
forever;
[22] a heritage to his servant Israel,
for his steadfast love endures
forever.

[23] It is he who remembered us in
our low estate,
for his steadfast love endures
forever;
[24] and rescued us from our foes,
for his steadfast love endures
forever;
[25] who gives food to all flesh,

l Or *Sea of Reeds* *m* Or *Sea of Reeds*

for his steadfast love endures
forever.

[26] O give thanks to the God of
heaven,
for his steadfast love endures
forever.

Psalm 137

Lament over the Destruction of Jerusalem

1 By the rivers of Babylon—
there we sat down and there we
wept
when we remembered Zion.
2 On the willows[n] there
we hung up our harps.
3 For there our captors
asked us for songs,
and our tormentors asked for
mirth, saying,
"Sing us one of the songs of
Zion!"

4 How could we sing the LORD's
song
in a foreign land?
5 If I forget you, O Jerusalem,
let my right hand wither!
6 Let my tongue cling to the roof
of my mouth,
if I do not remember you,
if I do not set Jerusalem
above my highest joy.

7 Remember, O LORD, against the
Edomites
the day of Jerusalem's fall,
how they said, "Tear it down!
Tear it down!
Down to its foundations!"
8 O daughter Babylon, you
devastator![o]
Happy shall they be who pay
you back
what you have done to us!
9 Happy shall they be who take
your little ones
and dash them against the
rock!

Psalm 138

Thanksgiving and Praise

Of David.

1 I give you thanks, O LORD, with
my whole heart;
before the gods I sing your
praise;
2 I bow down toward your holy
temple
and give thanks to your name
for your steadfast love
and your faithfulness;
for you have exalted your name
and your word
above everything.[p]
3 On the day I called, you
answered me,
you increased my strength of
soul.[q]

4 All the kings of the earth shall
praise you, O LORD,

---

n Or *poplars* *o* Or *you who are devastated*
p Cn: Heb *you have exalted your word above all your name* *q* Syr Compare Gk Tg: Heb *you made me arrogant in my soul with strength*

for they have heard the words
of your mouth.
5 They shall sing of the ways of
the LORD,
for great is the glory of the
LORD.
6 For though the LORD is high, he
regards the lowly;
but the haughty he perceives
from far away.

7 Though I walk in the midst of
trouble,
you preserve me against the
wrath of my enemies;
you stretch out your hand,
and your right hand delivers
me.
8 The LORD will fulfill his
purpose for me;
your steadfast love, O LORD,
endures forever.
Do not forsake the work of
your hands.

Psalm 139

The Inescapable God

To the leader. Of David. A Psalm.

1 O LORD, you have searched me
and known me.
2 You know when I sit down and
when I rise up;
you discern my thoughts from
far away.
3 You search out my path and my
lying down,
and are acquainted with all my
ways.
4 Even before a word is on my
tongue,
O LORD, you know it
completely.
5 You hem me in, behind and
before,
and lay your hand upon me.
6 Such knowledge is too
wonderful for me;
it is so high that I cannot attain
it.

7 Where can I go from your
spirit?
Or where can I flee from your
presence?
8 If I ascend to heaven, you are
there;
if I make my bed in Sheol, you
are there.
9 If I take the wings of the
morning
and settle at the farthest limits
of the sea,
10 even there your hand shall lead
me,
and your right hand shall hold
me fast.
11 If I say, "Surely the darkness
shall cover me,
and the light around me
become night,"
12 even the darkness is not dark to
you;
the night is as bright as the
day,
for darkness is as light to
you.

13 For it was you who formed my
inward parts;

you knit me together in my
mother's womb.
14 I praise you, for I am fearfully
and wonderfully made.
Wonderful are your works;
that I know very well.
15 My frame was not hidden from
you,
when I was being made in
secret,
intricately woven in the
depths of the earth.
16 Your eyes beheld my unformed
substance.
In your book were written
all the days that were formed
for me,
when none of them as yet
existed.
17 How weighty to me are your
thoughts, O God!
How vast is the sum of them!
18 I try to count them—they are
more than the sand;
I come to the end[r]—I am still
with you.

19 O that you would kill the
wicked, O God,
and that the bloodthirsty would
depart from me—
20 those who speak of you
maliciously,
and lift themselves up against
you for evil![s]
21 Do I not hate those who hate
you, O LORD?
And do I not loathe those who
rise up against you?
22 I hate them with perfect hatred;
I count them my enemies.
23 Search me, O God, and know
my heart;
test me and know my
thoughts.
24 See if there is any wicked[t] way
in me,
and lead me in the way
everlasting.[u]

Psalm 140

Prayer for Deliverance from Enemies

To the leader. A Psalm of David.

1 Deliver me, O LORD, from
evildoers;
protect me from those who are
violent,
2 who plan evil things in their
minds
and stir up wars continually.
3 They make their tongue sharp
as a snake's,
and under their lips is the
venom of vipers. *Selah*

4 Guard me, O LORD, from the
hands of the wicked;
protect me from the violent
who have planned my
downfall.
5 The arrogant have hidden a trap
for me,
and with cords they have
spread a net,[v]
along the road they have set
snares for me. *Selah*

---

r Or *I awake* *s* Cn: Meaning of Heb uncertain
t Heb *hurtful* *u* Or *the ancient way.* Compare
Jer 6.16 *v* Or *they have spread cords as a net*

6 I say to the LORD, "You are my
God;
give ear, O LORD, to the voice
of my supplications."
7 O LORD, my Lord, my strong
deliverer,
you have covered my head in
the day of battle.
8 Do not grant, O LORD, the
desires of the wicked;
do not further their evil plot.[w]
Selah

9 Those who surround me lift up
their heads;[x]
let the mischief of their lips
overwhelm them!
10 Let burning coals fall on them!
Let them be flung into pits,
no more to rise!
11 Do not let the slanderer be
established in the land;
let evil speedily hunt down the
violent!

12 I know that the LORD maintains
the cause of the needy,
and executes justice for the
poor.
13 Surely the righteous shall give
thanks to your name;
the upright shall live in your
presence.

Psalm 141

Prayer for Preservation from Evil

A Psalm of David.

1 I call upon you, O LORD; come
quickly to me;
give ear to my voice when I
call to you.
2 Let my prayer be counted as
incense before you,
and the lifting up of my hands
as an evening sacrifice.

3 Set a guard over my mouth,
O LORD;
keep watch over the door of
my lips.
4 Do not turn my heart to any
evil,
to busy myself with wicked
deeds
in company with those who
work iniquity;
do not let me eat of their
delicacies.

5 Let the righteous strike me;
let the faithful correct me.
Never let the oil of the wicked
anoint my head,[y]
for my prayer is continually[z]
against their wicked
deeds.

---

w Heb adds *they are exalted* *x* Cn Compare Gk: Heb *those who surround me are uplifted in head*; Heb divides verses 8 and 9 differently *y* Gk: Meaning of Heb uncertain *z* Cn: Heb *for continually and my prayer*

6 When they are given over to
those who shall condemn
them,
then they shall learn that my
words were pleasant.
7 Like a rock that one breaks
apart and shatters on the
land,
so shall their bones be strewn at
the mouth of Sheol.[a]

8 But my eyes are turned toward
you, O GOD, my Lord;
in you I seek refuge; do not
leave me defenseless.
9 Keep me from the trap that they
have laid for me,
and from the snares of
evildoers.
10 Let the wicked fall into their
own nets,
while I alone escape.

Psalm 142

Prayer for Deliverance from Persecutors

A Maskil of David. When he was in the cave. A Prayer.

1 With my voice I cry to the
LORD;
with my voice I make
supplication to the LORD.
2 I pour out my complaint before
him;
I tell my trouble before him.
3 When my spirit is faint,
you know my way.
In the path where I walk
they have hidden a trap for
me.
4 Look on my right hand and
see—
there is no one who takes notice
of me;
no refuge remains to me;
no one cares for me.

5 I cry to you, O LORD;
I say, "You are my refuge,
my portion in the land of the
living."
6 Give heed to my cry,
for I am brought very low.

Save me from my persecutors,
for they are too strong for
me.
7 Bring me out of prison,
so that I may give thanks to
your name.
The righteous will surround me,
for you will deal bountifully
with me.

Psalm 143

Prayer for Deliverance from Enemies

A Psalm of David.

1 Hear my prayer, O LORD;
give ear to my supplications
in your faithfulness;
answer me in your
righteousness.

---

a Meaning of Heb of verses 5–7 is uncertain

[2] Do not enter into judgment with
your servant,
for no one living is righteous
before you.

[3] For the enemy has pursued me,
crushing my life to the
ground,
making me sit in darkness
like those long dead.
[4] Therefore my spirit faints
within me;
my heart within me is
appalled.

[5] I remember the days of old,
I think about all your deeds,
I meditate on the works of
your hands.
[6] I stretch out my hands to you;
my soul thirsts for you like a
parched land. *Selah*

[7] Answer me quickly, O LORD;
my spirit fails.
Do not hide your face from me,
or I shall be like those who
go down to the Pit.
[8] Let me hear of your steadfast
love in the morning,
for in you I put my trust.
Teach me the way I should go,
for to you I lift up my soul.

[9] Save me, O LORD, from my
enemies;
I have fled to you for refuge.[b]
[10] Teach me to do your will,
for you are my God.
Let your good spirit lead me
on a level path.

[11] For your name's sake, O LORD,
preserve my life.
In your righteousness bring
me out of trouble.
[12] In your steadfast love cut off
my enemies,
and destroy all my
adversaries,
for I am your servant.

Psalm 144

Prayer for National Deliverance and Security

Of David.

[1] Blessed be the LORD, my rock,
who trains my hands for war,
and my fingers for battle;
[2] my rock[c] and my fortress,
my stronghold and my
deliverer,
my shield, in whom I take
refuge,
who subdues the peoples[d]
under me.

[3] O LORD, what are human beings
that you regard them,
or mortals that you think of
them?
[4] They are like a breath;
their days are like a passing
shadow.

b One Heb Ms Gk: MT *to you I have hidden*
c With 18.2 and 2 Sam 22.2: Heb *my steadfast love* d Heb Mss Syr Aquila Jerome: MT *my people*

5 Bow your heavens, O Lord,
and come down;
touch the mountains so that
they smoke.
6 Make the lightning flash and
scatter them;
send out your arrows and rout
them.
7 Stretch out your hand from on
high;
set me free and rescue me
from the mighty waters,
from the hand of aliens,
8 whose mouths speak lies,
and whose right hands are false.

9 I will sing a new song to you,
O God;
upon a ten-stringed harp I will
play to you,
10 the one who gives victory to
kings,
who rescues his servant
David.
11 Rescue me from the cruel
sword,
and deliver me from the hand
of aliens,
whose mouths speak lies,
and whose right hands are false.

12 May our sons in their youth
be like plants full grown,
our daughters like corner
pillars,
cut for the building of a palace.
13 May our barns be filled,
with produce of every kind;
may our sheep increase by
thousands,
by tens of thousands in our
fields,
14 and may our cattle be heavy
with young.
May there be no breach in the
walls,[e] no exile,
and no cry of distress in our
streets.

15 Happy are the people to whom
such blessings fall;
happy are the people whose
God is the Lord.

Psalm 145

The Greatness and the Goodness of God

Praise. Of David.

1 I will extol you, my God and
King,
and bless your name forever
and ever.
2 Every day I will bless you,
and praise your name forever
and ever.
3 Great is the Lord, and greatly
to be praised;
his greatness is unsearchable.

4 One generation shall laud your
works to another,
and shall declare your mighty
acts.
5 On the glorious splendor of
your majesty,
and on your wondrous works,
I will meditate.

---

e Heb lacks *in the walls*

[6] The might of your awesome
deeds shall be proclaimed,
and I will declare your
greatness.
[7] They shall celebrate the fame of
your abundant goodness,
and shall sing aloud of your
righteousness.

[8] The LORD is gracious and
merciful,
slow to anger and abounding
in steadfast love.
[9] The LORD is good to all,
and his compassion is over
all that he has made.

[10] All your works shall give
thanks to you, O LORD,
and all your faithful shall
bless you.
[11] They shall speak of the glory of
your kingdom,
and tell of your power,
[12] to make known to all people
your[f] mighty deeds,
and the glorious splendor of
your[g] kingdom.
[13] Your kingdom is an everlasting
kingdom,
and your dominion
endures throughout all
generations.

The LORD is faithful in all his
words,
and gracious in all his deeds.[h]
[14] The LORD upholds all who are
falling,
and raises up all who are bowed
down.
[15] The eyes of all look to you,
and you give them their food in
due season.
[16] You open your hand,
satisfying the desire of every
living thing.
[17] The LORD is just in all his ways,
and kind in all his doings.
[18] The LORD is near to all who call
on him,
to all who call on him in truth.
[19] He fulfills the desire of all who
fear him;
he also hears their cry, and
saves them.
[20] The LORD watches over all who
love him,
but all the wicked he will
destroy.

[21] My mouth will speak the praise
of the LORD,
and all flesh will bless his
holy name forever and
ever.

Psalm 146

Praise for God's Help

[1] Praise the LORD!
Praise the LORD, O my soul!
[2] I will praise the LORD as long as
I live;
I will sing praises to my God
all my life long.

[3] Do not put your trust in princes,

f Gk Jerome Syr: Heb *his* *g* Heb *his* *h* These two lines supplied by Q Ms Gk Syr

in mortals, in whom there is no
help.
4 When their breath departs, they
return to the earth;
on that very day their plans
perish.

5 Happy are those whose help is
the God of Jacob,
whose hope is in the LORD their
God,
6 who made heaven and earth,
the sea, and all that is in them;
who keeps faith forever;
7 who executes justice for the
oppressed;
who gives food to the hungry.

The LORD sets the prisoners
free;
8 the LORD opens the eyes of the
blind.
The LORD lifts up those who are
bowed down;
the LORD loves the righteous.
9 The LORD watches over the
strangers;
he upholds the orphan and
the widow,
but the way of the wicked he
brings to ruin.

10 The LORD will reign forever,
your God, O Zion, for all
generations.
Praise the LORD!

Psalm 147

Praise for God's Care for Jerusalem

1 Praise the LORD!
How good it is to sing praises
to our God;
for he is gracious, and a song of
praise is fitting.
2 The LORD builds up Jerusalem;
he gathers the outcasts of Israel.
3 He heals the brokenhearted,
and binds up their wounds.
4 He determines the number of
the stars;
he gives to all of them their
names.
5 Great is our Lord, and abundant
in power;
his understanding is beyond
measure.
6 The LORD lifts up the
downtrodden;
he casts the wicked to the
ground.

7 Sing to the LORD with
thanksgiving;
make melody to our God on the
lyre.
8 He covers the heavens with
clouds,
prepares rain for the earth,
makes grass grow on the hills.
9 He gives to the animals their
food,
and to the young ravens when
they cry.
10 His delight is not in the strength
of the horse,

nor his pleasure in the speed of a runner;[i]
11 but the LORD takes pleasure in those who fear him,
in those who hope in his steadfast love.

12 Praise the LORD, O Jerusalem!
Praise your God, O Zion!
13 For he strengthens the bars of your gates;
he blesses your children within you.
14 He grants peace[j] within your borders;
he fills you with the finest of wheat.
15 He sends out his command to the earth;
his word runs swiftly.
16 He gives snow like wool;
he scatters frost like ashes.
17 He hurls down hail like crumbs—
who can stand before his cold?
18 He sends out his word, and melts them;
he makes his wind blow, and the waters flow.
19 He declares his word to Jacob,
his statutes and ordinances to Israel.
20 He has not dealt thus with any other nation;
they do not know his ordinances.
Praise the LORD!

Psalm 148

Praise for God's Universal Glory

1 Praise the LORD!
Praise the LORD from the heavens;
praise him in the heights!
2 Praise him, all his angels;
praise him, all his host!

3 Praise him, sun and moon;
praise him, all you shining stars!
4 Praise him, you highest heavens,
and you waters above the heavens!

5 Let them praise the name of the LORD,
for he commanded and they were created.
6 He established them forever and ever;
he fixed their bounds, which cannot be passed.[k]

7 Praise the LORD from the earth,
you sea monsters and all deeps,
8 fire and hail, snow and frost,
stormy wind fulfilling his command!

9 Mountains and all hills,
fruit trees and all cedars!
10 Wild animals and all cattle,

i Heb *legs of a person* *j* Or *prosperity*
k Or *he set a law that cannot pass away*

creeping things and flying
birds!

[11] Kings of the earth and all
peoples,
princes and all rulers of the
earth!
[12] Young men and women alike,
old and young together!

[13] Let them praise the name of the
LORD,
for his name alone is exalted;
his glory is above earth and
heaven.
[14] He has raised up a horn for his
people,
praise for all his faithful,
for the people of Israel who are
close to him.
Praise the LORD!

Psalm 149

Praise for God's Goodness to Israel

[1] Praise the LORD!
Sing to the LORD a new song,
his praise in the assembly of the
faithful.
[2] Let Israel be glad in its Maker;
let the children of Zion rejoice
in their King.
[3] Let them praise his name with
dancing,
making melody to him with
tambourine and lyre.
[4] For the LORD takes pleasure in
his people;
he adorns the humble with
victory.
[5] Let the faithful exult in glory;
let them sing for joy on their
couches.
[6] Let the high praises of God be
in their throats
and two-edged swords in
their hands,
[7] to execute vengeance on the
nations
and punishment on the
peoples,
[8] to bind their kings with fetters
and their nobles with chains
of iron,
[9] to execute on them the
judgment decreed.
This is glory for all his
faithful ones.
Praise the LORD!

Psalm 150

Praise for God's Surpassing Greatness

[1] Praise the LORD!
Praise God in his sanctuary;
praise him in his mighty
firmament![l]
[2] Praise him for his mighty
deeds;
praise him according to his
surpassing greatness!

[3] Praise him with trumpet sound;
praise him with lute and
harp!

l Or *dome*

4 Praise him with tambourine and
dance;
praise him with strings and
pipe!
5 Praise him with clanging
cymbals;
praise him with loud clashing
cymbals!
6 Let everything that breathes
praise the LORD!
Praise the LORD!